PARTNERSHIP TAXATION

Introductory and Advanced

STUDENT EDITION

PHILIP F. POSTLEWAITE

Harry R. Horrow Professor of Law
Director of the Tax Program
Northwestern University School of Law

ROBERT R. WOOTTON

Senior Lecturer of Law
Northwestern University
School of Law

Volume 1—Cases, Materials, and Problems

(2012-2013 Edition)

For Student Use Only

WG&L

This publication is designed to provide accurate and authoritative information in regard to the subject matter covered. It is sold with the understanding that neither the author(s) nor the publisher is engaged in rendering legal, account-ing, or other professional service. If legal advice or other expert assistance is required, the services of a competent professional should be sought.

In response to IRS Circular 230 requirements, Thomson Reuters advises that any discussions of federal tax issues in its publications and products, or in third-party publications and products on its platforms, are not intended to be used and may not in fact be used to avoid any penalties under the Internal Revenue Code, or to promote, market, or recommend any transaction or sub-ject addressed therein.

PRINTED IN THE UNITED STATES OF AMERICA

THOMSON REUTERS

Ode to the Ruler

The linear manner in which the metallic instrument
Faces its tasks is consistently reliable
And its smooth, sometimes transparent complexion remains
Unimpaired, despite kids anxiously and impatiently
Flailing it. Undoubtedly, the ruler is the most underestimated tool
Within the overcrowded desk drawers of teachers,
Stuffed in backpacks of striving students, and perhaps lost on the locker room
Floor. I commend it for its loyalty and for forging a path to success.

With its metallic blade as powerful as the indestructible Mjolnir,
But especially the amount of pressure it withstands from society.
Rulers guide us; measure the world, our world,
And, if elected, these figures change the world.
They grasp the impossible tasks with which our world may cower
To face. Rulers improve the foundation of society with binding promises
To repair the dysfunctional systems within; however,
They might with a slight bite and a quick lash of failure
Betray, like a teacher who lashes an immature student.

Matthew Postlewaite
March 5, 2012

For all the joy you have given me!

Love,
Dad

To our wonderful students at Northwestern Law,
and particularly the Tax Program,
without whose exuberant errors and inspiring misconceptions
this book would be less than we hope it to be.

RRW

Preface

This text differs from current partnership tax coursebooks in a number of respects. Student casebooks offer the traditional materials for study—cases, rulings, etc.—but frequently fail to offer the detailed analysis of these materials within their statutory framework necessary to understand a complex area such as partnership taxation. The other type of student coursebook—the abridged student version of a professional treatise—denies both the student and the instructor the benefit of reading and considering for themselves the primary sources of partnership taxation. Our efforts meld these competing instructional modes and afford the instructor the greatest latitude in structuring his or her course. This coursebook is in two volumes—Volume 1 contains rulings, cases, problems, and other materials and Volume 2 contains an abridged version of the professional treatise, Partnership Taxation (Thomson Reuters/WG&L, 7th edition 2012).

Volume 1 stresses a problem-solving approach through the use of numerous short problems interspersed among the relevant materials. This problem-solving approach parallels a "real world" experience and thus helps students develop legal and analytic skills. Each chapter is organized into three sections—(1) a brief textual introduction to the area, (2) a few relevant materials such as cases and rulings, and (3) a set of problems intended to introduce the student to the significant issues in the area. At the start of each Volume 1 problem area, the student is given a reading assignment in Volume 2 which addresses the particular issues under examination.

The first 17 chapters address different stages of the life cycle of a partnership. This material serves as an introduction to, and an overview of, the basics of partnership taxation. In our experience, this material is well-suited, both in length and coverage, to an introductory course in partnership taxation. Chapters 18 through 25 consider more advanced topics. We have developed these chapters for use in the instruction of an advanced course in partnership taxation, either to follow the introductory course or for the instruction of students who already have some knowledge of the area. Alternatively, one or more of these advanced chapters (or individual problems from these chapters) can be assigned as additional work in an introductory course, time and temperament permitting.

Each of the advanced chapters is topically related to one or more of the introductory chapters. The following guide may assist instructors (and their students) in understanding these relationships.

Topic	Introductory	Advanced
Partnership Classification	Problem Area 1	Problem Area 18
Section 704(c)	Problem Area 7	Problem Area 19
Property Contributions	Problem Area 2	Problem Area 20
Service Contributions	Problem Area 3	Problem Area 21
Allocations of Debt-Financed Deductions	Problem Area 7	Problem Area 22
Transfers of Interests	Problem Areas 11 and 15	Problem Area 23
Distributions	Problem Areas 9, 12 and16	Problem Area 24
Terminations	Problem Area 17	Problem Area 25

In order to ease the reading of the cases and other material contained in Volume 1, some citations have been omitted without the use of ellipses. In some instances, footnotes in cases and other quoted material have been eliminated without indication. Any footnotes that are not deleted retain their original numbers.

The material in the Student Edition and its accompanying Teacher's Manual, both of which are current through March 1, 2012, reflect the valuable assistance of a variety of people to whom the authors express their thanks. The authors wish to thank the fine staffs of Northwestern University School of Law and Warren, Gorham & Lamont of Thomson Reuters, Tax and Accounting. All have been particularly helpful and cooperative. Further appreciation goes to the members of the Partnership Taxation classes of the Tax Program at Northwestern University School of Law, upon whom various drafts of this text have been inflicted. That usage, accompanied by student comments and reactions to the materials, have permitted a far better refinement of the product than we would have attained operating in a vacuum.

Table of Contents

Volume 1

Problem Area 1   Partnership Classification

Problem Area 2   Partnership Formation—Acquisition of a Partnership Interest in Exchange for a Contribution of Property

Problem Area 3   Partnership Formation—Acquisition of a Partnership Interest (Other Than a Profits Interest) in Exchange for a Contribution of Services

Problem Area 4   Basis of a Partner's Partnership Interest

Problem Area 5   Taxing Partnership Operations— Characterization and Computation of Partnership Income

Problem Area 6   Taxing Partnership Operations— Partnership Taxable Years

Problem Area 7   Taxing Partnership Operations— Determining the Partners' Distributive Shares

Problem Area 8   Taxing Partnership Operations— Transactions Between Related Parties

Problem Area 9   Partnership Distributions—Current Distributions That Do Not Change Partners' Interests in Tainted Assets

Problem Area 10   Transfers of Partnership Interests— Sales of Interests in Partnerships That Do Not Hold Tainted Assets

Problem Area 11   Transfers of Partnership Interests— Sales of Interests in Partnerships Holding Tainted Assets

Problem Area 12 Partnership Distributions—Liquidating Distributions That Do Not Change Partners' Interests in Tainted Assets

Problem Area 13 Partnership Distributions—Liquidating Distributions That Change Partners' Interests in Tainted Assets

Problem Area 14 Death or Retirement of a Partner— Payments in Liquidation of the Interest of a Retired Partner

Problem Area 15 Adjustments to the Bases of Partnership Assets—Adjustments When Partnership Interests Are Transferred

Problem Area 16 Adjustments to the Bases of Partnership Assets—Adjustments in Connection With Distributions

Problem Area 17 Taxing Partnership Operations— Termination of a Partnership Other Than By Division or Merger

Problem Area 18 Hybrid Entities

Problem Area 19 Section 704(c)

Problem Area 22 Allocation of Partnership Debt and Debt-Financed Losses and Deductions

Problem Area 23 Transfers of Partnership Interests: Special Topics

Problem Area 24 Distributions: Marketable Securities, Basis Shifting, and Mixing Bowls

Problem Area 25 Partnership Mergers and Divisions

CHAPTER 1

Partnership Classification

PROBLEM AREA 1

INTRODUCTION

Business activity may occur in a number of different forms ranging from the conduct of operations as a sole proprietorship to the use of a corporation. Along that continuum, there are tenancies in common, general partnerships, limited partnerships, limited liability partnerships, limited liability companies, publicly traded partnerships, S corporations, professional corporations, and C corporations.

The choice between organizing a business as a non-corporate or corporate entity is governed primarily by three considerations: the applicable commercial law, the tax treatment of the business form chosen, and the investment and business preferences of the parties involved.

For tax purposes, there are three relevant classification categories: (1) individual, (2) partnership, and (3) corporation. The importance of the distinction between an individual (even a group of individuals operating in concert but *not* as a partnership) and a partnership is not so much tax liability as it is the record keeping and reporting requirements. For example, individuals who are tenants in common record their business or investment-oriented activity directly on their personal books and tax returns, while partners are required under §§ 702 and 703 to determine their overall activity at the partnership level and those results are then allocated among the members according to their interests in the partnership.

The distinction between a partnership and a C corporation is more dramatic in terms of overall tax liability. The income of a partnership is allocated among the partners and, thus, is taxed only once at the partner level, while a C corporation, recognized as an entity separate and distinct from its shareholders, is itself subject to tax as the income is earned and the shareholders are taxed again when the corporate earnings are distributed—the proverbial double taxation feature of corporations.

The Internal Revenue Code broadly defines a partnership to include "a syndicate, group, pool, joint venture, or other unincorporated organization through or by means of which any business, financial operation, or venture is carried on, and which is not, within the meaning of this title, a corporation or a trust or estate." IRC §§ 761(a) and 7701(a)(2). At the very least, a partnership requires three elements: two or more persons who (1) carry on a business, (2) for profit, (3) as co-owners. The failure to meet any one of these elements may result in the relationship being classified as something other than a partnership, *e.g.*, co-tenants, lessor-lessee, employer-employee, lender-borrower, etc.

The Regulations specify that a joint undertaking does not always constitute a partnership for tax purposes. Reg. § 301.7701-1(a)(2). For example, an agreement merely to share expenses is not a partnership because it lacks a profit motive. Likewise, even where a profit orientation exists, co-ownership may be absent given the relationship of the parties. For example, property which is maintained, kept in repair, and rented or leased to another for a share of the possessor's profits does not constitute a partnership, but rather a lessor-lessee relationship.

The existence of co-ownership is determined by a facts-and-circumstances approach and is evidenced by activities such as the contribution of capital to the enterprise, the rendition of services, the exercise of management or control of the business, and an agreement to share in business losses. To be classified as a partnership, even a profit-oriented co-ownership must engage in business activity. For example, tenants in common may be classified as partners if they actively carry on a trade, business, financial operation, or venture and divide the profit therefrom. The crucial factor distinguishing a tenancy in common from a partnership is the active pursuit of a business.

Historically a business entity was classified for federal income tax purposes as either a partnership or a corporation under the "resemblance" test first enunciated by the Supreme Court in *Morrissey v. Commissioner*, 296 US 344 (1935), and subsequently adopted in modified form by Regulations. If an entity more closely resembled a corporation than another type of business organization, it was classified as such and taxed accordingly. Of course, the resemblance text was subject to congressional alteration—for example, S corporations are treated as the functional equivalent of partnerships under §§ 1361–1371 and publicly traded partnerships are taxed as corporations under § 7704.

Under the resemblance text, the Regulations identified four characteristics associated with the corporate form of doing business. They were: (1) continuity of life, (2) centralized management, (3) limited liability, and (4) free transferability of interests. An entity was treated as a corporation for federal income tax purposes if more corporate characteristics than non-corporate characteristics were present. Therefore, under the Regulations, unless the entity possessed three of the four corporate characteristics, it was classified as a partnership.

The Service in 1995 issued Notice 95-14, 1995-1 CB 297, indicating its interest in altering the existing classification Regulations. The Service subsequently promulgated Regulations §§ 301.7701-1, 301.7701-2, and 301.7701-3, which eliminated the classification criteria for qualifying business entities.

These Regulations, colloquially dubbed the "check the box" rules, permit an eligible business entity that has at least two members to elect classification as an association (taxable as a corporation) or as a partnership. For purposes of the check-the-box rules, an eligible business entity is an organization which is recognized as an entity for federal tax purposes and is not a trust or an entity otherwise subject to special tax treatment under the Code. Nevertheless, eight categories of enterprises are specifically excluded by the Regulations. Of particular importance, enterprises incorporated under state or Federal law are not entitled to elect partnership status. In addition, some (but not all) enterprises incorporated under foreign law are not entitled to elect partnership status. The definitive list of such foreign enterprises, frequently referred to as "per se corporations," is set forth in the Regulations.

The Regulations also provide a default rule applicable in cases where an otherwise qualifying entity does not make the election. Under the default rule, a domestic eligible business entity with two or more members is taxed as a partnership, whereas a foreign eligible business entity is taxed as a partnership only if at least one member does not have limited liability for the entity's debts.

PROBLEM 1

QUESTIONS

1. A is producing a Broadway play and approaches B to participate in the lead role. B agrees to accept the position in return for 20 percent of the gross receipts. What is their relationship for tax purposes?

2. A sells a hardware business to B for $10,000 plus 20 percent of the net profits from the business for five years. A demands to serve as a management consultant to the business with certain veto rights to ensure that B does not dissipate any of the assets of the business. What is the relationship between A and B?

3. A and B each owns an undivided one-half interest in a tract of raw land. In discussing each of the following cumulative facts, determine how the operation should be classified for tax purposes and the opportunity, if any, for electing out of partnership status under § 761(a). Would it make any difference if A and B each owned individually a part of the tract instead of each owning an undivided interest in the whole?

   a. A and B construct a parking lot on the property, which they lease to C for $2,000 per month. C operates a parking business. A and B divide the profit equally.

   b. Some time later, A and B construct an apartment building on the property which they lease through an agent. The agent provides customary tenant services such as electricity, hot and cold water, parking stalls, heat and air conditioning, maintenance, cleaning of the public areas, and the like.

   c. Several years thereafter, A and B construct an athletic club for the tenants of the apartment building that includes a swimming pool and tennis courts as well as a health facility with a sauna, steam room, and complete gym. The tenants are required to pay fees for the use of these extra facilities in addition to their regular rents.

4. The ABCZ partnership was formed for the purpose of developing tracts of land. A, B, and C are individual limited partners and Z, a corporation, is the sole general partner. The corporation has a 20 percent interest in the partnership and has substantial assets other than its partnership interest.

The partnership agreement provides that limited partners can transfer their income interests only with the consent of the general partner and further provides that the limited partners can freely transfer their capital interests only after first offering such interests to other members of the partnership at fair market value. The partnership agreement also provides that the partnership will continue for 30 years, notwithstanding the death, insanity, bankruptcy, retirement, resignation, or expulsion of any member of the partnership.

How is ABCZ classified for tax purposes?

5. X is organized as a limited liability company (LLC) under the provisions of the New Jersey Limited Liability Company Act. Under its operating agreement, X may engage in any and all business activity permitted by New Jersey. It has a single member, individual A, who is also its sole manager. X's operating agreement grants exclusive management authority to its designated manager. Under the New Jersey Act, no member, manager, employee, or agent is obligated personally for any of an LLC's debts, obligations, or liabilities. How is X classified for tax purposes?

6. Q, Inc. is incorporated under the laws of Illinois by its two shareholders, A and B. How is Q, Inc. classified for tax purposes? What result if A and B elect S corporation status for Q, Inc.?

7. X, a Delaware business corporation, is the sole owner of L, an Austrian GmbH, a form of business organization that provides limited liability to all of its owners. X and L form P, a United Kingdom Private Company, which also offers the protection of limited liability to all of its owners. What is the United States federal income tax classification of P?

8. Mid-American Pipeline, L.P. is a limited partnership with approximately 500 limited partners. Its general partner is MAP Management, Inc., a Delaware business corporation. Mid-American Pipeline operates a network of gas pipelines throughout the Great Plains and into Canada and substantially all of its revenues consists of fees received for gas shipments through these pipelines. Limited partnership interests are traded on the New York and Toronto stock exchanges. How is Mid-American Pipeline classified for tax purposes?

MATERIALS

TIFD III-E, Inc. v. United States
459 F3d 220 (2d Cir. 2006)

LEVAL, Circuit Judge.

This appeal tests the power of the Internal Revenue Service to examine and recharacterize an interest which accords with its ostensible classification only in illusory or insignificant respects. The taxpayer-plaintiff TIFD III-E, Inc. (the "taxpayer" or "TIFD III-E"), a subsidiary of General Electric Capital Corporation ("GECC"), brought suit in the United States District Court for the District of Connecticut . . . to challenge adjustments made by the Internal Revenue Service ("IRS") to the tax returns for 1993 to 1998 of a partnership named Castle Harbour Limited Liability Company ("Castle Harbour" or the "partnership"), for which the taxpayer was the tax-matters partner. The IRS's adjustments added $62 million to the taxpayer's tax bill. After an eight-day bench trial, the court ruled in favor of the taxpayer, and the government brought this appeal. We reverse the judgment of the district court.

The litigation turns primarily on the propriety of the partnership's ostensible allocation of its income as between the taxpayer and two Dutch banks, ING Bank N.V. and Rabo Merchant Bank N.V. (the "Dutch banks" or the "banks"), which invested in the partnership. The Dutch banks do not pay taxes to the United States. The partnership's "Operating Agreement" allocates to them 98 percent of the "Operating Income," which comprises the great majority of the partnership's income. The Operating Income, calculated for tax purposes, however, vastly exceeded the amounts the banks would actually receive. The net Operating Income, of which 98 percent would go to the banks, was drastically reduced by huge depreciation deductions which the IRS would not recognize, as the assets in question had already been fully depreciated. The effects of the ostensible allocation of the majority of the partnership's income to the non-taxpaying Dutch banks were to shelter most of the partnership's income from taxation and to redirect that income tax-free to the taxpayer. What the Dutch banks were in fact to receive from the partnership was dictated by provisions of the partnership agreement calling for the reimbursement of their initial investment at an annual rate of return of 9.03587 percent (or, in some circumstances, 8.53587 percent), subject to the possibility of small adjustments and to the possibility of a slight increase in the event of unexpectedly great partnership earnings. The banks' reimbursement at the agreed rate of return was formidably secured by a variety of contractual undertakings by the taxpayer and its parent GECC. . . .

The provisions of the immensely complex partnership agreements are analyzed in the district court's thorough, comprehensive, and detailed opinion. The court essentially acknowledged that the creation of the partnership was largely tax-motivated. The court nonetheless found that the partnership had other bona fide purposes, and some genuine economic effect. It therefore rejected the government's contention that the partnership's construct was a sham, which should be disregarded. The court concluded that the Dutch banks were, for tax purposes, partners of Castle Harbour.

While the government raises several arguments on appeal, we focus primarily on its contention that the Dutch banks should not be treated as equity partners in the Castle Harbour partnership because they had no meaningful stake in the success or failure of the partnership. In its analysis of this question, the district court made several errors of law which undermined the soundness of its conclusions. The facts of the allocation of partnership resources, as set forth in the partnership documents (and as found by the district court), compel the conclusion that the IRS correctly determined that the Dutch banks were not bona fide equity participants in the partnership. We accordingly reverse the judgment.

I. Background . . .
A. Overview

GECC has long been in the business of owning commercial aircraft which it leased to airlines. The economic benefits of aircraft ownership are primarily two—the revenues produced by employment of the aircraft in the business of air transportation, and the depreciation deductions the aircraft generate, which can substantially reduce the owner's tax liability. However, once an owner has taken depreciation covering its full investment in the aircraft, no further depreciation deductions may be claimed. GECC had long produced revenue by leasing the aircraft to airlines and realized beneficial tax relief through depreciation. Eventually, however, GECC found itself in the position of owning a fleet of aircraft that had been fully depreciated and could thus no longer serve as the basis for depreciation deductions. By reason of its inability to take further depreciation, its ownership of these aircraft had become less remunerative. GECC solicited proposals from investment banks for financing of these aircraft.

The Castle Harbour partnership, which is the subject of this litigation, resulted from a proposal presented to GECC by Babcock & Brown, to which GECC paid $9 million for its assistance in the creation and execution of the plan. Following Babcock & Brown's proposal in 1993, GECC caused the formation of an eight-year partnership, later named Castle Harbour, and solicited foreign financial companies, which are not subject to tax in the United States, as investors in the partnership. GECC caused its subsidiaries to transfer the ownership of a fleet of fully depreciated aircraft under lease to airlines to the Castle Harbour partnership, in which its subsidiary TIFD III-E, the taxpayer in this action, became the tax-matters partner. The assets transferred by GECC entities to the partnership were the fleet of aircraft, with a market value of $272 million, $22 million in receivables from aircraft-rental agreements, and $296 million in cash, making a total investment of $590 million. Shortly thereafter, the two Dutch banks contributed $117.5 million in cash to the partnership. The district court found that the taxpayer contributed 82 percent of the partnership's capital and the Dutch banks contributed 18 percent. The Dutch banks' participation in the partnership was to be passive. They were to exercise no role in the management, which was assigned entirely to the taxpayer. The documents of the partnership characterize the Dutch banks as equity partners. This characterization is the main focus of this dispute. . . .

In short, the Dutch banks, which contributed about 18 percent of the partnership's capital and contributed nothing to its management, were allocated, for tax purposes, 98 percent of most of its taxable income. The actual distributions to be made to the banks, however, were arranged so that they would receive, according to a previously agreed schedule, the reimbursement of their investment, plus an annual return at an agreed rate near 9 percent, plus a small share in any unexpectedly large profits. . . . The Dutch banks' interest in the eight-year partnership was essentially as follows: (1) They were promised the reimbursement, on a previously agreed schedule, of their initial $117.5 million investment at an agreed annual rate of return; (2) their repayment at the agreed rate of return was secured by the personal guaranty of GECC; (3) they were fully protected against risk of loss, except as to a tiny amount in highly unlikely circumstances; and (4) their ability to earn in excess of the agreed annual rate by participation in unexpected gains was, as a practical matter, capped at $2,854,493 (less than 2.5 percent of their investment), plus 1 percent. . . .

II. Discussion
A. Errors of Law in the District Court's Analysis

We find that the district court erred as a matter of law in several respects. In rejecting the government's contention that the Dutch banks were not bona fide equity partners for tax purposes, the court relied essentially upon the sham-transactions test to the exclusion of the test of totality-of-the-circumstances set forth by the Supreme Court in *Commissioner v. Culbertson*, 337 U.S. 733 (1949). In examining the related question whether the banks' interest was more in the nature of debt or equity, the court erred in several respects—primarily by accepting at face value the appearances and labels created by the partnership, rather than assessing the underlying economic realities. . . . In sum, the Dutch banks' interest was overwhelmingly in the nature of a secured lender's interest, which would neither be harmed by poor performance of the partnership nor significantly enhanced by extraordinary profits. The banks had no meaningful stake in the success or failure of Castle Harbour. While their interest was not totally devoid of indicia of an equity participation in a partnership, those indicia were either illusory or insignificant in the overall context of the banks' investment. The IRS appropriately rejected the equity characterization.

i. Failure To Employ the *Culbertson* Test

The court should not have rejected the government's contention that the Dutch banks' interest was not a bona fide equity partnership participation without examining the question under the all-facts-and-circumstances test of *Culbertson*. The court relied on the sham-transaction doctrine, which accepts the taxpayer's characterization of an interest as controlling unless that characterization is determined to be a sham—that is, altogether without economic substance. ("[T]he 'sham transaction' doctrine...is the test by which a court is to scrutinize the partnership structure."). Using this test, the court determined that because, in addition to the strong and obvious tax motivations, the taxpayer had some additional non-tax motivation to raise equity capital, the transaction could not be considered a sham.

The IRS, however, is entitled in rejecting a taxpayer's characterization of an interest to rely on a test less favorable to the taxpayer, even when the interest has economic substance. This alternative test determines the nature of the interest based on a realistic appraisal of the totality of the circumstances. We do not mean to imply that it was error to consider the sham test, as the IRS purported to rely in part on that test. The error was in failing to test the banks' interest also under *Culbertson* after finding that the taxpayer's characterization survived the sham test.

In *Culbertson*, the Supreme Court ruled that a partnership exists when, "considering all the facts—the agreement, the conduct of the parties in execution of its provisions, their statements, the testimony of disinterested persons, the relationship of the parties, their respective abilities and capital contributions, the actual control of income and the purposes for which it is used, and any other facts throwing light on their true intent—the parties in good faith and acting with a business purpose intended to join together in the present conduct of the enterprise." This test turns on the fair, objective characterization of the interest in question upon consideration of all the circumstances. The IRS's challenge to the taxpayer's characterization is not foreclosed merely because the taxpayer can point to the existence of some business purpose or objective reality in addition to its tax-avoidance objective. The district court recognized the existence of the *Culbertson* test, but did not conduct a *Culbertson* analysis of whether the banks' interest was a bona fide equity partnership participation. This was error.

ii. Errors in Determining the Nature of the Dutch Banks' Interest

Consideration whether an interest has the prevailing character of debt or equity can be helpful in analyzing whether, for tax purposes, the interest should be deemed a bona fide equity participation in a partnership. Although questioning the usefulness of the inquiry, the district court did consider whether the Dutch banks' interest was more akin to debt than to equity and concluded it was not. In making this analysis, however, the court made errors of law, which undermined its conclusion. In large part these errors consisted in accepting at face value artificial constructs of the partnership agreement without examining all the circumstances to determine whether powers granted to the taxpayer effectively negated the apparent interests of the banks.

Neither the Internal Revenue Code nor the Regulations provide for definitions of debt and equity. We have noted that Congress appears to have intended that "the significant factor" in differentiating between the two be whether "the funds were advanced with reasonable expectations of repayment regardless of the success of the venture or were placed at the risk of the business." . . .

a. The Banks' Share in the Upside Potential of the Partnership.

The district court recognized that the banks ran no meaningful risk of being paid anything less than the reimbursement of their investment at the Applicable Rate of return. The court concluded on the other hand that the banks were given a meaningful and unlimited share of the upside potential of the partnership. This conclusion played a major role in supporting the district court's conclusion that the banks' interest was clearly in the nature of equity. The problem with this determination is that it depended on the fictions projected by the partnership agreement, rather than on assessment of the practical realities. The realistic possibility of upside potential—not the absence of formal caps—is what governs this analysis.

It is true that the partnership agreement placed no formal upper limit on the banks' receipt of 98 percent of the Operating Income of the partnership. On the other hand, as a practical matter, the banks enjoyed only a narrowly circumscribed ability to participate in profits in excess of their Applicable Rate of return. The limitations of the banks' ability to share meaningfully in the profits of the partnership resulted, as noted above, from three provisions of the agreements. First, the taxpayer, which held the full power to manage the partnership, had the right, by transferring productive assets to the CHLI subsidiary of the partnership, to reclassify the income produced by those assets from the category of Operating Income (in which the banks would take 98 percent) to Disposition Gains (in which the banks' share was 1 percent, over and above approximately $2.85 million). Second, the taxpayer could reduce drastically the net Operating

Income, in which the banks took a 98 percent share, by redepreciating the already fully depreciated aircraft, which had the effect of transferring the revenue covered by the depreciation from the banks to the taxpayer. Finally, the taxpayer could at any time, and at negligible cost, terminate the partnership.

As a practical matter, therefore, the Dutch banks' opportunity to participate in unexpected and extraordinary profits (beyond the reimbursement of their investment at the Applicable Rate of return) was capped at $2.85 million, plus 1 percent. Full realization of the $2.85 million potential, on an investment of $117.5 million, would have increased the banks' *total* return by less by 2.5 percent—a relatively insignificant incremental return over the projected eight-year life of the partnership. In short, the district court's conclusion that the banks enjoyed a meaningful and unlimited share of the partnership's upside potential was erroneously based on the fictions established by the partnership documents, and did not take account of the practical reality of the taxpayer's powers to restrict the banks' share of profits.

b. The Relevance of a "Sum Certain."

In conducting its analysis, the district court relied upon IRS Notice 94-47, 1994-19 IRB 9 (Apr. 18, 1994), which sets forth a nonexhaustive list of eight factors to be considered in distinguishing between debt and equity. This Notice directs consideration "whether there is an unconditional promise on the part of the issuer to pay a sum certain." In considering this factor, the court concluded that the banks were not owed a sum certain. The court therefore concluded that this factor argued against a finding of kinship to debt and in favor of kinship to equity. We believe the court erred, for reasons already discussed, in reaching its conclusion, or at least in the significance the court attached to it. As noted above, the court reasoned that, although "their potential downside was limited [by the partnership agreements] their upside was not." . . . "They were to receive 98 percent of the net Operating Income, whatever that might be . . . . Thus, although they were guaranteed a minimum return, they were not guaranteed a maximum—or, more to the point, a *certain* return . . . . [A]n investor with unlimited upside potential has a significant interest in the performance of the entity in question, because performance directly affects the amount of her return."

It is not entirely clear what the court meant by this analysis. The court could have meant either that (i) *any* potential share in profits results in an obligation to pay something other than a sum certain, and therefore tends to indicate an equity interest, rather than debt; or (ii) that a *substantial* share in potential profits, such as represented by the banks' 98 percent share of the Operating Income, indicates an equity interest rather than debt, even though downside risk may be eliminated. We think the district court probably meant the latter, both because it emphasized the 98 percent share and spoke of an investor with *unlimited* upside potential, and because the court repeatedly asserted that trivial interests should play no role in its analysis. Either meaning would be mistaken, although for different reasons.

If the court intended the first meaning (which we think unlikely)—that any deviation from a sum certain, no matter how trivial, argues against a finding of debt— this would misunderstand the basic purpose of the analysis. The purpose of the analysis is to bypass appearances and focus instead on practical realities. While an obligation to pay a sum certain indicates debt, it does not follow that any insignificant deviation from a sum certain indicates equity. The purpose of the test is to determine as a practical matter whether the interest created is *more akin* to equity or debt. Thus, the closer the amount owed comes to being a sum certain, the more it would tend to indicate debt. Trivial or insignificant deviations from a sum certain would do little to argue against a finding of debt.

If the court meant the latter—that the banks' unlimited upside potential, represented by their 98 percent share in the partnership's Operating Income, indicated a meaningful stake in the profits of the venture and thus argued against a finding of debt—this was error for the reasons discussed above: It failed to take account of the power of the taxpayer to direct the profits to itself by various devices, rather than to the banks.

The banks had essentially bargained for and received a secure guaranty of the reimbursement of their investment at the agreed Applicable Rate of return. Their apparent 98 percent share of partnership income was largely defeasible by the taxpayer, and was more in the nature of window dressing designed to give ostensible support to the characterization of equity participation, which was essential to the dominant tax objective, than a meaningful stake in the profits of the venture. The possibility of a small share in extraordinary profits was not a significant feature of their investment. While the amount owed to the banks was not exactly a "sum certain," it was not significantly different; it was more akin to the characteristic repayment of debt than to a real equity stake in the venture.

c. Whether the Banks' Interest Was Subordinated to General Creditors of the Partnership.

IRS Notice 94-74 lists as a factor to be considered in determining whether an interest is more akin to debt or equity "whether the rights of the holders of the instruments are subordinate to the rights of general creditors." The court concluded that the Dutch banks' interest was subordinate. While this conclusion was in a sense technically correct, it was erroneous as a practical matter because it overlooked the realities of the security provided to protect the banks' interest.

It is true that no partnership document overtly provided that repayment of the banks would take priority over payment of general creditors of the partnership. If the inquiry were limited to disposition of assets of Castle Harbour, we see no reason to doubt that general creditors would take prior to the banks. In fact, however, the repayment of the banks' interest was even more securely protected than by priority over the general creditors. The banks did not need to rely on assets of Castle Harbour or the taxpayer for reimbursement. They had the guaranty of the taxpayer's far more solvent parent GECC. Upon consideration of all the facts and circumstances, it is clear that, far from being subordinate to the general creditors, the Dutch banks were secured in such manner that they would be repaid in full with interest from a source to which the general creditors had no access. The apparent subordination found by the district court was a fiction overridden by GECC's guaranty.

d. Right To Enforce Payment of Principal and Interest.

The IRS Notice also lists as a pertinent factor "whether holders of instruments possess the right to enforce the payment of principal and interest." The district court erred in its consideration of this factor. Although the partnership arrangements do give to the banks the power to enforce the repayment of their principal and interest by terminating the partnership, the court did not deem this factor as supporting a finding of debt, but rather deemed it a factor that "deserve[s] little weight." The court explained that

> though a creditor with no right to enforce the payment of principal or interest . . . looks suspiciously like an equity holder, an equity holder with a right to force a buyout of his share is perfectly normal. In the partnership context, the default rule is that any partner can force a liquidation of the partnership, *i.e.*, force her investment to be returned to her (plus her gains or minus her losses).

The issue raised by the factor, however, is not whether the Dutch banks had a right to force a buyout of their share, giving account to the profits they had gained and losses they had suffered during their participation. It is rather whether they had the right to force the payment of what was effectively their principal and interest. They did. The partnership agreements gave the banks the power to terminate and receive the reimbursement of their $117.5 million investment at the agreed annual rate of return. As the district court elsewhere recognized, the banks were protected against any meaningful diminution of such repayment. And to the extent they were entitled to a share of profits over and above the return of their principal plus interest, this was, as explained above, a negligible interest (which, furthermore, did not detract from the fact that they were empowered to force the payment of their invested principal and interest). The position of the Dutch banks was thus very different from an ordinary equity partner's ability to force liquidation of a partnership. It was error for the district court to treat this factor as one without significance in the debt/equity analysis.

e. Management Rights.

The court likewise erred in its consideration of "whether the instruments give the holders the right to participate in the management of the issuer." Although recognizing that the banks had no right to participate in management, the district court did not deem this factor as favoring kinship to debt, but rather dismissed it as without significance. The court explained: "Possession of management rights by an alleged creditor…indicates the creditor may really be an owner, but the reverse is not true. The average stockholder of a publicly traded corporation has no management rights, but there is little doubt he holds equity."

The explanation is inapposite. In the first place, the Dutch banks were not like the "average stockholder" as they had invested nearly 20 percent of the partnership's assets. Furthermore, if the average stockholder of a publicly traded corporation has no practical influence on management, that is not because he possesses no management rights, but rather because his voting right is small in relation to the total electorate. Every share of stock in the typical publicly traded corporation carries with it one vote for the directors of the corporation. The banks, in contrast, although they had contributed a sizeable share of the partnership's capital, exercised no such vote. The failure to exercise management rights is certainly not conclusive. A holder of a bona fide minority equity interest in a partnership or corporation may well have no practical ability to influence management and may even have no vote as a formal matter. Nonetheless, it seems clear that the denial of participation in management to an investor is a factor which tends, even if only slightly, to favor a conclusion that the interest resembles debt. . . .

B. Whether the IRS Properly Determined that the Interest of the Banks Was Not a Bona Fide Equity Participation.

The ultimate question is whether the IRS properly determined in its FPAAs that the interest of the banks was not a bona fide equity participation. The errors of law made by the district court in considering this question invalidate its conclusion. We are accordingly compelled to vacate the judgment. The question remains whether we should remand for new findings or undertake ourselves to answer in the first instance the question of bona fide equity participation. We conclude that consideration of this question under *Culbertson's* mandate to appraise the totality of the circumstances compels the conclusion that, for tax purposes, the banks were not bona fide equity partners in Castle Harbour. Accordingly, there is no reason to remand for new findings.

The transaction consisted, as a practical matter, of an advance by the Dutch banks of $117.5 million. The partnership undertook to repay the advance at an agreed rate of return, pursuant to a previously agreed payment schedule. In the event of a missed payment, the banks had the power to liquidate the partnership and to receive the return of their principal at the agreed rate of return. These payments were to be made regardless of the fortunes of the partnership. Furthermore, because the payments were guaranteed by GECC, the banks were secured in the receipt of the payments, regardless of whether the partnership profited or lost money. Because of this guaranty, the banks had effective priority over the general creditors of the partnership. In all these respects, the banks were, for all intents and purposes, secured creditors. It is true that the banks' interest took on some aspect of equity participation in that they ran a small risk of a shortfall in event of catastrophic loss—a risk so small that the district court disregarded it—and that they were given in addition a participation in extraordinary unforeseen profits of the partnership. As for participation in unexpected profits, for the reasons explained above, the taxpayer was as a practical matter empowered to limit the banks' participation to an amount that was insignificant in the context of the banks' $117.5 million eight-year investment.[18] This was not a significant participation in the profits of the partnership.

We recognize that if the Dutch banks had a sufficiently sizable share in the profit potential of the partnership, they might appropriately be deemed equity participants for tax purposes, notwithstanding the guaranteed repayment of their initial investment at an agreed rate of return. See *Hunt v. Comm'r*, 59 TCM (CCH) 635 (1990) (noting that a bona fide equity interest can exist even where a minimum return is guaranteed). On different facts a difficult question would arise whether an investor's right to a share of profits was sufficient to make its interest a bona fide equity participation for tax purposes notwithstanding the secured guaranty of the return of its principal plus interest. This is not such a case. Here the banks were accorded the *appearance* of a meaningful interest in the potential profits of the partnership, which was effectively nullified by the taxpayer's ability to limit their participation in such profits to an insignificant amount.

---

[18] An additional return of $2.85 million over eight years would have increased the bank's rate of return by approximately one-third of one percent.

In following the approach of *Culbertson*, we are compelled to look not so much at the labels used by the partnership but at true facts and circumstances. The Dutch banks' interest was in the nature of a secured loan, with an insignificant equity kicker. Only in a negligible fashion was their well-secured interest intertwined with the fortunes of the business. The facts and circumstances presented, considered in their totality, compel the conclusion that the Dutch banks' interest was, for tax purposes, not a bona fide equity participation. . . .

> [On remand from the preceding decision of the Second Circuit Court of Appeals, the District Court again found in favor of the taxpayer, relying heavily on the statutory identification of a partner found in § 704(e)(1). *TIFD III-E v. United States,* 660 F Supp 2d 367 (D. Conn. 2009). This decision is itself on appeal to the Second Circuit.]

Littriello v. United States
484 F3d 372 (6th Cir. 2006)

MARTHA CRAIG DAUGHTREY, Circuit Judge.
In this appeal from a grant of summary judgment to the government, we are presented with a case of first impression regarding the validity of the Treasury Department's so-called "check-the-box" regulations, promulgated in 1996 to simplify the classification of business entities for tax purposes.

The plaintiff, Frank Littriello, was the sole owner of several Kentucky limited liability companies (LLCs), the operation of which resulted in unpaid federal employment taxes totaling $1,077,000. Because Littriello was the sole member of the LLCs and had not elected to have the businesses treated as "associations" (*i.e.,* corporations) under Treasury Regulations §§ 301.7701-3(a) and (c), the LLCs were "disregarded" as separate taxable entities and, instead, were treated for federal tax purposes as sole proprietorships under Treasury Regulation § 301.7701-3(b)(1)(ii). When Littriello, as sole proprietor, failed to pay the outstanding employment taxes, the IRS filed notices of determination and, eventually, notified him of its intent to levy on his property to enforce previously filed tax liens. Littriello responded by initiating complaints for judicial review in district court, contending that the regulations in question (1) exceed the authority of the Treasury to issue regulatory interpretations of the Internal Revenue Code; (2) conflict with the principles enunciated by the Supreme Court in *Morrissey v. Commissioner,* 296 U.S. 344 (1935); and (3) disregard the separate existence of an LLC under Kentucky state law. . . . After the cases were consolidated for disposition, the district court held that the "check-the-box regulations" are " a reasonable response to the changes in the state law industry of business formation," upheld them under *Chevron* analysis [*Chevron U.S.A., Inc. v. Natural Res. Def. Council, Inc.,* 467 U.S. 837 (1984)], and held that the plaintiff was individually liable for the employment taxes at issue. We conclude that the district court's analysis was correct and affirm. . . .

DISCUSSION

The Treasury Regulations at the heart of this litigation were issued in 1996 to clarify the rules for determining the classification of certain business entities for federal tax purposes, replacing the so-called "*Kintner* regulations." The earlier regulations had been developed to aid in classifying business associations that were not incorporated under state incorporation statutes but that had certain characteristics common to corporations and were thus subject to taxation as corporations under the federal tax code. Corporate income is, of course, subject to "double taxation"—once at the corporate level and again at the individual-shareholder level. In contrast, partnership income benefits from "pass-through" treatment—it is taxed once, not at the business level but only after it passes through to the individual partners and is taxed as income to them. A sole proprietorship—in which a single individual owns all the assets, is liable for all debts, and operates in an individual capacity—is also taxed only once.

The *Kintner* regulations built on an even earlier standard, set out by the Supreme Court in *Morrissey*, in which the Court addressed the tax code provision that included an "association" within the definition of a corporation, in order to determine whether a "business trust" qualified as an "association" for federal tax purposes. *Morrissey* identified certain characteristics as those typical of a corporation, including the existence of associates, continuity of the entity, centralized management, limited personal liability, transferability of ownership interests, and title to property. However, the Court did not hold that a specific number of those characteristics had to be present in order to establish the business entity as a corporation, nor did it address the consequence of a partnership having some of those characteristics, leaving the distinctions between and among the various defined entities less than clear.

Meant to clarify some of the confusion created in the wake of *Morrissey*, the *Kintner* regulations developed four essential characteristics of a corporate entity and provided that an unincorporated business would be treated as an "association"—and, therefore, as a corporation rather than a partnership—if it had three of those four identifying characteristics. The *Kintner* regulations, adequate to provide a measure of predictability at the time of their promulgation in 1960 and for several decades afterward, proved less than adequate to deal with the new hybrid business entities—limited liability companies, limited liability partnerships, and the like—developed in the last years of the last century under various state laws. These unincorporated business entities had the characteristics of both corporations and partnerships, combining ease of management with limited liability, and were increasingly structured with the *Kintner* regulations in mind, in order to take advantage of whatever classification was thought to be the most advantageous. The "Kintner exercise" required skillful lawyering by business entities and case-by-case review by the IRS; it quickly came to be seen as squandering of resources on both sides of the equation.

As a result, the IRS undertook to replace the *Kintner* regulations with a more practical scheme, consistent with existing tax statutes and with a new provision in § 7704 treating publicly-traded entities as corporations, regardless of their structure or status under state law. As to the unincorporated business associations not covered by § 7704, including the newly emerging hybrid entities, the IRS proposed to allow an election by the taxpayer to be treated as a corporation or, in the absence of such an election, to be "disregarded," *i.e.*, deemed a partnership (for entities with multiple members) or a sole proprietorship (for those with a single member). After a period for notice and comment, the new regulations were issued and became effective on January 1, 1997, implementing the definitional provisions of §§ 7701(a)(2) and (3). The regulations were particularly helpful with regard to the tax status of the new hybrids, because the hybrid entities were not, and still are not, explicitly covered by the definitions set out in § 7701. What was avoided by the resulting "check-the-box" provisions was the necessity of forcing those hybrids to jump through the *Kintner* regulation "hoops" in order to achieve a desired—and perfectly legal—classification for federal tax purposes.

The district court noted that Littriello's unincorporated businesses had not elected to be treated as corporations under the new regulations and were, therefore, deemed by the IRS to be sole proprietorships. This result provided Littriello with a major tax advantage: his income from the healthcare facilities would be taxed to him only once. But, of course, it also meant that he would be responsible not only for taxes on business income but also for those federal employment taxes that were required by statute and that had not been paid for the years in question.

The district court found that the regulations were a reasonable interpretation by the IRS of a tax statute (§ 7701) that was otherwise ambiguous, upheld them under *Chevron* analysis, after noting that it was apparently the first court asked to review those regulations, and held Littriello individually liable for the amounts assessed by the IRS. In doing so, the district court rejected Littriello's arguments that the Secretary of the Treasury had exceeded his authority in promulgating the entity-classification regulations, that the regulations are invalid under *Morrissey*, and that they impermissibly altered the legal status of his state-law-created LLC. . . .

A. Chevron Analysis

The first two arguments raised by Littriello are intertwined. He contends that the statute underlying the "check-the-box" regulations is unambiguous and that the district court's invocation of *Chevron* was, therefore, erroneous. Under *Chevron*, a court reviewing an agency's interpretation of a statute that it administers must first determine "whether Congress has directly spoken to the precise question at issue." If congressional intent is clear, then "that is the end of the matter; for the court, as well as the agency, must give effect to the unambiguously expressed intent of Congress." However, "if the statute is silent or ambiguous with respect to the specific issue, the question for the court is whether the agency's answer is based on a permissible construction of the statute."

Littriello . . . posits that the regulations run afoul of *Morrissey*, "the seminal case on § 7701," which he reads to hold that the IRS is legally required to determine the classification of a taxpayer-business within the definitions set out in the statute and may not "abdicate the responsibility of making that determination to the taxpayer itself" by permitting an election of classification such as a "check-the-box" option.

Although the plaintiff's *Morrissey* argument is not a model of clarity, it seems to depend on the proposition that the terms defined in § 7701 ("corporation," "association," "partnership," etc.) are not ambiguous but "[have been] in common usage in Anglo American law for centuries" and, as a corollary, that "*Morrissey* provides a test of identification [that is itself] unambiguous." Hence, the argument goes, it is the "check-the-box" regulations that " render whole portions of the Internal Revenue Code ambiguous" and are therefore " in direct conflict with the decision of the Supreme Court in *Morrissey*" in the absence of Congressional amendment to § 7701.

It is unnecessary, in our judgment, to engage in an exegesis of *Chevron* here. The perimeters of that opinion and its directive to courts to give deference to an agency's interpretation of statutes that the agency is entrusted to administer and to the rules that govern implementation, as long as they are reasonable, are clear, and are clearly applicable in this case. Moreover, the argument that *Morrissey* has somehow cemented the interpretation of § 7701 in the absence of subsequent Congressional action or Supreme Court modification is refuted by *Chevron,* in which the Court suggested that an agency's interpretation of a statute, as reflected in the regulations it promulgates, can and must be revised to meet changing circumstances. Even more to the point, the Court in *Morrissey* observed that the Code's definition of a corporation was less than adequate and that, as a result, the IRS had the authority to supply rules of implementation that could later be changed to meet new situations. . . .

In short, we agree with the district court's conclusions: that § 7701 is ambiguous when applied to recently emerging hybrid business entities such as the LLCs involved in this case; that the Treasury regulations developed to fill in the statutory gaps when dealing with such entities are eminently reasonable; that the "check-the-box" regulations are a valid exercise of the agency's authority in that respect; that the plaintiff's failure to make an election under the "check-the-box" provision dictates that his companies be treated as disregarded entities under those regulations, thereby preventing them from being taxed as corporations under the Internal Revenue Code; and that he is, therefore, liable individually for the employment taxes due and owing from those businesses because they constitute sole proprietorships under § 7701, and he is the proprietor.

B. Status Under State Law . . .

The federal government has historically disregarded state classifications of businesses for some federal tax purposes. . . . [T]he United States Supreme Court held that Massachusetts trusts were "associations" within the meaning of the Internal Revenue Code despite the fact they were not so considered under state law. As courts have repeatedly observed, state laws of incorporation control various aspects of business relations; they may affect, but do not necessarily control, federal tax provisions. See, e.g., *Morrissey* (explaining that common law definitions of certain corporate forms do not control interpretation of federal tax code). As a result, Littriello's single-member LLCs are entitled to whatever advantages state law may extend, but state law cannot abrogate his federal tax liability. . . .

CONCLUSION

For the reasons set out above, we reject the plaintiff's challenge to the "check-the-box" regulations and AFFIRM the district court's grant of summary judgment to the defendant.

[On remand from the preceding decision of the Second Circuit Court of Appeals, the District Court again found in favor of the taxpayer, holding that the Dutch banks owned capital interests in a capital-intensive partnership, and were therefore partners under § 704(e)(1). *TIFD III-E, Inc. v United States,* 660 F. Supp. 2d 367 (D. Conn. 2009). This decision was reversed by the Second Circuit, which held that "the same evidence which, on our last review, compelled the conclusion that the banks' interest was so markedly in the nature of debt that it does not qualify as bona fide equity participation also compels the conclusion that the banks' interest was not a capital interest under § 704(e)(1)." *TIFD III-E, Inc. v United States,* No. 10-70-cv (2d Cir., filed January 24, 2012).]

Revenue Ruling 75-374
1975-2 C.B. 261

Advice has been requested whether, under the circumstance described below, the co-owners of an apartment project would be treated as a partnership for Federal income tax purposes.

X, a life insurance company, and Y, a real estate investment trust, each own an undivided one-half interest in an apartment project. X and Y entered into a management agreement with Z, an unrelated corporation, and retained it to manage, operate, maintain, and service the project.

Generally, under the management agreement Z negotiates and executes leases for apartment units in the project; collects rents and other payments from tenants; pays taxes, assessments, and insurance premiums payable with respect to the project; performs all other services customarily performed in connection with the maintenance and repair of an apartment project; and performs certain additional services for the tenants beyond those customarily associated with maintenance and repair. Z is responsible for determining the time and manner of performing its obligations under the agreement and for the supervision of all persons performing services in connection with the carrying out of such obligations.

Customary tenant services, such as heat, air conditioning, hot and cold water, unattended parking, normal repairs, trash removal, and cleaning of public areas are furnished at no additional charge above the basic rental payments. All costs incurred by Z in rendering these customary services are paid for by X and Y. As compensation for the customary services rendered by Z under the agreement, X and Y each pay Z a percentage of one-half of the gross rental receipts derived from the operation of the project.

Additional services, such as attendant parking, cabanas, and gas, electricity, and other utilities are provided by Z to tenants for a separate charge. Z pays the costs incurred in providing the additional services, and retains the charges paid by tenants for its own use. These charges provide Z with adequate compensation for the rendition of these additional services.

Section 761(a) . . . provides that the term "partnership" includes a syndicate, group, pool, joint venture or other unincorporated organization through or by means of which any business, financial operation, or venture is carried on, and which is not a corporation or a trust or estate.

Section 1.761-1(a) of the . . . Regulations provides that mere co-ownership of property that is maintained, kept in repair, and rented or leased does not constitute a partnership. Tenants in common may be partners if they actively carry on a trade, business, financial operation, or venture and divide the profits thereof. For example, a partnership exists if co-owners of an apartment building lease space and in addition provide services to the occupants either directly or through an agent.

The furnishing of customary services in connection with the maintenance and repair of the apartment project will not render a co-ownership a partnership. However, the furnishing of additional services will render a co-ownership a partnership if the additional services are furnished directly by the co-owners or through their agent. In the instant case by reason of the contractual arrangement with Z, X and Y are not furnishing the additional services either directly or through an agent. Z is solely responsible for determining the time and manner of furnishing the services, bears all the expenses of providing these services, and retains for its own use all the income from these services. None of the profits arising from the rendition of these additional services are divided between X and Y.

Accordingly, X and Y will be treated as co-owners and not as partners for purposes of section 761 of the Code.

CHAPTER 2

Partnership Formation— Acquisition of a Partnership Interest in Exchange for a Contribution of Property

PROBLEM AREA 2

INTRODUCTION

A partner can acquire a partnership interest from the partnership itself in exchange for the contribution of either property or services. Such a contribution of property or services can occur upon formation of the partnership or at a later time involving an already existing partnership. This Problem Area focuses on the tax consequences of a contribution of property. Problem Area 3 concerns the receipt of a partnership interest in return for services.

Section 721(a) provides that "no gain or loss shall be recognized to a partnership or to any of its partners in the case of a contribution of property to the partnership in exchange for an interest in the partnership." This non-recognition treatment does not apply, however, to contributions to an investment partnership under § 721(b) or to contributions arising in an international context under §§ 721(c) and 721(d).

For a contribution of property to qualify for non-recognition of gain or loss, the partner must transfer property to the partnership. Neither § 721 nor its Regulations defines "property." Money clearly is considered property for this purpose. Real property and tangible personal property qualify if title is transferred to the partnership. Services do not constitute property for § 721 purposes. Other types of rights and interests are not as easily classified. For example, in *Oden v. Commissioner*, which follows, the taxpayer's personal note constituted property for purposes of § 721. The taxpayer had a zero basis in the note, which carried over to the partnership. If the taxpayer had made any payments on the note, the court evidently would have increased his basis for the partnership interest by the amount of such payments. Intangible rights, including various forms of intellectual property, pose similar classification issues.

The non-recognition treatment of § 721 may be undercut by other judicial and statutory doctrines. For example, the assignment-of-income doctrine, the potential application of §§ 1245 and 1250 regarding depreciation recapture, and § 453B regarding the disposition of installment obligations must be considered. Furthermore, gain may result from the contribution of property that is subject to a liability as a result of the shifting of the contributing partner's share of the liability through its assumption by the partnership.

When a contribution to a partnership qualifies under § 721, the basis of the contributing partner's partnership interest is determined under § 722. Notwithstanding the fact that the partners, not the partnership, are responsible on their personal returns for the earnings or losses from operations, an entity approach is employed whereby the partners maintain a basis for their partnership interests. The basis of the contributing partner's partnership interest is equal to the amount of money contributed plus the adjusted basis of any property contributed. An increase in basis is available for the amount of any gain recognized under § 721(b) by the contributing partner.

Section 723 provides for the determination of the partnership's basis for the contributed assets. The partnership's basis for the contributed property is the adjusted basis of the property to the contributing partner at the time of the contribution. Essentially, the partnership takes a transferred basis from the partner and will recognize gain or loss upon the ultimate disposition of the property. The effect of these rules is that the aggregate basis of property in the hands of the partnership, the so-called "inside basis," equals the aggregate basis of the partners' interest in the partnership, the so-called "outside basis." Inside and outside basis will frequently run in tandem and may remain equal even after years of operations. The rules of § 1223 generally provide for "tacking" when calculating the holding period both for property contributed to the partnership and for the contributing partner's partnership interest.

The non-recognition treatment afforded by § 721 may be jeopardized if the partnership makes a distribution to the contributing partner in connection with his contribution. If the contribution and the distribution are sufficiently linked, they may constitute a disguised sale of the property to the partnership under § 707(a)(2)(B) and the Regulations thereunder. The effect of this characterization is to cause the partner to recognize gain or loss with respect to the portion of the contributed property deemed sold and to give the partnership a full cost basis and new holding period therein. More detailed study of these complex rules is deferred to Problem Area 20.

If § 707(a)(2)(B) does not apply to the distribution, the excess of any money that is distributed or deemed distributed to a partner in connection with the contribution of property to the partnership over the adjusted basis of the partner's partnership interest constitutes taxable gain under § 731(a). Such a situation could occur upon the formation of the partnership when the contributing partner transfers encumbered property or the partnership otherwise assumes an individual liability of the contributing partner. Under § 752(a), a partner is deemed to contribute money to a partnership to the extent of his share of the partnership's liabilities. Additionally, under § 752(b), if the partnership assumes the liability of a partner, *e.g.*, by a transfer of encumbered property, the partner is deemed to receive a distribution of money in that amount. Thus, when the amount of the *net* liability relief exceeds the basis for the partner's partnership interest, gain will be generated under § 731.

PROBLEM 2

QUESTIONS

1. A, B, and C agree to form a real estate investment partnership. They decide to form an equal, cash-method, general partnership, with each contributing property worth $300,000. A contributes cash in that amount; B contributes raw land purchased for $100,000 and held for two years; and C contributes publicly traded stock purchased for $400,000 and held for six months. The parties anticipate a serious exploration of the real estate market and will either hold the real estate and any subsequently acquired real estate for appreciation or will construct an apartment building for rental purposes.

    a. What gain or loss is recognized by each partner as a result of these contributions?

    b. What is the tax basis of each partner's interest in the partnership?

    c. What is the partnership's basis in each asset?

    d. What is each partner's holding period for his partnership interest?

    e. What is the partnership's holding period for its assets?

2. Same as question 1. above, except that, two years after formation of the partnership, D acquires an interest in the partnership in exchange for contributing a parcel of land that adjoins the partnership's original property. D purchased this parcel for $200,000, and it is worth $400,000 at the time of contribution. At that time, the partnership's original land has appreciated in value to $500,000, the stock contributed by C has recovered to $400,000 in value, and the partnership continues to hold $300,00 in cash as its only other asset.

    a. What is D's percentage interest in the partnership?

    b. What gain or loss is recognized by D as a result of her contribution?

    c. What gain or loss is recognized by the other partners as a result of D's contribution?

3. Same as question 1. above, except that B contributes publicly traded stock rather than land.

4. A, B, and C are sole proprietors, each individually engaged in the business of freelance court reporting. All three individuals report their income on the cash method. They decide to form an equal, cash-method, general partnership to provide court reporting services. A, B, and C each contributes the following property worth $30,000 to the partnership.

A contributes:

    • $20,000.
    • A's personal note for $15,000 with a $10,000 value.

B contributes:

- Xerox duplicator-collator held several years. Value $30,000, recomputed basis $40,000, adjusted basis $10,000. Three years remaining useful life.

C contributes:

- $25,000 in § 453 installment obligations acquired three months ago from the sale of property held for three years. Value $20,000, adjusted basis $15,000.
- Accounts receivable from his sole proprietorship valued at $10,000, attributable to services rendered over the preceding months.

a. What gain or loss is recognized by each partner as a result of these contributions?

b. What is the tax basis of each partner's interest in the partnership?

c. What is the partnership's basis in each asset?

d. What is each partner's holding period for his partnership interest?

e. What is the partnership's holding period for its assets?

f. Would it make any difference if B had held the Xerox duplicator for five months?

5. a. What is the tax basis of B's partnership interest in question 4. above if the partnership assumes a recourse liability of B in the amount of (i) $9,000 or (ii) $18,000? Assume, in both situations, (i) an increase in the gross value of the Xerox machine so that the *net* value on contribution remains $30,000, and (ii) no change in the recomputed basis or adjusted basis of the Xerox machine, which remain $40,000 and $10,000, respectively. Ignore the possible application of § 707(a)(2)(B).

b. What is the effect of the liabilities on the partnership's adjusted basis in the property contributed by B?

c. What is the amount and character of any gain resulting to B from the contribution of the Xerox duplicator if the partnership assumes B's recourse liability of (i) $9,000 or (ii) $18,000?

MATERIALS

Oden v. Commissioner
TC Memo 1981-184

IRWIN, Judge.

OPINION

. . . The issue presented for our determination focuses upon the propriety of petitioners' claimed partnership loss of $30,789. This loss was mainly attributable to alleged intangible drilling costs deducted by the Ohio Producers partnership pursuant to an election under section 263(c).

Respondent bases his denial of the claimed partnership loss in excess of $16,250 on the following grounds: (1) Petitioner has not established that intangible drilling costs in an amount in excess of $65,000 were actually incurred in connection with the Chamberlain well. Thus, petitioner, with a one-fourth interest in the well, may not deduct more than $16,250 for intangible drilling costs; (2) petitioner, according to respondent, did not acquire an operating interest in the Chamberlain well until after the well had been drilled to production. Thus, respondent relies on *Haass v. Commissioner*, 55 T.C. 43 (1970), which holds that a working or operating interest in a specific well must be acquired prior to the incursion of drilling and development expenses in order that expenses be deductible to the holder of such an interest; and (3) petitioner has not established that he had a higher basis than $16,250 in his partnership interest.

Petitioner argues that the issue of the amount of intangible drilling costs incurred by the Ohio Producers partnership was not raised in the notice of deficiency and hence constitutes new matter regarding which the burden of proof rests on respondent. This burden, petitioner asserts, has not been satisfied. Petitioner further maintains that he acquired his partnership interest prior to the time that intangible drilling costs were incurred respecting the Chamberlain well. Petitioner claims that his basis in the Ohio Producers partnership was $35,000 and accordingly the claimed partnership loss of $30,789 is allowable.

We hold for respondent for the reason that petitioner's basis in his partnership interest has not been shown to be greater than $16,250 and accordingly any partnership loss in excess of that amount must be disallowed.

Section 722 provides in pertinent part that the basis of an interest in a partnership acquired by a contribution of property, including money, to the partnership shall be the amount of such money and the adjusted basis of such property to the contributing partner at the time of the contribution. A partner's distributive share of partnership loss (including capital loss) shall be allowed only to the extent of the adjusted basis of such partner's interest in the partnership at the end of the partnership year in which the loss occurred. Section 704(d). Petitioner's cash contribution to the Ohio Producers partnership was $16,250. Additionally, he argues that he tendered a note for $18,750 at the time of the creation of the partnership. Petitioner claims that under section 742 he is entitled to a $35,000 basis in his partnership interest.

Petitioner's application of section 742 to the instant case is in error. That section provides that a transferee's initial basis in his partnership interest is determined under the rules generally applicable to acquisitions of other types of property. See section

1.742-1, Income Tax Regs. Accordingly, if a partnership interest is purchased or acquired in a taxable exchange, the transferee's basis is his cost under section 1012. Where, however, the partnership interest is acquired by a contribution of property to the partnership, the contributor's basis in the acquired interest is determined by reference to the adjusted basis of the property so contributed.

Petitioner urges that we determine that his basis in the Ohio Producers partnership includes the face amount ($18,750) of a note allegedly executed and delivered by him to the partnership. Petitioner has not shown that any payments were made on the note during 1971.

Petitioner advances an elaborate argument which points to the alleged transfer of his own note to the partnership. He emphasizes that the note created a bona fide indebtedness to the partnership, while he minimizes the importance of the question of whether the note was recourse or nonrecourse. While we agree that it is irrelevant in the present context whether the note was either recourse or nonrecourse, we believe that such irrelevancy stems from the fact that petitioner's basis in his partnership interest is to be determined under section 722. Since petitioner incurred no cost in making the note, its basis to him was zero. Petitioner has not shown that any payments on the note were made in 1971. Thus, pursuant to the mandate of section 722, petitioner is not entitled to increase his partnership basis by the face amount of the allegedly transferred note. Accordingly, petitioner is not entitled to deduct any partnership loss in excess of his cash contribution of $16,250. Section 704(d).

Other arguments aired by the parties are rendered moot by our holding above and thus we do not address them.

Decision will be entered for the respondent.

Internal Revenue Service
Field Service Advice Memorandum 1998-481

Issues

Whether a transfer of a "non-exclusive" right to use and have access to manufacturing technology and the exclusive right to use and have access to related technology to a partnership is a "contribution of property" for purposes of section 721. . . .

Conclusions

The Service's position regarding whether "property" is "contributed" in exchange for a partnership interest for purposes of section 721(a) is that the contributor must transfer all substantial rights in the underlying property. However, serious consideration must also be given to the adverse precedent in *E.I. du Pont de Nemours & Co. v. United States*, 471 F.2d 1211 (Ct. Cl. 1973) and *United States v. Stafford*, 727 F.2d 1043, 1048 (11th Cir. 1984), which suggests that a court could hold [in these circumstances] that taxpayer "contributed property" for purposes of section 721 . . . .

Facts

A is a worldwide manufacturing company that has developed a unique, cost efficient process for manufacturing product F. The process technology is commonly known as B. . . .

On Date 1, A and D entered into a "Joint Venture Agreement," which became effective on Date 2. The Joint Venture Agreement will be hereinafter referred to as "the Agreement." D is an entity organized under the laws of country E and is classified as a corporation for U.S. tax purposes. Pursuant to the Agreement, A and D agreed to produce and market product F in Europe and agreed to form G, a business entity organized under the laws of country E and classified as a partnership for U.S. tax purposes. D contributed plant, equipment, spare parts, and customer lists in exchange for a 50 percent interest in G. A . . . contribute[d] certain interests in the B process technology in exchange for A's 50 percent interest in G. The interest in the B process technology consisted of: (1) the non-exclusive right to use and have access to the B process technology under terms and conditions of a separate agreement between [A] and G; and (2) the exclusive right to have access to and to use a related technology in a specifically delineated area. G did not have the right to sublicense the technology in either instance.

Law and Analysis . . .

Contributions of property to a partnership in exchange for a partnership interest therein are governed specifically by section 721. There are no precise, consistent definitions for the terms "contribution," "property," and "exchange" included in section 721(a). Section 351 is analogous to section 721 because section 351 addresses property transfers to corporations in exchange for stock in such corporations. Section 351 is not, however, the Subchapter C mirror image of section 721 because section 351 only governs transfers by "controlling" shareholders. Exchanges involving "non-controlling" shareholders are governed by sections 118 and 1032. . . . Notwithstanding these differences, we believe that the standards for an exchange of property for purposes of sections 721 and 351 are similar.

Under section 351, no gain or loss will be recognized if one or more persons transfer property to a corporation solely in exchange for stock in the corporation and, immediately after the exchange, such person or persons are in control of the corporation. The Service interprets this language to mean that, under section 351, a person must "transfer property to a corporation solely in exchange for stock" in a manner consistent with section 1001. Consequently, if the rights to be transferred to the transferee corporation were sold to a third party for cash, gain or loss would have to be realized under section 1001 and section 61(a)(3) in order for the transfer to qualify for nonrecognition under section 351.

Rev. Rul. 69-156, 1969-1 C.B. 101, illustrates the Service's position with respect to the granting of a non-exclusive license to use patent rights. In that ruling, the Service held that the grant of patent rights to a corporation in exchange for stock will constitute a transfer of property under section 351 only if the grant consists of all substantial rights in the patent and would constitute a sale or exchange of property rather than a license. The Service has applied a similar analysis to rights other than patents (see Rev. Proc. 83-59, 1983-2 C.B. 575, 578, sections 4.023(4) (copyrights and trade secrets) and 4.023(5) (franchises, trademarks, and trade names)), and we see no basis for distinguishing the rights transferred to the partnership by the taxpayer in the present case.

Notwithstanding the above, serious consideration must be given to case law interpreting the Service's position, before proposing adjustments in the statutory notice of deficiency. In *E.I. du Pont de Nemours & Co. v. United States*, 471 F.2d 1211 (Ct. Cl. 1973), the United States Court of Claims held that a "carved out" right to a non-exclusive license would qualify for non-recognition under section 351. In so holding, the court rejected the Service's position set forth in Rev. Rul. 69-156 and held that there is no basis for limiting non-recognition under section 351 to transfers which constitute sales or exchanges under section 1001. Because *du Pont* was decided in the predecessor of the United States Court of Federal Claims, its precedential effect is not confined to a specific geographical area. Further, the Service has not successfully litigated any cases concerning this issue since 1973. . . .

We also note that in *United States v. Stafford*, 727 F.2d 1043, 1048 (11th Cir. 1984), the court held that a partner's transfer of a letter of intent, which was unenforceable under state law, qualified for non-recognition under section 721. In reaching this conclusion, the court relied on precedent under section 351 to determine the scope of the term "property" under section 721. The court reasoned that the purpose of section 721 is similar to the purpose of section 351, which is to facilitate the flow of property into entities which will use the property productively. . . .

Case Development, Hazards and Other Considerations:

Under all the circumstances of this case, we believe that, in light of *du Pont*, *Stafford*, and the rationale adopted by the courts therein, a court would be very likely to conclude that the transfer of a non-exclusive license and the related technology in the present case should qualify for non-recognition under section 721. Accordingly, we recommend accepting the taxpayer's characterization as a contribution to the partnership pursuant to section 721(a).

CHAPTER **3**

Partnership Formation— Acquisition of a Partnership Interest (Other Than a Profits Interest) in Exchange for a Contribution of Services

PROBLEM AREA 3

INTRODUCTION

A partner may acquire a partnership interest in exchange for services rendered, or a promise of services to be rendered, to the partnership. In contrast to the general rule applicable to contributions of property, the receipt of a partnership interest in exchange for services may result in income to the recipient partner. Traditionally, partnership interests have been divided between capital interests (*i.e.*, a partner's right to proceeds on liquidation) and profits interests (*i.e.*, a partner's right to future realized income, gains, or losses) for purposes of this analysis, with only the former being subject to tax on receipt.

More recently, Proposed Regulations have suggested that all partnership interests ought to be subject to the same set of rules, but have hastily added a safe harbor through which service partners and partnerships can attach a zero valuation to a profits interest, thereby assuring that the service provider is not subject to immediate taxation on receipt. In recognition of the traditional dichotomy between capital interests and profits interests, and the difference in tax consequences to the service provider of receiving one or the other, Problem Area 3 focuses solely on capital interests. The treatment of profits interests and other more advanced topics is reserved for Problem Area 21.

Regulation § 1.721-1(b)(1) provides that the transfer of an interest in partnership capital to a partner as compensation for services constitutes income to the partner under § 61. Proposed Regulation § 1.721-1(b)(1), in contrast, identifies such a transaction as a transfer of property which is taxable to the service provider under § 83 and the Regulations thereunder. This brings into play the more fully developed rules of § 83, including those relating to property which is subject to a substantial risk of forfeiture.

Under the § 83 regime, a compensatory partnership interest is includable in the service partner's gross income at an amount equal to the fair market value of the partnership interest determined when the partner's rights in the interest are not subject to a substantial risk of forfeiture. Under § 83, the service partner is not treated as a partner for tax purposes while such restrictions or conditions are in force. However, the § 83(b) election permits the recipient to accelerate the time for including the value of the capital interest in gross income and possibly minimize the amount of income includable as ordinary income.

Upon making this election, the service partner is considered to be a partner for tax purposes, creating the possibility that he or she will be allocated shares of partnership items during the period prior to vesting that will be forfeited if vesting never occurs. Proposed Regulation §§ 1.704-1(b)(4)(xii) and 1.706-3 anticipate this possibility and provide for "forfeiture allocations" to address it. This advanced topic is examined in Problem Area 21.

The § 83 regime also affects the timing of the deduction available to the partnership for whom services are rendered. Assuming that a deduction is otherwise available under § 162 or § 212, the partnership is entitled to deduct the same amount as the service provider includes in income with respect to his receipt of a compensatory partnership interest. The deduction is allowed in the partnership's taxable year in which or with which ends the taxable year of the service provider in which he includes the amount as compensation income. Reg. § 1.83-6(a)(1).

Prior to the issuance of the Proposed Regulations in 2003, many believed (although no court opinion or Ruling had addressed the issue) that the share of partnership assets to which the service partner would be entitled upon liquidation of his capital interest should be considered to have been paid to the partner (thereby resulting in gain or loss to the partnership if the assets were appreciated or depreciated) and subsequently contributed by the distributee/service partner to the partnership for his partnership interest. Proposed Regulation § 1.721-1(b)(2) adopts an entity, rather than an aggregate, approach to the issue and provides that the partnership recognizes no gain or loss on the compensatory transfer of a partnership interest.

PROBLEM 3

QUESTIONS

1. On January 1, Year 1, A, B, and C join together to form an equal partnership. A and B contribute $30,000 each to the partnership. C does not make a capital contribution, but instead agrees to act as the manager of the partnership's business. Each of A, B, and C receives a one-third interest in the capital, profits, and losses of the partnership. What are the tax consequences to C on the transfer of the partnership capital interest, including (a) the amount of income, gain, or loss and its character for tax purposes and (b) the adjusted basis and holding period of the interest received? What are the tax consequences to the partnership on the transfer, including (c) the income, gain, or loss realized and (d) deductions? Assume, in each case, that the value of the partnership interest transferred to C is $20,000.

2. What if, in question 1. above, C previously negotiated a contract to purchase a new office building in which to locate the business of the partnership and contributes the contract to the partnership?

3. In question 1. above, what result if A and B each contributes property with a basis of $10,000 and a fair market value of $30,000 instead of money?

4. In question 3. above, what result if C receives his capital interest for services he has provided in the past to A and B?

5. Since October, Year 1, A and B have operated an equal law partnership. Each partner contributed $30,000 cash at the partnership's formation with which it purchased the small office building where the partners practice in a suburban community. The building is now worth $120,000 and has an adjusted basis of $55,000. In December, Year 3, the partners seek to persuade C, a highly respected tax attorney, to join them as a partner. C has no money or property to contribute. Nevertheless, A and B are willing to give him a one-third interest in the capital, profits, and losses of the partnership. C agrees to join the firm and to establish and conduct a tax department. What are the tax consequences of the transaction to all parties? Assume that the building is the partnership's only asset and that the value of the partnership interest transferred to C is $40,000.

6. In question 5. above, what are the tax effects to C and the partnership if the partnership agreement provides that C cannot sell his partnership interest unless he has performed services for the partnership until the earlier of his death or five years from the date he entered the partnership?

7. In question 6., above, compare the current and future tax consequences to C if he:

a. Reports the partnership interest as income by electing § 83(b).

b. Does not elect to report income under § 83(b).

MATERIALS

United States v. Frazell
335 F2d 487 (5th Cir. 1964)

TUTTLE, Chief Judge.

This is an appeal by the Government from a judgment in favor of the taxpayer. As the largely undisputed facts are set out at length in the opinion of the district court, only a summary will be presented here. On February 9, 1951, William Frazell, a geologist, entered into a contract with the N. H. Wheless Oil Company, a partnership, and W. C. Woolf, under which Frazell was to check certain areas to determine whether potentially productive oil and gas properties might be procured there. He was to recommend those properties he found suitable to Wheless and Woolf, and upon their joint approval, he was to attempt to acquire such properties, taking title thereto in the names of Wheless and Woolf in equal shares. In return for these services, Frazell was to receive "a monthly salary or drawing account," plus expenses, and specified interests in the property acquired. It was agreed, however, "that Frazell shall not be entitled to, nor shall he be considered as owning, any interest in said properties until such time as Wheless and Woolf shall have recovered their full costs and expenses of said properties" including the amounts paid out to Frazell.

The arrangement proved successful, and it was evident in the early part of 1955 that Wheless and Woolf would fully recover their costs and expenses by the end of November of that year. In April 1955, the 1951 contract was terminated, and by contract dated April 20, 1955, all the properties acquired under the earlier arrangement were transferred to the W.W.F. Corporation, a Delaware corporation formed specifically to acquire these properties in return for the issuance of debentures to Wheless and Woolf and of stock to Wheless, Woolf, and Frazell. Frazell received 6,500 shares of W.W.F. stock (13% of the total issued), having a fair market value of $91,000, but he included no part of this amount in his 1955 income tax return. The Commissioner ruled that the $91,000 should have been included in income and assessed a deficiency, which Frazell paid under protest and seeks to recover here.

Frazell contends that he received the W.W.F. stock in a tax-free exchange within the terms of section 351(a), Internal Revenue Code of 1954. That section provides:

> No gain or loss shall be recognized if property is transferred to a corporation by one or more persons solely in exchange for stock or securities in such corporation and immediately after the exchange such person or persons are in control . . . of the corporation. For purposes of this section, stock or securities issued for services shall not be considered as issued in return for property.

The district court agreed that section 351(a) is applicable in this case. This was said to follow from that court's finding that the 1951 contract created a "joint venture" among the three participants. We take no issue with the trial court's finding of fact in this matter, but it does not follow from the categorization of the 1951 arrangement as a "joint venture" that the April 1955 transactions resulted in no taxable income to Frazell.

It is fundamental that "compensation for services" is taxable as ordinary income under the Internal Revenue Code of 1954. § 61(a)(1). This principle applies whether the one compensated for his services is an employee receiving a salary, fees, or commission (ibid.), one receiving corporate securities (§ 351(a)), or a "service partner" receiving an interest in the partnership. (§ 721; Reg. § 1.721-1(b)(1)).

The regulation pertaining to partnerships provides that:

> the value of an interest in such partnership capital so transferred to a partner as compensation for services constitutes income to the partner under section 61. The amount of such income is the fair market value of the interest in capital so transferred . . . at the time the transfer is made for past services . . . . The time when such income is realized depends on all the facts and circumstances, including any substantial restrictions or conditions on the compensated partner's right to withdraw or otherwise dispose of such interest.

This rule would have been directly applicable had the 1951 contract continued in effect through November 1955, the date on which Wheless and Woolf would have fully recovered their costs in the venture. The contract made it clear that Frazell would "not have the right to dispose of any rights which may accrue to him" before those costs were recovered. But after November, he would have received a largely unrestricted interest in about 13 percent of the partnership properties. That this interest was primarily, if not entirely, in return for Frazell's services to the enterprise is undisputed. Thus, so much of the interest Frazell was to receive in November 1955 as could be attributed to his services for the oil venture would have been ordinary income to him in the year of receipt.

The applicable rule is in no way changed by Frazell's contention that his interest in the enterprise was a "carried interest." There are three recognized varieties of "carried interest," and each "may be created under varied circumstances, *e.g.*, . . . as compensation for services rendered, *e.g.*, by a geologist . . . ." The interest created by the 1951 contract most nearly fits into the "Menahan" category of "carried interests;" that is, "a springing executory interest . . . conveyed by the carrying party [Wheless and Woolf] to the carried party [Frazell], such interest to become possessory upon the satisfaction of . . . [the carrying party's] costs." Even if Frazell is taken to have had some sort of interest in the properties in question from their first acquisition, his interest would not have become possessory until November 1955. Under Treasury Regulation § 1.721-1(b) (1), the value of that interest would have been taxable to him at that time.

The fact that the contract was terminated prior to November 1955 should have no effect on the tax consequences of Frazell's arrangements. The transactions of April 1955 may be viewed in either of two ways: (1) If Frazell's partnership interest became possessory immediately upon the termination of the 1951 contract, so much of that interest received as compensation for services was taxable to him under the rule of Treasury Regulation § 1.721-1(b) (1). Thereafter, the transfer of his interest for W.W.F. stock was tax-free under section 351(a). (2) If the $91,000.00 of W.W.F. stock was given in substitution for the partnership interest originally contemplated, so much of that stock received in compensation for services was taxable to Frazell under section 351(a). As either view of the 1955 transactions results in ordinary income to Frazell, there is no reason for us to split hairs and choose between them.

This is not to say that the full $91,000.00 is ordinary income. The trial court found that, just as Wheless and Woolf contributed large amounts of capital, "Frazell supplied to the venture a very valuable oil map which was his private property." Indeed the record shows that prior to entering into the 1951 contract Frazell had acquired several maps which apparently proved very helpful to the work of the venture. Among the reasons given by Mr. Wheless for desiring to employ Frazell was that "he had accumulated maps, geological data and various information that was valuable to the arrangement that it would have taken a long time for someone else just moving into the territory to accumulate." And Frazell himself testified that he "had contributed considerable information and maps which resulted in the discovery and production of oil . . . . "Although it is clear that the greater part of the 13 percent interest received by Frazell was received as compensation for services, the court's finding and the cited testimony suggest that some part of that interest might have been received in return for "property;" namely, the maps. That part of the property Frazell received in 1955 attributable to his contribution of maps is not taxable in 1955 no matter whether we view the interest received as a partnership interest vesting on the termination of the 1951 contract (§ 721) or as shares of W.W.F. stock given in substitution therefor. (§ 351(a).)

Before the nonrecognition rule can be applied to the maps in this case, however, two factual determinations must be made: (1) Did Frazell contribute the maps in question to the oil venture or did he keep them as his own personal property? (2) If he contributed them to the venture, what was their value at the time they were contributed? As the burden of proof on both of these issues lies with the taxpayer, it might be argued that he is foreclosed in these issues because of the silence of the record on these points. However, we prefer to remand the case to the district court to permit it to make findings on these two issues. This disposition is in accord with the action of this court in a number of recent cases.

The judgment is therefore reversed and the case remanded to the district court to determine whether the maps introduced at the original trial were contributed by Frazell to the oil venture created by the 1951 contract. If the court finds that the maps were so contributed, it shall determine their value as of the time of their contribution. Such part of $91,000.00 as exceeds the value of the maps as determined by the trial court is properly taxable to Frazell as ordinary income.

Reversed and remanded.

Schneer v. Commissioner
97 TC 643 (1991)

GERBER, Judge.

FINDINGS OF FACT

. . . Petitioners resided at Croton-On-Hudson, New York, at the time the petition was filed in this case. Stephen B. Schneer . . . was a practicing attorney during the years 1983, 1984, and 1985. Until February 25, 1983, petitioner was an associate with the law firm of Ballon, Stoll & Itzler (BSI). BSI was a partnership. Petitioner was not a partner in BSI and he did not share in general partnership profits. Petitioner's financial arrangement with BSI consisted of a fixed or set salary and a percentage of any fees which arose from clients petitioner brought or referred to the firm.

BSI did not have a written partnership agreement, and no written agreement existed in connection with petitioner's relationship as an associate with BSI. When petitioner left BSI he had an understanding that he would continue to receive his percentage of fees which arose from clients he had referred when he was an associate with BSI. Petitioner was expected to consult regarding clients he referred to BSI and whose fees were to be shared by petitioner. Petitioner would have become entitled to his percentage of the fees even if he had not been called upon to consult.

After petitioner left BSI and while he was a partner of two other law partnerships (other than BSI) he consulted on numerous occasions concerning BSI clients. Most of the 1984 and 1985 fees received under this agreement were attributable to Terri Girl and Prince, clients that petitioner had brought to BSI. Neither the remaining BSI attorneys nor petitioner had contemplated whether petitioner would receive the fees if he refused to consult concerning the clients referred by petitioner. For the years under consideration, petitioner consulted with BSI attorneys on each occasion his services were requested. The services provided by petitioner to BSI consisted of legal advice and consultation on legal matters.

Late in February 1983, petitioner became a partner in the law firm of Bandler & Kass (B&K), and on August 1, 1985, petitioner became a partner in the law firm of Sylvor, Schneer, Gold & Morelli (SSG&M). BSI, B&K, SSG&M, and petitioner, at all pertinent times, kept their books and reported their income on the cash method of accounting. Neither B&K nor SSG&M had written partnership agreements. The agreement between the partners of B&K was that each partner would receive a percentage of the partnership profits derived from all fees received beginning the date the partner joined the partnership. In addition, petitioner agreed to turn over to the partnership all legal fees received after joining the partnership, regardless of whether the fees were earned in the partnership's name or from the partnership's contractual relationship with the client. The same agreement existed between the partners of SSG&M, including petitioner.

During 1984 and 1985, BSI remitted $21,329 and $10,585 to petitioner. The amounts represented petitioner's percentage of fees from BSI clients that he had referred to BSI at a time when he was an associate with BSI. With the exception of $1,250 for the 1984 taxable year, all of the fees received during 1984 and 1985 were for work performed after petitioner left BSI. Petitioner, pursuant to his agreements with B&K and SSG&M, turned those amounts over to the appropriate partnership. B&K and SSG&M, in turn, treated the amounts as partnership income which was distributed to each partner (including petitioner) according to the partner's percentage share of partnership profits.

BSI's 1984 records reflect that of the $21,329 total, $944 was attributable to Prince and $17,060 was attributable to Terri Girl. The remainder of the $21,329 remitted for 1984 ($3,325) was attributable to BSI clients for which petitioner had not consulted since leaving BSI during February 1983. The 1985 records of BSI reflect that the entire amount ($10,585) was attributable to Prince. BSI records reflect that billings and fees were made and received from BSI clients at various times during the year, but that petitioner received one annual aggregate payment.

OPINION

We consider here basic principles of income taxation. There is agreement that the amounts paid to petitioner by his former employer-law firm are income in the year of receipt. The question is whether petitioner (individually) or the partners of petitioner's partnerships (including petitioner) should report the income in their respective shares.

The parties have couched the issue in terms of the anticipatory assign-ment-of-income principles. Equally important to this case, however, is the viability of the principle that partners may pool their earnings and report partnership income in amounts different from their contribution to the pool. See sec. 704(a) and (b). The parties' arguments bring into focus potential conflict between these two principles and compel us to address both.

First, we examine the parties' arguments with respect to the assign-ment-of-income doctrine. Respondent argues that petitioner earned the income in question before leaving BSI, despite the fact that petitioner did not receive that income until he was a partner in B&K and, later, SSG&M. According to respondent, by entering into partnership agreements requiring payment of all legal fees to his new partner-ships, petitioner anticipatorily assigned to those partnerships the income earned but not yet received from BSI . . . .

Petitioner contends that the income in question was not earned until after he left BSI and joined B&K and SSG&M. He argues that the income received from BSI is reportable by the partners of the B&K and SSG&M partnerships (including petitioner) in their respective shares. Petitioner also points out that partnership agreements, which like the ones in issue allocate and redistribute partners' income, have received the approval of respondent in Rev. Rul. 64-90, 1964-1 C.B. (Part 1) 226. Petitioner argues that he was obligated to consult with BSI in order to be entitled to the BSI fees. Petitioner concedes that, for some of the income in question, no consultation was performed or requested. He emphasizes, however, that a substantial amount (about 90 percent) of the fees involved clients of BSI for whom consultation was performed. Finally, petitioner believes that his failure to consult would have resulted in loss of the fees.

The principle of assignment of income, in the context of Federal taxation, first arose in *Lucas v. Earl*, where the Supreme Court, interpreting the Revenue Act of 1918, held that income from a husband-taxpayer's legal practice was taxable to him, even though he and his wife had entered into a valid contract under State law to split all income earned by each of them. In so holding, Justice Holmes, speaking for the Court, stated:

> There is no doubt that the statute could tax salaries to those who earned them and provide that the tax could not be escaped by anticipatory arrangements and contracts however skillfully devised to prevent the salary when paid from vesting even for a second in the man who earned it.

From that pervasive and simply stated interpretation, a plethora of cases and learned studies have sprung forth. . . .

In this case, petitioner was not entitled to the referral fees unless the work for the referred clients had been successfully completed. On the other hand, petitioner would be entitled to the fees if the work was completed or if at the time of the assignment there was nothing contingent in petitioner's right to collect his percentage of the fees. Additionally, the majority of the services had not been performed prior to petitioner's leaving BSI. In this regard services had been performed with respect to $1,250 prior to 1984. With respect to $3,325 of the $21,329 of fees received in 1984, petitioner did not consult and was not required to do anything subsequent to leaving BSI to be entitled to those fees. With respect to the remainder of the $21,329 for 1984 and all of the 1985 fees, petitioner was called upon to and did consult while he was a partner of B&K or SSG&M.

We must decide whether petitioner had earned the fees in question prior to assigning them to the B&K or the SSG&M partnerships. Although petitioner was on the cash method, the principles that control use of the cash method are not suited to this inquiry. For purposes of the assignment-of-income doctrine, it must be determined whether the income was earned prior to an assignment. The principles underlying the cash method do not focus upon when income is earned, the focus is upon when income is actually or constructively received. The accrual method, however, involves a question of when income is earned, rather than when it is received. We accordingly consider the principles underlying the accrual method for the purpose of determining whether petitioner had "earned" the income in question prior to the time he agreed to turn it over to the B&K or SSG&M partnerships. . . .

The transaction under consideration is one where petitioner had an agreement under which he would receive a percentage of fees received by BSI from clients who were referred by petitioner while he was an employee of BSI. Inherent in petitioner's unconditional right to payment is the condition precedent that billable services have been performed for the referred client. Additionally, petitioner's right to payment may also be subject to a second condition precedent that he may be required to consult and be involved in performing the services to be billed. Finally, there is the conditional aspect of payment. If the referred client does not pay for services rendered, then petitioner will not receive his percentage.

The possibility that the client might not pay his obligation once services are performed is insufficient to cause the deferral of income for an accrual method taxpayer. On the other hand, the prerequisite of performance of the services prior to any liability on the part of the obligor is an essential to satisfying the all-events test. The right to receive income cannot become fixed before the obligor has an obligation to pay. Recognition of liability by the obligor is the essence of accrual.

The record in this case reflects that, with the exception of $1,250 of services performed in prior years, the billings and payments in question were performed and collected subsequent to the time of assignment of the income. The requirement that petitioner may have been called upon to consult is part of the contingency relating to the performance of the work prior to liability being established or fixed. The absence of consulting by petitioner is not decisive in the setting of this case. Additionally, as a corollary to the income principles, under section 461(h) a taxpayer is not entitled to a deduction under the accrual method unless there has been economic performance, i.e., the services have been performed or the property delivered.

With these principles as our guide, we hold that petitioner had not earned the fees in question prior to leaving BSI, with the exception of the $1,250 received for services performed in an earlier year. More specifically, we hold that petitioner earned the income in question while a partner of a partnership to which he had agreed to pay such income. With respect to substantially all of the fees in issue, BSI records reflect that clients were billed and payment received during the years in issue. Moreover, if petitioner had refused a request for his consultation, it was, at very least, questionable whether he would have received his share of the fee if the work had been successfully completed without him. Petitioner was requested to and did provide further services with regard to clients from which about 90 percent of the fees were generated. We note that BSI did not request consultation with respect to $3,325 remitted during 1984.

However, that amount was not earned as of the time of the assignment because the work had not yet been performed for the BSI clients (irrespective of whether or not petitioner would be called upon to consult). Accordingly, with the exception of $1,250 for petitioner's 1984 taxable year, we hold that petitioner had not earned the income in question prior to leaving BSI and did not make an anticipatory assignment of income which had been earned.

Two additional related questions remain for our consideration. First, respondent argues that irrespective of when petitioner earned the income from BSI, "there was no relationship . . . [between] the past activity of introducing a client to . . . [BSI], and the petitioner's work as a partner with . . . [B&K or SSG&M]." According to respondent, petitioner should not be allowed to characterize as partnership income fees that did not have a requisite or direct relationship to a partnership's business. In making this argument, respondent attempts to limit and modify his longstanding and judicially approved position in Rev. Rul. 64-90, 1964-1 C.B. (Part 1) 226. Second, while we generally hold that petitioner did not make an assignment of income already earned, the possibility that this was an assignment of unearned income was not foreclosed.

These final two questions bring into focus the true nature of the potential conflict in this case—between respondent's revenue ruling and the assignment-of-income doctrine. Both questions, in their own way, ask whether any partnership agreement—under which partners agree in advance to turn over to the partnership all income from their individual efforts—can survive scrutiny under the assignment-of-income principles.

Rev. Rul. 64-90, 1964-1 C.B. (Part 1) at 226–227, in pertinent part, contains the following:

> Federal income tax treatment of compensation received by a partner and paid over to a partnership where the partner, who uses the cash receipts and disbursements method of accounting, files his returns on a calendar year basis and the partnership, which also uses the cash method, files its returns on a fiscal year basis.
>
> Advice has been requested regarding the Federal income tax consequences of a change in the terms of a partnership agreement to provide that all compensation received by the partners will be paid over to the partnership immediately upon receipt.
>
> In the instant case, several individuals formed a partnership for the purpose of engaging in the general practice of law. Aside from the partnership business, each of the partners has performed services from time to time in his individual capacity and not as a partner. The several partners have always regarded the fees received for such services as compensation to the recipient as an individual. . . .
>
> *In the instant case, the general practice of the partnership consists of rendering legal advice and services. Consequently, fees received by a partner for similar services performed in his individual capacity will be considered as partnership income if paid to the partnership in accordance with the agreement. Those fees need not be reported separately by the partner on his individual return. However, the partner's distributive share of the partnership's taxable income which he must report on his individual return will include a portion of such fees.* [Emphasis supplied.]

A key requirement of this ruling is that the services for which fees are received by individual partners must be *similar* to those normally performed by the partnership. Cases dealing with similar partnership agreement situations have also enforced this requirement. Respondent now attempts to add to this requirement by arguing that the fees here in question were earned through activity, which was admittedly legal work, but was not sufficiently related to the work of petitioner's new partnerships. In other words, respondent argues that the income here was earned in BSI's business activity and not B&K's or SSG&M's business activity. . . .

There is no need for us to adopt a broader view of petitioner's partnership in this case. His referral fee income was clearly earned through activities "within the ambit" of the business of his new partnerships. Their business was the practice of law as was petitioner's consulting activity for BSI. His work was incident to the conduct of the business of his partnerships. We decline to adopt respondent's more narrow characterization of the business of petitioner's new partnerships. Neither the case law nor respondent's rulings support such a characterization.

Thus, we arrive at the final question in this case. We have already held that petitioner had not yet earned the majority of the income in question when he joined his new partnerships. Additionally, petitioner's fee income from his BSI clients qualifies, under the case law and respondent's rulings, as income generated by services sufficiently related to the business conducted by petitioner's new partnerships. If we decide that petitioner's partnerships should report the income in question, petitioner would be taxable only to the extent of his respective partnership share. This would allow petitioner, through his partnership agreements with B&K and SSG&M, to assign income not yet earned from BSI. Thus, the case law and respondent's rulings permit (without explanation), in a partnership setting, the type of assignment addressed by *Lucas v. Earl*. We must reconcile the principle behind Rev. Rul. 64-90, 1964-1 C.B. (Part 1) 226, with *Lucas v. Earl*. The question is whether income not yet earned and anticipatorily assigned under certain partnership agreements are without the reach of the assignment-of-income principle.

The Internal Revenue Code of 1954 provided the first comprehensive statutory scheme for the tax treatment of partners and partnerships. No section of the 1954 Code, successive amendments or acts, nor the legislative history specifically addresses the treatment of income earned by partners in their individual capacity but which is pooled with other partnership income. It is implicit in subchapter K, however, that the pooling of income and losses of partners was intended by Congress. This question is more easily answered where the partnership contracts with the client for services which are then performed by the partner. The question becomes more complex where the partner contracts and performs the services when he is a partner.

Moreover, no opinion contains a satisfactory rationale as to why partnership pooling agreements do not come within the holding of *Lucas v. Earl*. Even in *Mayes* and *Hamm* (where the attempted pooling of income was treated as a prohibited assignment of income) it is suggested that in the appropriate circumstances, a partnership agreement that effectuates anticipatory assignments of income should be respected for tax purposes. Indeed, other opinions contain similar holdings.

The fundamental theme penned by Justice Holmes provides that the individual who earns income is liable for the tax. It is obvious that the partnership, as an abstract entity, does not provide the physical and mental activity that facilitates the process of "earning" income. Only a partner can do so. The income earned is turned over to the partnership due solely to a contractual agreement, i.e., an assignment, in advance, of income.

The pooling of income is essential to the meaningful existence of subchapter K. If partners were not able to share profits in an amount disproportionate to the ratio in which they earned the underlying income, the partnership provisions of the Code would, to some extent, be rendered unnecessary.

The provisions of subchapter K tacitly imply that the pooling of income is permissible. Said implication may provide sufficient reason to conclude that a partnership should be treated as an entity for the purpose of pooling the income of its partners. Under an entity approach, the income would be considered that of the partnership rather than the partner, even though the partner's individual efforts may have earned the income. If the partnership is treated as an entity earning the income, then assignment-of-income concepts would not come into play. . . .

The theory concerning partnerships as entities is not easily defined. It is well established that the partnership form is a hybrid—part separate entity, part aggregate. The difficulty lies in deciding whether a particular set of circumstances relate to one end or the other of the partnership hybrid spectrum. The Supreme Court in *Basye* stated that "partnerships are entities for purposes of calculating and filing informational returns but. . . . they are conduits through which the taxpaying obligation passes to the individual partners in accord with their distributive shares." This analysis provides some foundation for the idea that partners should report their distributive share, rather than the fruits of their personal labors. But it does not provide any guidance concerning the type of income or service that should be brought within the entity concept as it relates to partnerships.

The principle we must analyze in this case involves the role of the partnership with respect to the function of earning income. A general partnership is "an association of two or more persons to carry on as co-owners a business for profit." Uniform Partnership Act sec. 6(1). Either a partnership or a corporation may enter into a contract with clients to perform services. In a partnership, however, either the entity or the individual may enter into contracts. The question we seek to answer is whether this distinction should be treated differently.

For purposes of an entity concept approach to partnerships, we must consider the type and source of income which should be included. Because we have already determined that the type of activity generating the income is relevant to an assignment-of-income analysis in the partnership setting, we focus our analysis of partnerships as entities on situations where the income is of a type normally earned by the partnership. Only in such situations has a partner acted as part of the partnership entity.

The entity concept as it relates to partnerships is based, in part, on the concept that a partner may further the business of the partnership by performing services in the name of the partnership or individually. The name and reputation of a professional partnership plays a role in the financial success of the partnership business. If the partners perform services in the name of the partnership or individually they are, nonetheless, associated with the partnership as a partner. This is the very essence of a professional service partnership, because each partner, although acting individually, is furthering the business of the partnership. . . .

The lack of structure inherent in the partnership form does not lend itself to easy resolution of the assignment-of-income question. A partnership's characteristics do, however, militate in favor of treating a partner's income from services performed in an individual capacity, which are contractually obligated to the partnership for allocation in accord with the preestablished distributive shares, in the same manner as income earned through partnership engagement.

Accordingly, in circumstances where individuals are not joining in a venture merely to avoid the effect of *Lucas v. Earl*, it is appropriate to treat income earned by partners individually, as income earned by the partnership entity, i.e., partnership income, to be allocated to partners in their respective shares. To provide the essential continuity necessary for the use of an entity concept in the partnership setting, the income should be earned from an activity which can reasonably be associated with the partnership's business activity. In the setting of this case, with the exception of $1,250 in 1984, petitioner was a partner of B&K or SSG&M when the fees were earned. Additionally, about 90 percent of the fees were, in part, earned through petitioner's efforts while he was a partner of B&K or SSG&M.

There is no apparent attempt to avoid the incidence of tax by the formation or operation of the partnerships in this case. Petitioner, in performing legal work for clients of another firm, was a partner with the law firms of B&K and SSG&M. In view of the foregoing, we hold that, with the exception of $1,250 for 1984, the fee income from BSI was correctly returned by the two partnerships in accord with the respective partnership agreements. . . .

Decision will be entered under Rule 155.

CHAPTER 4

Basis of a Partner's Partnership Interest

PROBLEM AREA 4

INTRODUCTION

The basis for a partner's partnership interest initially is determined under § 722, which provides that the basis for the interest is the amount of money contributed and the adjusted basis to the contributing partner of any property contributed. The basis mechanism for a partnership employs an entity concept. Income is computed at the partnership level but is taxed at the partner level. However, those earnings upon which the partner is taxed may not have been distributed to the partner. Consequently, adjustments to the basis for the partner's partnership interest are required in order to avoid double tax consequences upon the sale or liquidation of the interest.

Section 705(a) adjusts the partner's basis to reflect the operations of the partnership. The basis is *increased* by the partner's distributive share for the taxable year of: (1) taxable income of the partnership, (2) partnership income exempt from income tax, and (3) other miscellaneous adjustments. Similarly, the basis is *decreased*, but not below zero, by: (1) distributions by the partnership, (2) the partner's distributive share of partnership losses, (3) expenditures of the partnership not deductible in computing its taxable income and not properly chargeable to capital account, and (4) other miscellaneous adjustments. For example, if a partner contributes $200 cash for the partnership interest and the partner's share of *undistributed* partnership earnings for the year upon which she is taxed is $300, the basis is increased to $500. These adjustments ensure that upon a sale or liquidation of the interest she is not taxed again on that amount.

An additional aspect of the basis concept is the limitation of § 704(d) which restricts the deduction of a partner's share of partnership losses to the amount of the basis for the partner's partnership interest. Thus, for example, a partner with a $1,000 share of losses, but only a $400 basis, will have the deduction of $600 of those losses deferred until such time as the partner has sufficient basis (after all adjustments are made in the current year) against which to deduct such losses.

The basis of a partnership interest also is adjusted to reflect partnership liabilities. Under § 752(a), a partner's share of any partnership liabilities is treated as a contribution of money by the partner to the partnership which increases the adjusted basis of the partnership interest. Likewise, under § 752(b), a reduction of a partner's share of partnership liabilities is treated as a distribution from the partnership to the partner which reduces the adjusted basis of the partnership interest. If the amount treated as distributed is greater than the partner's basis, the excess is recognized as gain under § 731 from the sale or exchange of the interest. In order to determine a partner's share of the partnership liabilities, both the nature of the partnership (general, limited, or limited liability company ("LLC")) and the nature of the liability (recourse or nonrecourse) must be considered.

Regulations §§ 1.752-1 to 1.752-4 establish the boundaries of the liability allocation rules. Different sharing rules apply depending on the nature of the liability. Recourse liabilities are allocated according to the partners' economic risk of loss on the liability—in large part because that is the funding agreement for the liability in case of default and an inadequacy of partnership assets. However, personal liability does not exist for nonrecourse liabilities in the event of default. Consequently, nonrecourse liabilities will be funded with partnership capital and earnings and are generally allocated among the partners based on their profit ratios. The profit ratio specified for such a liability in the partnership agreement generally is determinative, after taking into account priorities for any portion of the liability attributable to minimum gain or minimum § 704(c) gain. Thus, a partner with a ten percent interest in profits and a 15 percent interest in losses often would have a $10,000 share in a $100,000 nonrecourse liability and a $15,000 share in a $100,000 recourse liability.

The above sharing rules are fully applicable to limited partnerships and LLCs as well as to general partnerships, but the liability shares that result from the application of these rules may vary due to the differing economic positions of general partners, limited partners, and LLC members. With regard to recourse liabilities, limited partners and LLC members are protected under state law (except to the extent they are obligated by contract to make additional contributions to the partnership) against liability to the partnership creditors. Thus, where a limited partner or LLC member has no obligation to contribute any amount beyond his initial capital, he will not share in recourse liabilities. Instead, the liability will be allocated exclusively to the general partner in accordance with the risk of loss. If the limited partner is obligated to the partnership for additional contributions, he is entitled to his portion of the liability if he bears the economic risk of loss. However, with respect to nonrecourse liabilities, as no partner (not even a general partner) or LLC member is liable upon default, the Regulations in keeping with the policy described above generally allocate such liabilities to all partners, including limited partners and LLC members, pursuant to their profit ratios, or, should the parties agree, in other permissible manners described in the Regulations.

It is quite common for partners or LLC members to utilize "hybrid" financing arrangements to effectuate their desired allocation formula. For example, because limited partners require nonrecourse financing for basis purposes, a partnership unable to procure nonrecourse financing might instead enter into a nonrecourse agreement while simultaneously having its general partners execute a guaranty. However, the courts, the Service, and Congress attacked such financing devices by identifying the party who bore the risk of loss and determining the partners' shares of the liability accordingly. Consequently, in cases of hybrid financing, the hybrid arrangement is "bifurcated" into its recourse and nonrecourse components. The above-described sharing rules are applied separately to each component.

As is evident from the above discussion, basis may be generated through various partnership borrowings thereby avoiding the § 704(d) limitation on loss availability. However, as regards partnership losses, two other limitations on loss availability must be confronted. The at-risk rules of § 465 deny the deduction of losses in excess of the amount for which a partner is at risk. A partner is at risk to the extent of any money contributed to the partnership, the adjusted basis of any property contributed thereto, and the partner's share of partnership recourse liabilities. Generally, nonrecourse liabilities do not constitute amounts at risk. Thus, a limited partner or LLC member may have basis under §§ 752 and 704(d) through nonrecourse financing but not be at risk for such amounts. Therefore, the loss would not be available for use on the partner's personal return. An exception exists for "qualified nonrecourse financing" with regard to real estate activities. For example, limited partners participating in a limited partnership or members of an LLC investing in an apartment complex with qualified nonrecourse financing would have an equivalent total of basis and at-risk amounts.

The final limitation with regard to partnership losses is the passive-loss limitation of § 469. Prior to the disposition of a passive activity, losses derived from the activity may be deducted only against passive income. Subject to regulatory exceptions, a limited partnership interest is deemed to be a passive activity. In contrast, under developing case law, the dividing line between active and passive in the case of an LLC appears to depend not on whether the LLC member takes an active role in the management of the entity.

PROBLEM 4

QUESTIONS

1. A and B are equal partners in a general partnership. A has a basis of $30,000 in his partnership interest. B has a basis of $10,000 in her partnership interest. What is the effect of each of the following events on the basis of each partner's partnership interest? When is the effect taken into account?

a. The partnership makes a charitable contribution of $5,000.

b. Each partner's distributive share of the partnership's taxable income is $10,000.

c. The partnership has $8,000 in interest income from tax-exempt municipal bonds.

d. The partnership makes a cash distribution of $10,000 to each partner.

e. The partnership exchanges rental real estate with a fair market value of $100,000 and an adjusted basis of $30,000 for other real estate worth $100,000 in a § 1031 exchange.

f. During the year, a lease is terminated. The partnership's lessee expended $30,000 in improvements which were not substitutes for rent during the lease period. The fair market value of the improvements is $50,000 on the date the partnership takes possession of the leased premises.

g. The partnership pays $2,000 in life insurance premiums to insure the lives of key employees, with the partnership named as beneficiary.

2.   **a.** Same as question 1. above, except that item b. is a distributive share of partnership loss (instead of income) in the amount of $10,000 to each partner. If all of the loss is not allowed to a partner, what is the character of the disallowed loss?

b. Same as question 1. above, except that the partnership's charitable contribution is property with a value of $2,500 and an adjusted basis of $1,000.

c. Same as question 1. above, except that the partnership's charitable contribution is $30,000 in cash.

3. Using the facts of question 2a. above, assume that on January 1 of the next year, B sells her partnership interest to C for $10,000. Assume that the AC partnership has no income or deductions for that year. Does C succeed to B's carryover loss? What if B in the following year repurchases the partnership interest from C?

4. AB, an equal cash-method partnership with cash-method partners, ordered stationery and other secretarial supplies in the amount of $300. Before payment but after transfer of title, is there any effect on the tax basis of each partner's partnership interest? What if the liability were for services already performed but not yet paid?

5 a. A and B form AB, an equal general partnership. Each contributes $10,000 to the capital of the partnership. The partnership purchases a $100,000 building for $20,000 cash and $80,000 borrowed on a recourse basis. What are the partners' respective bases in their partnership interests? What if the partnership liability is nonrecourse?

b. In a. above, assume that the partnership liability is recourse and A and B share profits in a 40:60 ratio and losses in a 70:30 ratio. Assume further that these "special allocations" will be respected for federal tax purposes. What are the partners' respective bases in their partnership interests? What if the liability is nonrecourse?

c. In a. above, assume that AB is an equal limited partnership with B as the limited partner. Furthermore, assume that the partnership agreement provides that all losses will be allocated to A, the general partner, once the limited partner's capital account has been reduced to zero, taking into account any obligation the limited partner has to restore a deficit in the limited partner's capital account. Assume further that these allocations will be respected for federal tax purposes. What are the partners' respective bases in their partnership interests, assuming, alternatively in each case, that the liability is either recourse or nonrecourse?

(i) B has no obligation to make additional capital contributions to the partnership.

(ii) B is obligated under the partnership agreement to contribute an additional $30,000.

(iii) B agrees to pay up to $40,000 if A actually pays off the partnership's liability from his personal funds.

(iv) B agrees to guarantee $40,000 of the partnership's liability directly to the lender.

d. Assume that the partnership in a. above is formed as a limited liability company taxed as a partnership in which A and B have equal interests. The $80,000 partnership liability is secured by a pledge of all of the partnership's assets and the loan documentation states that the lender's only recourse is to such assets. What are the partners' shares of this liability? What if the loan documentation is silent on this point?

MATERIALS

Revenue Ruling 96-11
1996-1 CB 140

ISSUE

If a partnership makes a charitable contribution of property, are the partners' bases in their partnership interests decreased to reflect the contribution?

FACTS

A and *B* each contributes an equal amount of cash to form *PRS*, a general partnership. Under the *PRS* agreement, each item of income, gain, loss, and deduction of the partnership is allocated 50 percent to *A* and 50 percent to *B*. *PRS* has unencumbered property, *X*, with a basis of $60x and a fair market value of $100x. *PRS* contributes *X* in a transaction that qualifies as a charitable contribution under § 170(c) of the Internal Revenue Code. The charitable contribution is not subject to the limitations of § 170(e)(1).

LAW AND ANALYSIS

Section 170(a) allows as a deduction any charitable contribution (as defined in § 170(c)) payment of which is made within the taxable year. The deduction provided by § 170(a) is subject to the limitations of § 170(b).

Section 1.170A-1(c)(1) of the Income Tax Regulations provides that, if a charitable contribution is made in property other than money, the amount of the contribution is the fair market value of the property at the time of the contribution. . . .

Section 703(a)(2)(C) provides that the taxable income of a partnership is computed in the same manner as in the case of an individual except that the deduction for charitable contributions provided in § 170 is not allowed to the partnership. However, under § 702(a)(4) each partner takes into account separately the partner's distributive share of the partnership's charitable contributions (as defined in § 170(c)).

Section 1.170A-1(h)(7) provides that a partner's distributive share of charitable contributions actually paid by a partnership during its taxable year may be allowed as a deduction in the partner's separate return for the partner's taxable year with or within which the taxable year of the partnership ends, to the extent that the aggregate of the partner's share of the partnership contributions and the partner's own contributions does not exceed the limitations in § 170(b).

Section 705(a)(1) provides that the adjusted basis of a partner's interest in a partnership shall be increased by the sum of the partner's distributive share for the taxable year and prior taxable years of: (1) taxable income of the partnership as determined under § 703(a); (2) income of the partnership exempt from income tax; and (3) the excess of the deductions for depletion over the basis of the property subject to depletion.

Section 705(a)(2) provides that the adjusted basis of a partner's interest in a partnership shall be decreased (but not below zero) by distributions by the partnership and by the sum of the partner's distributive share for the taxable year and prior taxable years of: (1) losses of the partnership; and (2) expenditures of the partnership not deductible in computing its taxable income and not properly chargeable to capital account.

The adjustments to the basis of a partner's interest in a partnership under § 705 are necessary to prevent inappropriate or unintended benefits or detriments to the partners. Generally, the basis of a partner's interest in a partnership is adjusted to reflect the tax allocations of the partnership to that partner. This ensures that the income and loss of the partnership are taken into account by its partners only once. In addition, as provided in §§ 705(a)(1)(B) and 705(a)(2)(B), adjustments must also be made to reflect certain nontaxable events in the partnership. For example, a partner's share of nontaxable income (such as exempt income) is added to the basis of the partner's interest because, without a basis adjustment, the partner could recognize gain with respect to the tax-exempt income, for example, on a sale or redemption of the partner's interest, and the benefit of the tax-exempt income would be lost to the partner. Similarly, a partner's share of nondeductible expenditures must be deducted from the partner's basis in order to prevent that amount from giving rise to a loss to the partner on a sale or a redemption of the partner's interest in the partnership.

In determining whether a transaction results in exempt income within the meaning of § 705(a)(1)(B), or a nondeductible, noncapital expenditure within the meaning of § 705(a)(2)(B), the proper inquiry is whether the transaction has a permanent effect on the partnership's basis in its assets, without a corresponding current or future effect on its taxable income. Pursuant to § 703(a)(2)(C), the contribution of *X* by *PRS* is not taken into account by *PRS* in computing its taxable income. Consequently, the contribution results in a permanent decrease in the aggregate basis of the assets of *PRS* that is not taken into account by *PRS* in determining its taxable income and will not be taken into account for federal income tax purposes in any other manner. Therefore, for purposes of § 705(a)(2)(B), the contribution of *X*, and the resulting permanent decrease in partnership basis, is an expenditure of the partnership not deductible in computing its taxable income and not properly chargeable to capital account . . . .

Reducing the partners' bases in their partnership interests by their respective shares of the permanent decrease in the partnership's basis in its assets preserves the intended benefit of providing a deduction. . . . for the fair market value of appreciated property without recognition of the appreciation. By contrast, reducing the partners' bases in their partnership interests by the fair market value of the contributed property would subsequently cause the partners to recognize gain (or a reduced loss), for example, upon a disposition of their partnership interests, attributable to the unrecognized appreciation in *X* at the time of this contribution.

Under the *PRS* agreement, partnership items are allocated equally between *A* and *B*. Accordingly, the basis of *A*'s and *B*'s interests in *PRS* is each decreased by $30*x*.

HOLDING

If a partnership makes a charitable contribution of property, the basis of each partner's interest in the partnership is decreased (but not below zero) by the partner's share of the partnership's basis in the property contributed.

Revenue Ruling 88-77
1988-2 CB 128

ISSUE

For purposes of computing the adjusted basis of a partner's interest in a cash basis partnership, are accrued but unpaid expenses and accounts payable "liabilities of a partnership" or "partnership liabilities" within the meaning of section 752 of the Internal Revenue Code?

FACTS

A is a partner in P partnership. P files returns on a calendar year basis and uses the cash receipts and disbursements method of accounting. At the close of the taxable year at issue, P's accrued expenses and accounts payable consisted of 100x dollars for interest expense and accounts payable of 200x dollars for services received.

LAW AND ANALYSIS

Section 722 of the Code provides that a partner's basis is increased by the amount of money the partner contributes to the partnership.

Section 752(a) of the Code provides that any increase in a partner's share of the liabilities of a partnership, or any increase in a partner's individual liabilities by reason of the assumption by the partner of partnership liabilities, is treated as a contribution of money by the partner to the partnership.

Rev. Rul. 60-345, 1960-2 C.B. 211, holds that, for purposes of section 752 of the Code, the term "liabilities" includes a cash basis partnership's obligations for the payment of outstanding trade accounts, notes, and accrued expenses.

The present issue is similar to that arising under section 357(c) of the Code when property and liabilities are contributed to a controlled corporation in exchange for stock. For purposes of determining the basis of the stock received in the exchange under section 358 and any gain that must be recognized on the exchange under section 357(c), section 357(c)(3) provides that the term "liabilities" shall not include obligations the payment of which would give rise to a deduction or that would constitute a guaranteed payment under section 736(a). This rule is subject to an exception found in section 357(c)(3)(B) for liabilities the incurrence of which resulted in the creation of, or an increase in, the basis of any property....

The legislative history accompanying the amendment to section 704(c) made by the Tax Reform Act of 1984 explicitly rejected the conclusion reached in Revenue Ruling 60-345 in favor of an interpretation of section 752 that is consistent with section 357(c). See H.R. Rep. No. 861, 98th Cong., 2d Sess. 856-857 (1984), 1984-3 (Vol. 2) C.B. 110, 111.

Under P's method of accounting, P's obligations to pay amounts incurred for interest and services are not deductible until paid. For purposes of section 752 of the Code, the terms "liabilities of a partnership" and "partnership liabilities" include an obligation only if and to the extent that incurring the liability creates or increases the basis to the partnership of any of the partnership's assets (including cash attributable to borrowings), gives rise to an immediate deduction to the partnership, or, under section 705(a)(2)(B), currently decreases a partner's basis in the partner's partnership interest. The preceding sentence uses the term "assets" to include capitalized items that are properly allocable to future periods, such as organizational expenses and construction period expenses.

The liabilities incurred by P for interest expense and services do not create or increase the basis of a partnership asset or give rise to a deduction when incurred. Therefore, for purposes of computing A's adjusted basis in P, A may not treat P's accrued expenses and accounts payable as a liability of the partnership.

HOLDING

For purposes of computing the adjusted basis of a partner's interest in a cash basis partnership, accrued but unpaid expenses and accounts payable are not "liabilities of a partnership" or "partnership liabilities" within the meaning of section 752 of the Code.

Pleasant Summit Land Corp. v. Commissioner
863 F2d 263 (3d Cir. 1988)

GREENBERG, Circuit Judge.

Appellants, Pleasant Summit Land Corporation (PSLC) and George and Sharon Prussin, appeal from adverse decisions entered by the Tax Court following a consolidated trial on their petitions to redetermine deficiencies determined by the Commissioner of Internal Revenue. PSLC challenges the Tax Court's conclusion that it was a "personal holding company" subject to the tax on personal holding companies in its tax year in issue. Resolution of its appeal depends on whether its sale of the Summit House apartments in West Orange, New Jersey, was of a capital asset and thus resulted in a capital gain, as it claims, or whether the Summit House was a property it held primarily for sale to customers in the ordinary course of its trade or business so that its sale resulted in ordinary gross income.

George Prussin is an investor in a limited partnership, Pleasant & Summit Associates (PSA), which indirectly purchased Summit House from PSLC. The Prussins challenge the Tax Court's conclusions that: (1) nonrecourse financing of the Summit House purchase exceeded its fair market value; (2) the nonrecourse financing would not support depreciation and interest deductions which they claimed by reason of George Prussin's limited partnership interest in PSA; and (3) these deductions would be disallowed in full rather than only to the extent that they were the product of financing in excess of the fair market value of Summit House. . . .

We will affirm the Tax Court's decision with respect to PSLC. We will reverse the Tax Court's decision to the extent it completely disallowed the Prussins' deductions and will remand for a determination of the fair market value of Summit House and for calculation of the appropriate deductions allowable to the Prussins. . . .

I. BACKGROUND

A. *The Underlying Business Transaction* On May 3, 1978, in an arm's length transaction, PSLC entered into an agreement to purchase the Summit House, a property on Summit Street, West Orange, New Jersey, containing two apartment buildings and a small separate resident manager's apartment for $4,200,000. The purchase was closed on or about June 1, 1978 and the consideration was paid by

$250,000 in cash, by delivery of a $1,350,000 note secured by a purchase money mortgage, and by PSLC taking title subject to a previously existing $2,600,000 nonrecourse mortgage.

Contemporaneously with the purchase, PSLC created a wholly owned subsidiary, Mount Orange Realty Corp. (MORC), to which it then sold the Summit House buildings while retaining the land beneath them. The sale price to MORC was $5,200,000, consisting of $500,000 in cash which MORC borrowed or owed and a $4,700,000 nonrecourse mortgage which wrapped around and was subject to the prior two mortgages. The note which this mortgage secured permitted accumulation of interest and principal through December 31, 1988, except that annual interest payments were required up to the available cash flow. This conveyance of the property placed the depreciable buildings in one entity while leaving the nondepreciable land in another.

PSLC then sold its MORC stock to the newly created PSA, which was organized to acquire the Summit House, for $2,559,200, paid in the form of a nonrecourse note secured by the MORC shares, for which a mortgage of Summit House to PSLC was immediately substituted. This note had provisions for accumulation of interest and principal through December 31, 1988, similar to those in the $4,700,000 note. PSA then dissolved MORC, took direct ownership of the Summit House buildings and took over MORC's obligations including the $500,000 due on the purchase of the Summit House and the $4,700,000 nonrecourse wraparound mortgage. Thus, the cost to PSA for acquisition of Summit House was the $2,559,200 indebtedness for the purchase of the MORC shares, assumption of MORC's $500,000 obligation, and assumption of MORC's $4,700,000 nonrecourse wraparound mortgage for a total of $7,759,200. The record, however, does not clearly establish that PSA paid the $500,000. Of course, this assumption of obligations did not transform the nonrecourse debts to recourse obligations. The consequence of these transactions was to leave PSA with large debts with interest charges and a substantial depreciable asset, a situation setting up the possibility for it to claim large tax deductions. Additionally, PSLC leased the land under the buildings to PSA for $10,000 a year under an agreement allowing rent to be accumulated and deferred at a fixed rate of interest. This provision caused PSA to generate additional tax deductions for the interest which accrued on the unpaid rent.

PSA sold thirty limited partnership units to a group of investors including George Prussin for a total of $1,980,000 paid with down payments and subsequent installments. The offering memorandum to the investors indicated that the $500,000 due on the sale from PSLC would be paid from the investors' down payments, leading the Commissioner in his brief to indicate that it appears that MORC's $500,000 obligation for its down payment was satisfied from the investors' funds. Inexplicably, the agreement for sale of the MORC shares between PSLC and PSA included a warranty by PSLC that MORC had no liabilities. Some months after PSA acquired Summit House, a new nonrecourse mortgage was substituted for the prior $2,600,000 mortgage but this did not enhance PSA's risk in the transaction. Most of the foregoing transactions were nearly contemporaneous and thus they formed part of one large structured undertaking.

PSA reported losses on its income tax returns for 1978 and 1979, and later years, largely attributable to interest deductions and depreciation. These losses were passed through to the limited partners who used them to off-set income on their individual tax returns. On December 19, 1985 an unrelated third party purchased the Summit House land from PSLC and the buildings and lease from PSA for a total of $7,000,000. . . .

IV. THE PRUSSINS' APPEAL. The Prussins, as limited partners in PSA, claimed a deduction for their distributive share of PSA's depreciation and interest deductions which the Commissioner, upheld by the Tax Court, completely disallowed. . . . [W]e must decide whether the Tax Court's finding of fact that PSA's nonrecourse indebtedness substantially exceeded the fair market value of Summit House was clearly erroneous. . . . [W]e must consider which of the following approaches should be followed: (1) the excess nonrecourse indebtedness may support the claimed deductions; (2) the presence of excess nonrecourse indebtedness requires a complete disallowance of the claimed deductions; or (3) only deductions attributable to the non recourse indebtedness to the extent that it was excessive should be disallowed . . . .

B. *Whether PSA's Nonrecourse Indebtedness Exceeded the Fair Market Value of Summit House* If we assume, even though the record is unclear on this point, that PSA paid the $500,000 which MORC was to have paid to PSLC, PSA's purchase price for Summit House was $7,759,200, of which no more than $500,000 was paid other than by creation of nonrecourse indebtedness. Otherwise it was $7,259,200. It is this investment which must be compared to the fair market value of Summit House.

The Prussins challenge Judge Cohen's finding of the maximum fair market value. At trial they had the burden of proof on the issue. But they introduced no significant evidence of valuation and they produced no expert testimony on this point.

While normally the parties to a real estate transaction have adverse economic interests and thus can be expected to establish fair market value themselves, Judge Cohen explained that here "[s]ales subsequent to PSLC's acquisition of the property. . . . were not at arm's length, and provide no evidence of the property's fair market value." This determination rested on her perception of the motivation for the conveyances: "in a transaction entered into primarily to generate tax benefits, the interests of the buying and selling parties are not necessarily adverse."

The Prussins challenge this line of reasoning by asserting that not paying money out is almost *always* better than getting a deduction. Thus, PSA would not pay an excessive amount for the property. While their reasoning is generally true, the Tax Court cited PSA's own projected tax benefits to demonstrate that this transaction did indeed provide deductions sufficient to compensate for the additional money paid out. In addition, there was no evidence that PSA had attempted to negotiate the sales price. We conclude that Judge Cohen was justified in considering indications other than what PSA paid to determine the fair market value of Summit House.

The Tax Court did consider the following indicia of fair market value: (1) PSLC had paid $4,200,000 for the improvements *and the land* in an arm's length transaction immediately before selling the improvements to PSA for over $7,700,000; (2) the assessed value of the improvements for property tax purposes suggested a fair market value of $1,522,500; (3) the improvements were insured for $2,745,000; and (4) the improvements and land were sold in 1985 for $7,000,000.

The Prussins argue that the Tax Court erroneously ignored oral testimony regarding the anticipated increase in value of Summit House provided it could be marketed as originally envisioned as cooperatives or condominiums, a purpose frustrated by a change of local law. We, however, see no reason to accept this assertion in view of Judge Cohen's analysis of the evidence in the record. Further, the facts of this case demonstrate the peril in relying on anticipated changes in a property to support an enhanced value. In short, Judge Cohen did not have to reject solid evidence showing a maximum fair market value because of a speculative projected new use.

The Prussins erroneously assert that Judge Cohen held that PSLC's purchase price was conclusive of fair market value in PSA's subsequent purchase. She, however, did not hold that Summit House could be worth no more to PSA than PSLC had paid for the property. What she did hold was that the Prussins had failed to meet their burden of proof on value and that only the sale to PSLC on the record provided evidence of the value of Summit House. Furthermore, she did not find that fair market value was $4,200,000; she concluded that fair market value could not have been more than that sum.

Given her consideration of many different bases for finding fair market value and the Prussins' failure to present expert testimony on value, we conclude that Judge Cohen's findings as to the maximum fair market value were not clearly erroneous. Accordingly, we will not disturb her finding that the non-recourse financing exceeded the fair market value of Summit House.

C. *The Appropriate Legal Standard* The Internal Revenue Code does not expressly provide in any section germane to this case for any adjustment of deductions when non-recourse debt exceeds fair market value. Thus, it is necessary to analyze the overall statutory framework and legal precedents to understand the significance of the Tax Court's finding that PSA's nonrecourse debt exceeded the fair market value of Summit House.

1. *The Statutory Framework* The Internal Revenue Code allows a deduction for "a reasonable allowance for the exhaustion, wear and tear" of property used in the taxpayer's trade or business and of property held for the production of income. I.R.C. § 167(a). This depreciation deduction is calculated using the adjusted basis of the property used to calculate gain under section 1011. See I.R.C. § 167(g). The basis of the property for purposes of calculating gain under section 1011 is ultimately defined in section 1012. Section 1012 provides that generally the "basis of property shall be the cost of such property."

The cost of property includes the amount of indebtedness incurred or assumed by the purchaser as part of the purchase transaction. However, several courts of appeals have held that non-recourse debt in excess of fair market value is not included in the cost of property for purposes of calculating the depreciation deduction. See, e.g., *Odend'hal v. Commissioner*, 748 F.2d 908, 912–14 (4th Cir. 1984), cert. denied, 471 U.S. 1143 (1985); *Estate of Franklin v. Commissioner*, 544 F.2d 1045, 1049 (9th Cir. 1976).

Section 163(a) of the Internal Revenue Code allows a deduction for all interest paid or accrued within the taxable year on indebtedness. This provision allows a deduction for interest paid on non-recourse debt. It has been held, however, that when "both the purchase price and the lesser principal amount of the non-recourse note which makes up a portion of such purchase price unreasonably exceed the value of the property acquired, then no 'genuine indebtedness' exists and no 'investment in the property' occurs." *Flowers v. Commissioner*, 80 T.C. 914, 942 (1983); see also *Odend'hal*, 748 F.2d at 912–14; *Estate of Franklin*, 544 F.2d at 1049.

Although separate statutory provisions govern interest and depreciation deductions, the case law typically merges issues relating to their allowance. Thus, when nonrecourse debt is excluded from the basis for purposes of calculation of depreciation, it is not treated as genuine indebtedness for determination of interest deductions.

2. *Whether the Nonrecourse Indebtedness is Included In PSA's Basis and Whether it is "Genuine Indebtedness."* Although this court has not previously addressed this issue, decisions of other courts of appeals have disallowed deductions for interest and depreciation in circumstances similar to those here. Some of these cases specifically involve investments in real estate and improvements.

Of the cases decided by other courts of appeals, that most similar to this case is *Odend'hal v. Commissioner*, 748 F.2d 908. *Odend'hal* stands for the proposition that if the fair market value of property is less than its non-recourse financing, the principal of the nonrecourse financing in excess of fair market value is not included in the basis for the purpose of claiming depreciation. Moreover, *Odend'hal* holds this excess nonrecourse debt does not sustain a deduction for interest payments.

The facts of *Odend'hal* were as follows. Ten taxpayers purchased a warehouse and food processing facility. As in this case, the taxpayers acquired only the improvements and a long term lease on the land. The purchase took place in December of 1972 for a total consideration of $4,000,000 of which $80,000 was paid in cash and $3,920,000 was financed by nonrecourse debt. Interest on the nonrecourse debt was to be serviced currently but the principal was due in a balloon payment at the end of a fifteen year period.

The promoter of this investment represented that based on a depreciable lifespan of fourteen-and-a-half years, the income earned from leasing the property would not equal the total of the cost of leasing the land, mortgage interest, and depreciation. However, he explained that the interest and depreciation deductions would generate additional tax benefits so that an investor in the 50% tax bracket would convert the investment income loss into an after-tax gain.

Although the taxpayers purchased the property for $4,000,000, the Tax Court concluded that its fair market value was only $2,000,000. Because of the wide discrepancy between the face value of the nonrecourse debt and the fair market value, the Tax Court held that the nonrecourse note did not represent genuine indebtedness. Thus, it did not allow the taxpayers to include the non-recourse debt in their basis for purposes of depreciation. In addition, the taxpayers were allowed to deduct interest and other expenses only to the extent of their income from the property.

The taxpayers appealed to the United States Court of Appeals for the Fourth Circuit, arguing that the Tax Court's determination of fair market value was clearly erroneous and that, as a matter of law, the Tax Court was bound to recognize the entire nonrecourse indebtedness when computing depreciation and interest deductions. The Court of Appeals rejected both contentions.

In finding that the Tax Court's valuation of the property was not clearly erroneous, the Court of Appeals relied, in part, on the fact that the same property had been conveyed for $2,670,000 in an arm's length sale five years before it was sold to the group of ten taxpayers. Once the fair market value was established the court turned to the issue of the excessive non-recourse debt. It stated:

> If, as a matter of fact, the fair market value of the property is less than that financed by a nonrecourse loan, the authorities hold that the principal of the non

recourse loan which exceeds fair market value does not represent a real investment in the property by a taxpayer and he may not include that non-recourse amount in his basis for depreciation. In addition, the interest paid on the loan is not allowable as an interest deduction. Basis for depreciation usually includes the amount of any indebtedness incurred or assumed by the purchaser in connection with the purchase of the property, because the taxpayer has an obligation to pay the debt. When the debt is a nonrecourse loan, the principal amount of the loan is included in the taxpayer's basis so long as the fair market value of the property is at least equal to the amount of the non-recourse debt at the time it was incurred, because the taxpayer, even though he has no personal liability at stake, has an economic incentive to pay off the debt rather than to lose the collateral. But if the stated price financed by non-recourse debt exceeds the fair market value of the property, to the extent of the excess, the taxpayer has no equity in the property to protect and no economic incentive to pay off the debt.

Under this analysis taxpayers are able to claim depreciation and interest deductions to the extent that non-recourse debt does not exceed fair market value.

Odend'hal ultimately relied on *Estate of Franklin*, 544 F.2d 1045, which imposed similar limits on deductions supported by nonrecourse debt. In *Estate of Franklin* the owner of a motel agreed to sell it for $1,224,000 with the entire purchase price to be paid by a note secured by a nonrecourse mortgage with monthly principal and interest installments of $9,045.36. A balloon payment of $975,000 was due ten years from the sale. The property was leased back to the seller for a monthly rental equal to the $9,045.36 monthly debt service. The seller was responsible for operating the motel and paying all expenses. The buyers' only cash payment was $75,000 of prepaid interest.

The buyers claimed that they could take interest and depreciation deductions for the ten years and then either make the balloon payment and complete the purchase or back out of the purchase. The Tax Court characterized this transaction as a ten year option to purchase and accordingly disallowed the deductions for interest and depreciation.

The Court of Appeals for the Ninth Circuit considered the case from a different perspective. It held that if the transaction met two criteria it would not be considered a sale for tax purposes and thus no interest or depreciation deductions would be allowed. The first test was whether the value on which the transaction was based exceeded the fair market value of the property. The second factor was whether the transaction was financed with non-recourse debt which exceeded the fair market value of the underlying property. The Court of Appeals concluded that the transaction in *Estate of Franklin* met these two criteria and thus it affirmed the Tax Court.

The Prussins attempt to distinguish *Odend'hal* and *Estate of Franklin* on two rationales. First, they argue cash represented only three percent of the purchase price in *Odend'hal* and just over six percent of the purchase price in *Estate of Franklin*, as opposed to their own more substantial investment in PSA. Second, they contend the large balloon payments in *Odend'hal* and *Estate of Franklin* demonstrate that the transactions were mere options to purchase and that here there are no such balloon payments.

Each of these attempts to distinguish *Odend'hal* and *Estate of Franklin* must fail. With regard to the first objection, the appropriate comparison with *Odend'hal* and *Estate of Franklin* is the proportion of cash to nonrecourse debt paid by PSA rather than the amount of the individual limited partners' cash investments. Based on a purchase price of $7,759,200 and a $500,000 cash payment, assuming it was made, this calculation would indicate that 6.44% of the purchase price was paid in cash. This analysis reveals the similarity of this case to the precedents rather than providing a basis to distinguish them. Of course, the Prussins' argument is even weaker if the $500,000 was not paid.

The Prussins' second rationale partially misstates the terms of PSA's obligations. As we have indicated, principal payments on the mortgages were substantially postponed. But even if they were not, it is the existence of deferred nonrecourse indebtedness in excess of the value of the property that creates the economic disincentive to pay the debt. While there may be less incentive to make a balloon payment at the end of a term as compared with earlier structured payments, the proper analysis must be predicated on a comparison of the nonrecourse debt to the fair market value of the property at its acquisition.

The Prussins attempt to distinguish other cases applying *Estate of Franklin* to real estate investments. Both *Beck v. Commissioner*, 678 F.2d 818 (9th Cir. 1982), and *Narver v. Commissioner*, 75 T.C. 53 (1980), aff'd per curiam, 670 F.2d 855 (9th Cir. 1982), are supposedly inapplicable in light of the small percentage of the purchase price paid in a form other than nonrecourse debt and the great overvaluing of the property. But the Prussins' attempt to distinguish these cases must fail for the same reason that *Odend'hal* and *Estate of Franklin* cannot be distinguished: that is, the Prussins are not comparing the same parts of the different transactions as they are looking to the limited partners' investment rather than that of PSA. The Summit House purchase price was substantially paid by PSA with non-recourse obligations.

While we regard *Odend'hal* and *Estate of Franklin* as the appropriate precedents, we do not consider them as authority to eliminate all deductions for interest and depreciation. While we realize that a taxpayer holding property subject to a nonrecourse debt in excess of the market value of the property may have no incentive to pay off any portion of the debt, including the amount not exceeding the fair market value of the property, it is equally logical to recognize that the creditor holding the debt has no incentive to take back the property if the taxpayer offers to pay the debt up to the value of the property. For example, if a creditor held a nonrecourse debt for $1,500,000 on a property with a fair market value of $1,000,000, he would have a disincentive to foreclose if his defaulting debtor offered to settle the debt for not less than $1,000,000. Thus, it is appropriate to disregard only the portion of non-recourse debt in excess of the fair market value of the property when it was acquired for purposes of calculations of the depreciation and interest deductions and to regard the nonrecourse debt as genuine indebtedness to the extent it is not disregarded. Moreover, there is precedent for disallowing deductions based on nonrecourse debt only insofar as attributable to the excess of debt over the fair market value.

Unquestionably, the record compels the conclusion that Summit House, though not exceeding $4,200,000 in fair market value, had a substantial value. Thus, under our analysis the Tax Court's determination that the deductions should be disallowed in full cannot be sustained. Accordingly, we will remand the case to the Tax Court for a determination of fair market value of Summit House at the time of PSA's acquisition.

We also conclude that the actual cash investment of PSA in the purchase of Summit House, if there was any, should be disregarded in the calculation of the fair market value as it obviously was at risk. While Judge Cohen inferred that the $500,000 was not paid by PSA, we are not satisfied that this was necessarily correct, particularly in view of the Commissioner's brief in which it is recited that it appears that the $500,000 was paid from the investor's funds. According to the Prussins, the absence of evidence establishing that the $500,000 was paid is attributable to the fact that there was no issue at trial raised regarding this point. On the remand it may be definitively ascertained whether the payment was made. The significance of the cash investment is that there is an economic reason to pay off a nonrecourse debt when there is some equity in the property, even though the total debt when added to the equity exceeds the value of the property, as the alternative to paying the debt is the loss of the equity. Thus, if there is a $500,000 equity in a property worth $4,000,000, the owner of the property should logically be willing to pay off up to $4,000,000 in nonrecourse debt to save the property because his loss in that case will not exceed $500,000 but his loss in giving up the property will be $500,000. . . .

Revenue Ruling 94-4
1994-1 CB 195

ISSUE

If a deemed distribution of money under § 752(b) of the Internal Revenue Code occurs as a result of a decrease in a partner's share of the liabilities of a partnership, is the deemed distribution taken into account at the time of the distribution or at the end of the partnership taxable year?

LAW

Under § 752(b), a decrease in a partner's share of partnership liabilities is considered a distribution of money to the partner by the partnership. The partner will recognize gain under § 731(a)(1) if the distribution of money exceeds the adjusted basis of the partner's interest immediately before the distribution.

Section 1.731-1(a)(1)(ii) of the Income Tax Regulations provides that for purposes of §§ 731 and 705, advances or drawings of money or property against a partner's distributive share of income are treated as current distributions made on the last day of the partnership taxable year with respect to that partner.

Rev. Rul. 92-97, 1992-2 C.B. 124, treats a deemed distribution of money to a partner resulting from a cancellation of debt as an advance or drawing under § 1.731-1(a)(1)(ii) against that partner's distributive share of cancellation of indebtedness income.

HOLDING

A deemed distribution of money under § 752(b) resulting from a decrease in a partner's share of the liabilities of a partnership is treated as an advance or drawing of money under § 1.731-1(a)(1)(ii) to the extent of the partner's distributive share of income for the partnership taxable year. An amount treated as an advance or drawing of money is taken into account at the end of the partnership taxable year. A deemed distribution of money resulting from a cancellation of debt may qualify for advance or drawing treatment under this revenue ruling and under Rev. Rul. 92-97.

CHAPTER 5

Taxing Partnership Operations— Characterization and Computation of Partnership Income

PROBLEM AREA 5

INTRODUCTION

Although a partnership is not a taxable entity, it is required to compute its taxable income as though it were a taxpayer. Under § 703(a), a partnership calculates taxable income in the same manner as an individual taxpayer. However, § 703(a)(2) denies certain deductions in computing partnership taxable income because these deductions are allowed to the individual partners on their separate tax returns. To afford the partnership a deduction on such items would result in a double benefit. For example, personal exemptions provided by § 151 are not deductible by the partnership, but are taken by the partners individually.

In order to determine his personal tax liability, each partner takes into account separately his distributive share of the partnership's income, gain, loss, deduction, or credit. Section 702(a) requires separate statement of six specifically enumerated items (capital gains and losses, § 1231 gains and losses, charitable contributions, etc.), a seventh category of items as required by the Regulations, and a final catch-all category of all other items, often referred to as "bottom-line profit or loss."

Separate statement is required for the categories of §§ 702(a)(1)–702(a)(7) because the tax effects of those items are dependent upon the factual particulars of each partner. For example, a capital loss of $10,000 for each partner will be of limited utility to a partner with no capital gain but will be fully available to a partner with $10,000 or more of capital gain. Separate statement allows the capital-loss limitation of § 1211 to be applied separately to each partner. Each item of separately stated partnership income, gain, loss, deduction, or credit is separately reported on schedule K for the partnership and schedule K-1 for each partner.

The entity characteristic of a partnership is emphasized by § 702(b), which provides that the tax character of items constituting each partner's distributive share is fixed at the partnership level, without regard to the trade or business of each partner. Thus, for example, a disposition of property by a partnership will be characterized by the nature of the partnership's activities with respect to that property—holding period, capital-asset status, etc. The professions and individual activities of the member partners are irrelevant to such a determination. However, it must be remembered that a partnership acts through its partners. Therefore, the actions of a partner may prove relevant to the characterization issue if taken on behalf of the partnership.

PROBLEM 5

QUESTIONS

1. A is a chemist who never has owned real estate. B subdivides real estate as her primary business activity. They form a partnership which purchases several parcels of real property. Two years later, the partnership sells one of its real properties at a gain after extensive marketing efforts. What are the tax consequences to A and B?

2. Same as question 1. above, except that the real property sold is one that B contributed to the partnership at its formation. Does this change the tax consequences to the partners?

3. The ABC limited partnership is composed of individual limited partners A and B and corporate general partner C. Each has a one-third interest in each item of income and deduction. A also operates a sole proprietorship. Determine each partner's distributive share of income and deductions, assuming the following receipts and expenditures:

   a. $10,000 in long-term capital gain.

   b. $3,000 in dividends from a domestic corporation.

   c. $2,000 of a bad debt recovery.

   d. $20,000 expenditure for property qualifying for § 179.

   e. $40,000 in depreciation expense, the first $10,000 of which is specially allocated to the limited partners by the partnership agreement.

   f. $30,000 in investment interest expense.

   g. $200,000 treasure trove (under Regulation § 1.61-14).

   h. $43,000 of § 162 expense.

4. D, a wealthy individual, and H, Inc. form a limited partnership in which they share profits, losses, and capital in a 99:1 ratio. The primary purpose for selecting the limited partnership vehicle is to maximize protection from personal liability, while avoiding an additional tax at the entity level. Does such an arrangement violate the partnership anti-abuse Regulation?

MATERIALS

Podell v. Commissioner
55 TC 429 (1970)

QUEALY, Judge.

. . .The only question presented for decision is whether amounts received by petitioner on the sale of certain real estate are taxable as ordinary income under section 61 or as capital gain . . . .

During each of the years 1964 and 1965, Hyman Podell (hereinafter referred to as petitioner) entered into an oral agreement with Mr. Cain Young (hereinafter referred to as Young), a real estate operator located in Brooklyn, New York, whereby petitioner advanced various amounts of money to Young to be used for the purchase and renovation of certain residential real estate. Young was to provide the actual management for the project. Petitioner entered into the agreement with Young in each of the years in the hope that the renovation of the buildings purchased pursuant to the agreement would help in the rehabilitation of certain slum areas in Brooklyn.

Pursuant to the aforesaid agreement, Young purchased various buildings in the Bedford-Stuyvesant, Crown Heights, and other areas of Brooklyn, New York. Young renovated the buildings, refinanced them, and sold them at the best possible price obtainable. In 1964, petitioner and Young purchased, renovated, and sold nine buildings. In 1965, petitioner and Young purchased, renovated, and sold five buildings. In other years, the number was less. The aforesaid activities constituted only a portion of the total activities carried on by Young.

Young held the aforementioned buildings for sale in the ordinary course of business. In addition, petitioner and Young shared equally in the profit or loss on the sale of each of the buildings. In 1964, petitioner's share of the net gain realized from his agreement with Young was $4,198.03. In 1965, petitioner's share of the net gain realized from his agreement with Young was $2,903.41.

Petitioner is engaged in the full-time practice of law, and he has paid regular taxes on his earnings as an attorney. He did not actively participate in the purchase, the renovation, or the sale of the real estate.

ULTIMATE FINDING OF FACT

The oral agreements entered into between petitioner and Young in 1964 and 1965 established a joint venture for the purpose of purchasing, renovating, and selling certain residential real estate in the ordinary course of trade or business.

OPINION

In this case, during each of the years 1964 and 1965, petitioner entered into an oral agreement with Young for the purchase, renovation, and sale of certain residential real estate. Profit and loss realized on the sale of such property was shared equally by petitioner and Young.

Section 1221, which defines "capital asset," provides in pertinent part:

For purposes of this subtitle, the term "capital asset" means property held by the taxpayer (whether or not connected with his trade or business), but does not include—

(1) stock in trade of the taxpayer or other property of a kind which would properly be included in the inventory of the taxpayer if on hand at the close of the taxable year, *or property held by the taxpayer primarily for sale to customers in the ordinary course of his trade or business;* [Emphasis supplied.]

Petitioner maintains that the properties sold were capital assets and that any gains on those sales should be taxed as capital gains.

Respondent argues that the oral agreements between petitioner and Young established a partnership or joint venture for the purposes of purchasing, renovating, and selling real estate in the ordinary course of business, and that consequently, the gains arose from the sale of noncapital assets and are to be treated as ordinary income.

We have found as an ultimate fact that the agreement between petitioner and Young gave rise to a joint venture. Under section 761(a), a joint venture is included within the definition of a "partnership" for purposes of the internal revenue laws (henceforth in this opinion, the terms are used interchangeably). Section 761(a) provides:

(a) PARTNERSHIP.—For purposes of this subtitle, the term "partnership" *includes* a syndicate, group, pool, *joint venture* or other unincorporated organization through or by means of which any business, financial operation, or venture is carried on, and which is not, within the meaning of this title [subtitle], a corporation or a trust or estate. [Emphasis supplied.]

A joint venture has been defined as a "special combination of two or more persons, wherein some specific venture a profit is jointly sought without any actual partnership or corporate designation."

The elements of a joint venture are: (a) A contract (express or implied) showing that it was the intent of the parties that a business venture be established; (b) an agreement for joint control and proprietorship; (c) a contribution of money, property, and/or services by the prospective joint venturers; and (d) a sharing of profits, but not necessarily of losses (although some jurisdictions require that there be a sharing of losses).

In many respects, the concept of joint venture is similar to the concept of partnership, and many of the principles of partnership law are applicable to joint ventures. A primary distinction between the two concepts is that a joint venture is generally established for a single business venture (even though the business of managing the venture to a successful conclusion may continue for a number of years) while a partnership is formed to carry on a business for profit over a long period of time.

It is undisputed that petitioner and Young joined in an agreement establishing a joint business venture to acquire, improve, and resell residential property at a profit, and it is immaterial that the petitioner was motivated, in part, by social objectives. There was a contribution to the business of property, services, or money by each of the parties involved. Petitioner and Young also agreed to share equally in any resulting gain or loss.

The fact that petitioner did not exercise as much managerial control over the day-to-day activities relating to the purchase, renovation, and sale of the real estate as Young is not sufficient reason for this Court to find against the existence of a joint venture. While petitioner gave Young discretion with respect to all aspects of the purchase, renovation, and sale of the real estate in question, petitioner retained the power to approve of the steps undertaken by Young to execute their agreement through his control over his continued contributions of funds to the venture.

The real estate acquired by the joint venture is to be considered partnership property for purposes of taxation. Section 702(a) provides, in part:

> (a) GENERAL RULE.—In determining his income tax, each partner shall take into account separately *his distributive share of the partnership's*—
>
> > (1) gains and losses from sales or exchanges of capital assets held for not more than 6 months,
> >
> > (2) gains and losses from sales or exchanges of capital assets held for more than 6 months,
>
> [Emphasis supplied.]

Section 702(b) establishes the "conduit rule" for the income taxation of partnerships and provides:

> (b) CHARACTER OF ITEMS CONSTITUTING DISTRIBUTIVE SHARE.—The character of any item of income, gain, loss, deduction, or credit included in a partner's distributive share . . . shall be determined as if such item were realized directly from the source from which realized by the partnership, or incurred in the same manner as incurred by the partnership.

In essence, the "conduit rule" requires that for the purpose of determining the nature of an item of income, gain, loss, deduction, or credit in the hands of the partnership before distribution or a partner (joint venturer—henceforth in this opinion the terms "partner" and "joint venturer" are used interchangeably) after distribution, the partnership is to be viewed as an entity and such items are to be characterized from the viewpoint of the partnership rather than from the viewpoint of an individual partner. Thus, the phrase "his trade or business" in section 1221(1) clearly refers to the trade or business of the partnership, despite the fact that under section 701 partnerships are not subject to income tax. It is the intent of the partnership and not that of any specific partner which is determinative in characterizing the income for purposes of taxation.

The trade or business of the joint venture or partnership in this case during the years in question was the purchase, renovation, and sale of certain residential real estate irrespective of and separately from the various businesses or professions of the individual joint venturers. The real estate sold by the joint venture was held for sale to the customers of the joint venture in the ordinary course of the joint venture's business with the consequence that the residential real estate parcels were not capital assets in the hands of the joint venture. Consequently, the income realized by the joint venture on the sale of the real estate was ordinary income. Therefore, applying the "conduit rule" of section 702(b), this income remained ordinary income in the hands of the joint venturers.

The cases of *United States v. Rosebrook*, 318 F.2d 316 (C.A. 9, 1963), and *Riddell v. Scales*, 406 F.2d 210 (C.A. 9, 1969), which look to the purposes of the joint venturers in determining the character of the income, are readily distinguishable from the case before us. In *Rosebrook*, there was direct ownership of the property in question by the taxpayer even though her interest had been committed to a joint venture. Furthermore, the taxpayer had succeeded involuntarily to ownership of the property and participation in the joint venture through her father. In the case before us, these factors are not present. In *Riddell v. Scales*, supra, the joint venture as an entity was not engaged in the real estate business.

Petitioner relies heavily on *Austin v. Commissioner*, 263 F. 2d 460 (C.A. 9, 1959), to support his position. His reliance is without foundation. The facts of *Austin* are entirely distinguishable from the case at hand. In *Austin*, the taxpayer was an attorney who individually sold vacant lots over a period of years. He was not a participant in a joint venture that had as its primary purpose the purchase, renovation, and sale of residential real estate to its customers in the ordinary course of its business. In the case before us, petitioner was engaged in such a joint venture, and the character of the income in his hands is determined by the character it would have had if it had remained with the joint venture. Since it would be ordinary income to the joint venture, it is ordinary income to petitioner. In short, *Austin* is irrelevant in terms of the facts of this case.

Decision will be entered for the respondent.

Baumgart v. Commissioner
TC Memo. 1983-738, 47 TCM 592

WHITAKER, Judge.

After concessions by both parties the issues remaining are (1) whether the petitioner's sale of railroad cars in 1975 is subject to ordinary income or long-term capital gain treatment . . . .

Prior to the years at issue, petitioner was in the business of providing marketing and consulting services to American manufacturers desiring to sell their products to foreign purchasers. The business was in the form of two sole proprietorships called B Associates and Gateway International Company (Gateway International). . . . Although his businesses were sole proprietorships, petitioner did some of his business with the assistance of another individual named Kenneth R. McGuire (McGuire).

Through his business contacts, petitioner discovered that there might be a good business opportunity in the leasing of used railroad cars. He discovered that Greenville Steel Car Company (Greenville) had such cars for sale. On September 17, 1974, petitioner and McGuire formed GILCO, a general partnership, for the purpose of acquiring used railroad cars to be owned, leased, and operated by GILCO. The cars were to be acquired from Greenville pursuant to the exercise of a previously negotiated (but not yet formalized) option.

The option agreement was formalized on September 24, 1974. It granted GILCO an option to purchase from Greenville 549 Twin Hopper cars for $5,500 per car . . . .

The railroad cars were under lease to the Pittsburgh & Shawmut Railroad Company (P & S), and Greenville was to transfer the cars to GILCO upon termination of the lease in July 1975 if GILCO exercised the option.

During the negotiations with Greenville, the GILCO partners discussed the possibility of obtaining title to the cars during the term of the P & S lease and of leasing the cars after the P & S lease expired. After obtaining the option, petitioner tried unsuccessfully to arrange a lease of the cars to a business contact for future date. He then ran ads in the Wall Street Journal and contracted people who might be interested in purchasing or leasing the cars. In letters dated between September 27, 1974, and October 11, 1974, petitioner followed up telephone calls with written offers to sell the cars for $7,100 per car or to lease them for $4.75 per car per day.

On October 18, 1974, International Minerals and Chemical Corporation (IMC) responded to petitioner's September 27, 1974, letter by offering to purchase the cars for $7,025 per car, or a total of $3,856,725. On October 21, 1974, GILCO gave notice to Greenville that it planned to exercise the option to purchase the cars and would open the letter of credit securing the payment of $15,000 by November 9, 1974.

On November 8, 1974, GILCO sold the cars upon which it has an option to IMC for $7,025 each. On the same day, GILCO notified Greenville that GILCO was exercising the option to purchase the cars, and thereafter the option became a purchase agreement. GILCO had a letter of credit issued to secure the purchase price. GILCO purchased no other railroad cars after that date. In keeping with a condition of the sales agreement between GILCO and IMC (sales agreement), IMC saw that two irrevocable letters of credit were issued, one to Greenville for $3,019,500, which satisfied GILCO's obligation under the purchase agreement (i.e., GILCO's cost of the cars) and another to GILCO for $837,225 (GILCO's profit). GILCO thus did not have to provide any cash for the purchase and sale of the cars. . . .

Petitioner reported the gain from the sale of the cars to IMC as gain from the sale of an asset used in the trade or business of leasing railroad cars, which he claims resulted in capital gain here. In the statutory notice of deficiency, respondent reclassified the gain as ordinary income.

Respondent's position in support of its determination is that the railroad cars were property held primarily for sale to customers in the ordinary course of a trade or business and thus were excluded from capital gain treatment under section 1231(b) and from the definition of a capital asset by reason of section 1221(1). Therefore, it is contended, profit from their sale gives rise to ordinary income. Petitioner argues that the cars were used in the trade or business of leasing railroad cars and that they were not held primarily for sale. For the reasons which follow, we find that the sale of the railroad cars resulted in ordinary income to the petitioner.

Section 1221 defines a capital asset broadly as "property held by the taxpayer," but limits this expansive language by excluding, inter alia, "property held by the taxpayer primarily for sale to customers in the ordinary course of his trade or business." Section 1231 provides preferential capital gain treatment for "property used in the trade or business," but also excludes property "held by the taxpayer primarily for sale to customers in the ordinary course of his trade or business." The function of this exclusion, according to the Supreme Court,

> is to differentiate between the "profits and losses arising from the everyday operation of a business" on the one hand . . . and "the realization of appreciation in value accrued over a substantial period of time" on the other.

First, we hold that petitioner fails to qualify for the favorable treatment of section 1231 because the railroad cars do not constitute property used in petitioner's trade or business. Petitioner claimed on his return that the cars were used in his business of leasing railroad cars, but we do not believe that petitioner was in the leasing business. The rental of the cars was pursuant to a pre-existing lease that was not arranged by petitioner and was nothing more than a mere fortuity. Moreover, his rental of the cars was an interim proposition, since the ultimate sale was a foregone fact at the time of purchase from Greenville. . . .

Petitioner also argues that the instant transaction should not be excluded from capital gain treatment under either section 1221 or 1231 because the rental shows that the cars were not "property held . . . primarily for sale." But we believe that petitioner held the cars primarily for sale within the meaning of these sections. . . .

But in order to be excluded from the definition of a capital asset the cars also must have been held for sale in the course of petitioner's business. Petitioner argues that his activities with respect to the railroad cars were not part of his existing business, because the structure of the instant transaction as a purchase and sale differed substantially from his activities in his existing business, where he sold property on behalf of others for a commission. He further contends that his existing business was not dealing in personal property and that it involved different products in a different market from the instant transaction. Respondent, on the other hand, contends that the purchase and sale of the railroad cars was in substance so similar to petitioner's existing business that it should be considered to be a part of it—or at least an enlargement or modification of that business.

We note initially that petitioner's ownership of the railroad cars was technically by means of a one-half interest in GILCO, a partnership. The record contains no evidence as to the reason why the instant transaction was effected through a separate entity from the sole proprietorship through which he conducted his business. We find, however, that the existence of the partnership entity is not material for purposes of the instant discussion—and the parties apparently were of the same view, as their briefs contain virtually no discussion of its relevance.

We have held in previous cases that the existence of a trade or business for various purposes is to be determined at the partnership level. This rule—which we reaffirm here—is based upon the familiar principle enunciated by the Supreme Court in *United States v. Basye*, 410 U.S. 441, 448 (1973), that "the partnership is regarded as an independently recognizable entity apart from the aggregate of its partners" for purposes of determining the character of partnership income. See section 702(b). Thus in *Brannen v. Commissioner*, we held that, in determining whether an activity was engaged in for profit within the meaning of section 183, profit motive should be analyzed at the partnership level. In Madison Gas & *Electric Co. v. Commissioner*, we held that the businesses of the partners could not be imputed to the partnership to transform nondeductible start-up costs of the entity into deductible business expenses of the partners. And in G*oodwin v. Commissioner*, we reaffirmed our *Madison Gas* holding with regard to similar pre-business expenses.

Our present comparison of petitioner's business activities in and outside of the partnership is fully consistent with those cases, because we here focus not upon whether the activities of GILCO rose to the level of a trade or business as in these cases—we will address that question later. Rather, our present emphasis is upon petitioner's intent: specifically, we are inquiring whether he intended by purchasing and selling these railroad cars to continue in an expanded form of his existing business or to enter into a wholly separate investment endeavor. Therefore, it is completely appropriate for us to examine petitioner's activities in both his existing business and the partnership to ascertain whether they were so similar that they constituted one business.

The partnership was not merely an investment by petitioner in a completely unrelated venture. It was in reality no different from his existing commission business, largely because in the activities of GILCO petitioner did not bear any risks of ownership. The purchase and sale for the cars were structured so that at no point did petitioner or GILCO have to supply any cash to finance the transaction; petitioner thus was not subject to a cash flow risk. Petitioner's sales contract with IMC provided that petitioner would sell as many cars as it could deliver by a certain date; therefore there was no risk of a suit by IMC for nondelivery. While petitioner makes several conclusory claims concerning the "contingent" nature of his contract, we fail to see how he could possibly be subject to the rise and fall of the marketplace when he sold the cars simultaneously with his purchase of them. . . .

This virtually risk-free nature of the purchase and sale makes it very similar to petitioner's commission arrangements in his existing business, where his profit was assured and similarly was due solely to the personal services he performed in putting together a willing buyer and seller. . . .

Therefore, we find that the purchase and sale of the railroad cars constituted an extension of petitioner's existing business.

Petitioner alternatively claims that the transaction did not constitute a separate, independent trade or business because it was an isolated, speculative, nonrecurring sale, which is not properly treated as a trade or business. Respondent contends, on the other hand, that the instant transaction did constitute a trade or business in its own right and that capital gain treatment is inappropriate because, where property is acquired specifically for sale pursuant to a preexisting sale arrangement, that property is held for sale in the ordinary course of a trade or business. For purposes of completeness we will deal with these contentions.

In determining whether a trade or business exists, each case necessarily will turn upon the totality of circumstances. In examining these circumstances, the courts have, over the years, developed a series of factors that have proven to be helpful in determining whether a particular endeavor rises to the level of a trade or business. These factors include the purpose for which the taxpayer acquired and held the property, the extent of improvements made to facilitate its sale, the activity of the taxpayer in promoting sales, the frequency and continuity of sales, the length of time the property was held between purchase and sale, and the relative income to the taxpayer from the sale of the property, compared with his other income.

After a careful examination of the facts in this case, we find that petitioner's activities in connection with the railroad cars rose to the level of a trade or business. The evidence clearly shows that petitioner exercised a good degree of personal effort and control over the purchase and sale of the railroad cars. Petitioner also was active in the maintenance of the railroad cars during the period between the exercise of the option on November 8, 1974, and final delivery to IMC in December 1975. The fact that there was such a short period of ownership of the cars also is indicative of business rather than investment behavior. With regard to frequency of sales, while there was only one sales contract with IMC, the seven separate deliveries of the railroad cars to

IMC were treated by the parties as separate "sales." And, when some of the cars were rejected by IMC because they had been inadequately maintained, petitioner threatened to sue P & S until he worked out the repurchase agreement with Greenville. When viewed together, all of these facts show a substantial degree of involvement by petitioner in the purchase, maintenance and sale of the railroad cars and a distinct lack of passive "investment" intent or behavior. . . . These facts lead us to conclude that petitioner was engaged in the trade or business of selling railroad cars. . . .

For these reasons, petitioner's claim for capital gain treatment will be denied.

United States v. Basye
410 US 441 (1973)

MR. JUSTICE POWELL delivered the opinion of the Court:

This is a partnership income tax case brought here by the United States on a petition for writ of certiorari from the Court of Appeals for the Ninth Circuit. Respondents, physicians and partners in a medical partnership, filed suit in the District Court for the Northern District of California seeking the refund of income taxes previously paid pursuant to a deficiency assessed by the Commissioner of Internal Revenue. The case was heard on an agreed statement of facts and the District Court ruled in respondents' favor. 295 F. Supp. 1289 (1968). The Government appealed to the Ninth Circuit and that court affirmed the lower court's judgment. 450 F. 2d 109 (1971). We agreed to hear this case to consider whether, as the Government contends, the decision below is in conflict with precedents of this Court. 405 U.S. 1039 (1972). Because we find that the decision is incompatible with basic principles of income taxation as developed in our prior cases, we reverse.

I.

Respondents, each of whom is a physician, are partners in a limited partnership known as Permanente Medical Group, which was organized in California in 1949. Associated with the partnership are over 200 partner physicians, as well as numerous nonpartner physicians and other employees. In 1959, Permanente entered into an agreement with Kaiser Foundation Health Plan, Inc., a nonprofit corporation providing prepaid medical care and hospital services to its dues-paying members.

Pursuant to the terms of the agreement, Permanente agreed to supply medical services for the 390,000 member-families, or about 900,000 individuals, in Kaiser's Northern California Region which covers primarily the San Francisco Bay area. In exchange for those services, Kaiser agreed to pay the partnership a "base compensation" composed of two elements. First, Kaiser undertook to pay directly to the partnership a sum each month computed on the basis of the total number of members enrolled in the health program. That number was multiplied by a stated fee, which originally was set at a little over $2.60. The second item of compensation—and the one that has occasioned the present dispute—called for the creation of a program, funded entirely by Kaiser, to pay retirement benefits to Permanente's partner and nonpartner physicians.

The pertinent compensation provision of the agreement did not itself establish the details of the retirement program; it simply obligated Kaiser to make contributions to such a program in the event that the parties might thereafter agree to adopt one. As might be expected, a separate trust agreement establishing the contemplated plan soon was executed by Permanente, Kaiser, and the Bank of America Trust and Savings Association, acting as trustee. Under this agreement Kaiser agreed to make payments to the trust at a predetermined rate, initially pegged at 12 cents per health plan member per month. Additionally, Kaiser made a flat payment of $200,000 to start the fund and agreed that its pro rata payment obligation would be retroactive to the date of the signing of the medical service agreement.

The beneficiaries of the trust were all partner and nonpartner physicians who had completed at least two years of continuous service with the partnership and who elected to participate. The trust maintained a separate tentative account for each beneficiary. As periodic payments were received from Kaiser, the funds were allocated among these accounts pursuant to a complicated formula designed to take into consideration on a relative basis each participant's compensation level, length of service, and age. No physician was eligible to receive the amounts in his tentative account prior to retirement, and retirement established entitlement only if the participant had rendered at least 15 years of continuous service or 10 years of continuous service and had attained age 65. Prior to such time, however, the trust agreement explicitly provided that no interest in any tentative account was to be regarded as having vested in any particular beneficiary. The agreement also provided for the forfeiture of any physician's interest and its redistribution among the remaining participants if he were to terminate his relationship with Permanente prior to retirement. A similar forfeiture and redistribution also would occur if, after retirement, a physician were to render professional services for any hospital or health plan other than one operated by Kaiser. The trust agreement further stipulated that a retired physician's right to receive benefits would cease if he were to refuse any reasonable request to render consultative services to any Kaiser-operated health plan.

The agreement provided that the plan would continue irrespective either of changes in the partnership's personnel or of alterations in its organizational structure. The plan would survive any reorganization of the partnership so long as at least 50 percent of the plan's participants remained associated with the reorganized entity. In the event of dissolution or of a nonqualifying reorganization, all of the amounts in the trust were to be divided among the participants entitled thereto in amounts governed by each participant's tentative account. Under no circumstances, however, could payments from Kaiser to the trust be recouped by Kaiser: once compensation was paid into the trust it was thereafter committed exclusively to the benefit of Permanente's participating physicians.

Upon the retirement of any partner or eligible nonpartner physician, if he had satisfied each of the requirements for participation, the amount that had accumulated in his tentative account over the years would be applied to the purchase of a retirement income contract. While the program thus provided obvious benefits to Permanente's physicians, it also served Kaiser's interests. By providing attractive deferred benefits for Permanente's staff of professionals, the retirement plan was designed to "create an incentive" for physicians to remain with Permanente and thus "insure" that Kaiser would have a "stable and reliable group of physicians."

During the years from the plan's inception until its discontinuance in 1963, Kaiser paid a total of more than $2,000,000 into the trust. Permanente, however, did not report these payments as income in its partnership returns. Nor did the individual partners include these payments in the computations of their distributive shares of the partnership's taxable income. The Commissioner assessed deficiencies against each partner-respondent for his distributive share of the amount paid by Kaiser. Respondents, after paying the assessments under protest, filed these consolidated suits for refund.

The Commissioner premised his assessment on the conclusion that Kaiser's payments to the trust constituted a form of compensation to the partnership for the services it rendered and therefore was income to the partnership. And, notwithstanding the deflection of those payments to the retirement trust and their current unavailability to the partners, the partners were still taxable on their distributive shares of that compensation. Both the District Court and the Court of Appeals disagreed. They held that the payments to the fund were not income to the partnership because it did not receive them and never had a "right to receive" them. They reasoned that the partnership, as an entity, should be disregarded and that each partner should be treated simply as a potential beneficiary of his tentative share of the retirement fund. Viewed in this light, no presently taxable income could be attributed to these cash basis taxpayers because of the contingent and forfeitable nature of the fund allocations.

We hold that the courts below erred and that respondents were properly taxable on the partnership's retirement fund income. This conclusion rests on two familiar principles of income taxation, first, that income is taxed to the party who earns it and that liability may not be avoided through an anticipatory assignment of that income, and, second, that partners are taxable on their distributive or proportionate shares of current partnership income irrespective of whether that income is actually distributed to them. The ensuing discussion is simply an application of those principles to the facts of the present case.

II.

Section 703 of the Internal Revenue Code of 1954, insofar as pertinent here, prescribes that "[t]he taxable income of a partnership shall be computed in the same manner as in the case of an individual." § 703(a). Thus, while the partnership itself pays no taxes, § 701, it must report the income it generates and such income must be calculated in largely the same manner as an individual computes his personal income. For this purpose, then, the partnership is regarded as an independently recognizable entity apart from the aggregate of its partners. Once its income is ascertained and reported, its existence may be disregarded since each partner must pay a tax on a portion of the total income as if the partnership were merely an agent or conduit through which the income passed.[8]

In determining any partner's income, it is first necessary to compute the gross income of the partnership. One of the major sources of gross income, as defined in § 61(a)(1) of the Code, is "compensation for services, including fees, commissions, and

---

[8] There has been a great deal of discussion in the briefs and in the lower court opinions with respect to whether a partnership is to be viewed as an "entity" or as a "conduit." We find ourselves in agreement with the Solicitor General's remark during oral argument when he suggested that "[i]t seems odd that we should still be discussing such things in 1972." The legislative history indicates, and the commentators agree, that partnerships are entities for purposes of calculating and filling informational returns but that they are conduits through which the taxpaying obligation passes to the individual partners in accord with their distributive shares.

similar items." There can be no question that Kaiser's payments to the retirement trust were compensation for services rendered by the partnership under the medical service agreement. These payments constituted an integral part of the employment arrangement. The agreement itself called for two forms of "base compensation" to be paid in exchange for services rendered—direct per-member, per-month payments to the partnership and other, similarly computed, payments to the trust. Nor was the receipt of these payments contingent upon any condition other than continuation of the contractual relationship and the performance of the prescribed medical services. Payments to the trust, much like the direct payments to the partnership, were not forfeitable by the partnership or recoverable by Kaiser upon the happening of any contingency.

Yet the courts below, focusing on the fact that the retirement fund payments were never actually received by the partnership but were contributed directly to the trust, found that the payments were not includable as income in the partnership's returns. The view of tax accountability upon which this conclusion rests is incompatible with a foundational rule, which this Court has described as "the first principle of income taxation: that income must be taxed to him who earns it." The entity earning the income—whether a partnership or an individual taxpayer—cannot avoid taxation by entering into a contractual arrangement whereby that income is diverted to some other person or entity. Such arrangements, known to the tax law as "anticipatory assignments of income," have frequently been held ineffective as means of avoiding tax liability. The seminal precedent, written over 40 years ago, is Mr. Justice Holmes' opinion for a unanimous Court in *Lucas v. Earl*, 281 US 111 (1930). There the taxpayer entered into a contract with his wife whereby she became entitled to one-half of any income he might earn in the future. On the belief that a taxpayer was accountable only for income actually received by him, the husband thereafter reported only half of his income. The Court, unwilling to accept that a reasonable construction of the tax laws permitted such easy deflection of income tax liability, held that the taxpayer was responsible for the entire amount of his income . . . .

The principle of *Lucas v. Earl*, that he who earns income may not avoid taxation through anticipatory arrangements no matter how clever or subtle, has been repeatedly invoked by this Court and stands today as a cornerstone of our graduated income tax system. And, of course, that principle applies with equal force in assessing partnership income.

Permanente's agreement with Kaiser, whereby a portion of the partnership compensation was deflected to the retirement fund, is certainly within the ambit of *Lucas v. Earl*. The partnership earned the income and, as a result of arm's-length bargaining with Kaiser, was responsible for its diversion into the trust fund. The Court of Appeals found the *Lucas* principle inapplicable because Permanente "never had the right itself to receive the payments made into the trust as current income." In support of this assertion, the court relied on language in the agreed statement of facts stipulating that "[t]he payments . . . were paid solely to fund the retirement plan, and were not otherwise available to [Permanente] . . . ." Emphasizing that the fund was created to serve Kaiser's interest in a stable source of qualified, experienced physicians, the court found that Permanente could not have received that income except in the form in which it was received.

The court's reasoning seems to be that, before the partnership could be found to have received income, there must be proof that "Permanente agreed to accept less direct compensation from Kaiser in exchange for the retirement plan payments." Apart from the inherent difficulty of adducing such evidence, we know of no authority imposing this burden upon the Government. Nor do we believe that the guiding principle of *Lucas v. Earl* may be so easily circumvented. Kaiser's motives for making payments are irrelevant to the determination whether those amounts may fairly be viewed as compensation for services rendered. Neither does Kaiser's apparent insistence upon payment to the trust deprive the agreed contributions of their character as compensation. The Government need not prove that the taxpayer had complete and unrestricted power to designate the manner and form in which his income is received. We may assume, especially in view of the relatively unfavorable tax status of self-employed persons with respect to the tax treatment of retirement plans, that many partnerships would eagerly accept conditions similar to those prescribed by this trust in consideration for tax-deferral benefits of the sort suggested here. We think it clear, however, that the tax laws permit no such easy road to tax avoidance or deferment. Despite the novelty and ingenuity of this arrangement, Permanente's "base compensation" in the form of payments to a retirement fund was income to the partnership and should have been reported as such.

III.

Since the retirement fund payments should have been reported as income to the partnership, along with other income received from Kaiser, the individual partners should have included their shares of that income in their individual returns. §§ 61(a)(13), 702, 704. For it is axiomatic that each partner must pay taxes on his distributive share of the partnership's income without regard to whether that amount is actually distributed to him. *Heiner v. Mellon*, 304 US 271 (1938), decided under a predecessor to the current partnership provisions of the Code, articulates the salient proposition. After concluding that "distributive" share means the "proportionate" share as determined by the partnership agreement, the Court stated:

> The tax is thus imposed upon the partner's proportionate share of the net income of the partnership, and the fact that it may not be currently distributable, whether by agreement of the parties or by operation of law, is not material.

Few principles of partnership taxation are more firmly established than the principle that no matter the reason for nondistribution, each partner must pay taxes on his distributive share. Treas. Reg. § 1.702-1.

The courts below reasoned to the contrary, holding that the partners here were not properly taxable on the amounts contributed to the retirement fund. This view, apparently, was based on the assumption that each partner's distributive share prior to retirement was too contingent and unascertainable to constitute presently recognizable income. It is true that no partner knew with certainty exactly how much he would ultimately receive or whether he would in fact be entitled to receive anything. But the existence of conditions upon the actual receipt by a partner of income fully earned by the partnership is irrelevant in determining the amount of tax due from him. The fact that the courts below placed such emphasis on this factor suggests the basic misapprehension under which they labored in this case. Rather than being viewed as responsible contributors to the partnership's total income, respondent-partners were seen only as contingent beneficiaries of the trust. In some measure, this misplaced focus on the considerations of uncertainty and forfeitability may be a consequence of the erroneous manner in which the Commissioner originally assessed the partners' deficiencies. The Commissioner divided Kaiser's trust fund payments into two categories: (1) payments earmarked for the tentative accounts of *nonpartner* physicians; and (2) those allotted to *partner* physicians. The payments to the trust for the former category of nonpartner physicians were correctly counted as income to the partners in accord with the distributive-share formula as established in the partnership agreement. The latter payments to the tentative accounts of the individual partners, however, were improperly allocated to each partner pursuant to the complex formula in the retirement plan itself, just as if that agreement operated as an amendment to the partnership agreement.

The Solicitor General, alluding to this miscomputation during oral argument, suggested that this error "may be what threw the court below off the track." It should be clear that the contingent and unascertainable nature of each partner's share under the retirement trust is irrelevant to the computation of his distributive share. The partnership had received as income a definite sum which was not subject to diminution or forfeiture. Only its ultimate disposition among the employees and partners remained uncertain. For purposes of income tax computation it made no difference that some partners might have elected not to participate in the retirement program or that, for any number of reasons, they might not ultimately receive any of the trust's benefits. Indeed, as the Government suggests, the result would be quite the same if the "potential beneficiaries included no partners at all, but were children, relatives, or other objects of the partnership's largesse." The sole operative consideration is that the income had been received by the partnership, not what disposition might have been effected once the funds were received.

IV.

In summary, we find this case controlled by familiar and long-settled principles of income and partnership taxation. There being no doubt about the character of the payments as compensation, or about their actual receipt, the partnership was obligated to report them as income presently received. Likewise, each partner was responsible for his distributive share of that income. We, therefore, reverse the judgments and remand the case with directions that judgments be entered for the United States.

It is so ordered.

Revenue Ruling 68-79
1968-1 CB 310

Advice has been requested whether a partner's distributive share of partnership capital gains resulting under the circumstances described below is long-term capital gain. A, B and C were equal partners in ABC partnership. On June 1, 1966, the partnership acquired 300 shares of X corporation stock as an investment. On February 1, 1967, A sold his partnership interest to new partner D. On May 1, 1967, the partnership sold at a gain the 300 shares of X stock (at which time D's holding period for his partnership interest was not more than six months).

Section 1222(1) of the Internal Revenue Code of 1954 defines the term "short-term capital gain" as gain from the sale or exchange of a capital asset held for not more than six months, if and to the extent such gain is taken into account in computing gross income.

Section 1222(3) of the Code defines the term "long-term capital gain" as gain from the sale or exchange of a capital asset held for more than six months, if and to the extent that such gain is taken into account in computing gross income.

Section 702(a) of the Code provides that in determining his income tax, each partner shall take into account separately his distributive share of the partnership's gains and losses from sales or exchanges of capital assets held for more than six months.

Section 702(b) of the Code provides that the character of any item of income, gain, loss, deduction, or credit included in a partner's distributive share under paragraphs (1) through (8) of subsection (a) shall be determined as if such item were realized directly from the source from which realized by the partnership, or incurred in the same manner as incurred by the partnership.

The character of any item of income, gain, loss, deduction, or credit included in a partner's distributive share under paragraphs (1) through (8) of section 702(a) of the Code is determined at the partnership level. Compare Revenue Ruling 67-188, 1967-1 C.B. 216.

Since the ABC partnership held the X stock for more than six months, the gain realized by the partnership is long-term capital gain.

Accordingly, in computing his gross income, D should take into account separately in his return, as long-term capital gain, his distributive share of the partnership's long-term capital gain arising from the sale by the partnership of X corporation stock held by it as an investment for more than six months, notwithstanding that D has a holding period for his partnership interest of not more than six months.

Revenue Ruling 86-138
1986-2 CB 84

ISSUE

Under section 703(a) of the Internal Revenue Code, is a subsidiary partnership in a multi-tiered arrangement required to state separately items of income, gain, loss, deduction, or credit if separate statement of these items could affect the tax liability of a partner in a higher-tier partnership in the multi-tiered arrangement but not the tax liability of a partner of the subsidiary partnership?

FACTS

S, a limited partnership, engages in construction activities. X, a corporation, is the sole general partner of S. P, a limited partnership, is the sole limited partner of S. The partners of P are all individuals. S and P are classified as partnerships under section 7701(a)(2) of the Code.

In the taxable year in question, S paid interest expense on indebtedness incurred to purchase property held for investment within the meaning of section 163(d)(3)(D) of the Code. S did not separately state the investment interest expense or the investment income in informing its partners of their distributive share of income, gain, loss, deduction, or credit on schedule K-1 (Form 1065) (Partner's Share of Income, Credits, Deductions, etc.) for the taxable year.

LAW AND ANALYSIS

Section 701 of the Code provides that a partnership as such shall not be subject to the income tax imposed by Chapter 1 of the Code. Persons carrying on business as partners shall be liable for income tax only in their separate or individual capacities.

Section 702(a) of the Code provides that, in determining a partner's income tax, each partner must take into account separately the partner's distributive share of items enumerated in section 702(a)(1) through, (8). Under section 702(a)(7), a partner must take into account separately those items of income, gain, loss, deduction, or credit prescribed by regulations.

Section 1.702-1(a)(8)(ii) of the Income Tax Regulations provides that each partner must take into account separately the partner's distributive share of any partnership item which if separately taken into account by any partner would result in an income tax liability for that partner different from that which would result if that partner did not take the item into account separately.

Section 702(b) of the Code provides that the character of any item included in a partner's distributive share under paragraphs (1) through (7) of section 702(a) is determined as if the item were realized directly from the source from which realized by the partnership, or incurred in the same manner as incurred by the partnership.

Section 703(a)(1) of the Code provides that a partnership shall separately state the items described in section 702(a) of the Code in computing its taxable income.

Section 163(a) of the Code allows a deduction for all interest paid or accrued within the taxable year on indebtedness.

Section 163(d)(1) of the Code provides that, in the case of a taxpayer other than a corporation, the amount of investment interest otherwise deductible is limited to (A)

$10,000 ($5,000, in the case of a separate return by a married individual), plus (B) the amount of the net investment income (as defined in section 163(d)(3)(A)), plus an additional amount in the case of net leases. Section 163(d)(3)(D) defines "investment interest" as interest paid or accrued on indebtedness incurred or continued to purchase or carry property held for investment.

Rev. Rul. 84-131, 1984-2 C.B. 37, concludes that in the case of a partnership whose partners are individuals, the partners must take into account separately their distributive shares of investment interest under section 163(d)(3)(D) of the Code.

The limitation on investment interest expense under section 163(d) of the Code does not apply to corporations. Under section 701, a partnership is not subject to the income tax. Because S has only a corporation and a partnership as partners, the tax liability of S's partners cannot be affected by the section 163(d) limitation. However, P, the limited partner of S, has partners that are individuals. The tax liability of these individual partners of P may be affected by the section 163(d) limitation, and they therefore need a separate statement of their distributive share of investment income and investment interest expenses of S and P. See Rev. Rul. 84-131, 1984-2 C.B. 37. The fact that an item flows through an intermediate partnership does not change the character of the item. Therefore, in order to give effect to section 702(a)(8) and section 1.702-1(a)(8)(ii), S and P must separately state investment interest expense and investment income under section 703 of the Code.

HOLDING

Under section 703(a) of the Code, a subsidiary partnership in a multi-tiered arrangement must separately state those items of income, gain, loss, deduction, and credit which if separately taken into account by any partner of any partnership in the multitiered structure would result in an income tax liability for that partner different from that which would result if that partner did not take those items into account separately.

Revenue Ruling 89-7
1989-1 CB 178

[ISSUE]

If a partner's distributive share of the partnership's expenses under section 179 of the Internal Revenue Code is not fully deductible by the partner because, when combined with the partner's section 179 expenses from other sources, the partner's section 179 expenses from all sources exceed the maximum amount allowable to the partner under section 179(b)(1), is the partner's basis in the partnership interest reduced by the partner's full distributive share of the partnership's section 179 expenses, including the partnership's section 179 expenses that the partner cannot deduct?

FACTS

In 1988, AB, a partnership, elected under section 179(a) of the Code to expense the entire cost of certain qualifying property that it purchased and placed in service during that year. A similar election was made by another partnership, AC. With respect to each of the partnerships, A had a three-fifths interest in each item of partnership income, gain, deduction, loss, and credit. The partnerships separately stated each partner's distributive share of section 179 expenses for that year. The sum of A's distributive share of section 179 expenses from AB and AC exceeded $10,000. AB and AC reduced the basis of the specific property to which the section 179 election applied by the total amount of section 179 expenses allocated to the partners as required by section 1.179-1(f)(2) of the Income Tax Regulations. The partnerships are both calendar year partnerships. But for the limitation contained in section 179(b)(1), A, AB, and AC each meet all the other limitations and restrictions of section 179.

LAW AND ANALYSIS

Section 179(a) of the Code provides that a taxpayer may elect to treat the cost of any section 179 property as an expense that is not chargeable to capital account. Any cost so treated shall be allowed as a deduction for the taxable year in which the section 179 property is placed in service. Under section 1.179-1(a) of the regulations, taxpayers may elect to treat as an expense all or a portion of the cost of section 179 property.

Section 179(b)(1) of the Code provides that the aggregate cost of property that may be taken into account under section 179(a) shall not exceed $10,000.

Section 179(d)(1) of the Code provides that the term "section 179 property" means any recovery property that is section 38 property and that is acquired by purchase for use in the active conduct of a trade or business.

Section 179(d)(8) of the Code and section 1.179-2(c) of the regulations provide that, in the case of a partnership, the dollar limitation contained in section 179(b)(1) shall apply with respect to the partnership and with respect to each partner.

Section 1.179-1(f)(2) of the regulations provides that, generally, the basis of a partnership's section 179 property must be reduced to reflect the amount of the section 179 expense elected by the partnership. This reduction must be made even if the section 179(b) dollar limitation prevents a partner from deducting all or a portion of the amount allocated by the partnership.

Section 1.179-1(h) of the regulations provides that the election to expense the cost of section 179 property is made by the partnership.

Section 702(a)(7) of the Code provides that in determining a partner's income tax, each partner shall take into account separately the partner's distributive share of the partnership's items of income, gain, loss, deduction, and credit (in addition to those items specifically listed in section 702(a)(1) through 702(a)(6)) to the extent provided by regulations prescribed by the Secretary. Section 1.702-1(a)(8)(ii) of the regulations provides that each partner must take into account separately the distributive share of any partnership item that if separately taken into account by any partner would result in an income tax liability for the partner different from that which would result if that partner did not take the item into account separately.

Section 703(a) of the Code provides that the taxable income of a partnership is computed in the same manner as in the case of an individual, except that the items described in section 702(a) must be separately stated and certain deductions specified in section 703(a)(2) are not allowed to the partnership. The deduction allowable under section 179 is not among the deductions disallowed under section 703(a)(2).

Section 705(a) of the Code provides, in part, that the adjusted basis of a partner's interest in a partnership shall be the basis of such interest determined under section 722 (relating to contributions to a partnership) or section 742 (relating to transfers of partnership interests) increased by the partner's distributive share for the taxable year and prior taxable years of taxable income of the partnership as determined under section 703(a) and decreased (but not below zero) by distributions by the partnership as provided in section 733 and by the sum of the partner's distributive share for the taxable year and prior taxable years of losses of the partnership and expenditures of the partnership not deductible in computing its taxable income and not properly chargeable to capital account.

The deduction allowable under section 179 of the Code must be separately stated under section 702(a)(7) because a partner's income tax liability may differ depending on whether or not this deduction is separately stated by the partnership. In compliance with section 179(d)(8) of the Code and section 1.179-2(c) of the regulations, A deducted only $10,000 of the total section 179 expenses separately stated and allocated to A by the partnerships.

Under section 703(a) of the Code, the deductible section 179 expenses of a partnership for a taxable year reduce the taxable income or increase the taxable loss of the partnership for the year. In addition, the section 179 expenses of a partnership that are not deductible in computing the partnership's taxable income or loss for a taxable year by reason of the application of the section 179(b) limitations to the partnership constitute expenditures of the partnership that are not properly chargeable to capital account. Accordingly, A's distributive share of the section 179 expenses of the partnerships will be reflected in the adjusted basis of A's interest in each partnership through the basis adjustments required by section 705(a), whether or not A is allowed a deduction for such expenses.

HOLDING

The adjusted basis of A's interest in AB and AC must be reduced under section 705 by A's distributive share of the section 179 expenses of the partnerships even though A may be prohibited from deducting all or a portion of such expenses under section 179(b)(1).

Revenue Ruling 2008-39
2008-2 CB 252

ISSUE

Under the facts described below, how are the management fees incurred by each of the lower tier partnerships (LTPs) and the management fee incurred by the upper tier partnership (UTP) taken into account in computing the tax liability of an individual who is a limited partner (LP) of UTP?

FACTS

LP, an individual, owns a limited partnership interest in UTP. UTP owns limited partnership interests in several LTPs. Each LTP is engaged in the business of trading in securities and such business constitutes a trade or business within the meaning of § 162 of the Internal Revenue Code (Code). UTP's activities consist solely of acquiring, holding, and disposing of interests in LTPs, and such activities, without regard to the activities of LTPs, do not constitute a trade or business within the meaning of § 162. Instead, UTP's activities (without regard to the activities of LTPs) consist of holding limited partnership interests in LTPs for the production of income within the meaning of § 212. UTP and each LTP pay an annual management fee to their respective managers in consideration for management services performed for their benefit. Each management fee is computed as a specified percentage of the value of the net assets owned by UTP and each LTP, as the case may be.

The management fee paid or incurred by each LTP is an ordinary and necessary business expense within the meaning of § 162 in carrying on its trade or business. The management fee paid or incurred by UTP, without regard to the activities of LTP, is an ordinary and necessary expense in carrying on its investment activities. UTP's management fee is not paid or incurred by UTP on behalf of any LTP in connection with an LTP's trade or business. None of the management fees are properly capitalized under § 263.

Under the terms of the partnership agreement of each LTP, UTP receives a distributive share of the items of income, gain, loss, deduction and credit of each LTP. Under the terms of UTP's partnership agreement, LP receives a distributive share of UTP's items of income, gain, loss, deduction and credit.

LAW AND ANALYSIS

Section 162(a) provides, in part, that there shall be allowed as a deduction all the ordinary and necessary expenses paid or incurred during the taxable year in carrying on any trade or business.

Section 212 provides that in the case of an individual, there shall be allowed as a deduction all the ordinary and necessary expenses paid or incurred during the taxable year (1) for the production or collection of income, (2) for the management, conservation, or maintenance of property held for the production of income, or (3) in connection with the determination, collection, or refund of any tax.

Section 1.212-1(d) of the Income Tax Regulations provides that expenses, to be deductible under § 212, must be "ordinary and necessary." Thus, such expenses must be reasonable in amount and must bear a reasonable and proximate relation to the production or collection of taxable income or to the management, conservation, or maintenance of property held for the production of income.

Section 1.212-1(g) provides that fees for services of investment counsel and similar expenses paid or incurred by a taxpayer in connection with investments held by the taxpayer are deductible under § 212 if they are paid or incurred for the production of income and they are ordinary and necessary under the circumstances.

Section 702(a)(8) provides that, in determining the partner's income tax, each partner shall take into account the partner's distributive share of the partnership's taxable income or loss, exclusive of the items requiring separate computation under § 702(a)(1) through (7). Section 702(a)(1) through (6) lists specific items of income, gain, loss, deduction or credit that must be separately stated by a partnership. Section 702(a)(7) provides that other items of income, gain, loss, deduction or credit also must be separately stated if required by regulations prescribed by the Secretary.

Section 702(b) provides that the character of any item of income, gain, loss, deduction, or credit included in a partner's distributive share under paragraphs (1) through (7) of § 702(a) shall be determined as if such item were realized directly from the source from which realized by the partnership, or incurred in the same manner as incurred by the partnership.

Section 703(a) provides that the taxable income of a partnership shall be computed in the same manner as in the case of an individual, except that the items listed in § 702(a) shall be separately stated and the deductions listed in paragraph (2) of § 703(a) shall not be allowed.

Section 703(a)(2)(E) provides that the additional itemized deductions for individuals in part VII of subchapter B of the Code, including expenses described in § 212, are not allowed to the partnership.

Section 1.702-1(a)(1) through (a)(8)(i) lists specific items of income, gain, loss, deduction or credit that must be separately stated by a partnership. Specifically, § 1.702-1(a)(8)(i) provides, in part, that each partner shall take into account separately the partner's distributive share of the partnership's non-business expenses that are described in § 212.

In *Butler v. Commissioner*, 36 T.C. 1097 (1961), the Tax Court held that, because loans made by a limited partner to a partnership were a vital factor in the existence and furtherance of the partnership's business and were proximately related to the business activities of the partnership, the limited partner was entitled to a business bad debt deduction. The Tax Court noted its agreement with other cases that "[b]y reason of being a partner in a business petitioner was individually engaged in business." Other courts have permitted a general partner to deduct as a trade or business expense amounts paid on behalf of the business of the partnership. In *Ward v. Commissioner*, 20 T.C. 332 (1953), *aff'd*, 224 F.2d 547 (9th Cir. 1955), following the termination of a general partnership, a general partner paid medical expenses of a partnership employee. The court held that the partner was individually engaged in business by reason of being a partner. Because of the termination of the partnership, the fact that the partner was no longer in business at the time of the expense did not mean the deduction was denied. A similar result was reached in *Flood v. United States,* 133 F. 2d 173 (1st Cir. 1943).

In *Goodwin v. Commissioner*, 75 T.C. 424 (1980), *aff'd*, 691 F.2d 490 (3d Cir. 1982), the Tax Court concluded that, for the purpose of characterizing partnership expenses for purposes of § 162, a partnership must be viewed as a substantive economic entity clearly distinct from its partners. In *Goodwin,* the taxpayer was individually engaged in real estate activities and attempted to claim deductions under § 162(a) for his distributive share as a limited partner of certain startup costs incurred by two limited partnerships formed to construct housing projects. The taxpayer argued that his activities as a partner constituted an expansion or continuation of his existing trade or business. The Tax Court, citing *Madison Gas and Electric Co. v. Commissioner,* 72 T.C. 521 (1979), *aff'd,* 633 F.2d 512 (7th Cir. 1980), held that in the context of § 162, the character of deductions incurred by the partnership, *i.e.,* whether the deductions are incurred in the course of a trade or business, must be resolved at the partnership level. The partnership was not yet carrying on a trade or business at the time the startup costs were paid or incurred. Accordingly, the Tax Court determined that the taxpayer's share of the startup costs were not deductible under § 162 regardless of the taxpayer's individual activities.

The Tax Court in *Goodwin* distinguished the question of whether a partnership expense was an ordinary and necessary expense incurred in carrying on the trade or business of a partnership from the question of whether a partner may deduct unreimbursed amounts paid by the partner on behalf of the partnership. It was the latter question that the Tax Court concluded was the issue in *Butler, Ward,* and *Flood.* In *Goodwin,* the Tax Court interpreted *Butler, Ward,* and *Flood* to stand for the proposition that, under certain facts, a partner may be entitled to individually deduct under § 162 as an ordinary and necessary expense an amount paid by the partner on behalf of the partnership for which the partner is not reimbursed. *See also Cropland Chemical v. Commissioner,* 75 T.C. 288 (1980); *Klein v. Commissioner,* 25 T.C. 1045 (1956); and Rev. Rul. 70-253, 1970-1 C.B. 31.

UTP's management fee is not an ordinary and necessary expense paid or incurred by UTP on behalf of the LTPs in carrying on the trading business of the LTPs. Thus, the reasoning and conclusions in *Butler, Ward,* and *Flood* are inapposite to the facts presented in this ruling.

Further, the reasoning and conclusions in Rev. Rul. 98-15, 1998-1 C.B. 718, do not apply to the question presented in this ruling. Rev. Rul. 98-15 addresses whether, under the facts described in that ruling, an organization that operates an acute care hospital continues to qualify for exemption from federal income tax as an organization described in § 501(c)(3) when it forms a limited liability company (LLC) with a for-profit corporation and then contributes its hospital and all of its other operating assets to the LLC, which then operates the hospital. The question addressed in Rev. Rul. 98-15 is distinguishable from the question presented in this ruling.

Accordingly, under *Goodwin,* the question of whether the management fee paid or incurred by UTP may be deducted under § 162 or § 212 must be resolved solely by reference to the activities of UTP. Because UTP itself is not engaged in a trade or business within the meaning of § 162 and because the management fee is not paid or incurred on behalf of any LTP in connection with an LTP's trade or business, the management fee is not deductible under § 162. Instead, UTP's annual management fees are ordinary and necessary expenses described in § 212 paid or incurred in connection with UTP's investment activities. Accordingly, LP's share of the UTP's management fee is deductible under § 212. Pursuant to § 703(a)(2)(E) , UTP does not take into account UTP's management fees in computing UTP's taxable income. Instead, § 1.702-1(8)(a)(i) requires that UTP separately state UTP's management fees and that LP take into account separately LP's distributive share of UTP's management fees.

Because the management fee of each LTP is an ordinary and necessary expense paid or incurred in carrying on the trade or business of the LTP, the management fee is deductible under § 162. As a result, each LTP takes its management fee into account in computing its taxable income or loss described in § 702(a)(8), and UTP takes into account its distributive share of the taxable income or loss of each LTP in computing UTP's own taxable income or loss described in § 702(a)(8). LP takes into account its distributive share of UTP's taxable income or loss in computing LP's tax liability.

HOLDING

UTP's management fee is not an ordinary and necessary expense paid or incurred by UTP on behalf of the LTPs in carrying on their trading business. The management fee paid or incurred by UTP constitutes an expense described in § 212. This expense is not taken into account in computing UTP's taxable income or loss described in § 702(a)(8). Instead, the management fee must be separately stated by UTP and separately taken into account by LP in computing LP's tax liability.

The management fee paid or incurred by an LTP constitutes an expense described in § 162 and is taken into account in computing the LTP's taxable income or loss described in § 702(a)(8). UTP's distributive share of taxable income or loss of an LTP is taken into account in computing UTP's taxable income or loss described in § 702(a)(8). In computing LP's tax liability, LP takes into account LP's distributive share of UTP's taxable income or loss.

CHAPTER **6**

Taxing Partnership Operations—Partnership Taxable Years

PROBLEM AREA 6

INTRODUCTION

According to § 706(a), a partner must include his distributive share of partnership income, gain, loss, deduction, or credit "for any taxable year of the partnership ending within or with the taxable year of the partner." As a consequence, if the partnership's taxable year is different from that of its partners, potential tax savings can arise from the deferral of partnership income into a subsequent year of the partner. For example, if A and B, calendar-year taxpayers, were equal partners in a partnership that selected a fiscal year ending January 31, deferral benefits would arise because partnership income from 11 months of the first year would not be taxable to the partners until the end of the second year.

Historically, such a procedural election for the partnership was available. Congress began limiting such possibilities through the enactment of § 706 in 1954, which sought in many cases to bring the tax-reporting periods for the partners and the partnership into harmony. In 1986, Congress further amended § 706(b)(1) to reduce the deferral of partners' income through the use of a taxable year for the partnership that is different from that of the partners.

Section 706(b)(1)(B) establishes priority rules for determining the taxable year of the partnership. First, a partnership must have the same taxable year as the common taxable year of the partner or partners who have an aggregate interest in partnership profits and capital greater than 50 percent.

If there is no partner or combination of partners with the same taxable year owning a majority in interest of the partnership, the partnership must adopt the common taxable year of all of the principal partners of the partnership. A principal partner is a person owning an interest of five percent or greater in partnership capital or profits. Like the majority-interest requirement, the intent of the principal-partners requirement is to conform the partnership taxable year to the same taxable year as that of the partners who own the greatest interest in the partnership and have a common taxable year.

Finally, if the partnership is unable to determine its taxable year by reference to either the majority-interest requirement or the principal-partners requirement, it must adopt the year prescribed by Regulation. In this case, the adoption of a calendar year may not be effective in reducing the deferral of the partners' income. Consequently, Regulation § 1.706-1 provides that the partnership taxable year will be the taxable year of one or more partners that results in the least aggregate deferral of income to the partners.

As a practical matter, most partnerships will use a calendar year for tax purposes because most are composed of individual partners who employ a calendar year rather than a fiscal year. However, partnerships composed of entities that do not utilize the calendar year may well find that a taxable year other than the calendar year minimizes deferral.

Notwithstanding the taxable year dictated by § 706(b)(1)(B), under § 706(b)(1)(C) the partnership may use any other taxable year if an acceptable business purpose is established. Revenue Ruling 87-57, reproduced below, contains examples of circumstances that may or may not constitute valid business purposes. For example, maintaining record-keeping consistency (*e.g.*, a fiscal-year partnership forced by § 706 onto a calendar year) is not acceptable, while the adoption of a year reflecting the enterprise's business cycle is a valid business purpose. Because of the deferral benefits of such a period, a business purpose is established only if the non-tax reasons for the use of the requested year are compelling.

Finally, § 444 permits a partnership to elect an initial fiscal year that results in a deferral period not in excess of three months, provided the payment requirements of § 7519 are met. Thus, a partnership which under the standards of § 706 would be a calendar-year partnership, if willing to comply with the deposit provisions of § 7519, could elect an initial fiscal year ending September 30, October 31, or November 30. If, however, the partnership had already established a fiscal year, § 444(b)(2) would prohibit a change to another fiscal year that offered more deferral than the partnership's existing fiscal year.

PROBLEM 6

QUESTIONS

1. The Law Firm is a newly formed partnership with 25 equal partners. Each partner has a four percent interest in capital and profits. All partners are calendar-year taxpayers. What is the taxable year of the partnership? Instead, assume that all partners are on the same fiscal year (a non-calendar year). May the partnership adopt that fiscal year?

2. A has a fiscal year ending in October. B has a fiscal year ending in October. C has a calendar year. They form the ABC partnership with the following interests in capital and profits: A and B each has 48 percent, and C has four percent. What is the partnership's taxable year? What result if the partnership desires to adopt a fiscal year ending September 30?

3. Same as question 2. above, except that on July 31, B has a fiscal year ending in June.

4. Same as question 2. above, except that B sells her interest in the partnership to D, who has a fiscal year ending in June.

5. The Cannery, a calendar-year partnership, desires to change from a calendar year to a fiscal year ending November 30. The partnership has a canning season which extends from June 1 to November 1. All partners are calendar-year taxpayers. Is the approval of the Service needed to make this change? Why might the partnership seek such approval? Is it likely to be granted?

MATERIALS

Revenue Procedure 2006-46
2006-2 CB 859

SECTION 1.
PURPOSE

This revenue procedure provides the exclusive procedures for a partnership . . . to obtain automatic approval to adopt, change, or retain its annual accounting period under § 442 of the Internal Revenue Code and § 1.442-1(b) of the Income Tax Regulations. . . . A partnership . . . complying with the applicable provisions of this revenue procedure will be deemed to have established a business purpose and obtained the approval of the Commissioner of Internal Revenue to adopt, change, or retain its annual accounting period under § 442 and the regulations thereunder.

SECTION 2.
BACKGROUND

.01 *Taxable Year Defined.*

(1) *In general.* Section 441(b) and § 1.441-1(b)(1) provide that the term "taxable year" generally means the taxpayer's annual accounting period, if it is a calendar year or fiscal year, or, if applicable, the taxpayer's required taxable year.

(2) *Annual accounting period.* Section 441(c) and § 1.441-1(b)(3) provide that the term "annual accounting period" means the annual period (calendar year or fiscal year) on the basis of which the taxpayer regularly computes its income in keeping its books.

(3) *Required taxable year.*

(a) *In general.* Section 1.441-1(b)(2) provides that certain taxpayers must use the particular taxable year that is required under the Code or regulations thereunder. Exceptions to the required taxable year are provided for certain taxpayers . . . .

(b) *Partnerships.* Section 706(b) and § 1.706-1(b)(2) generally provide that a partnership's taxable year must be its required taxable year. However, a partnership may have a taxable year other than its required taxable year if it makes an election under § 444, elects to use a 52-53-week taxable year that ends with reference to its required taxable year or a taxable year elected under § 444, or establishes a business purpose for having a different taxable year and obtains the approval of the Commissioner under § 442. The required taxable year for a partnership is:

(i) the taxable year of one or more of its partners who have an aggregate interest in partnership profits and capital of greater than 50 percent;

(ii) if there is no taxable year described in clause (i), the taxable year of all the principal partners of the partnership (*i.e.*, all the partners having an interest of 5 percent or more in partnership profits or capital); or

(iii) if there is no taxable year described in clause (i) or (ii), the taxable year that results in the least aggregate deferral of income to the partners. . . .

.02 *Adoption of a Taxable Year.* A newly-formed partnership . . . may adopt its required taxable year, a taxable year elected under § 444, or a 52-53-week taxable year ending with reference to its required taxable year or a taxable year elected under § 444 without the approval of the Commissioner pursuant to § 441. If, however, a partnership . . . wants to adopt any other taxable year, it must establish a business purpose and obtain approval under § 442. *See* § 1.441-1(c).

.03 *Change in Taxable Year.*

(1) *In general.* Section 1.442-1(a) generally provides that a taxpayer that wants to change its annual accounting period and use a new taxable year must obtain the approval of the Commissioner.

(2) *Annualization of short period return.* Section 443(b) and § 1.443-1(b)(1)(i) generally provide that if a return is made for a short period resulting from a change of an annual accounting period, the taxable income for the short period must be placed on an annual basis by multiplying the income by 12 and dividing the result by the number of months in the short period. Unless § 443(b)(2) and § 1.443-1(b)(2) apply, the tax for the short period generally is the same part of the tax computed on an annual basis as the number of months in the short period is of 12 months. But see §§ 1.706-1(b)(8)(i)(B) . . . for exceptions to this general rule for partnerships . . . .

(3) *No retroactive change in annual accounting period.* Unless specifically authorized by the Commissioner, a taxpayer may not request, or otherwise make, a retroactive change in annual accounting period, regardless of whether the change is to a required taxable year.

.04 *Retention of a Taxable Year.* In certain cases, a partnership . . . will be required to change its taxable year unless it establishes a business purpose and obtains the approval of the Commissioner under § 442, or makes an election under § 444, to retain its current taxable year. *See* § 1.441-1(d). For example, . . . a partnership using a taxable year that corresponds to its required taxable year gener-ally must obtain the approval of the Commissioner to retain that taxable year if its required taxable year changes as a result of a change in ownership. *But see* § 706(b)(4)(B). However, a partnership that previously has established a business purpose to the satisfaction of the Commissioner to use a particular fiscal year is not required to obtain the approval of the Commissioner to retain such fiscal year if its required taxable year changes provided such fiscal year currently qualifies as a permitted taxable year.

.05 *Approval of an Adoption, Change, or Retention.* Section 1.442-1(b) pro-vides, in part, that in order to secure the approval of the Commissioner to adopt, change, or retain an annual accounting period, a taxpayer must file an application, generally on Form 1128, "Application to Adopt, Change, or Retain a Tax Year," with the Commissioner within such time and in such manner as is provided in administrative procedures published by the Commissioner. In general, an adoption, change, or retention in annual accounting period will be approved if the taxpayer establishes a business purpose for the requested annual accounting period and agrees to the Commissioner's prescribed terms, conditions, and adjustments for effecting the adoption, change, or retention.

.06 *Business Purpose.*

(1) *Sufficient business purposes.* Section 1.442-1(b)(2) provides that the requirement of a business purpose generally will be satisfied, and adjustments to neutralize any tax consequences will not be required, if the requested annual accounting period coincides with the taxpayer's required taxable year, ownership taxable year, or natural business year. Section 1.442-1(b)(2) also provides that, in the case of a partnership . . .deferral of income to partners . . . will not be treated as a business purpose.

(2) *Natural business year.* A taxpayer is deemed to have established a natural business year if it satisfies the "25-percent gross receipts test" described in section 5.07 of this revenue procedure.

.07 *Section 444 Elections.* A partnership . . . generally can elect under § 444 to use a taxable year other than its required taxable year, but only if the deferral period of the taxable year elected is not longer than the shorter of 3 months or the deferral period of the taxable year being changed. A partnership . . . with a § 444 election must make required payments under § 7519 that approximate the amount of deferral benefit . . . . A taxpayer may automatically adopt, change to, or retain a taxable year permitted under § 444 by filing a Form 8716, "Election to Have a Taxable Year Other Than a Required Taxable Year." A taxpayer that wants to terminate its § 444 election must follow the automatic procedures under § 1.444-1T(a)(5) to change to its required taxable year or establish a business purpose for using a different taxable year pursuant to § 442, the regulations thereunder, Rev. Proc. 2002-39, 2002-1 C.B. 1046 (or any successor), or this revenue procedure (whichever is applicable). . . .

SECTION 4.
SCOPE

.01 *Applicability.* Except as provided in section 4.02, this revenue procedure, which is the exclusive procedure for a taxpayer (as defined in section 5.01 of this revenue procedure) within its scope to secure the Commissioner's approval, applies to:

(1) *Required taxable year.* A partnership . . . that wants to change to its required taxable year (as defined in section 5.05 of this revenue procedure), or a partnership . . . that wants to change to a 52-53-week taxable year ending with reference to such required taxable year;

(2) *Natural business year.* A partnership . . . that wants to change to or retain a natural business year that satisfies the 25- percent gross receipts test described in section 5.07 of this revenue procedure, or to a 52-53-week taxable year ending with reference to such taxable year; . . .

   (4) *Certain 52-53-week taxable years.* A partnership . . . that wants to change from a 52-53-week taxable year that references a particular calendar month to a non-52-53-week taxable year that ends on the last day of the same calendar month that is a permitted taxable year, and vice versa;

   (5) *Certain taxpayers that are required to make concurrent changes.* Notwithstanding any limitation in this revenue procedure to the contrary (including any limitations in section 4.02 of this revenue procedure) or any conflicting testing date provisions, this revenue procedure applies to a taxpayer that is required to concurrently change its annual accounting period as a term and condition for the approval of a related taxpayer's change of annual accounting period. . . .

   .03 *Nonautomatic Changes.* Any taxpayer that wants to adopt, change to, or retain an annual accounting period that cannot do so automatically under this revenue procedure (because the requested taxable year is not described in section 4.01 or because of any application of section 4.02) or pursuant to a provision in the Code, regulations, or other published administrative procedures, must obtain the approval of the Commissioner. *See* § 1.442-1(b) and Rev. Proc. 2002-39 (or any successor) for rules relating to nonautomatic changes of annual accounting periods by partnerships . . . .

SECTION 5.
DEFINITIONS

   The following definitions apply solely for purposes of this revenue procedure: . . .

   .05 *Required Taxable Year.* The "required taxable year" is the taxable year determined under § 706(b) in the case of a partnership . . . without taking into account any taxable year that is allowable by reason of a business purpose (including a grandfathered fiscal year as defined in section 5.09 of this revenue procedure) or a § 444 election.

   .06 *Permitted Taxable Year.* A "permitted taxable year" is the required taxable year; a natural business year; . . . a taxable year elected under § 444; a 52-53-week taxable year that references the required taxable year, natural business year, ownership taxable year, or a taxable year elected under § 444; or any other taxable year for which the taxpayer establishes a business purpose to the satisfaction of the Commissioner.

   .07 *Natural Business Year.* A "natural business year" is a year for which a partnership . . . satisfies the following "25-percent gross receipts test":

   (1) *25-percent gross receipts test.* Except as provided in (2) below, the 25-percent gross receipts test is satisfied if each of the results described in (a) and (b) below equals or exceeds 25-percent:

   (a) Gross receipts from sales and services for the most recent 12-month period that ends with the last month of the requested annual accounting period are totaled and then divided into the amount of gross receipts from sales and services for the last 2 months of this 12-month period.

(b) The same computation as in (1)(a) above is made for the two preceding 12-month periods ending with the last month of the requested annual accounting period.

(2) *Exception.* The taxpayer must determine whether any annual accounting period other than the requested annual accounting period also meets the 25-percent test described in (1). If one or more other annual accounting periods produce higher averages of the three percentages (rounded to $1/100$ of a percent) described in (1) than the requested annual accounting period, then the requested annual accounting period will not qualify as the taxpayer's natural business year.

(3) *Special rules.*

(a) To apply the 25-percent gross receipts tests for any particular taxable year, the taxpayer must compute its gross receipts from sales and services under the method of accounting used to prepare its federal income tax returns for such taxable year.

(b) If a taxpayer has a predecessor organization and is continuing the same business as its predecessor, the taxpayer must use the gross receipts from sales and services of its predecessor for purposes of computing the 25-percent gross receipts test.

(c) If the taxpayer (including any predecessor organization) does not have a 47-month period of gross receipts (36-month period for requested taxable year plus additional 11-month period for comparing requested taxable year with other potential taxable years), then it cannot establish a natural business year under this revenue procedure.

(d) If the requested taxable year is a 52-53-week taxable year, the calendar month ending nearest to the last day of the 52-53-week taxable year is treated as the last month of the requested taxable year for purposes of computing the 25-percent gross receipts test. . . .

.09 *Grandfathered Fiscal Year.* A "grandfathered fiscal year" is a fiscal year (other than a year that resulted in a three-month or less deferral of income) that a partnership . . . received permission to use on or after July 1, 1974, by a letter ruling (*i.e.*, not by automatic approval).

.10 *First Effective Year.* The "first effective year" is the first taxable year for which an adoption, change, or retention in annual accounting period is effective. The first effective year generally is the short period required to effect the change. In the case of a short period of 6 days or less, the first effective year is the taxable year that includes such short period under § 1.441-2(b)(2)(ii). The first effective year is also the first taxable year for complying with all the terms and conditions set forth in this revenue procedure necessary to effect the adoption, change, or retention in annual accounting period.

.11 *Short Period.* In the case of a change in annual accounting period, a taxpayer's "short period" is the period beginning with the day following the close of the old taxable year and ending with the day preceding the first day of the new taxable year. . . .

SECTION 6.
TERMS AND CONDITIONS OF CHANGE

.01 *In General.* An adoption, change, or retention in annual accounting period filed under this revenue procedure must be made pursuant to the terms and conditions provided in this revenue procedure. . . .

.03 *First Effective Year Tax Return.*

(1) *When to file.* The taxpayer generally must file a federal income tax return for the first effective year by the due date of that return, including extensions, in accordance with § 1.443-1(a).

(2) *Annualization.* If the taxpayer is a PSC or a trust, the taxpayer's taxable income for the short period must be annualized and the tax must be computed in accordance with the provisions of § 443(b) and § 1.443-1(b). However, for changes to (or from) a 52-53-week taxable year referencing the same month as the current (or requested) taxable year, see special rules in § 1.441-2

.04 *Subsequent Year Tax Returns.* Returns for subsequent taxable years generally must be made on the basis of a full 12 months (or on a 52-53-week basis) ending on the last day of the requested taxable year, unless the taxpayer secures the approval of the Commissioner to change that taxable year.

.05 *Changes in Natural Business Year.* If a partnership, S corporation, electing S corporation, or PSC changes to or retains a natural business year and that year no longer qualifies as a permitted taxable year, the taxpayer is using an impermissible annual accounting period and must change to a permitted taxable year. Taxpayers qualifying under section 4 of this revenue procedure may request automatic approval for the change under the provisions of this revenue procedure. Other taxpayers must request approval under Rev. Proc. 2002-39 (or any successor).

.06 *Changes in Ownership Taxable Year.* An S corporation or electing S corporation that adopts, changes to, or retains an ownership taxable year under this revenue procedure must change to a permitted taxable year, or request approval to retain its current taxable year, if, as of the first day of any taxable year, its ownership taxable year changes. S corporations qualifying under section 4 of this revenue procedure may request automatic approval for the change or retention under the provisions of this revenue procedure. Other taxpayers must request approval under Rev. Proc. 2002-39 (or any successor).

.07 *52-53-week Taxable Years.* If applicable, the taxpayer must comply with § 1.441-2(e) (relating to the timing of taking items into account in those cases where the taxable year of a pass- through entity or PSC ends with reference to the same calendar month as one or more of its partners, shareholders, or employee-owners).

.08 *Creation of Net Operating Loss or Capital Loss.* In the case of a PSC changing its annual accounting period, if the PSC generates a net operating loss (NOL) or capital loss (CL) in the short period required to effect the change in annual accounting period, the PSC may not carry the NOL or CL back, but must carry it over in accordance with the provisions of §§ 172 and 1212, respectively, beginning with the first taxable year after the short period. However, except as provided in § 280H and the regulations thereunder, the short period NOL or CL must be carried back or carried over in accordance with § 172 or 1212, respectively, if it is either (a) $50,000 or less; or (b) less than the NOL or CL, respectively, generated for the full 12-month period beginning with the first day of the short period. The taxpayer must wait until this 12-month period has expired to determine whether the taxpayer qualifies for the exception in (b) above.

.09 *Creation of General Business Credits.* In the case of a PSC changing its annual accounting period, if there is an unused general business credit or any other unused credit generated in the short period, the PSC must carry that unused credit forward. An unused credit from the short period may not be carried back.

SECTION 7.
GENERAL APPLICATION PROCEDURES

.01 *Approval.* Approval is hereby granted to any taxpayer within the scope of this revenue procedure to adopt, change, or retain its annual accounting period, provided the taxpayer complies with all the applicable provisions of this revenue procedure. Approval is granted beginning with the first effective year. A taxpayer granted approval under this revenue procedure to adopt, change to, or retain an annual accounting period other than its required year is deemed to have established a business purpose for the adoption, change, or retention to the satisfaction of the Commissioner. . . .

Revenue Ruling 87-57
1987-2 CB 117

ISSUE

In the situations described below, has a partnership, an S Corporation, or a personal service corporation established, to the satisfaction of the Secretary, a business purpose for adopting, retaining, or changing its tax year?

FACTS

In each of these situations, the taxpayer is a partnership, an S corporation, or a personal service corporation. In addition, in each instance the owners of the taxpayer have tax years that differ from the tax year requested by the taxpayer. The requested tax year is not a "grandfathered fiscal year" within the meaning of section 5.01(2) of Rev. Proc. 87-32 [predecessor of Revenue Procedure 2006-46] . . . .

Situation 1

The taxpayer desires to use a January 31 tax year. The taxpayer's reason for the requested tax year is that that year corresponds to the natural business year for the taxpayer's type of business as suggested by the Natural Business Year Committee of the American Institute of Certified Public Accountants (AICPA) in an official release published in 100 *Journal of Accountancy* 59 (December 1955). In addition, the taxpayer is using a January 31 fiscal year for financial reporting purposes.

Situation 2

The taxpayer desires to use a September 30 tax year. The taxpayer's reasons for the requested tax year are that the taxpayer's accountant is extremely busy during the first six months of the year and that, if the taxpayer were to have a September 30 tax year, the taxpayer would receive a reduced charge for the accountant's services.

Situation 3

The taxpayer desires to retain its November 30 tax year. The taxpayer's reasons for the requested tax year are that the taxpayer has used a November 30 tax year since the inception of its business 15 years ago and that, if the taxpayer is required to change its tax year, it would lose its recordkeeping consistency and thus would suffer a financial hardship in changing the records to another year.

Situation 4

The taxpayer desires to use a tax year ending September 30. The taxpayer's reason for the requested tax year is that the taxpayer desires to issue timely tax information (for example, Schedules K-1, Form 1065 Partner's Share of Income, Credits, Deductions, Etc.) to its owners to facilitate the filing of timely returns by its owners.

Situation 5

The taxpayer desires to use a November 30 tax year. The taxpayer can establish a natural business year ending on January 31 under section 4.01(1) of Rev. Proc.

87-32. If the taxpayer had not satisfied the natural business year test for January 31, it would have met the natural business year test for November 30.

Situation 6

The taxpayer desires to use a June 30 tax year. The taxpayer's reason for the requested tax year is that it coincides with the taxpayer's natural business year. For this taxpayer, June 30 is not a "natural business year," within the meaning of section 4.01(1) of Rev. Proc. 87-32. This failure to satisfy section 4.01(1) of Rev. Proc. 87-32 is caused by unusual gross receipts figures for several months during the 47-month period (36-month period for requested tax year plus additional 11-month period for comparing requested tax year with other potential tax years) covered by the test. The figures for those months were unusual because a labor strike closed the taxpayer's business during a period that included its normal peak season. The taxpayer has data for the most recent five years demonstrating that the requested tax year would have satisfied the definition of a natural business year within the meaning of section 4.01(1) of Rev. Proc. 87-32, if the strike had not occurred.

Situation 7

The taxpayer desires to use a May 31 tax year. The taxpayer's reason for the requested tax year is that due to weather conditions the business is operational only during the period of September 1 through May 31. For the 10 years it has been in business, the taxpayer has had insignificant gross receipts for the period June 1 through August 31. The facility used by the taxpayer is not used for any other purpose during the three months of insignificant gross receipts. This taxpayer does not have a "natural business year," within the meaning of section 4.01(1) of Rev. Proc. 87-32.

Situation 8

The taxpayer desires to continue to use a March 31 tax year. The taxpayer changed its method of accounting to the accrual method for the tax year ended March 31, 1987. The taxpayer's reason for the requested tax year is that it coincides with the taxpayer's natural business year. For this taxpayer, March 31 is not a "natural business year," within the meaning of section 4.01(1) of Rev. Proc. 87-32. The 25-percent test in section 4.01(1) of Rev. Proc. 87-32 requires the taxpayer to compute the gross receipts on the basis of the method of accounting used to file its return for each year of the test. Therefore, the taxpayer must compute gross receipts on the cash method of accounting for tax years prior to the tax year ended March 31, 1987. The taxpayer has audited financial statements that were prepared on the basis of an accrual method that is acceptable for tax purposes. The taxpayer's gross receipts based on the accrual method would satisfy the 25-percent test for a tax year ending March 31.

LAW AND ANALYSIS

Section 441(b)(1) of the Internal Revenue Code provides that the term "taxable year" generally means the taxpayer's annual accounting period, if it is a calendar year or a fiscal year. Section 441(c) provides that the term "annual accounting period" means the annual period on the basis of which the taxpayer regularly computes its income in keeping its books. Section 441(d) defines the term "calendar year" as a period of 12 months ending on December 31. Section 441(e) defines the term "fiscal year" as a period of 12 months ending on the last day of any month other than December or a 52–53 week period as described in section 441(f). *See also* sections 1.441-1 and 1.441-2 of the Income Tax Regulations. . . .

Prior to the Act, Rev. Proc. 74-33, 1974-2 C.B. 489, set forth the factors considered in determining if a "natural business year" existed for purposes of granting a request for a change in accounting period. The Conference Report for the Act, 2 H.R. Rep. No. 99-841 (Conf. Rep.), 99th Cong., 2d Sess. II-319 (1986), states that the conferees intend that any partnership that received permission under the provisions of Rev. Proc. 74-33 to use a fiscal tax year (other than a tax year that resulted in a three-month-or-less deferral of income) will be allowed to continue to use such tax year without obtaining the approval of the Secretary. Similarly, any S corporation that received permission to use a fiscal tax year (other than a tax year that resulted in a three-month-or-less deferral of income) which permission was granted on or after the effective date of Rev. Proc. 74-33 will be allowed to continue to use such tax year without obtaining the approval of the Secretary. *See* Rev. Proc. 87-32, which defines the term "grandfathered fiscal year" to include tax years for which a taxpayer received the permission described in the Conference Report. None of the taxpayers in the factual situations here is requesting to retain a grandfathered fiscal year.

With respect to the establishment of a business purpose for the use of a tax year, the Conference Report states that the Secretary may prescribe tests to be used to establish the existence of a business purpose if, in the discretion of the Secretary, such tests are desirable and expedient towards the efficient administration of the tax laws. Rev. Proc. 87-32 sets forth a mechanical natural business year test and an ownership tax year test that, if either is satisfied, establish, to the satisfaction of the Secretary, a business purpose (as described in sections 441(i), 706(b)(1)(C), and 1378(b)(2)) for a taxpayer to retain, and in limited situations, adopt or change to a tax year.

A taxpayer that cannot satisfy any of the tests set forth in Rev. Proc. 87-32 must establish a business purpose based on consideration of all the facts and circumstances, including the tax consequences. The tax consequences to be considered include: (1) deferring a substantial portion of a taxpayer's income or shifting a substantial portion of a taxpayer's deductions from one year to another to reduce substantially a taxpayer's tax liability; (2) causing a similar deferral or shift in the case of any other person, such as a partner, a beneficiary, or a shareholder in an S corporation; and (3) creating a short period in which there is a substantial net operating loss.

The Conference Report lists various nontax factors that will ordinarily not be sufficient to establish that the business purpose requirement for a particular tax year has been met. These factors are: (1) the use of a particular year for regulatory or financial accounting purposes; (2) the hiring patterns of a particular business—for example, the fact that a firm typically hires staff during certain times of the year; (3) the use of a particular year for administrative purposes, such as the admission or retirement of partners or shareholders, promotion of staff, and compensation or retirement arrangements with staff, partners, or shareholders; and (4) the fact that a particular business involves the use of price lists, a model year, or other items that change on an annual basis.

Both tax factors and nontax factors must be considered for purposes of determining whether a taxpayer has established a business purpose for the requested tax year. In this context, the Conference Report demonstrates the significant weight that must be assigned to tax factors. The four nontax factors that the report identifies as ordinarily insufficient all involve issues of convenience for the taxpayer. Accordingly, if a requested tax year creates deferral or distortion, the taxpayer's nontax factors must demonstrate compelling reasons for the requested tax year.

The taxpayer in each of the eight situations must establish, to the satisfaction of the Secretary, a business purpose for the use of the requested tax year. Each taxpayer has nontax, business reasons for the use of the requested tax year. However, because the requested tax year is different from the tax year of the taxpayer's owners, the taxpayer's use of the requested tax year would inherently create deferral or distortion. Under these circumstances, the taxpayer can establish, to the satisfaction of the Secretary, a business purpose for the requested tax year only if the nontax reasons for the use of that year are compelling.

The taxpayer's reason for the requested tax year in *Situation 1* is that the requested tax year is the natural business year suggested by the Natural Business Year Committee of the AICPA and the taxpayer uses the requested tax year for financial statement purposes. As stated in the Conference Report, the use of a particular year for financial accounting purposes is not sufficient to establish that the business purpose requirement for that year has been met. In addition, the natural business year suggested by the AICPA is not based upon the taxpayer's own facts and circumstances.

In *Situations 2–4*, the taxpayers' reasons for the requested tax years are to take advantage of an accountant's reduced rate *(Situation 2)*, to have recordkeeping consistency *(Situation 3)*, and to issue timely tax information forms to partners *(Situation 4)*. The reasons given in these three situations are ones of convenience to the taxpayers. Although the reasons are not among those specifically enumerated in the Conference Report, they are very similar to the convenience reasons listed there as being insufficient to establish that the business purpose requirement for a requested tax year has been met.

The taxpayer's reason in *Situation 5* is that the requested November 30 tax year would be a natural business year but for the fact that the January 31 year produces a higher percentage under the 25-percent test of Rev. Proc. 87-32. Because a November 30 fiscal year satisfies the 25-percent test and results in less deferral to the shareholders than January 31, the Commissioner, in his discretion, considers it desirable and expedient for the efficient administration of the tax laws for this taxpayer to use November 30 as its tax year. Accordingly, the taxpayer has established a business purpose for using the requested tax year.

The taxpayer's reasons in *Situation 6* are that the requested tax year coincides with the taxpayer's natural business year and that, if the strike had not occurred, the requested year would have been a natural business year according to the test set forth in Rev. Proc. 87-32. The taxpayer's failure to establish a natural business year under the 25-percent test is due to unusual circumstances that occurred during the test period and that were beyond the taxpayer's control. The historical data support the taxpayer's contention that, in the absence of these unusual circumstances, the requested year would have qualified as the taxpayer's natural business year. Thus, the Commissioner is satisfied that the taxpayer has established a business purpose for the requested tax year.

The taxpayer's reason in *Situation 7* is that the requested May 31 tax year coincides with the time the taxpayer has closed down operations for the past 10 years. That closing is not within the taxpayer's control. Accordingly, the taxpayer has established a business purpose for using the requested tax year.

The taxpayer's reason in *Situation 8* is that the requested March 31 tax year coincides with the taxpayer's natural business year and that, if the taxpayer had used the accrual method of accounting, the requested year would have been a natural business year according to the test set forth in Rev. Proc. 87-32. The taxpayer has changed its method of accounting to the accrual method. Therefore, it is reasonable for the Commissioner to allow the taxpayer to use a March 31 tax year if the accrual method, which will be used for all future tax years, would establish a natural business year ending on March 31.

HOLDING

Each taxpayer in *Situations 1-4* has failed to establish, to the satisfaction of the Secretary, a business purpose for the use of its requested tax year. Each taxpayer in *Situations 5-8* has established, to the satisfaction of the Secretary, a business purpose for the use of its requested tax year.

CHAPTER 7

Taxing Partnership Operations—Determining the Partners' Distributive Shares

PROBLEM AREA 7

INTRODUCTION

As discussed in Problem Area 5, a partner's distributive share of partnership income, gain, or loss under § 702 is reported on the partner's personal tax return. Under § 704(a), a partner's distributive share for any taxable year is determined by the partnership agreement, which under § 761(c) includes any amendments thereto up to the date required for the filing of the partnership return for the year (usually three and one-half months following the close of the taxable year). If the partnership agreement does not address a particular item or if the allocation provided for in the agreement does not have substantial economic effect, a partner's distributive share under § 704(b) is determined "in accordance with the partner's interest in the partnership" (a facts and circumstances analysis).

One of the hallmarks of the use of the partnership entity is the emphasis on flexibility which is permitted in Subchapter K. Section 704(a) illustrates such treatment. Thereunder, any specific item (income, gain, loss, deduction, or credit) can be allocated for a particular year in a fashion different from the other items. Additionally, item allocations as well as allocations of overall results (bottom-line profit or loss) can vary on a yearly basis.

However, this flexibility is subject to the limitation that the allocations must possess substantial economic effect. In essence, the statutory standard seeks to match tax effects with economic effects and thus requires economic benefit in return for the allocation of a tax gain and economic burden in return for the allocation of a tax loss. The Regulations stipulate in detailed fashion various requirements for meeting the economic effect test and the substantiality test.

For the economic effect test, the Regulations mandate that the partnership maintain capital accounts which reflect the allocations, that liquidation rights be governed by the capital accounts, and that partners be obligated to return to the partnership any deficit balances in their capital accounts. (A partnership agreement can satisfy the third requirement by reducing capital accounts by certain expected amounts and including a "qualified income offset" in any case in which the deficit-restoration obligation is less than unconditional.) Through such requirements, the partner receiving a tax allocation also will bear the financial benefit or burden. For example, assume that A and B form an equal partnership with a $10 cash contribution by each. Accordingly, each has a capital account balance of $10. If the partnership experiences a $10 loss for the year and the partners agree that it is to be allocated exclusively to B, the allocation will possess economic effect if it is reflected in the capital accounts, because B's capital account will be reduced to $0. If there is a liquidation of the partnership, which after the loss has assets of $10, A will receive the $10 and B will receive nothing. In essence, B's receipt of the extra $5 of deductions cost her $5 in liquidation proceeds.

If, in the second year of partnership operations, another $10 loss is incurred and is allocated to B, B will have a $10 deficit capital account while A will have a $10 positive account. The partnership has no assets and upon liquidation would have nothing to distribute. However, provided a deficit payback agreement exists, B will be required to contribute an additional $10 to the partnership, thereby bringing her capital account up to $0. The contributed funds will then be distributed to A in satisfaction of his positive capital account balance. In all, B will have paid $10 for the extra $10 of deductions. If a deficit payback provision were missing, such would not be the case, and the allocation of the last $10 of loss to B would not be permitted.

Even if an allocation possesses economic effect, it will not be respected for § 704(b) purposes unless it meets the substantiality requirement as well. The allocation must affect substantially the dollar amounts to be received by the partners from the partnership, independent of tax consequences. An allocation will not meet this test if it is a "shifting" allocation (offsetting allocations within a single year), a "transitory" allocation (offsetting allocations over a number of years), or an allocation under which at least one partner may benefit, and no partner stands to be harmed, on an after-tax, present-value basis.

With regard to shifting and transitory allocations, the focus of the Regulations is whether the effects on the capital accounts are similar to those that would be obtained if the allocation in question had not been made, but the overall tax liabilities of the partners are reduced. For example, if the AB partnership had a $10,000 § 1231 loss and a $10,000 ordinary loss and A in his personal capacity had a $10,000 § 1231 gain and B did not, an allocation of the § 1231 loss to B and the ordinary loss to A would be a shifting allocation. The decreases in the capital accounts of both partners would be identical to the decreases which would have occurred if both types of losses had been allocated equally to A and B, but the overall tax liabilities of the parties would be reduced compared to those that would arise if the losses were allocated on an equal basis.

With regard to the more general test (often referred to as the "overall tax effect test"), if the allocation is of disparate capital account amounts but the overall tax liabilities of the partners are reduced (e.g., an allocation of tax-exempt income to one partner and a greater amount of ordinary income to the other partner who has an expiring net operating loss), the allocation may fail the substantiality test. In such a case, the after-tax position of each partner must be compared with his after-tax position in the absence of the special allocation. If one partner (for instance, the partner receiving a lesser amount of income that is tax-favored) may be better off, and there is a strong likelihood that the other partner (receiving a greater allocation of income that is tax-disfavored) will not be worse off, the economic effect of the special allocation will be found to be insubstantial.

Should an allocation fail either test (economic effect or substantiality), the items in question will be reallocated according to the partners' interests in the partnership. While this standard employs a facts-and-circumstances analysis, the Regulations emphasize the partners' shares of partnership contributions, rights to cash flow, liquidation rights, and *economic* profit and loss allocations as relevant to such a determination.

While most tax allocations are susceptible of compliance with the § 704(b) requirements, some items are pure tax items—credits, depreciation recapture, tax preference items, and deductions attributable to nonrecourse financing—incapable of possessing economic effect. For example, if A and B contribute $10 each to a partnership which purchases an asset for $20 and thereby generates a $2 credit, the partners' capital accounts will remain at $10 each regardless of how the credit is allocated. Nevertheless, the § 704(b) Regulations deem allocations of such items to be in accordance with a partner's interest in the partnership if specified standards of the Regulations for such an allocation are met. Often the controlling standard employs a "piggyback" approach permitting an allocation of that item if it follows an underlying allocation which is susceptible of, and possesses, economic effect.

An important example of this concern involves nonrecourse deductions. Nonrecourse deductions are those deductions or expenditures that are attributable to nonrecourse liabilities of the partnership or limited liability company (LLC). For this purpose, nonrecourse liabilities of a partnership or LLC are those for which no partner or member bears the economic risk of loss. This is the case if the partnership or LLC itself is not liable for repayment beyond the value of the property securing the liability. It is also the case for all liabilities of an LLC, whether or not the creditor's rights are limited to particular property of the LLC, because under state law no member of an LLC is personally responsible for its debts. Thus, all losses and deductions of an LLC which are debt-financed are nonrecourse deductions. The allocation of nonrecourse deductions among the partners or members cannot have economic effect, because any economic burden in connection with them will not fall on the partners or members but will be borne exclusively by the creditor. (Problem Area 22 considers the more advanced topic of "partner nonrecourse deductions," which are deductions funded by debt that is nonrecourse in the sense that the liability of the partnership incurring the debt is limited to the value of specific property securing the liability, but with respect to which one or more partners have assumed personal responsibility via a guarantee or other credit-enhancement device.)

Under the Regulations, nonrecourse deductions must be allocated among the partners in accordance with their interests in the partnership. The Regulations provide that an allocation of nonrecourse deductions that meets a "safe harbor" test will be deemed to be in accordance with the partners' interests in the partnership.

The "safe harbor" standard is met upon compliance with the following four-factor test:

1. At all times, the partnership agreement must require that the capital accounts be maintained in compliance with the Regulations and liquidating distributions be made in accordance with the capital accounts, and the partnership agreement must contain either an unlimited deficit-restoration obligation or a qualified income offset.
2. Allocations of nonrecourse deductions must be reasonably consistent with allocations, which have substantial economic effect, of some other significant partnership item attributable to the property securing the nonrecourse debt.
3. The partnership agreement must provide for a minimum gain chargeback.
4. All other material allocations and capital account adjustments must be recognized under Regulation § 1.704-1(b).

Under this standard, the allocation will be upheld if it "piggybacks" a significant allocation with substantial economic effect attributable to the financed property and if a process (the minimum gain chargeback) exists which ensures that the recipient of the deductions will bear an offsetting tax, although not economic, burden when the property is sold or foreclosed upon.

Among the tax allocations that cannot have economic effect is pre-contribution gain or loss in property contributed to the partnership, because typically such property is valued for capital-account purposes at its value rather than its basis. For example, if A and B form a partnership and A contributes cash of $30 and B contributes an asset with a basis of $10 and a value of $30, each will have a capital account of $30. Sale of the contributed property for $30 will produce a tax gain of $20, which will not affect the partners' capital accounts regardless of how it is allocated. Such settings are addressed by § 704(c), which generally mandates that pre-contribution gain or loss be allocated to the contributor of the property. This prevents income-shifting or loss-shifting through the use of the partnership vehicle. Similarly, if the contributed property is depreciable and if its transferred basis does not produce tax depreciation equal to book depreciation, allocation of an amount of tax depreciation to a non-contributing partner that is less (or more) than his share of book depreciation can also accomplish a shifting of pre-contribution gain (or loss) to such partner. In this circumstance, § 704(c) requires that each non-contributing partner receive allocations of tax depreciation from the contributed property that are equal to the allocations of book depreciation. If the "ceiling rule" under the traditional method of allocation thwarts this goal, the partnership may elect to make curative or remedial allocations to the extent necessary to correct this effect. Finally, § 724 ensures that the contributor cannot employ a partnership for character conversion through the contribution of assets. For example, if a partner who is a dealer with respect to certain property could contribute it to a non-dealer partnership, the ordinary income taint could be removed upon the partnership's subsequent sale of the property. Section 724 safeguards against these potential abuses by forcing character retention for the contributed property for five years.

PROBLEM 7

QUESTIONS

1. Q and R form the QR general partnership, each contributing $30,000. During its first year of operation, the partnership loses $10,000. Q and R agree that the loss should be allocated to R. What requirements must be met for the allocation to have economic effect? What are the tax and capital-account effects of the allocation?

2. A and B form the AB general partnership with cash contributions of $50,000 each. Each partner has a one-half interest in the capital, profits, and losses of the partnership and an unlimited obligation to restore any deficit balance in the partner's capital account on liquidation. The partnership purchases an apartment building for $100,000 on January 1, Year 1. A wishes to shelter income from non-partnership activities, so the partnership agreement allocates to A the entire depreciation deduction of $5,000 per year. The partners agree to reflect the depreciation allocation by appropriately adjusting A's capital account and to distribute proceeds on liquidation in accordance with their capital accounts. Assume that other expenses exactly equal income. Does the allocation possess economic effect? What cash would be distributed to the partners on January 1, Year 4, if the property were sold alternatively for $85,000, $100,000, or $70,000 and the partnership subsequently liquidated? What additional provisions should be included in the partnership agreement in the event that the partners do not agree to restore any deficit balances in their capital accounts?

3. A and B form an equal AB general partnership, each contributing $5,000. The partnership agreement requires the partners to restore any deficit balance in their respective capital accounts upon liquidation. The partnership borrows $90,000 on a recourse basis and purchases a building for $100,000 on January 1, Year 1. Assuming the depreciation expense is $5,000 per year and the parties agree that all depreciation will be allocated to A, what are their capital accounts on January 1, Year 4? What are their tax bases? What results if the building is sold alternatively for $85,000, $100,000, or $70,000 and thereafter the partnership satisfies the liability?

4. At the end of the partnership year, when the amounts and character of income and deductions are certain, the equal AB partnership allocates all items equally between its two partners, except for $100 of tax-exempt interest, which it allocates entirely to A, and $100 of fully taxable interest, which it allocates entirely to B. Assuming the capital accounts are properly adjusted and the partnership agreement provides that distributions will be in accordance with the capital accounts, will the allocation have substantial economic effect if A and B are similarly situated taxpayers? What if the partners wanted to reallocate distributive shares on an amended tax return or a late return?

5. A and B enter into a partnership agreement on January 1, Year 1. A contributes $25,000 cash and agrees to devote his full-time services to the partnership. B, who is and expects to continue to be in a higher tax bracket than A, contributes $500,000 in cash. The agreement provides that 99 percent of all deductions and taxable losses will be allocated to B until there is net taxable income, whereupon B will be allocated an amount of income equal to her prior allocated losses. Thereafter, all taxable income or loss will be allocated equally. Determine the substantiality of the partnership's allocation scheme under the following circumstances:

a. The partnership is formed for wildcat oil drilling of a particular piece of property.

b. The partnership is formed to acquire and lease machinery. Because of the nature of the machinery and its depreciable life, as well as the predictable nature of the income expected from machinery leases entered into by the partnership, there is a strong likelihood at the time of formation that B's allocations will be offset completely by December 31, Year 4.

c. In b. above, assume that the allocations are not expected to be offset completely until December 31, Year 10.

6. What result in question 2. above where the property is sold alternatively for $85,000, $100,000, or $70,000, if A and B agree that any gain (to the extent of prior depreciation allocations) arising on the disposition of the property will be credited to A? Do the original allocations and chargeback allocation have economic effect? Is this effect substantial?

7. Determine the validity of the allocations set forth in the equal AB partnership agreement.

a. All depreciation deductions related to § 1245 property are allocated to A and all gain on disposition up to the aggregate depreciation is charged back to A. Depreciation recapture is not allocated to either partner by the partnership agreement. At a time when a computer (recomputed basis $10,000) has an adjusted basis of $3,600, it is sold for $12,000. How is the depreciation recapture shared between the partners? How does this answer change if the partnership's depreciable property is a building and the sale generates $6,400 of unrecaptured § 1250 gain?

b. Assume in question 3. above that the partnership borrows on a nonrecourse basis, that A is a limited partner, with no obligation to restore any deficit balance in his capital account, that there is a qualified income offset in the partnership agreement, and that the building declines in value to $85,000, at which time the partnership forfeits ownership rights.

8. A, B, and C decide to form the ABC partnership on January 1, Year 1. Each partner has a one-third interest in capital, profits, and losses.

A contributes a personal automobile with a holding period of more than one year, value of $20,000, and a basis of $15,000. The partnership elects to depreciate it on a straight-line basis with a five-year recovery period for tax purposes and a five-year useful life for book purposes.

B contributes $20,000 in cash.

C contributes $10,000 in cash plus land with a value of $10,000, basis of $4,000, and a holding period in excess of one year, held by C and the partnership as an investment. The following are alternative situations.

a. Assume the partnership sells the land contributed by C at its fair market value of $10,000. What is the effect on the income, basis, and capital account of each partner?

b. How are the annual book and tax depreciation amounts ($4,000 and $3,000, respectively) allocated among the partners? What is the effect on the income, basis, and capital account of each partner?

c. In a. above, assume that the partnership sells the land for $7,000. What result?

d. Assume that the automobile contributed by A has a basis of $10,000. How are the annual book and tax depreciation amounts ($4,000 and $2,000, respectively) allocated among the partners? What is the effect on the income, basis, and capital account of each partner? Why might B and C wish to receive allocations of tax depreciation equal to the book depreciation allocated to them? Is this possible?

e. In c. above, why might A and B wish to receive allocations of tax loss equal to the book losses allocated to them? Is this possible?

f. Assume in a. above that the land is inventory property within the meaning of § 751(d) as to C but is investment property as regards the partnership. What result to the parties if the land is sold for $13,000 in Year 2? What result if it is sold for $13,000 in Year 6?

g. Assume that B contributes a capital asset with a basis of $35,000 and fair market value of $20,000 instead of a cash contribution of $20,000 and that the partnership is a dealer with regard to that property. What result if the property is sold for $22,000 in the next year? What result if the property is sold for $18,000 in the next year?

MATERIALS

Goldfine v. Commissioner
80 TC 843 (1983)

PARKER, Judge.

. . . Blackard and Goldfine entered into a joint venture to own and operate an apartment complex. Each contributed one-half of the initial capital. Under the terms of their agreement, each was to share equally the proceeds of the sale of the joint venture assets, and any net proceeds on liquidation. Each actually shared equally certain cash distributions representing proceeds from refinanced loans. Each was equally liable for cash losses (i.e., any losses computed without depreciation). However, the joint venture agreement allocated to Goldfine all of the depreciation deductions, and allocated to Blackard all of the net income computed without depreciation. We must decide whether the principal purpose of these allocations was the avoidance or evasion of income taxes.

Partners must report as income their distributive shares of partnership income. Sec. 702(a). Section 704 grants partners great latitude in determining themselves by their partnership agreement what their distributive shares will be. Normally, a partner's distributive share of income, gain, loss, deduction, or credit will be determined by the terms of the partnership agreement. Sec. 704(a). However, section 704(b) imposes certain limitations upon the partners' right to fix their distributive shares. For pre-1976 taxable years, those limitations were phrased in terms of a tax-avoidance test, namely, that allocations of an "item" of income, gain, loss, deduction, or credit would be disregarded if the principal purpose of the allocation was avoidance or evasion of tax (sec. 704(b)(2)). That tax-avoidance test did not differ significantly from the "substantial economic effect" test that was adopted in 1976. And both before and after 1976, an allocation of bottom line income or loss (sec. 704(a)(9) before 1976) must likewise have economic substance in the sense that it reflects the *actual* division of income or loss among the partners when viewed from the standpoint of economic, rather than tax, consequences.

In a pre-1976 situation, as here, under the express language of section 704(b) "a partner's distributive share of any item of income is determined in accordance with his distributive share of taxable income or loss unless the partnership agreement provides special allocations, in which case the allocations are effective for Federal tax purposes unless the principal purpose of the allocation is the avoidance or evasion of income tax." If the special allocation is disregarded, the partners' shares of the item are determined in accordance with the ratio by which the partners, themselves, divide the general profits and losses of the partnership. . . .

The most important of these tests, and the sole test after 1976 is "substantial economic effect," by which we look to see that the partner to whom the item is specially allocated for tax purposes also bears the economic burdens and benefits of that specially allocated item. If a partner's allocation of an item of income or deduction is reflected in his capital account and if the liquidation proceeds of the entity are distributed in accordance with the capital account balances, the allocation has substantial economic effect. Moreover, where a partner's capital account registers a deficit, he must have the obligation upon liquidation to restore that deficit. Absent such an obligation, the other partner or partners would have to bear part of the economic cost of the special allocations that resulted in the deficit capital account. We will apply the above "capital accounts analysis" to the facts of the instant case.

It is apparent that the allocation of depreciation to Goldfine lacks substantial economic effect. While the special allocation is reflected in Goldfine's capital account, the partnership agreement does not provide that the partners are liable to restore deficits in their capital accounts. Petitioners argue that the Illinois Uniform Partnership Act imposes such an obligation upon the partners. We do not believe that the Uniform Partnership Act makes any express provision for such restoration, but we need not address petitioners' argument. Even assuming that Goldfine must restore his deficit, it is clear from the partnership agreement that the assets on dissolution are not to be distributed on the basis of the balances in the partners' capital accounts. Rather, upon liquidation, the partnership agreement plainly calls for an equal division of the net proceeds. The agreement, drafted by Goldfine himself, expressly provided that upon sale of the assets "the gain shall be divided equally between the parties hereto, meaning sales price less mortgage balance due, taxes, and costs of the sale and then equally sharing the net proceeds of the sale." Similarly, the agreement expressly provided for equal division of the net proceeds in the event of termination, defining net proceeds as "the sales or agreed appraised price, less the mortgage indebtedness and taxes." Thus, under the "capital accounts analysis," Goldfine does not bear the economic burden of the depreciation deductions allocated to him.

However, petitioners argue that the allocation nonetheless has substantial economic effect because in fact Goldfine would actually have borne any losses that might have resulted. Petitioners argue that since Blackard was insolvent at the time of the agreement, Goldfine's guarantee of Blackard's indebtedness upon Yorkshire made certain that Goldfine, alone, would actually pay any loss. We disagree. The record is inadequate to support a finding that Blackard was in fact insolvent at the time the parties executed their agreement. Moreover, petitioners' argument ignores Richard's guarantee of one of the five promissory notes. We conclude that the special allocation of depreciation to Goldfine lacked substantial economic effect. . . .

In light of the lack of substantial economic effect, the lack of business purpose or business validity apart from the tax consequences, the fact of Goldfine's actual knowledge of the amounts of depreciation deductions that would be allocated to him over the 10-year period, and the fact of Goldfine's express admission that without the allocation of depreciation deductions he would not have entered into the agreement, we conclude that the principal purpose of the special allocation of depreciation deductions to Goldfine was the avoidance or evasion of income taxes.

The joint venture agreement also allocated to Blackard all of Black-Gold's net income computed without depreciation. . . .

Accordingly, we are free to apply the factors in section 1.704-1(b), Income Tax Regs., quoted above, to determine whether the special allocations to Blackard were made principally for tax-avoidance purposes. These allocations were made subject to normal business risks and their amounts were not subject to reasonable estimation. The allocations to Blackard of net cash flow, and net income without depreciation, were dependent solely upon Black-Gold's success. The fluctuations in net income without depreciation reported by Blackard, and cash distributions (including management fees) to Blackard between 1971 and 1979, demonstrate that these amounts could not be reasonably estimated at the outset of the venture. Blackard apparently wanted the positive cash flow to service its other debts, and this factor could perhaps indicate a business purpose on the part of one of the partners, independent of that partner's tax concerns. However, these are only three of the several factors we must consider in determining whether the principal purpose of the allocations was tax avoidance.

As indicated above, however, the crucial factor is whether allocations have "substantial economic effect." It is here that the allocations to Blackard must fail. Although the allocations and distributions to Blackard are reflected in its capital account, the partnership agreement expressly provides that the net proceeds on liquidation are to be divided equally between Blackard and Goldfine, not on the basis of their capital account balances. During Black-Gold's 1972 tax year, Blackard with-drew funds representing Black-Gold's cash flow in the amount of $6,502, while it was charged with $22,150 in net income. During Black-Gold's 1973 tax year, Blackard withdrew $8,092 representing Black-Gold's cash flow while being charged with net income of $11,881. Thus, in both years, the amount of Black-Gold's cash flow distributed to Blackard did not equal the total amount of income that was charged to and reported by Blackard. Equal distributions to Blackard and Goldfine of net liquida-tion proceeds would result in Goldfine's receiving profits charged and taxed to Blackard. Likewise, after reallocating back to Blackard its distributive share of the partnership depreciation deductions improperly allocated to Goldfine, an equal distri-bution of the net liquidation proceeds to Blackard and Goldfine might not restore to Blackard all of the items charged to its capital account. In either case, the special allocations do not affect the partners' actual division of profits and losses, and therefore lack substantial economic effect.

Finally, the overall tax consequences to Blackard and Goldfine also indicate a tax-avoidance purpose. Blackard was allocated "net income" upon which Blackard paid no taxes because it was offset against Blackard's net operating losses from its other operations. Goldfine reported large depreciation losses which offset large portions of his income from his law practice otherwise subject to tax at a 50-percent marginal rate. Thus, the actual tax effect of the allocations, if permitted, would be to minimize the parties' overall tax burdens. After weighing all the facts, we conclude that the principal purpose of the allocations to Blackard, as with the special allocation to Goldfine, was the avoidance or evasion of income taxes . . . .

As discussed above, the allocations to Blackard have no real effect on the actual manner in which the partners divided Black-Gold's profits and losses. Accordingly, we conclude that the allocation to Blackard was not bona fide because it did not affect the actual economic rights and obligations of the partners and did not reflect the *actual* division of income or loss between the partners when viewed from the standpoint of economic, rather than tax, consequences.

Finally, having invalidated for tax purposes the special allocation of depreciation to petitioner and the allocations to Blackard, we should consider the proper distributive share upon which Goldfine is taxable. Each partner contributed an equal amount of capital and, under the agreement, each was to share equally in net proceeds from the sale of partnership assets and in the net proceeds from liquidation of the partnership. Moreover, each shared equally any "real" cash losses (i.e., losses computed without depreciation). In his notice of deficiency, respondent determined that Goldfine's distributive share of each partnership item was 50 percent, and the record is insuffi-cient to establish that Goldfine's distributive share is other than 50 percent. However, the partnership agreement entitled Blackard to all of the cash flow distributions and Blackard actually received those cash distributions. And it is not clear whether or not respondent took this factor into account in determining Goldfine's distributive share.[18] The parties may wish to consider this matter and may be able to attend to it in the computation under Rule 155 if that can be done without the necessity of reopening the record.

To reflect the parties' concessions and the foregoing,

Decision will be entered under Rule 155.

Interhotel Company Ltd. v. Commissioner
TC Memo 2001-151

JACOBS, Judge. (Supplemental Memorandum Opinion) . . .

---

[18] The treatment of cash flow special allocations is unsettled, and we express no view on the matter. We have found no cases directly dealing with the question, and the commentators are divided. Willis suggests that distributions of cash flow, even as a special allocation, should be governed by sec. 731, so that such cash flow distributions are taxable only to the extent they exceed the distributee partner's basis. 2 A. Willis, J. Pennell & P. Postlewaite, Partnership Taxation, sec. 82.16, at 82-40 to 82-43 (3d ed. 1982). Others suggest that where the cash flow allocations are not reflected in partner capital accounts upon which liquidation proceeds are to be distributed, the cash flow distributions may be—(1) taxable to the distributee partner under sec. 707(a) or 707(c) ; (2) a special allocation of gross receipts taxable as part of the distributive share under sec. 702 (with a commensurate reduction in basis under sec. 731 for the cash distribution); or (3) taxable as a "capital shift from the other partners." W. McKee, W. Nelson & R. Whitmire, Federal Taxation of Partnerships and Partners, pars. 10.07[2], 10.07[3], at 10-51 to 10-53; Solomon, "Current Planning for Partnership Start-up, Including Special Allocations, Retroactive Allocations and Guaranteed Payments," 37 N.Y.U. Tax. Inst., sec. 13.03[4], at 13-37 to 13-38 (1979).

Blackard is not a party to this litigation, but the tax treatment to it of the cash flow allocation and distributions would logically and consistently affect the manner in which those distributions should be considered in determining Goldfine's distributive share. If the cash flow distributions are treated solely under sec. 731, and thus not independently taxable, determining Goldfine's distributive share at 50 percent may result in unequal treatment for so-called equal partners— Blackard and Goldfine will have shared equally: (1) bottom line taxable income and loss, (2) loan refinancing distributions, (3) asset sale distributions, and (4) liquidation distributions, but Blackard will have received all of the cash flow distributions while Goldfine will have received nothing in return. One way to equalize their positions might be to give Goldfine an additional amount of Black-Gold's bottom line losses in an amount equal to Blackard's cash flow distributions, and then to divide the remaining taxable loss equally between Blackard and Goldfine. Thus, their hypothetical capital accounts would be reduced by equal amounts, maintaining their equal partnership. On the other hand, if the cash flow distributions are independently taxable to Blackard, as McKee and Solomon suggest, then there is no need to give Goldfine an additional amount of Black-Gold's bottom line loss since a determination of 50-percent distributive shares will maintain equality between the equal partners. The record does not indicate whether the cash flow distributions were taxed to Blackard independently of secs. 702 and 731. The record is singularly devoid of any information as to the tax treatment of Blackard.

Background

. . . Prior to 1985, Mr. Manchester formed two limited partnerships, Pacific Landmark Hotel, Ltd. (Landmark), and Pacific Gateway, Ltd. (Gateway), to construct, own, and manage two hotel facilities at the San Diego convention center. The two partnerships financed the construction of the hotels principally through the use of nonrecourse borrowing. For tax purposes, Landmark and Gateway utilized accelerated depreciation methods. These methods reduced the partnerships' tax bases in the hotel properties to amounts that were less than the amount of debts the partnerships had incurred to construct those properties.

Mr. Manchester formed IHCL to hold 35.354-percent limited partnership interests in Landmark and Gateway. Under the Agreement of Limited Partnership of IHCL, dated October 3, 1985 (the IHCL Original Agreement), Mr. Manchester held a .001-percent interest in IHCL. THEI held a 99.999-percent interest, both as a general and limited partner.

In November 1985, Dondi Properties (Dondi), which was then controlled by Vernon Savings and Loan Association (Vernon), invested in IHCL. Dondi received a 15-percent limited partnership interest in IHCL in exchange for its agreement to contribute $19.8 million to IHCL. Mr. Manchester then withdrew as a partner in IHCL. Following this transaction, THEI held an 85-percent interest in IHCL (an 84-percent limited partnership interest and a 1-percent interest as the general partner).

Dondi's entry into IHCL was reflected in a "Restated and Amended Agreement of Limited Partnership of IHCL", dated November 29, 1985 (the IHCL Restated Agreement). That agreement allocated 99 percent of IHCL's net losses to Dondi, and 1 percent to THEI as the general partner. The IHCL Restated Agreement further provided that after approximately 5 years, the net losses were to be allocated to the partners on a pro rata basis. Pursuant to the IHCL Restated Agreement, IHCL's net income was allocated to the partners in the same ratio as net losses until such time as the allocated amount of income equaled the amount of IHCL's cumulative net losses; thereafter, IHCL's income would be allocated to the partners pro rata.

Moreover, as part of Dondi's entry into IHCL, the limited partnership agreements of Landmark and Gateway were amended to allocate 90.91 percent of Landmark's and Gateway's net losses to IHCL.

IHCL maintained capital accounts for each of its partners. The partnership agreements of IHCL, Landmark, and Gateway all required that upon liquidation distributions to partners would be made in accordance with the partners' positive capital account balances.

By January 1986, Dondi had contributed $10.8 million of the required $19.8 million to IHCL and agreed to pay the balance due ($9 million) in subsequent quarterly installments. Dondi encountered financial difficulties and failed to make the installment payment due January 6, 1987. (By that time, the Federal Deposit Insurance Corporation (FDIC) had become the receiver for Vernon.) As a result, in April 1987, THEI gave Dondi written notice, under section 4.3.4.2(d) of the IHCL Restated Agreement, that Dondi's 99-percent allocation of IHCL's net losses was terminated. Pursuant to the IHCL Restated Agreement, IHCL's net losses were then allocated to the partners pro rata in accordance with the 85:15 ratio reflecting the two partners' interests. As a consequence, 15 percent of the losses were allocated to Dondi and 85 percent of the losses were allocated to THEI. The special allocation of IHCL's net income remained unchanged, and IHCL's Restated Agreement continued to allocate 99 percent of its net income to Dondi.

In October of 1987, the Marriott Corp. (Marriott) obtained a 5-percent general partnership interest in both Landmark and Gateway. Marriott also received an allocation of 95 percent of Landmark's net losses and 99 percent of Gateway's net losses. These allocations reduced the amount of losses Landmark and Gateway previously allocated to IHCL.

By the end of 1990, THEI's capital account in IHCL was a negative $5,920,614; principally, this was the result of the losses generated between Dondi's April 1987 default, and the reallocation of losses to Marriott 6 months later. In contrast, by the end of 1990, Dondi's capital account in IHCL grew to $14,879,392.

IHCL's balance sheet as of the end of 1990 revealed the following:

Cash	$7,955,796
Unamortized Organization costs	39,388
Investment in Pacific Gateway	2,328,218
Investment in Pacific Landmark	(1,358,431)
Liabilities	(6,193)
Subtotal	$8,958,778

On June 20, 1991, Dondi transferred its 15-percent limited partnership interest in IHCL to the FDIC, as receiver for Vernon. The FDIC transferred this interest in IHCL to Mr. Manchester in exchange for his $5 million payment. As a result, THEI held a 1-percent interest as general partner and an 84-percent interest as a limited partner. Mr. Manchester, as Dondi's successor, held the remaining 15-percent limited partnership interest and succeeded to Dondi's capital account.

On June 21, 1991, the parties executed a second amendment to the IHCL Restated Agreement. The second amendment provided that IHCL's net income would be allocated first to the partners who had negative capital account balances and, thereafter, to the partners pro rata.

At the end of 1991, the balance sheet of IHCL set forth its book value as follows:

Cash	$ 9,098,388
Unamortized organization costs	39,388
Note receivable from THEI	2,619,833
Investment in Pacific Gateway	2,660,677
Investment in Pacific Landmark	(3,967,304)
Liabilities	(1,847)
Subtotal	$10,449,135

IHCL filed a 1991 information return (Partnership Return of Income) reporting the allocation of 99 percent of its net income to Dondi through June 20, 1991, the date Dondi's interest was transferred to Mr. Manchester. The 1991 return further reflected that, after June 20, 1991, 100 percent of IHCL's net income was allocated to THEI.

Respondent challenged the allocation of 100 percent of IHCL's net income to THEI; respondent determined that for the period after June 20, 1991, Mr. Manchester should be allocated a portion of IHCL's net income. Specifically, respondent determined that Mr. Manchester's distributive share of IHCL's net income should be increased by $814,296 and that his share of tax preference items should be increased by $23,490. This reallocation of IHCL's net income reflects the pre-June 20, 1991, allocation of income and losses to Dondi: 1 percent to THEI and 99 percent to Mr.

Manchester, as Dondi's successor. The FPAA stated that "the adjustments in the distributive shares are determined in accordance with the partners' interest in the partnership as the partnership has not shown that the allocation per the return is an allowable allocation under the provisions of the Internal Revenue Code."

In Interhotel Co. I, we held that the allocation of 100 percent of IHCL's net income for 1991 to THEI lacked substantial economic effect and was inconsistent with the partners' interests in the partnership. Accordingly, we sustained respondent's reallocation of the majority of that income to Mr. Manchester. On appeal of our decision, the Court of Appeals for the Ninth Circuit stated:

> The Internal Revenue Service concedes that it erred in convincing the Tax Court to refrain from including a minimum gain chargeback in the court's calculations for purposes of the comparative liquidation test. Because of this concession, we Vacate the Tax Court's decision and Remand for further proceedings, findings, and conclusions.

Discussion

Section 704(a) provides the framework for the determination of a partner's distributive share of partnership income, gain, loss, deductions, or credits of the partnership. In general, the partnership agreement determines a partner's distributive share of these items. However, the partners' ability to allocate partnership items on a basis other than in accordance with the partners' interest in the partnership (i.e., non–pro rata basis) is not unrestricted. The allocation of partnership items on a non–pro rata basis (hereinafter referred to as a "special allocation") either (1) must have substantial economic effect (as opposed to the mere avoidance of tax), or if the allocation does not have substantial economic effect, then (2) the partner's distributive share of partnership items "shall be determined in accordance with the partner's interest in the partnership (determined by taking into account all facts and circumstances)". The regulations under section 704(b) describe in detail not only the circumstances in which a special allocation will have "substantial economic effect" but also the manner of determining a partner's "interest in the partnership".

(1) *The Basic Test of Economic Effect.* The basic test for economic effect (with respect to special allocations) is set forth in section 1.704-1(b)(2)(ii)(*b*). The test provides, in general, that a special allocation will have economic effect if the partnership agreement contains provisions that require: (1) The determination and maintenance of partners' capital accounts; (2) upon liquidation of the partnership, the proceeds of liquidation be distributed in accordance with the partners' positive capital account balances; and (3) upon liquidation of the partnership, all deficit capital accounts be restored to zero.

With regard to the matter before us, the parties agree that the IHCL Restated Agreement complies with the first two requirements. (The agreement provides that the partners' capital accounts will be properly maintained and that liquidation proceeds will be distributed to the partners in proportion to their positive capital account balances.) However, neither the IHCL Restated Agreement, nor any of its amendments, require partners having deficit capital account balances to restore the deficits to zero upon liquidation of the partnership. Accordingly, the special allocation of 100 percent of

IHCL's net income for 1991 to THEI did not meet all the requirements necessary to satisfy the basic test of substantial economic effect.

(2) *Alternative Test of Economic Effect.* Limited partnership agreements (such as the IHCL Original Agreement) usually provide specific limits upon the amount the limited partners are required to contribute to the partnership. These limits on liability, however, are inconsistent with the requirement in the basic test that upon liquidation each partner must agree to repay the deficit balance in that partner's capital account. Consequently, an alternative test for economic effect has been developed to provide that special allocations of partnership items may have economic effect even in the absence of an unlimited deficit restoration requirement.

The alternative test begins by incorporating the first two parts of the basic test. (As with the basic test, the partnership agreement must provide for properly maintained capital accounts. It must also provide that the proceeds of liquidation are to be distributed in accordance with the partners' positive capital account balances.) However, instead of a negative capital account makeup requirement, the alternative test mandates a hypothetical reduction of the partners' capital accounts. Specifically, the alternative test requires that capital accounts be reduced for any distributions that, as of the end of the year, are reasonably expected to be made, to the extent that such distributions exceed reasonably expected increases to the partners' capital accounts. By requiring a prospective reduction of capital accounts, the alternative test serves to preclude a limited partner from timing the receipt of deductible partnership expenses in a way that permits a partner to accumulate a negative capital account that the partner need not repay.

The alternative test also requires that the partnership agreement provide for a "qualified income offset" (QIO). A QIO provision automatically allocates income, including gross income and gain, to a limited partner who has an unexpected negative capital account, either as a result of partnership operations or as a result of making the adjustment for reasonably expected reductions. The QIO must operate "in an amount and manner sufficient to eliminate such deficit balance as quickly as possible."

In the present matter, neither the IHCL Original Agreement nor the IHCL Restated Agreement contains a provision requiring capital account adjustments for reasonably expected distributions or a "qualified income offset". Although the second amendment to the IHCL Restated Agreement does provide for a net income allocation to pay off THEI's deficit capital account, the second amendment falls short of providing a QIO. Rather, the second amendment allocates only net income, not "a pro rata portion of each item of partnership income" allocated "in an amount and manner sufficient to eliminate such deficit balance as quickly as possible." Consequently, the IHCL special allocation does not meet the alternative test of economic effect . . . .

(4) *Conclusion.* The special allocation of 100 percent of IHCL's net income for 1991 to THEI does not have substantial economic effect.

Partners' Interests in the Partnership

(1) *The General Rule.* Section 704(b) provides that an allocation of partnership income, gain, loss, deductions, or credit (or item thereof) that does not meet the requirements for substantial economic effect will be "determined in accordance with the partner's interest in the partnership". This requirement, although less specific than the test for economic effect, nevertheless requires that partnership allocations be

analyzed on the basis of their actual economic impact. Accordingly, the regulations provide that an examination of a partner's interest in the partnership "shall be made by taking into account all facts and circumstances relating to the economic arrangement of the partners."

    (2) *The Comparative Liquidation Test.* Pursuant to section 1.704-1(b)(3)(iii), a partner's interest in the partnership is determined by the "comparative liquidation test". When a partner's special allocation is consistent with the comparative liquidation test, the special allocation is deemed to be in accordance with the partners' interests in the partnership. This test applies only when a partnership's special allocations lack economic effect under the alternative test for economic substance.

    To satisfy the comparative liquidation test, the partnership agreement must meet the first two parts of the basic test for economic effect. That is, the partnership agreement must provide that (1) capital accounts are to be properly maintained, and (2) liquidating distributions will be made only to partners with positive capital account balances. When both conditions are satisfied, a partner's interest is measured by comparing the amount the partner would receive in a hypothetical liquidation at the end of the current year with the amount the partner would have received in a hypothetical liquidation at the end of the prior year . . . .

    Both parties rely on the comparative liquidation test to show their differing schemes.

    Respondent asserts that the comparative liquidation test of section 1.704-1(b)(3)(iii), supports the special allocation of all partnership income to Mr. Manchester . . . . First, respondent contends that if all of IHCL's assets had been sold at the end of 1990, the net liquidation proceeds would have been $8,958,778. Respondent computes this amount, using stipulated figures, as follows:

Assets

Cash	$7,955,796	
Investment in Landmark	(1,358,431)	
Investment in Gateway	2,328,218	
Unamortized organization costs	39,388	
Total assets		$ 964,971

Liabilities

Accounts payable	(6,193)	
Total liabilities		(6,193)
Net Proceeds		$ 958,778

    Next, respondent contends that if all of IHCL's assets had been sold at the end of 1991, the proceeds therefrom would be $10,449,135. This amount is computed as follows:

Assets

Cash	$9,098,388
Investment in Landmark	(3,967,304)
Investment in Gateway	2,660,677
Note receivable from THEI	2,619,833
Unamortized organization costs	39,388
Total assets	$10,450,982

Liabilities

Accounts payable	(1,847)
Total liabilities	(1,847)
Net proceeds	$10,449,135

Respondent asserts that, at the end of the first year (1990) all the liquidation proceeds would have gone to Dondi, which was the only partner to have a positive capital account. Further, respondent claims the amount available for distribution upon liquidation is $5,960,002 less than the positive capital account balance of $14,879,392 for Dondi.

At the end of the next year (1991, the year involved herein), the net book value of IHCL's assets was $10,449,135. Respondent contends that under the IHCL Restated Agreement, all of the increase in book value would have been distributed to Mr. Manchester, as successor to Dondi's interest in IHCL, because Mr. Manchester was the only partner with a positive capital account at the end of 1991. Respondent points out that the amount available for distribution is approximately $5 million less than the positive balance in Mr. Manchester's capital account.

Respondent concludes that the application of the comparative liquidation test supports the determination made in the FPAA—i.e., that because at the end of 1991 Mr. Manchester was the only partner having a positive capital account in IHCL, he would be the only partner eligible to receive IHCL's liquidation proceeds; accordingly, all the post-June 20, 1991, income of IHCL must be allocated to him.

Nonrecourse Debt Deductions

Petitioner disagrees with respondent's conclusion. Petitioner contends that respondent erroneously failed to include in the deemed liquidation proceeds approximately $7 million (relating to deductions that were based upon nonrecourse debt) for both 1990 and 1991. A brief discussion relating to tax principles involving the calculation of the basis of property acquired through nonrecourse debt financing and the calculation of gain required to be realized from the disposition of such property is deemed beneficial in understanding petitioner's position.

In a nonrecourse debt financing situation, the lender agrees that it will not maintain a collection action directly against the debtor. Rather, should the debtor default, the lender's only recourse is the institution of foreclosure proceedings with respect to the property securing the debt. Accordingly, if the value of the property securing the debt falls below the amount of the debt, it is the lender, not the debtor, who bears the risk of loss. Nevertheless, it is well settled that for tax purposes, nonrecourse debt incurred to acquire property constitutes a part of the debtor's cost basis in the property it has purchased. Accordingly, the amount of debt (even nonrecourse debt) increases the amount the debtor/taxpayer may claim for depreciation with respect to encumbered property. However, when the debtor disposes of the property, the debtor must include in the amount realized from the disposition of the property the amount of any remaining nonrecourse debt to which the property is subject. Thus, if the debtor has taken deductions (such as depreciation deductions) that have reduced its basis in the property to an amount less than the amount of the nonrecourse debt, the debtor must recognize gain at least to the extent that its basis is exceeded by the amount of debt secured by the property.

Minimum Gain and Minimum Gain Chargebacks

The aforementioned nonrecourse debt principles apply to partnerships. If a partnership has acquired properties with nonrecourse debt, the partnership's deduction of expenses associated with these properties—such as expenses for depreciation—may lead to a situation where the amount of nonrecourse debt exceeds the partnership's basis in the properties securing that debt. These deductions—called "non-recourse deductions"—per se do not have economic effect because the lender (and not the partnership or its partners) bears the economic risk of loss with respect to the nonrecourse deductions . . . .

"Minimum gain" is created when a partnership claims deductions that decrease the partnership's basis in a given property to an amount less than the balance of the nonrecourse debt incurred in the acquisition of that property.

The event that triggers a "minimum gain chargeback" is one which causes a decrease in partnership minimum gain. A triggering event therefore occurs when a partnership disposes of property in respect of which the partnership's nonrecourse indebtedness exceeds the partnership's basis. It is this type of event that, under *Tufts*, triggers the realization of gain by the partnership (at least to the extent the amount of the partnership's acquisition indebtedness exceeds the partnership's basis in that property). To illustrate, assume that a partnership owed $1 million in nonrecourse debt that it used to acquire depreciable property. If the partnership claimed $200,000 in depreciation deductions (which would lower its $1 million basis in the property to $800,000), the $200,000 (the amount by which the debt exceeds the partnership's basis) would be the "minimum gain." This $200,000 is the potential gain (sometimes called "phantom gain") that the partnership would realize when it disposes of that property. Thus, if the lender foreclosed upon the property, the partnership would realize at least a minimum gain of $200,000, even though the partnership received no gain in an economic sense.

The $200,000 "minimum gain chargeback" is the minimum gain that is allocated to the partners who had claimed (as pass throughs) the nonrecourse deductions. These allocations of minimum gain increase the partners' capital accounts as well as expose the partners to income taxation on the amount of gain.

Minimum Gain and the Comparative Liquidation Test

Petitioner maintains that the minimum gain chargeback provisions required IHCL to realize approximately $7 million in minimum gain chargebacks with respect to the comparative liquidation test. Petitioner's position is based on the following theory: although IHCL owned no property subject to nonrecourse debt, it had ownership interests in Landmark and Gateway, both of which did own such properties. IHCL's ownership of interests in these lower tier partnerships is, in effect, a proportionate ownership interest in the properties of those lower tier partnerships as well. In this regard, petitioner points to the regulations governing allocation of nonrecourse deductions, which expressly provide a "look-through" rule for situations involving tiered partnerships. Petitioner then posits that for purposes of the nonrecourse deductions, the "look-through" rule is designed to produce the same consequences for the upper tier partnership (here, IHCL) that would have resulted had IHCL directly held its proportionate share of the properties owned by Gateway and Landmark. Petitioner concludes that under these regulations, had Landmark or Gateway incurred minimum gains on the disposition of their property, IHCL would be required to realize its proportionate share of those gains.

Continuing, petitioner asserts that a deemed liquidation of IHCL under the comparative liquidation test would imply a deemed liquidation of Landmark and Gateway as well, and hence, a sale of their hotel properties. The result of the disposition of those properties would trigger minimum gain chargebacks to Landmark and Gateway, and through them, a proportionate share to IHCL.

Petitioner's application of the comparative liquidation test uses the same figures as respondent. However, petitioner augments those figures with substantial amounts of minimum gain chargebacks for both 1990 and 1991. As a first step, petitioner contends that if all of IHCL's assets had been liquidated at the end of 1990—the year prior to the taxable year—the net liquidation proceeds would have been $16,328,755. This amount is computed as follows:

Assets

Cash	$ 7,955,796
Unamortized organization costs	39,388
Investment in Pacific Gateway	2,328,218
Investment in Pacific Landmark	(1,358,431)
Liabilities	(6,193)
Subtotal	$ 8,958,778
1990 Minimum gain chargeback	7,369,977
Distributable liquidation proceeds at book value 1/1/91	$16,328,755

Petitioner contends that $5,920,614 of the minimum gain chargeback would be used first to eliminate THEI's negative capital account. The $1,449,353 balance of the minimum gain chargeback would then be allocated pursuant to the IHCL Restated Agreement as it was in effect during 1990. Thus, 85 percent (or $1,231,959) would be allocated to THEI and 15 percent (or $217,404) would be allocated to Dondi. These allocations, when added to the partners' capital accounts, yield a positive capital account of $1,231,959 for THEI and $15,096,769 for Dondi. Together, they reflect total partnership capital of $16,328,755—the amount of the previously identified liquidation proceeds.

As a second step, petitioner maintains that a liquidation of all of IHCL's assets at the end of 1991—the taxable year—would yield proceeds of $17,887,056. This amount is computed as follows:

12/31/91 Deemed Liquidation

Cash	$ 9,098,388
Organization costs	39,388
Note receivable from THEI	2,619,833
Investment in Pacific Gateway	2,660,677
Investment in Pacific Landmark	(3,967,304)
Liabilities	(1,847)
Subtotal	$10,449,135
1991 Minimum gain chargeback	7,437,891
Distributable liquidation proceeds at book value 12-31-91	$17,887,026

This $17,887,026 amount is $1,558,301 more than that for 1990, the prior year. This increase consists of an additional $67,914 in minimum gain chargebacks generated during 1991, plus partnership income for 1991 of $1,490,387. The total minimum gain would first be used to eliminate THEI's negative capital account of $5,920,614. The balance of $1,517,277 would be distributed in accordance with the partnership agreement—that is, 99 percent to Dondi and 1 percent to THEI until June 20, 1991, when 100 percent would be allocated to THEI.

Respondent's figures, showing a comparison of the partners' capital accounts that reflect minimum gain chargebacks, are as follows:

Date	THEI	Dondi/Manchester	Total
12-31-91	$2,092,861	$15,794,195	$17,887,056
12-31-90	1,231,959	15,096,796	16,328,755
Increase	$ 860,902	$ 697,399	$ 1,558,301

Respondent concludes that, because a deemed liquidation would produce the above results, its allocation of all the net income to THEI after June 20, 1991, reflects the partners' interests in the partnership.

The Issue Revisited

The contrast between respondent's and petitioner's theories of the comparative liquidations arises from petitioner's contention that a deemed liquidation of IHCL must also involve a deemed liquidation of Landmark and Gateway and the resulting minimum gain chargebacks.

In our initial examination of this issue, we agreed with respondent. In Interhotel I, we held that IHCL, as a minority owner of Landmark and Gateway, lacked the legal capacity to force Landmark and Gateway to dispose of the property that generated the nonrecourse deductions. Accordingly, upon liquidation, IHCL could only dispose of its partnership interests in Landmark and Gateway. Those partnerships, however, would continue to own the hotel properties. In the absence of some other event that triggered minimum gain chargebacks (such as a repayment of the principal of the nonrecourse loans with new capital or profits from operations), we concluded that a liquidation of IHCL under the comparative liquidation test would not increase the partners' capital accounts sufficiently to eliminate THEI's deficit account. Therefore, because Mr. Manchester would continue to have the only positive capital account on liquidation, we concluded that he alone would be entitled to the liquidation proceeds. Thus, we sustained respondent's determination that Mr. Manchester was chargeable with all of IHCL's income for 1991 under the comparative liquidation test.

Petitioner revised its argument on appeal to maintain that there need not be a deemed sale of the hotel properties in order to trigger the minimum gain chargebacks. On appeal, petitioner argued that to generate such chargebacks, it would suffice that IHCL, a pass-through beneficiary of the nonrecourse deductions, had terminated its pass-through connection to the properties. Respondent, having considered this revised argument, agreed. In view of respondent's concession as to the minimum gain chargebacks, the Court of Appeals vacated our earlier decision and remanded the case to us . . . .

It is apparent that respondent's concession effectively removes the basis for our original decision; namely, that a deemed liquidation of IHCL would not trigger a minimum gain chargeback. Petitioner now asserts that respondent's concession requires a determination in petitioner's favor. Petitioner maintains that a comparative liquidation of IHCL in 1990 and in 1991 would produce minimum gain chargebacks to THEI in both years, which chargebacks would be sufficient to eliminate THEI's negative capital account. The result is that both partners would have positive capital accounts. Accordingly, petitioner maintains, the requirement that liquidation proceeds be paid in accordance with positive capital accounts shows that its allocations reflect the partners' economic interests in the partnership. Respondent, however, contends that, notwithstanding his concession, our original decision was correct, based upon alternative evidentiary and legal arguments. . . .

Next, respondent contends that, even if petitioner has proved the amount of IHCL's partnership minimum gain, petitioner improperly included this amount in the liquidation proceeds. Respondent argues that the minimum gain chargeback is only an allocation of income, not income itself. Accordingly, respondent concludes that, absent evidence that a liquidation of IHCL would produce economic income or gain, it is improper to include minimum gain in the figures produced by a liquidation.

In our opinion, respondent misperceives the function of the minimum gain chargeback. Section 1.704-1T(b)(4)(iv)(a)(2) states that when the amount of nonrecourse liability exceeds the basis of the partnership's property securing it, "a disposition of such property *will generate gain* in an amount that is at least equal to such excess." (Emphasis supplied.) Although this "phantom" gain does not exist in the form of cash, it nevertheless is taken into account for tax purposes.

The regulations thus implement the *Tufts* doctrine that deductions based on nonrecourse financing will later be offset by increased income, even though that income is not realized in an economic sense. Here, IHCL had passed through nonrecourse deductions to its partners. The regulations require that a subsequent deemed liquidation of IHCL generates gains, albeit noncash, to offset previously claimed deductions. Those gains increase the upper tier partners' capital accounts pro tanto. Respondent's insistence that a deemed liquidation must produce actual economic gains to offset nonrecourse deductions is inconsistent with the logic of *Tufts*.

Other provisions of the regulations do not mandate a different result. Respondent refers to language of section 1.704-1T(b)(4)(iv)(e)(2), to the effect that if there is a net decrease in partnership minimum gain, then each partner "must be allocated items of income and gain for such year (and, if necessary, for subsequent years)". Respondent argues the parenthetical language refers to situations where the net decrease in partnership minimum gain in a taxable year exceeds the income and gain of the partnership for that taxable year. In such cases, respondent maintains, the excess amount of the decrease in minimum gain must be carried over and treated as a decrease in partnership minimum gain for the following years, at least to the extent there is equivalent partnership income and gain in those years. From this premise, respondent argues that the regulations restrict any minimum gain chargeback to the amount of partnership income or gain realized in a given taxable year. Accordingly, respondent asserts, "before it can charge back any of the net decrease in partnership minimum gain to the partners, petitioner must show that IHCL realized income or gain on the liquidation." Respondent then points to his earlier conclusion that IHCL would have a loss on liquidation, and concludes that, because there is not income or gain on the liquidation, no minimum gain chargeback is allowed.

We are not persuaded by respondent's argument. We believe that the quoted language does not apply to situations, such as that here, where minimum gain chargebacks are generated by the disposition of property in which the partnership's nonrecourse liabilities exceed its basis. In the latter situation, the regulations provide that sufficient gain will be generated automatically, by operation of the *Tufts* principle, to equal the amount of the minimum gain chargeback. As the regulations state, such dispositions of property will automatically generate gain "in an amount that is at least equal to" the minimum gain that must be charged back. There is thus no occasion to carry over any "excess" of a decrease in minimum gains.

Respondent also attacks petitioner's assumption that the allocation of minimum gain will suffice to offset IHCL's negative capital account. Respondent argues that even if THEI properly included IHCL's partnership minimum gain in the computation of the liquidation proceeds, IHCL improperly allocated enough of its partnership minimum gain to THEI to offset THEI's negative capital account. Respondent maintains that IHCL "has not computed each partner's share of partnership minimum gain."

We disagree. As noted above, petitioner has demonstrated to our satisfaction that IHCL's share of the minimum gain chargeback was $7,369,977 at the end of 1990, and $7,437,891 at the end of 1991. Moreover, the applicable regulations provide that each partner must be allocated items of income and gain to the extent of the *greater of* (1) the partner's share of the decrease in minimum gain allocable to the disposition of partnership property subject to nonrecourse liabilities, *or* (2) the deficit balance in such partner's capital account at the end of the year. Here, even according to respondent's calculations, THEI's share of the decrease in minimum gain allocable to the disposition of property is $3,042,812. THEI's negative capital account at the end of 1990, however, was $5,920,614. Under the regulations, THEI is allocated the greater of these amounts, that is, $5,920,614. Under the comparative liquidation test, allocation of the latter amount automatically is sufficient to eliminate THEI's negative capital account.

Nor are we persuaded by respondent's related contention that, before taking into account any minimum gain chargebacks, THEI's negative capital account of $5,920,614 must be increased by a deemed obligation to restore $3,042,812. As noted above, this amount represents respondent's computation of THEI's share of the decrease in minimum gain allocable to the disposition of property. Respondent contends that this restoration would provide a negative capital account of $2,877,802. Respondent then notes that section 1.704-1T(b)(4)(iv)(e)(2), requires that each partner must be allocated items of income and gain to the extent of the *greater of* (1) the partner's share of the decrease in minimum gain allocable to the disposition of partnership property subject to nonrecourse liabilities, *or* (2) the deficit balance in such partner's capital account at the end of the year. Under respondent's theory, THEI would be entitled to a minimum gain chargeback of only $3,042,812, its share of the minimum gain chargeback, because that amount would be greater than the recalculated deficit in its capital account of $2,877,802.

Respondent's argument that THEI must increase its capital account is based upon an erroneous reading of the regulations. . . .

This provision of the regulations is specifically designed to provide a means for nonrecourse deductions to meet the alternative test for economic substance, described supra. The regulations do so by treating a partner's share of a minimum gain chargeback as an amount the partner is required to restore to his or her capital account. In the present case, however, neither the IHCL Original Agreement nor the IHCL Restated Agreement meets the alternative test for economic substance because such agreements fail to provide a QIO. Accordingly, there is no "deemed obligation" that THEI restore to its capital account its alleged $3,042,812 share of the decrease in minimum gain allocable to the disposition of property. Even if THEI had such an obligation, that obligation would not operate to reduce the amount allocable to THEI under the minimum gain chargeback. The regulations provide that such a restoration obligation is performed only "(*after* taking into account . . . any changes during such year in partnership minimum gain and in the minimum gain attributable to any partner non-recourse debt)". In this case, the antecedent changes in such minimum gain were their total elimination by operation of the *Tufts* principle in the partnership regulations. *After* such changes, there was no minimum gain, and no partner could have a share of minimum gain to restore to its capital accounts.

Substantiality

The comparative liquidation test, is ineffective if the economic effect of the resulting allocations is "insubstantial". . . . In general, this requirement of substantiality requires "a reasonable possibility that the allocation (or allocations) will affect substantially the dollar amounts to be received by the partners from the partnership, independent of tax consequences." An allocation is not substantial under these regulations if the allocation enhances the after-tax economic position of at least one partner, and it is likely that the after-tax consequences of none of the other partners will be diminished.

The requirement of substantiality is another provision designed to ensure that allocations reflect economic reality. Here, IHCL has allocated its annual income away from Mr. Manchester, who succeeded to Dondi's large capital account, to THEI, which had a substantial negative capital account. This special allocation had an economic effect because it operated first to eliminate THEI's negative capital account and, by creating a positive capital account for THEI, then to increase THEI's share of IHCL's assets to be received on liquidation. The special allocation also ended Mr. Manchester's claims to additional income. The economic benefit to THEI and economic detriment to Mr. Manchester combined to prevent the reallocation from failing the requirement of the substantiality test. Accordingly, not only is the special allocation consistent with the partners' interests in the partnership, it is also "substantial" within the meaning of section 1.704-1(b)(3)(iii) . . . .

Decision will be entered under Rule 11.

Revenue Ruling 97-38
1997-2 CB 69

ISSUE

If a partner is treated as having a limited deficit restoration obligation under § 1.704-1(b)(2)(ii)(c) of the Income Tax Regulations by reason of the partner's liability to the partnership's creditors, how is the amount of that obligation calculated?

FACTS

In year 1, GP and LP, general partner and limited partner, each contribute $100x to form limited partnership LPRS. In general, GP and LP share LPRS's income and loss 50 percent each. However, LPRS allocates to GP all depreciation deductions and gain from the sale of depreciable assets up to the amount of those deductions. LPRS maintains capital accounts according to the rules set forth in § 1.704-1(b)(2)(iv), and the partners agree to liquidate according to positive capital account balances under the rules of § 1.704-1(b)(2)(ii)(b)(2).

Under applicable state law, GP is liable to creditors for all partnership recourse liabilities, but LP has no personal liability. GP and LP do not agree to unconditional deficit restoration obligations as described in § 1.704-1(b) (2)(ii)(b)(3) (in general, a deficit restoration obligation requires a partner to restore any deficit capital account balance following the liquidation of the partner's interest in the partnership); GP is obligated to restore a deficit capital account only to the extent necessary to pay creditors. Thus, if LPRS were to liquidate after paying all creditors and LP had a positive capital account balance, GP would not be required to restore GP's deficit capital account to permit a liquidating distribution to LP. In addition, GP and LP agree to a qualified income offset, thus satisfying the requirements of the alternate test for economic effect of § 1.704-1(b)(2)(ii)(d). GP and LP also agree that no allocation will be made that causes or increases a deficit balance in any partner's capital account in excess of the partner's obligation to restore the deficit.

LPRS purchases depreciable property for $1,000x from an unrelated seller, paying $200x in cash and borrowing the $800x balance from an unrelated bank that is not the seller of the property. The note is recourse to LPRS. The principal of the loan is due in 6 years; interest is payable semi-annually at the applicable federal rate. GP bears the entire economic risk of loss for LPRS's recourse liability, and GP's basis in LPRS (outside basis) is increased by $800x. See § 1.752-2.

In each of years 1 through 5, the property generates $200x of depreciation. All other partnership deductions and losses exactly equal income, so that in each of years 1 through 5 LPRS has a net loss of $200x.

LAW AND ANALYSIS

Under § 704(b) of the Internal Revenue Code and the regulations thereunder, a partnership's allocations of income, gain, loss, deduction, or credit set forth in the partnership agreement are respected if they have substantial economic effect. If allocations under the partnership agreement would not have substantial economic effect, the partnership's allocations are determined according to the partners' interests in the partnership. The fundamental principles for establishing economic effect require an allocation to be consistent with the partners' underlying economic arrangement. A partner allocated a share of income should enjoy any corresponding economic benefit, and a partner allocated a share of losses or deductions should bear any corresponding economic burden. *See* § 1.704-1(b)(2)(ii)(*a*).

To come within the safe harbor for establishing economic effect in § 1.704-1(b)(2)(ii), partners must agree to maintain capital accounts under the rules of § 1.704-1(b)(2)(iv), liquidate according to positive capital account balances, and agree to an unconditional deficit restoration obligation for any partner with a deficit in that partner's capital account, as described in § 1.704-1(b)(2)(ii)(*b*)(*3*). Alternatively, the partnership may satisfy the requirements of the alternate test for economic effect provided in § 1.704-1(b)(2)(ii)(*d*). *LPRS*'s partnership agreement complies with the alternate test for economic effect.

The alternate test for economic effect requires the partners to agree to a qualified income offset in lieu of an unconditional deficit restoration obligation. If the partners so agree, allocations will have economic effect to the extent that they do not create a deficit capital account for any partner (in excess of any limited deficit restoration obligation of that partner) as of the end of the partnership taxable year to which the allocation relates. Section 1.704-1(b)(2)(ii)(*d*)(*3*) (flush language).

A partner is treated as having a limited deficit restoration obligation to the extent of: (1) the outstanding principal balance of any promissory note contributed to the partnership by the partner, and (2) the amount of any unconditional obligation of the partner (whether imposed by the partnership agreement or by state or local law) to make subsequent contributions to the partnership. Section 1.704-1(b)(2)(ii)(*c*).

LP has no obligation under the partnership agreement or state or local law to make additional contributions to the partnership and, therefore, has no deficit restoration obligation. Under applicable state law, *GP* may have to make additional contributions to the partnership to pay creditors. However, *GP*'s obligation only arises to the extent that the amount of *LPRS*'s liabilities exceeds the value of *LPRS*'s assets available to satisfy the liabilities. Thus, the amount of *GP*'s limited deficit restoration obligation each year is equal to the difference between the amount of the partnership's recourse liabilities at the end of the year and the value of the partnership's assets available to satisfy the liabilities at the end of the year.

To ensure consistency with the other requirements of the regulations under § 704(b), where a partner's obligation to make additional contributions to the partnership is dependent on the value of the partnership's assets, the partner's deficit restoration obligation must be computed by reference to the rules for determining the value of partnership property contained in the regulations under § 704(b). Consequently, in computing *GP*'s limited deficit restoration obligation, the value of the partnership's assets is conclusively presumed to equal the book basis of those assets under the capital account maintenance rules of § 1.704-1(b)(2)(iv). *See* § 1.704-1(b)(2)(ii)(*d*) (value equals basis presumption applies for purposes of determining expected allocations and distributions under the alternate test for economic effect); § 1.704-1(b)(2)(iii) (value equals basis presumption applies for purposes of the substantiality test); § 1.704-1(b)(3)(iii) (value equals basis presumption applies for purposes of the partner's interest in the partnership test); § 1.704-2(d) (value equals basis presumption applies in computing partnership minimum gain).

The *LPRS* agreement allocates all depreciation deductions and gain on the sale of depreciable property to the extent of those deductions to *GP*. Because *LPRS*'s partnership agreement satisfies the alternate test for economic effect, the allocations of depreciation deductions to *GP* will have economic effect to the extent that they do not create a deficit capital account for *GP* in excess of *GP*'s obligation to restore the deficit balance. At the end of year 1, the basis of the depreciable property has been reduced to $800*x*. If *LPRS* liquidated at the beginning of year 2, selling its depreciable property for its basis of $800*x*, the proceeds would be used to repay the $800*x* principal on *LPRS*'s recourse liability. All of *LPRS*'s creditors would be satisfied and *GP* would have no obligation to contribute to pay them. Thus, at the end of year 1, *GP* has no obligation to restore a deficit in its capital account.

Because *GP* has no obligation to restore a deficit balance in its capital account at the end of year 1, an allocation that reduces *GP*'s capital account below $0 is not permitted under the partnership agreement and would not satisfy the alternate test for economic effect. An allocation of $200*x* of depreciation deductions to *GP* would reduce *GP*'s capital account to negative $100*x*. Because the allocation would result in a deficit capital account balance in excess of *GP*'s obligation to restore, the allocation is not permitted under the partnership agreement, and would not satisfy the safe harbor under the alternate test for economic effect. Therefore, the deductions for year 1 must be allocated $100*x* each to *GP* and *LP* (which is in accordance with their interests in the partnership).

The allocation of depreciation of $200*x* to *GP* in year 2 has economic effect. Although the allocation reduces *GP*'s capital account to negative $200*x*, while *LP*'s capital account remains $0, the allocation to *GP* does not create a deficit capital account in excess of *GP*'s limited deficit restoration obligation. If *LPRS* liquidated at the beginning of year 3, selling the depreciable property for its basis of $600*x*, the proceeds would be applied toward the $800*x* *LPRS* liability. Because *GP* is obligated to restore a deficit capital account to the extent necessary to pay creditors, *GP* would be required to contribute $200*x* to *LPRS* to satisfy the outstanding liability. Thus, at the end of year 2, *GP* has a deficit restoration obligation of $200*x*, and the allocation of depreciation to *GP* does not reduce *GP*'s capital account below its obligation to restore a deficit capital account.

This analysis also applies to the allocation of $200*x* of depreciation to *GP* in years 3 through 5. At the beginning of year 6, when the property is fully depreciated, the $800*x* principal amount of the partnership liability is due. The partners' capital accounts at the beginning of year 6 will equal negative $800*x* and $0, respectively, for *GP* and *LP*. Because value is conclusively presumed to equal basis, the depreciable property would be worthless and could not be used to satisfy *LPRS*'s $800*x* liability. As a result, *GP* is deemed to be required to contribute $800*x* to *LPRS*. A contribution by *GP* to satisfy this limited deficit restoration obligation would increase *GP*'s capital account balance to $0.

HOLDING

When a partner is treated as having a limited deficit restoration obligation by reason of the partner's liability to the partnership's creditors, the amount of that obligation is the amount of money that the partner would be required to contribute to the partnership to satisfy partnership liabilities if all partnership property were sold for the amount of the partnership's book basis in the property.

CHAPTER **8**

Taxing Partnership Operations—Transactions Between Related Parties

PROBLEM AREA 8

INTRODUCTION

Payments made by a partnership to a partner can be classified into three categories: (1) distributions of the partner's distributive share, as determined under § 704, of partnership income, (2) payments to a partner, engaged in a transaction with the partnership other than in the capacity of a member of the partnership (§ 707(a)), and (3) a guaranteed payment made to a partner, in the capacity of a partner, without regard to the income of the partnership in return for services or the use of capital (§ 707(c)). Thus, when a partner deals with the partnership, the schizophrenia between the entity and the aggregate approaches, so frequently encountered in the partnership area, returns.

Sections 707(a) and 707(c) adopt an entity approach with respect to transactions between a partner and the partnership. Under § 707(a), if a partner engages in a transaction with a partnership other than in the capacity of a member of the partnership, the transaction is treated as one between the partnership and a non-partner. Similarly, a § 707(c) guaranteed payment, made to a partner in the capacity of a partner and determined without regard to the income of the partnership, is afforded entity treatment. Thus, the recipient derives income under § 61, typically ordinary income except in the sales setting, and the partnership is entitled to a deduction, unless the payment is a capital expenditure under § 263.

Any other allocation and payment to a partner is a portion of the partner's distributive share as determined under § 704, which applies the entity approach generally for the measurement and calculation of income, but the aggregate approach for determining its taxation. The income is taxed to the partner when earned by the partnership, and its character is dependent upon its characterization at the partnership level. When the payment is made, even in a later year, it is treated as a distribution under § 731 and produces gain to the partner only if distributed in cash or marketable securities in an amount exceeding the adjusted basis of the partner's partnership interest.

In differentiating between the three categories of payments, the tax distinctions between a § 707(a) payment and a § 707(c) payment are minimal. In fact, the legislative history of § 707(a)(2)(A), relating to the performance of services for a partnership by one who is a partner, suggests that § 707(c) has been subsumed by § 707(a). The distinguishing factor between the two historically has been whether the services were rendered in a capacity of being a partner (a facts-and-circumstances test), yet in either case the recipient typically receives ordinary income while the partnership is entitled to an attendant deduction. The distinguishing feature between payments governed by §§ 704(a) and 731 and those governed by § 707(a) or § 707(c) is that the former are determined with respect to the income of the partnership. The Regulations highlight this fact by noting that an agreement among the partners under which one receives a one-third share of partnership income but not less than $21,000 does not give rise to a guaranteed payment if the partnership income for the year is at least $63,000. Unlike §§ 707(a) and 707(c), which always produce ordinary income to the service provider, a § 704(a) allocation to a service partner may consist of other items, such as capital gain or tax-exempt income.

With respect to one type of § 707(a) transaction, the sale of property between a partner and a partnership, the tax treatment of the parties differs significantly from the typical § 707(a) or § 707(c) payment. In these cases, the purchaser (*e.g.*, the partnership) must capitalize the sales price under §§ 263 and 1012 and recoup the purchase price, if at all, through depreciation and amortization deductions under §§ 167, 168, and 197. The seller of the property (*e.g.*, the partner) determines gain or loss characterized by the seller's personal factual particulars respecting holding period and capital-asset status. However, in some potentially abusive settings, the Code imposes rules for loss disallowance or character conversion. Section 707(b) addresses transactions between a partnership and a partner or a related person owning more than 50 percent of the capital or profits interests therein. In the case of losses, § 707(b) disallows the deduction and, in the case of certain gains, it transmutes potential capital gain into ordinary income. Furthermore, in cases where the partnership is not controlled and the sale takes place between the partnership and a person related to a partner, Regulation § 1.267(b)-1(b) employs an aggregate approach and disallows the loss realized by the partnership or such person, as the case may be, to the extent it is reflected in the related partner's distributive share of partnership loss or proportionate interest in the acquired assets.

PROBLEM 8

QUESTIONS

1. A is a partner in the ABC partnership. The partnership leases a building from A at an annual rent of $20,000 (its fair rental value). A continues to depreciate the building.

    a. How should the transaction be characterized?

    b. Assume that the ABC partnership uses an accrual method of accounting, that A is a cash-method taxpayer, that A and the partnership are calendar-year taxpayers, and that the payment is a § 707(a) payment. The partnership accrues the rental payment in Year 1 but does not make payment until April 1, Year 2. What result?

2. The ABC partnership (a law firm) agreement provides that A will receive a salary of $21,000 per year for his services as a lawyer without regard to the partnership's income, plus one-third of the taxable income or loss of the partnership after the deduction for A's salary. At the end of the year, before deducting A's salary, the partnership has net ordinary income of $12,000, long-term capital gain of $30,000, and short-term capital gain of $9,000. Before year-end, it pays $21,000 to A. The partnership and its partners are cash-method, calendar-year taxpayers. What are the results to A and to the partnership?

3. Assume alternatively in question 2. above that A is to receive one-third of the net ordinary income of the partnership, as determined after taking into account all expenses except any guaranteed payment, but not less than $21,000. In addition, he is to receive one-third of the net operating losses of the partnership, as determined after taking into account all expenses except any guaranteed payments. Capital gains and losses are to be shared equally among the three partners.

    a. What result if the net ordinary income of the partnership (before deducting any guaranteed payment) is $90,000?

    b. What result if the net ordinary income of the partnership (before deducting any guaranteed payment) is $30,000?

    c. What result if the net ordinary income of the partnership (before deducting any guaranteed payment) is $12,000?

4. Assume in question 2. above that the partnership is an accrual-method taxpayer which postpones the $21,000 salary payment to A until Year 2. What are the results to A and to the partnership?

5. A and B are brother and sister. A sells a computer used in his business, with an adjusted basis of $10,000, to the ABC partnership for $6,000. A, B, and C have equal interests in the capital, profits, and losses of the partnership. What are the results to A and the partnership?

6. Assume in question 5. above that the partnership subsequently sells the computer to an unrelated party. What are the results to A and the partnership if the sales price is:

    a. $7,000?

    b. $14,000?

7. Assume alternatively in question 5. above that D, the father of C, sells the computer to the partnership. What is the result to D? What is the result to the partnership?

8. A is a 90 percent partner in the AB partnership. A sells vacant land with an adjusted basis of $50,000 to the partnership for $200,000. The partnership begins subdividing the property into lots for sale. What are the tax consequences to A? What if A held the property primarily for sale?

9. Assume in question 8. above that A's mother, D, sells the vacant land to the partnership. What are the tax consequences to D?

10. AB is an equal partnership. CD is a partnership owned equally by the daughters of A and B. The AB partnership sells property to the CD partnership for use in its business. CD pays $10,000 for this property, which has an adjusted basis of $4,000 in AB's hands. What result?

MATERIALS

Revenue Ruling 81-300
1981-2 CB 143

ISSUE

Are the management fees paid to partners under the circumstances described below distributive shares of partnership income or guaranteed payments under section 707(c) of the Internal Revenue Code?

FACTS

The taxpayers are the general partners in a limited partnership formed to purchase, develop and operate a shopping center. The partnership agreement specifies the taxpayers' shares of the profit and loss of the partnership. The general partners have a ten percent interest in each item of partnership income, gain, loss, deduction, or credit. In addition, the partnership agreement provides that the general partners must contribute their time, managerial abilities and best efforts to the partnership and that in return for their managerial services each will receive a fee of five percent of the gross rentals received by the partnership. These amounts will be paid to the general partners in all events.

Pursuant to the partnership agreement, the taxpayers carried out their duties as general partners and provided the management services required in the operation of the shopping centers. The management fee of five percent of gross rentals were reasonable in amount for the services rendered.

LAW AND ANALYSIS

Section 707(a) of the Code provides that if a partner engages in a transaction with a partnership other than in the capacity of a member of such partnership, the transaction shall, except as otherwise provided in this section, be considered as occurring between the partnership and one who is not a partner.

Section 1.707-1(a) of the Income Tax Regulations provides that a partner who engages in a transaction with a partnership other than in the capacity of a partner shall be treated as if the partner were not a member of the partnership with respect to such transaction. The regulation's section further states that such transactions include the rendering of services by the partner to the partnership and that the substance of the transaction will govern rather than its form.

Section 707(c) of the Code provides that to the extent determined without regard to the income of the partnership, payments to a partner for services, termed "guaranteed payments", shall be considered as made to one who is not a member of the partnership, but only for purposes of section 61(a) and, subject to section 263, for purposes of section 162(a).

In Pratt v. Commissioner, 64 T.C. 203 (1975), aff'd in part, rev'd in part, 550 F.2d 1023 (5th Cir. 1977), under substantially similar facts to those in this case, both the United States Tax Court and the United States Court of Appeals for the Fifth Circuit held that management fees based on a percentage of gross rentals were not payments described in section 707(a) of the Code. The courts found that the terms of the partnership agreement and the actions of the parties indicated that the taxpayers were performing the management services in their capacities as general partners. Compare Rev. Rul. 81-301.

When a determination is made that a partner is performing services in the capacity of a partner, a question arises whether the compensation for the services is a guaranteed payment under section 707(c) of the Code or a distributive share of partnership income under section 704. In *Pratt*, the Tax Court held that the management fees were not guaranteed payments because they were computed as a percentage of gross rental income received by the partnership. The court reasoned that the gross rental income was "income" of the partnerships and, thus, the statutory test for a guaranteed payment, that it be "determined without regard to the income of the partnership," was not satisfied. On appeal, the taxpayer's argument was limited to the section 707(a) issue and the Fifth Circuit found it unnecessary to consider the application of section 707(c).

The legislative history of the Internal Revenue Code of 1954 indicates the intent of Congress to treat partnerships as entities in the case of certain transactions between partners and their partnerships. See S. Rep. No. 1622, 83d Cong., 2d Sess. 92 (1954). The Internal Revenue Code of 1939 and prior Revenue Acts contain no comparable provision and the courts had split on the question of whether a partner could deal with the partnership as an outsider. Compare Lloyd v. Commissioner, 15 B.T.A. 82 (1929) and Wegener v. Commissioner, 119 F.2d 49 (5th Cir. 1941). This resulted both in uncertainty and in substantial computational problems when an aggregate theory was applied and the payment to a partner exceeded the partnership income. In such situations, the fixed salary was treated as a withdrawal of capital, taxable to the salaried partner to the extent that the withdrawal was made from the capital of other partners. See, for example, Rev. Rul. 55-30, 1955-1 C.B. 430. Terming such treatment as unrealistic and unnecessarily complicated, Congress enacted section 707(a) and (c) of the Code of 1954. Under section 707(a) the partnership is considered an unrelated entity for all purposes. Under section 707(c), the partnership is considered an unrelated entity for purposes of sections 61 and 162 to the extent that it makes a guaranteed payment for services or for the use of capital.

Although a fixed amount is the most obvious form of guaranteed payment, there are situations in which compensation for services is determined by reference to an item of gross income. For example, it is not unusual to compensate a manager of real property by reference to the gross rental income that the property produces. Such compensation arrangements do not give the provider of the service a share in the profits of the enterprise, but are designed to accurately measure the value of the services that are provided.

Thus, in view of the legislative history and the purpose underlying section 707 of the Code, the term "guaranteed payment" should not be limited to fixed amounts. A payment for services determined by reference to an item of gross income will be a guaranteed payment if, on the basis of all of the facts and circumstances, the payment is compensation rather than a share of partnership profits. Relevant facts would include the reasonableness of the payment for the services provided and whether the method used to determine the amount of the payment would have been used to compensate an unrelated party for the services.

It is the position of the Internal Revenue Service that in *Pratt* the management fees were guaranteed payments under section 707(c) of the Code. On the facts presented, the payments were not disguised distributions of partnership net income, but were compensation for services payable without regard to partnership income.

HOLDING

The management fees are guaranteed payments under section 707(c) of the Code.

Revenue Ruling 81-301
1981-2 CB 144

ISSUE

Is an allocation based on a percentage of gross income paid to an advisor general partner subject to section 707(a) of the Internal Revenue Code, under the circumstances described below?

FACTS

ABC is a partnership formed in accordance with the Uniform Limited Partnership Act of a state and is registered with the Securities and Exchange Commission as an open-end diversified management company pursuant to the Investment Company Act of 1940, as amended. Under the partnership agreement, *ABC*'s assets must consist only of municipal bonds, certain readily-marketable temporary investments, and cash. The agreement provides for two classes of general partners: (1) "director general partners" (directors) who are individuals and (2) one "adviser general partner" (adviser) that is a corporate investment adviser registered as such in accordance with the Investment Advisers Act of 1940.

Under the partnership agreement, the directors are compensated and have complete and exclusive control over the management, conduct, and operation of *ABC*'s activities. The directors are authorized to appoint agents and employees to perform duties on behalf of *ABC* and these agents may be, but need not be, general partners. Under the partnership agreement, the adviser has no rights, powers, or authority as a general partner, except that, subject to the supervision of the directors, the adviser is authorized to manage the investment and reinvestment of *ABC*'s assets. The adviser is responsible for payment of any expenses incurred in the performance of its investment advisory duties, including those for office space and facilities, equipment, and any of its personnel used to service and administer *ABC*'s investments. The adviser is not personally liable to the other partners for any losses incurred in the investment and reinvestment of *ABC*'s assets.

The nature of the adviser's services are substantially the same as those it renders as an independent contractor or agent for persons other than *ABC* and, under the agreement, the adviser is not precluded from engaging in such transactions with others.

Each general partner, including the adviser general partner, is required to contribute sufficient cash to *ABC* to acquire at least a one percent interest in the partnership. The agreement requires an allocation of 10 percent of *ABC*'s daily gross income to the adviser. After reduction by the compensation allocable to the directors and the adviser, *ABC*'s items of income, gain, loss, deduction, and credit are divided according to the percentage interests held by each partner.

The adviser's right to 10 percent of *ABC*'s daily gross income for managing *ABC*'s investment must be approved at least annually by a majority vote of the directors or a majority vote of all the partnership interests. Furthermore, the directors may remove the adviser as investment manager at any time on 60 days written notice to the adviser. The adviser can terminate its investment manager status by giving 60 days written notice to the directors. The agreement provides that the adviser will no longer be a general partner after removal or withdrawal as investment manager, but will continue to participate as a limited partner in the income, gains, losses, deductions, and credits attributable to the percentage interest that it holds.

LAW AND ANALYSIS

Section 61(a)(1) of the Code provides that, except as otherwise provided by law, gross income means all income from whatever source derived, including compensation for services, including fees, commissions, and similar items.

Section 702(a) of the Code provides that in determining the income tax of a partner each partner must take into account separately such partner's distributive share of the partnership's items of income, gain, loss, deduction, or credit.

Section 707(a) of the Code provides that if a partner engages in a transaction with a partnership other than as a member of such partnership, the transaction shall, except as otherwise provided in section 707, be considered as occurring between the partnership and one who is not a partner.

Section 1.707-1(a) of the Income Tax Regulations provides that a partner who engages in a transaction with a partnership other than in the capacity as a partner shall be treated as if not a member of the partnership with respect to such transaction. Such transactions include the rendering of services by the partner to the partnership. In all cases, the substance of the transaction will govern rather than its form.

Section 707(c) of the Code provides that to the extent determined without regard to the income of the partnership, payments to a partner for services shall be considered as made to one who is not a member of the partnership, but only for purposes of section 61(a) and, subject to section 263, for purposes of section 162(a).

Although the adviser is identified in the agreement as an "adviser general partner," the adviser provides similar services to others as part of its regular trade or business, and its management of the investment and reinvestment of *ABC*'s assets is supervised by the directors. Also it can be relieved of its duties and right to compensation at any time (with 60 days notice) by a majority vote of the directors. Further, the adviser pays its own expenses and is not personally liable to the other partners for any losses incurred in the investment and reinvestment of *ABC*'s assets. The services performed by the adviser are, in substance, not performed in the capacity of a general partner, but are performed in the capacity of a person who is not a partner.

The 10 percent daily gross income allocation paid to the adviser is paid to the adviser in its capacity other than as a partner. Therefore, the gross income allocation is not a part of the adviser's distributive share of partnership income under section 702(a) of the Code or a guaranteed payment under section 707(c).

HOLDING

The 10 percent daily gross income allocation paid to the adviser is subject to section 707(a) of the Code and taxable to the adviser under section 61 as compensation for services rendered. The amount paid is deductible by the partnership under section 162, subject to the provisions of section 263.

Revenue Ruling 81-150
1981-1 CB 119

ISSUE

Is a management fee deductible in the year paid under the circumstances described below?

FACTS

P is a limited partnership organized to acquire an offshore drilling rig and to engage in contract drilling of oil and gas wells for major oil companies. The drilling rig will be constructed by a shipbuilding company, and will have a useful life of 10 years. The drilling rig is expected to be completed in July, 1981, at which time it will be placed in operation.

In 1980, P paid the managing partner a management fee of $325x$ dollars. The management fee is to compensate the managing partner for supervising construction and financing of the drilling rig and for managing the partnership during construction of the drilling rig.

P uses the cash method of accounting for receipts and expenditures and reports income on a calendar year basis. P proposes to deduct the management fee in the year paid.

LAW AND ANALYSIS

Section 162 of the Internal Revenue Code provides for a deduction of all ordinary and necessary expenses paid or incurred during the taxable year in carrying on a trade or business.

Section 263(a) of the Code provides, generally, that no deduction shall be allowed for capital expenditures.

Section 1.263(a)-2(a) of the Income Tax Regulations provides that the term capital expenditures includes the cost of acquisition, construction, or erection of buildings, machinery and equipment, furniture and fixtures, and similar property having a useful life substantially beyond the taxable year.

Section 195(a) of the Code provides that start-up expenditures paid or incurred after July 29, 1980, in taxable years ending after such date, may, at the election of the taxpayer, be treated as deferred expenses to be deducted over a period of not less than 60 months [now 15 years] as may be selected by the taxpayer (beginning with the month in which the business begins).

Section 195(b) defines "start-up expenditure" to mean any amount paid or incurred in connection with investigating the creation or acquisition of an active trade or business, or creating an active trade or business, and which, if paid in connection with the expansion of an existing trade or business, would be allowable as a deduction for the taxable year in which paid or incurred.

Section 195(c)(1) requires that an election under this section be made not later than the time prescribed by law for filing the return for the taxable year in which the business begins (including extensions thereof).

In Woodward v. Commissioner, 397 U.S. 572 (1970), the Supreme Court of the United States distinguished costs that are deductible under section 162 of the Code from costs that are capital expenditures. The court stated that: "It has long been recognized, as a general matter, that costs incurred in the acquisition or disposition of a capital asset are to be treated as capital expenditures."

In the present case, the management fee is to compensate the managing partner for supervising construction and financing of the drilling rig and for managing the partnership during construction of the drilling rig. The portion of the fee attributable to the supervision of construction and financing of the drilling rig is a cost incurred in the acquisition of a capital asset; as such, it is a capital expenditure, to be treated as part of the cost of the drilling rig. Such portion of the management fee is not a start-up expenditure within the meaning of section 195(b) of the Code.

With regard to the deductibility of the remaining portion of the management fee, it should be noted that, in order to qualify as a deductible business expense under section 162 of the Code, an expense must be (a) incurred in carrying on a trade or business, (b) ordinary and necessary, and (c) paid or incurred during the taxable year. See Commissioner v. Lincoln Savings and Loan Ass'n, 403 U.S. 345 (1971).

In Richmond Television Corporation v. United States, 345 F.2d 901 (4th Cir. 1965), the taxpayer, a corporation organized to operate a television station, applied for a broadcasting license in 1952. Prior to receipt of its broadcasting license and commencement of its broadcasting activities in 1956, the taxpayer incurred expenses in training prospective employees. The taxpayer deducted these expenses as business expenses under section 162 of the Code in taxable years 1952 through 1956.

In addressing the issue of the deductibility of business expenses, the court, in Richmond Television, stated that a taxpayer "has not 'engaged in carrying on a trade or business' within the intendment of section 162(a) until such time as the business has begun to function as a going concern and performed those activities for which it was organized." The court held that the taxpayer was not "engaged in carrying on a trade or business" until the broadcasting license was issued and broadcasting commenced. Because the expenditures for training prospective employees were made before the license was issued and before broadcasting commenced, the court held that they were capital expenditures and not deductible under section 162(a) of the Code.

In the present case, P will not be engaged in carrying on a trade or business until July, 1981, when the drilling rig will be completed and placed in operation. Because the management fee will be paid to the managing partner prior to July, 1981, the portion of the fee that is attributable to the management of the partnership during construction of the drilling rig will not be deductible as a business expense under section 162 of the Code. To the extent that such fee or portion thereof will be paid or incurred after July 29, 1980, however, it is a start-up expenditure within the meaning of section 195 of the Code because it was paid in creating an active trade or business and would have been currently deductible had the business already commenced operation. Should P make an election, in accordance with the provisions of section

195(c) of the Code, to treat the start-up expenditure as a deferred expense, it shall be allowed as a ratable deduction over such period of not less than 60 months [now 15 years] as may be selected by P beginning with July, 1981.

HOLDING

The portion of the management fee that is attributable to the supervision of construction and financing of the drilling rig is a capital expenditure, as defined in section 263 of the Code, and is treated as part of the cost of the drilling rig. The portion of the management fee that is attributable to the management of the partnership during construction of the drilling rig is not deductible in the year paid, under section 162 of the Code, but must be capitalized; that part of this amount paid or incurred after July 29, 1980, is a start-up expenditure which P may elect to deduct under section 195 of the Code.

Revenue Ruling 96-10
1996-1 CB 138

ISSUES

(1) If a loss on the sale of partnership property is disallowed under section 707(b)(1) of the Code, are the partners' bases in their partnership interests decreased under section 705(a)(2) to reflect the disallowed loss?

(2) If gain from the sale of partnership property is not recognized due to sections 707(b)(1) and 267(d), are the partners' bases in their partnership interests increased under section 705(a)(1) to reflect that gain?

FACTS

A and B contribute cash to form PRS, a general partnership. Under the partnership agreement, each item of income, gain, loss, and deduction of the partnership is allocated 75 percent to A and 25 percent to B. A is also a partner in PRS2, a general partnership. Under the partnership agreement, each item of income, gain, loss, and deduction of the partnership is allocated 60 percent to A and 40 percent to C. A, B, and C are unrelated to each other.

In year 1, PRS sells Property to PRS2 at its fair market value of $80x. The adjusted basis of Property at the time of the sale is $100x.

In year 5, PRS2 sells Property to an unrelated party for its fair market value of $90x. The adjusted basis of Property at the time of the sale is $80x.

LAW AND ANALYSIS

Section 1001(a) provides that the gain from the sale or other disposition of property shall be the excess of the amount realized therefrom over the adjusted basis and the loss shall be the excess of the adjusted basis over the amount realized. Section 1001(c) requires that the entire amount of this gain or loss be recognized, except as otherwise provided in subtitle A of the Code.

Section 707(b)(1) provides that no deduction shall be allowed for losses from sales or exchanges of property (other than an interest in the partnership) between a partnership and a person owning, directly or indirectly, more than 50 percent of the capital interest or the profits interest in the partnership or between two partnerships in which the same persons own, directly or indirectly, more than 50 percent of the capital interests or profits interests.

Section 707(b)(1) also provides that, in the case of a subsequent sale or exchange by a transferee described in section 707(b)(1), section 267(d) applies as if the loss were disallowed under section 267(a)(1). Section 267(d) provides that, if a taxpayer acquires property by sale or exchange from a transferor who, on the transaction, sustained a loss not allowable as a deduction by reason of section 267(a)(1), then any gain realized by the taxpayer on a sale or other disposition of the property shall be recognized only to the extent that the gain exceeds so much of the loss as is properly allocable to the property sold or otherwise disposed of by the taxpayer.

Section 705(a)(1) provides that the adjusted basis of a partner's interest in a partnership shall be increased by the sum of the partner's distributive share for the taxable year and prior taxable years of: (1) taxable income of the partnership as determined under section 703(a), (2) income of the partnership exempt from income tax, and (3) the excess of the deductions for depletion over the basis of the property subject to depletion.

Section 705(a)(2) provides that the adjusted basis of a partner's interest in a partnership shall be decreased (but not below zero) by distributions by the partnership and by the sum of the partner's distributive share for the taxable year and prior taxable years of: (1) losses of the partnership, and (2) expenditures of the partnership not deductible in computing its taxable income and not properly chargeable to capital account.

The adjustments to the basis of a partner's interest in a partnership under section 705 are necessary to prevent inappropriate or unintended benefits or detriments to the partners. Generally, the basis of a partner's interest in a partnership is adjusted to reflect the tax allocations of the partnership to that partner. This ensures that the income and loss of the partnership are taken into account by its partners only once. In addition, as provided in section 705(a)(1)(B) and (a)(2)(B), adjustments must also be made to reflect certain nontaxable events in the partnership. For example, a partner's share of nontaxable income (such as exempt income) is added to the basis of the partner's interest because, without a basis adjustment, the partner could recognize gain with respect to the tax- exempt income, for example, on the sale or redemption of the partner's interest, and the benefit of the tax-exempt income would be lost to the partner. Similarly, a partner's share of nondeductible expenditures must be deducted from the partner's basis in order to prevent that amount from giving rise to a loss to the partner on a sale or a redemption of the partner's interest in the partnership.

In determining whether a transaction results in exempt income within the meaning of section 705(a)(1)(B) or a nondeductible, noncapital expenditure within the meaning of section 705(a)(2)(B), the proper inquiry is whether the transaction has a permanent effect on the partnership's basis in its assets, without a corresponding current or future effect on its taxable income. PRS realizes a $20x loss on the sale of Property to PRS2 ($100x adjusted basis less $80x amount realized). Pursuant to section 707(b)(1), this loss is not deductible in computing taxable income because A owns more than 50 percent of the profits interest in both PRS and PRS2. Consequently, the sale results in a permanent decrease in the aggregate basis of the assets of PRS that is not taken into account by PRS in determining its taxable income and will not be taken into account for federal income tax purposes in any other manner. Therefore, for purposes of section 705(a)(2)(B), the loss on the sale of Property, and the resulting permanent decrease in partnership basis, is an expenditure of the partnership not deductible in computing its taxable income and not properly chargeable to capital account. Cf. section 1.704-1(b)(2)(iv)(i)(3) (losses disallowed under section 707(b) treated as section 705(a)(2)(B) expenditures for purposes of maintaining partners' capital accounts); section 1.701-2(f), Example 2 (requiring adjustments under section 705(a)(2)(B) for reductions in the basis of stock held by a partnership following an extraordinary dividend under section 1059).

Reducing the partners' bases in their partnership interests by their respective shares of the partnership's $20x loss preserves the intended detriment of not allowing losses from sales or exchanges between partnerships and related persons to be deducted. If the partners' bases in their partnership interests were not reduced by the amount of the partnership's disallowed loss, the partners could subsequently recognize this loss (or a reduced gain), for example, upon a disposition of their partnership interests.

Under the PRS agreement, A's distributive share of the partnership loss is $15x and B's distributive share is $5x. Accordingly, the basis of A's interest in PRS is decreased by $15x and the basis of B's interest in PRS is decreased by $5x.

PRS2 realizes a gain of $10x on the subsequent sale of Property ($90x amount realized less $80x adjusted basis). Pursuant to sections 707(b)(1) and 267(d), PRS2 must recognize the gain only to the extent that it exceeds the amount of PRS's disallowed loss. PRS2's gain on the sale ($10x) does not exceed PRS's disallowed loss ($20x) and, therefore, PRS2 does not recognize any gain on the sale of Property. Consequently, the sale of Property results in a permanent increase in the aggregate basis of the assets of PRS2 that is not taken into account by PRS2 in determining its taxable income and will not be taken into account for federal income tax purposes in any other manner. Therefore, for purposes of section 705(a)(1)(B), the gain realized but not recognized by PRS2 on the sale of Property, and the resulting permanent increase in basis, is income of the partnership exempt from tax.

Increasing the partners' bases in their partnership interests by their respective shares of the unrecognized gain on the sale of Property preserves the intended benefit of sections 707(b)(1) and 267(d). If the partners' bases in their partnership interests were not increased by the amount of the partnership's unrecognized gain, the partners could subsequently recognize this gain (or a reduced loss), for example, upon a disposition of their partnership interests.

Under the PRS2 agreement, A's distributive share of the partnership gain is $6x and C's distributive share is $4x. Accordingly, the basis of A's interest in PRS2 is increased by $6x and the basis of C's interest in PRS2 is increased by $4x.

HOLDINGS

(1) If a loss on the sale of partnership property is disallowed under section 707(b)(1), the basis of each partner's interest in the partnership is decreased (but not below zero) under section 705(a)(2) by the partner's share of that loss.

(2) If gain from the sale of partnership property is not recognized under sections 707(b)(1) and 267(d), the basis of each partner's interest in the partnership is increased under section 705(a)(1) by the partner's share of that gain.

Revenue Ruling 2007-40
2007-1 CB 1426

ISSUE

Is a transfer of partnership property to a partner in satisfaction of a guaranteed payment under section 707(c) a sale or exchange under section 1001, or a distribution under section 731?

FACTS

Partnership purchased Blackacre for $500x. A, a partner in Partnership, is entitled to a guaranteed payment under section 707(c) of $800x. Subsequently, when the fair market value of Blackacre is $800x and Partnership's adjusted basis in Blackacre is $500x, Partnership transfers Blackacre to A in satisfaction of the guaranteed payment to A.

LAW AND ANALYSIS

Section 731(b) provides that no gain or loss shall be recognized to a partnership on a distribution to a partner of property, including money.

Section 707(c) provides that, to the extent determined without regard to the income of the partnership, payments to a partner for services or for the use of capital are considered as made to one who is not a member of the partnership, but only for the purposes of § 61(a) (relating to gross income) and, subject to § 263, for purposes of § 162(a) (relating to trade or business expenses).

Section 61(a)(3) provides the general rule that gross income includes gains derived from dealings in property. In addition, section 1001(a) provides that the gain from the sale or other disposition of property shall be the excess of the amount realized over the adjusted basis provided in section 1011 for determining gain, and the loss shall be the excess of the adjusted basis over the amount realized.

Section 1001(b) further provides, in part, that the amount realized from the sale or other disposition of property shall be the sum of any money received plus the fair market value of the property (other than money) received.

A taxpayer that conveys appreciated or depreciated property in satisfaction of an obligation, or in exchange for the performance of services, recognizes gain or loss equal to the difference between the basis in the distributed property and the property's fair market value.

A transfer of partnership property in satisfaction of a partnership's obligation to make a guaranteed payment under section 707(c) is a sale or exchange under section 1001. Because the transfer is a sale or exchange under section 1001, it is not a distribution within the meaning of section 731. Accordingly, the nonrecognition rule in section 731(b) does not apply to the transfer.

Partnership realizes a $300x gain when Partnership transfers Blackacre in satisfaction of its section 707(c) guaranteed payment to A, the difference between the adjusted basis of the property ($500x) to the partnership and the property's fair market value ($800x).

HOLDING

A transfer of partnership property to a partner in satisfaction of a guaranteed payment under section 707(c) is a sale or exchange under section 1001, and not a distribution under section 731.

CHAPTER 9

Partnership Distributions— Current Distributions That Do Not Change Partners' Interests in Tainted Assets

PROBLEM AREA 9

INTRODUCTION

In the course of its operations, a partnership will make various distributions to its members. The most typical form of current (as opposed to liquidating) distribution is one of money. Under § 731, a partner does not recognize gain unless the amount of the distributed money exceeds the basis for the partner's partnership interest. In such a case, only the differential is treated as gain arising from the sale or exchange of a partnership interest and is characterized as capital. Oftentimes, cash distributions are funded by the current earnings of the partnership. Absent a termination of the partnership or a partner's interest therein, however, the allocation of the current year's income to a partner does not increase the basis of his interest in the partnership until the end of the partnership's regular tax year. This creates a risk that a partner whose basis in his interest at the beginning of the year is less than the amount of such distributions may be taxed twice, first on the distribution of the cash (without adequate basis to forestall taxation under § 731(a)(1)) and again when the corresponding income is allocated to the partner at year-end. Under the "drawings" rule of Regulation § 1.731-1(a)(1)(ii), however, such distributions may be treated as made on the last day of the partnership's taxable year, so that the basis increase attributable to the current year's earnings is available to offset them. The Service has ruled that the drawings rule also applies to deemed distributions of money resulting from liability shifts under § 752(b). See Revenue Ruling 94-4, 1994-1 CB 195, which is included in the materials for Problem Area 4.

With respect to distributions of property (other than money), no gain or loss is recognized. Generally, the basis of the distributed property to the distributee partner is the partnership's basis in the distributed property immediately prior to distribution. This rule applies under § 732(a)(1) unless the basis for the partnership interest of the distributee partner is less than the partnership's basis for the distributed asset, in which case the lesser amount will be its basis under § 732(a)(2). Thus, for example, if the basis for a partner's partnership interest is $20 and the partnership distributes currently property with a basis of $8 and fair market value of $15, the property will have a basis of $8 to the distributee partner. If, however, the distributee's basis for the partnership interest were $6, the distributed property would take a basis of $6. The basis for a partner's partnership interest is reduced under § 733 by the amount of money distributed or the basis of the distributed property under § 732.

Should both cash and property be distributed currently by a partnership, the Code and Regulations adopt a pro-taxpayer interpretation under which the cash is tested first for gain recognition under § 731 and thereafter the basis of the distributed property is determined under § 732. Thus, if cash of $20 and property with a basis to the partnership of $25 is distributed currently to a partner with a basis in his partnership interest of $30, no gain will be recognized under § 731 and the distributed property will take a basis of $10.

Under § 732(c), if unrealized receivables or inventory items are distributed in conjunction with other property, a priority rule accords basis first to those assets. Generally, such an approach is intended to preserve, but not overstate, the ordinary income because, under § 735, those assets will generate ordinary income upon their subsequent disposition and the priority allocation of basis to those assets under § 732(c) will in most cases preserve the amount of ordinary income as well. Absent such basis-stacking, the amount of ordinary income recognized on the subsequent collection or sale of unrealized receivables or inventory would be larger than that which the partnership itself would have recognized in every case in which the basis of the distributed assets is determined under § 732(a)(2).

The integrated and coordinated set of rules governing current distributions of property allow partnerships and their partners great flexibility in shifting the ownership of partnership properties among the partners with no current tax cost. In recent years, Congress has drawn the line in cases where a property distribution has the effect of changing a partner's ownership interest in property that he contributed to the partnership — in particular, a distribution of the contributed property to another partner or a distribution of other property to the contributing partner. These ownership-shifting transactions, addressed by § 704(c)(1)(B) and § 737, respectively, are of sufficient complexity to merit separate discussion, which can be found in Problem Area 24.

PROBLEM 9

QUESTIONS

1. A, B, C, and D are members of the ABCD partnership which has the following balance sheet:

	Adjusted Basis	Fair Market Value
Assets		
Cash	$ 80	$ 80
Accounts Receivable	0	40
Inventory	80	120
Land (investment)	40	120
Total	$200	$360
Capital		
A	$ 40	$ 90
B	30	90
C	20	90
D	10	90
Total	$100	$360

The partners have equal partnership interests, which they purchased from former partners at various times without precipitating a termination of the partnership. The partnership has never made an election under § 754. Each partnership interest has been held for more than one year. In the following questions, determine each partner's taxable gain or loss, basis in each distributed asset, basis in the partnership interest, and the results to the partnership.

a. ABCD distributes $20 in cash and a one-fourth undivided interest in the land to each partner.

b. ABCD distributes $10 in cash, one-fourth of the accounts receivable, and a one-fourth undivided interest in the land to each partner.

c. ABCD distributes $10 in cash, one-fourth of the inventory, and a one-fourth undivided interest in the land to each partner.

d. ABCD distributes one-fourth of the inventory and a one-fourth undivided interest in the land to each partner.

2. The ABC partnership is a dealer in land, and all of its assets consist of land held as inventory. B, an attorney, receives a current distribution of land from ABC on June 1, Year 2, which the partnership purchased on March 1, Year 2. The basis of the land to the partnership is $20 and its fair market value at the date of distribution is $25. B's basis in her partnership interest prior to the distribution is $50.

a. On July 1, Year 6, B sells the land for $30. What is the amount and character of B's gain?

b. In a. above, assume that B sells the land on July 1, Year 7. What is the amount and character of B's gain?

c. Assume that ABC purchases the land on June 1, Year 1 for $20 and distributes it to B on June 1, Year 2. B sells the land on July 1, Year 6 for $30. What is the amount and character of B's gain?

3. On January 1, the basis for A's partnership interest in the ABC partnership is $50. A draws $10 each month from the partnership during the year. The partnership is on a calendar year. All distributions are in cash. ABC has no profits from January to November, but has profits of $400 for December. A's share of the profits is 40 percent. Does A have taxable income or gain because of the withdrawals during the first 11 months of the partnership's taxable year? What financial accounting treatment regarding the draws would ensure the best tax consequences?

MATERIALS

Revenue Ruling 66-94
1966-1 CB 166

Advice has been requested as to the manner in which a partner should compute the basis of his partnership interest under section 705(a) of the Code for purposes of determining the extent to which his distributive share of partnership losses will be allowed as a deduction, and the extent to which gain will be realized by a partner upon the distribution of cash to him by the partnership.

During the taxable year, A, a member of the partnership, contributed $50x to the partnership as his initial capital contribution, and received $30x as a cash distribution from the partnership. A's distributive share of partnership losses at the end of its taxable year was $60x.

Section 705(a) of the Code provides, in part, that the adjusted basis of a partner's interest in a partnership shall be the basis of such interest determined under section 722 of the Code (relating to contributions to a partnership), (1) increased by the sum of his distributive share for the taxable year and prior taxable years of taxable income of the partnership, tax exempt income of the partnership, and the excess of depletion deductions over the basis of depletable property, and (2) decreased, but not below zero, by distributions by the partnership as provided in section 733 and by the sum of his distributive share of partnership losses and nondeductible partnership expenditures not chargeable to capital account.

Section 1.704-1(d)(1) of the Regulations provides, in part, that a partner's distributive share of partnership loss will be allowed only to the extent of the adjusted basis (before reduction by current year's losses) of such partner's interest in the partnership at the end of the partnership taxable year in which such loss occurred.

Section 1.704-1(d)(2) of the Regulations provides, in part, that in computing the adjusted basis of a partner's interest for the purpose of ascertaining the extent to which a partner's distributive share of partnership loss shall be allowed as a deduction for the taxable year, the basis shall first be increased under section 705(a)(1) of the Code and decreased under section 705(a)(2) of the Code, except for losses of the taxable year and losses previously disallowed.

Section 1.731-1(a) of the Regulations provides, in part, that where money is distributed by a partnership to a partner, no gain or loss shall be recognized to the partner except to the extent that the amount of money distributed exceeds the adjusted basis of the partner's interest in the partnership immediately before the distribution. For purposes of sections 731 and 705 of the Code, advances or drawings of money or property against a partner's distributive share of income shall be treated as current distributions made on the last day of the partnership taxable year with respect to such partner.

Based on the foregoing, it is concluded that:

(1) In computing A's adjusted basis for his interest in the partnership under section 705(a) of the Code, A's original basis, which is determined under section 722 relating to contributions to the partnership, should be decreased by first deducting distributions made to A by the partnership and thereafter by deducting his distributive share of partnership losses. However, A's basis for his interest in the partnership may not be reduced below zero. Thus:

A's contribution to the partnership	$50x
Deduct cash distributions made to A by the partnership	(30x)
	$20x
Deduct A's distributive share of losses ($60x) but only to the extent that A's basis is not reduced below zero	(20x)
A's basis for his interest in the partnership under section 705 of the Code	$ 0x

(2) In order to determine the extent to which A's distributive share of partnership losses will be allowed as a deduction, A's basis for his interest in the partnership computed in accordance with section 705(a) of the Code, should be determined without taking into account his distributive share of partnership losses for the taxable year. Thus:

A's contribution to the partnership	$50x
Deduct cash distributions made to A by the partnership	(30x)
	$20x
A's distributive share of partnership losses for the taxable year are not taken into account	(0x)
A's basis for determining the amount of his allowable partnership losses	$20x

(3) In order to determine the extent to which gain will be realized by A upon the distribution of cash to him by the partnership, A's basis for his interest in the partnership computed in accordance with section 705(a) of the Code, should be determined without taking into account cash distributions made to him by the partnership during its current taxable year. Thus:

A's contribution to the partnership	$50x
Cash distributions made by the partnership to A during the taxable year are not taken into account	(0x)
	$50x
Deduct A's distributive share of partnership losses to the extent allowed by section 704(d) of the Code. (See examples (1) and (2).)	(20x)
A's basis for determining the amount of gain be realized upon the distribution of cash to him by the partnership	$30x

A may deduct his distributive share of the partnership loss to the extent of $20x (see Example 2) and he realizes no gain from the cash distribution of $30x because his basis for determining the amount of gain upon such distribution is $30x (Example 3).

Revenue Ruling 79-205
1979-2 CB 255

ISSUES

When a partnership makes a nonliquidating distribution of property, (1) is a partner permitted to offset the increase in the partner's liabilities against the decrease in the partner's liabilities in determining the extent of recognition of gain or loss, and (2) is partnership basis adjusted before or after the property distribution?

FACTS

A and B are general partners in M, a general partnership, which was formed for the purposes of owning and operating shopping centers.

On December 31, 1977, M made nonliquidating distributions in a single transaction of a portion of its property to A and B. A and B are equal partners in M. M, A and B are calendar year taxpayers. No assets of the type described in section 751(a) of the Code were distributed by M to either A or B.

Immediately prior to the distribution A had an adjusted basis for A's interest in M of 1,000x dollars, and B had an adjusted basis for B's interest in M of 1,500x dollars. The property distributed to A had an adjusted basis to M of 2,000x dollars, and was subject to liabilities of 1,600x dollars. The property distributed to B had an adjusted basis to M of 3,200x dollars and was subject to liabilities of 2,800x dollars. A's individual liabilities increased by 1,600x dollars by reason of the distribution to A. B's individual liabilities increased by 2,800x dollars by reason of the distribution to B. A's share and B's share of the liabilities of M each decreased by 2,200x dollars ($1/2$ of 1,600x + $1/2$ of 2,800x dollars) by reason of the distributions. The basis and fair market value of the properties distributed were greater than the liabilities to which they were subject.

LAW

Section 705(a) of the Code provides, in part, that the adjusted basis of a partner's interest in a partnership shall be the basis of such interest determined under section 722 decreased (but not below zero) by partnership distributions as provided in section 733.

Section 722 of the Code provides, in part, that the basis of a partnership interest acquired by a contribution of money shall be the amount of such money.

Section 731(a)(1) of the Code provides that in the case of a distribution by a partnership to a partner gain shall not be recognized to such partner, except to the extent that any money distributed exceeds the adjusted basis of such partner's interest in the partnership immediately before the distribution.

Section 732(a)(1) of the Code provides that the basis of property (other than money) distributed by a partnership to a partner other than in liquidation of the partner's interest shall, except as provided in section 732(a)(2), be its adjusted basis to the partnership immediately before such distribution.

Section 732(a)(2) of the Code provides that the basis to the distributee partner of property to which section 732(a)(1) is applicable shall not exceed the adjusted basis of such partner's interest in the partnership reduced by any money distributed in the same transaction.

Section 733 of the Code provides that in the case of a distribution by a partnership to a partner other than in liquidation of a partner's interest, the adjusted basis to such partner of the interest in the partnership shall be reduced (but not below zero) by the amount of any money distributed to such partner and the amount of the basis to such partner of distributed property other than money, as determined under section 732.

Section 752(a) of the Code provides that any increase in a partner's share of the liabilities of a partnership, or any increase in a partner's individual liabilities by reason of the assumption by such partner of partnership liabilities, shall be considered as a contribution of money by such partner to the partnership.

Section 752(b) of the Code provides that any decrease in a partner's share of the liabilities of a partnership, or any decrease in a partner's individual liabilities by reason of the assumption by the partnership of such individual liabilities, shall be considered as a distribution of money to the partner by the partnership.

Section 752(c) of the Code provides that for purposes of section 752 a liability to which property is subject shall, to the extent of the fair market value of such property, be considered as a liability of the owner of the property.

ANALYSIS & HOLDING

In general, partnership distributions are taxable under section 731(a)(1) of the Code only to the extent that the amount of money distributed exceeds the distributee partner's basis for the partner's partnership interest. This rule reflects the Congressional intent to limit narrowly the area in which gain or loss is recognized upon a distribution so as to remove deterrents to property being moved in and out of partnerships as business reasons dictate. See S. Rep. No. 1622, 83rd Cong., 2nd Sess., page 96 (1954). Here, since partner liabilities are both increasing and decreasing in the same transaction offsetting the increases and decreases tends to limit recognition of gain, thereby giving effect to the Congressional intent. Consequently, in a distribution of encumbered property, the resulting liability adjustments will be treated as occurring simultaneously, rather than occurring in a particular order. Therefore, on a distribution of encumbered property, the amount of money considered distributed to a partner for purposes of section 731(a)(1) is the amount (if any) by which the decrease in the partner's share of the liabilities of the partnership under section 752(b) exceeds the increase in the partner's individual liabilities under section 752(a). The amount of money considered contributed by a partner for purposes of section 722 is the amount (if any) by which the increase in the partner's individual liabilities under section 752(a) exceeds the decrease in the partner's share of the liabilities of the partnership under section 752(b). The increase in the partner's individual liabilities occurs by reason of the assumption by the partner of partnership liabilities, or by reason of a distribution of property subject to a liability, to the extent of the fair market value of such property.

Because the distribution was part of a single transaction, the two properties are treated as having been distributed simultaneously to A and B. Therefore, all resulting liability adjustments relating to the distribution of the two properties will be treated as occurring simultaneously, rather than occurring in a particular order.

TREATMENT OF PARTNER A

A will be deemed to have received a net distribution of 600x dollars in money, that is, the amount by which the amount of money considered distributed to A (2,200x dollars) exceeds the amount of money considered contributed by A (1,600x dollars). Since 600x dollars does not exceed A's basis for A's interest in M immediately before the distribution (1,000x dollars), no gain is recognized to A.

Under section 732(a) of the Code, the basis to A of the property distributed to A is the lesser of (i) the adjusted basis of the property to the partnership (2,000x dollars), or (ii) the adjusted basis of A's partnership interest (1,000x dollars) reduced by the amount of money deemed distributed to A (600x dollars). Therefore, the basis of the property in A's hands is 400x dollars. Under section 733, the adjusted basis of A's partnership interest (1,000x dollars) is reduced by the amount of money deemed distributed to A (600x dollars) and by the basis to A of the distributed property (400x dollars). The adjusted basis of A's partnership interest is therefore reduced to zero.

TREATMENT OF PARTNER B

B will be deemed to have made a net contribution of 600x dollars, that is, the amount by which the amount of money considered contributed by B (2,800x dollars) exceeds the amount of money considered distributed to B (2,200x dollars). In applying sections 732(a) and 733 of the Code to B, the adjustment to B's basis in B's partnership interest attributable to the liability adjustments resulting from the distributions will be treated as occurring first, and the distribution of property to B as occurring second. By so doing, B's basis for the distributed property is increased and B's basis in B's partnership interest is decreased. This allocation gives greater effect to the general rule of section 732(a)(1), which provides for the partner to have the same basis in distributed property as the partnership had for that property.

Therefore, the first step is that B's basis for B's partnership interest (1,500x dollars) is increased under sections 722 and 705(a) by the amount of the net contribution deemed made by B (600x dollars), and is equal to 2,100x dollars. Next, under section 732(a) of the Code, the basis to B of the property distributed to B is the lesser of (i) the adjusted basis of the property to the partnership (3,200x dollars), or (ii) the adjusted basis of B's partnership interest (2,100x dollars) reduced by the amount of money deemed distributed to B (zero). Therefore, the basis of the property in B's hands is 2,100x dollars. Under section 733, the adjusted basis of B's partnership interest (2,100x dollars) is reduced by the amount of money deemed distributed to B (zero) and by the basis to B of the distributed property (2,100x dollars). The adjusted basis of B's partnership interest is therefore zero.

CHAPTER 10

Transfers of Partnership Interests—Sales of Interest in Partnerships That Do Not Hold Tainted Assets

PROBLEM AREA 10

INTRODUCTION

Upon the disposition of a partnership interest by sale or exchange, the partner's adjusted basis for the interest is offset against the amount realized, with the differential recognized as gain or loss. In determining the amount realized on the sale, § 752(d) requires that liabilities of the partnership be taken into account in a fashion similar to the treatment of liabilities in a non-partnership context. Thus, under the principles enunciated by the Supreme Court in *Crane v. Commissioner*, 331 US 1 (1947), and *Commissioner v. Tufts*, 461 US 300 (1983), a partner's share of the partnership liabilities as determined under § 752(b) will constitute an amount realized.

After a determination of the amount of the gain or loss recognized, characterization issues must be confronted. Except as provided in § 751(a), the topic discussed in Problem Area 11, § 741 provides that the gain or loss on such a sale is considered to be from the sale or exchange of a capital asset. Whether such capital gain or loss is long-term or short-term is determined by the partner's holding period for the interest, without reference to the partnership's holding period for any asset.

While the above-described principles are appropriate if the partnership interest is sold on the first day of the taxable year, a sale of the partner's entire partnership interest on any other day requires a preliminary calculation and basis adjustment to reflect the selling partner's share of the partnership's pre-sale operations for the year. If the selling partner disposes of his entire interest in the partnership, § 706(c)(2)(A) closes the partnership's taxable year with respect to the selling partner (but no other partner) on the date of the sale. Thus, under §§ 706(a) and 702(a), the partner reports his distributive share of the partnership's income, gain, or loss for such period and adjusts the basis for his partnership interest accordingly under § 705(a). In essence, the portion of the amount realized equivalent to the partner's distributive share of income or gain for the short taxable period ending with the sale is characterized by the nature of the partnership's operations, *i.e.*, ordinary income, short-term or long-term capital gain, and § 1231 gain, while the remainder of the transaction is addressed exclusively by § 741 (subject to § 751). Absent these rules, the selling partner would be able to convert his distributive share of partnership ordinary income into capital gain.

The varying interests rule, set forth in § 706(d) and developed in the Regulations thereunder, determines the selling partner's and the purchasing partner's distributive shares of the partnership's income, gain, or loss for the year of the sale. The Regulations permit a determination of the distributive share either by an interim closing of the books (which is the default method) or a proration of the results for the *entire* year between the seller and the purchaser based on the respective time periods of their ownership of the interest (which method may be adopted by agreement of the parties). A third option is the hybrid method, pursuant to which the income, gain, or loss from ordinary operations is prorated, while extraordinary items are allocated via an interim closing of the partnership's books.

The varying interests rule applies whether the selling partner disposes of his entire interest in the partnership or only a portion thereof. Despite its apparent prohibition of retroactive allocations, *i.e.*, allocations of income, gain, or loss from periods prior to an ownership change to the partners constituting the partnership after the ownership change, the same effect can often be achieved by special allocations having substantial economic effect under the rules of § 704(b).

If the selling partner disposes of less than his entire interest in the partnership, the partnership's tax year does not close with respect to the selling partner. Accordingly, his distributive share of the partnership's income, gain, and loss does not pass through to him until the end of the partnership's regular taxable year. Consistent with this approach, it appears that the adjustment of the basis of the selling partner's interest under § 705 does not take place until this time, and therefore is not taken into account in computing the selling partner's gain or loss on the sale of the partial interest.

PROBLEM 10

FACTS

A, B, and C are the original members of ABC, a cash-method, general partnership with a fiscal year ending January 31. Each partner has a one-third interest in the capital, profits, and losses of ABC. Each contributed $10 in cash to the partnership. The partnership has the following balance sheet.

	Adjusted Basis	Fair Market Value
Assets		
1	$20	$20
2	10	25
3	30	45
Total	$60	$90
Liabilities and Capital		
Liabilities		
Mortgage	$30	$30
Capital		
A	10	20
B	10	20
C	10	20
Total Liabilities and Capital	$60	$90

QUESTIONS

1. On February 1, Year 1, D purchase A's interest in ABC for $20 cash. Assume that ABC has no § 751(c) or § 751(d) assets and ignore the accrual of interest on the partnership's mortgage liability. What is the amount and character of A's gain or loss?

2. Assume that Asset 2 on the balance sheet consists of five separate items which are not inventory items within the meaning of § 751(d), each with a fair market value of $5 and an adjusted basis of $2. ABC's only transactions during its fiscal year ending on January 31, Year 2 are the sales of these items. These sales take place on February 1, April 1, June 1, September 1, and October 1, Year 1, and result in aggregate income of $15.

a. On August 1, Year 1, A sells his interest in ABC to D for $20 cash. What is A's share of the income of ABC for its fiscal year ending on January 31, Year 2? When must A report this income? What is the amount and character of A's gain or loss from the sale of his partnership interest?

b. What is the answer in question a. above if some of the records of ABC have been destroyed in a fire and it is impossible to determine the dates on which the items were sold other than that they were sold sometime during the year? What if it is merely inconvenient to close the books at the time of A's sale?

c. What is the answer in question a. above if A sells one-half of his interest in ABC to D on August 1, Year 1, for $10 cash?

d. Suppose in question a. above that A and D agreed that A would be responsible for 80 percent of the income attributable to the purchased interest for the fiscal year ending on January 31, Year 2 and that D would be responsible for the other 20 percent. Can the partnership achieve this result?

e. Suppose in question a. above that D demanded as a condition of her purchase of A's interest an allocation of 80 percent of the income attributable to that interest for the fiscal year ending on January 31, Year 2. Can the partnership accommodate this demand?

3. Assume in question 2. above that the partnership deducts $6 of interest on its mortgage liability for its fiscal year ending January 31, Year 2. How is this interest deduction allocated between A and D?

MATERIALS

Commissioner v. Tufts
461 US 300 (1983)

JUSTICE BLACKMUN delivered the opinion of the Court.

Over 35 years ago, in *Crane* v. *Commissioner*, 331 U.S. 1 (1947), this Court ruled that a taxpayer, who sold property encumbered by a nonrecourse mortgage (the amount of the mortgage being less than the property's value), must include the unpaid balance of the mortgage in the computation of the amount the taxpayer realized on the sale. The case now before us presents the question whether the same rule applies when the unpaid amount of the nonrecourse mortgage exceeds the fair market value of the property sold.

I

On August 1, 1970, respondent Clark Pelt, a builder, and his wholly owned corporation, respondent Clark, Inc., formed a general partnership. The purpose of the partnership was to construct a 120-unit apartment complex in Duncanville, Tex., a Dallas suburb. Neither Pelt nor Clark, Inc., made any capital contribution to the partnership. Six days later, the partnership entered into a mortgage loan agreement with the Farm & Home Savings Association (F&H). Under the agreement, F&H was committed for a $1,851,500 loan for the complex. In return, the partnership executed a note and a deed of trust in favor of F&H. The partnership obtained the loan on a nonrecourse basis: neither the partnership nor its partners assumed any personal liability for repayment of the loan. Pelt later admitted four friends and relatives, respondents Tufts, Steger, Stephens, and Austin, as general partners. None of them contributed capital upon entering the partnership.

The construction of the complex was completed in August 1971. During 1971, each partner made small capital contributions to the partnership; in 1972, however, only Pelt made a contribution. The total of the partners' capital contributions was $44,212. In each tax year, all partners claimed as income tax deductions their allocable shares of ordinary losses and depreciation. The deductions taken by the partners in 1971 and 1972 totalled $439,972. Due to these contributions and deductions, the partnership's adjusted basis in the property in August 1972 was $1,455,740.

In 1971 and 1972, major employers in the Duncanville area laid off significant numbers of workers. As a result, the partnership's rental income was less than expected, and it was unable to make the payments due on the mortgage. Each partner, on August 28, 1972, sold his partnership interest to an unrelated third party, Fred Bayles. As consideration, Bayles agreed to reimburse each partner's sale expenses up to $250; he also assumed the nonrecourse mortgage.

On the date of transfer, the fair market value of the property did not exceed $1,400,000. Each partner reported the sale on his federal income tax return and indicated that a partnership loss of $55,740 had been sustained. The Commissioner of Internal Revenue, on audit, determined that the sale resulted in a partnership capital gain of approximately $400,000. His theory was that the partnership had realized the full amount of the nonrecourse obligation.

Relying on *Millar* v. *Commissioner*, 577 F2d 212, 215 (CA3), cert. denied, 439 U.S. 1046 (1978), the United States Tax Court, in an unreviewed decision, upheld the asserted deficiencies. 70 T.C. 756 (1978). The United States Court of Appeals for the Fifth Circuit reversed. 651 F.2d 1058 (1981). That court expressly disagreed with the *Millar* analysis, and, in limiting *Crane* v. *Commissioner, supra*, to its facts, questioned the theoretical underpinnings of the *Crane*decision. We granted certiorari to resolve the conflict.

II

Section 752(d) of the Internal Revenue Code of 1954, 26 U.S.C. § 752(d), specifically provides that liabilities involved in the sale or exchange of a partnership interest are to "be treated in the same manner as liabilities in connection with the sale or exchange of property not associated with partnerships." Section 1001 governs the determination of gains and losses on the disposition of property. Under § 1001(a), the gain or loss from a sale or other disposition of property is defined as the difference between "the amount realized" on the disposition and the property's adjusted basis. Subsection (b) of § 1001 defines "amount realized": "The amount realized from the sale or other disposition of property shall be the sum of any money received plus the fair market value of the property (other than money) received." At issue is the application of the latter provision to the disposition of property encumbered by a nonrecourse mortgage of an amount in excess of the property's fair market value.

A

In *Crane* v. *Commissioner, supra*, this Court took the first and controlling step toward the resolution of this issue. Beulah B. Crane was the sole beneficiary under the will of her deceased husband. At his death in January 1932, he owned an apartment building that was then mortgaged for an amount which proved to be equal to its fair market value, as determined for federal estate tax purposes. The widow, of course, was not personally liable on the mortgage. She operated the building for nearly seven years, hoping to turn it into a profitable venture; during that period, she claimed income tax deductions for depreciation, property taxes, interest, and operating expenses, but did not make payments upon the mortgage principal. In computing her basis for the depreciation deductions, she included the full amount of the mortgage debt. In November 1938, with her hopes unfulfilled and the mortgagee threatening foreclosure, Mrs. Crane sold the building. The purchaser took the property subject to the mortgage and paid Crane $3,000; of that amount, $500 went for the expenses of the sale.

Crane reported a gain of $2,500 on the transaction. She reasoned that her basis in the property was zero (despite her earlier depreciation deductions based on including the amount of the mortgage) and that the amount she realized from the sale was simply the cash she received. The Commissioner disputed this claim. He asserted that Crane's basis in the property, under § 113(a)(5) of the Revenue Act of 1938 (the current version is § 1014 of the 1954 Code, was the property's fair market value at the time of her husband's death, adjusted for depreciation in the interim, and that the amount realized was the net cash received plus the amount of the outstanding mortgage assumed by the purchaser.

In upholding the Commissioner's interpretation of § 113(a)(5) of the 1938 Act, the Court observed that to regard merely the taxpayer's equity in the property as her basis would lead to depreciation deductions less than the actual physical deterioration of the property, and would require the basis to be recomputed with each payment on the mortgage. The Court rejected Crane's claim that any loss due to depreciation belonged to the mortgagee. The effect of the Court's ruling was that the taxpayer's basis was the value of the property undiminished by the mortgage.

The Court next proceeded to determine the amount realized under § 111(b) of the 1938 Act, (the current version is § 1001(b) of the 1954 Code). In order to avoid the "absurdity," see 331 U.S., at 13, of Crane's realizing only $2,500 on the sale of property worth over a quarter of a million dollars, the Court treated the amount realized as it had treated basis, that is, by including the outstanding value of the mortgage. To do otherwise would have permitted Crane to recognize a tax loss unconnected with any actual economic loss. The Court refused to construe one section of the Revenue Act so as "to frustrate the Act as a whole."

Crane, however, insisted that the nonrecourse nature of the mortgage required different treatment. The Court, for two reasons, disagreed. First, excluding the nonrecourse debt from the amount realized would result in the same absurdity and frustration of the Code. Second, the Court concluded that Crane obtained an economic benefit from the purchaser's assumption of the mortgage identical to the benefit conferred by the cancellation of personal debt. Because the value of the property in that case exceeded the amount of the mortgage, it was in Crane's economic interest to treat the mortgage as a personal obligation; only by so doing could she realize upon sale the appreciation in her equity represented by the $2,500 boot. The purchaser's assumption of the liability thus resulted in a taxable economic benefit to her, just as if she had been given, in addition to the boot, a sum of cash sufficient to satisfy the mortgage.

In a footnote, pertinent to the present case, the Court observed:

> Obviously, if the value of the property is less than the amount of the mortgage, a mortgagor who is not personally liable cannot realize a benefit equal to the mortgage. Consequently, a different problem might be encountered where a mortgagor abandoned the property or transferred it subject to the mortgage without receiving boot. That is not this case.

B

This case presents that unresolved issue. We are disinclined to overrule *Crane*, and we conclude that the same rule applies when the unpaid amount of the nonrecourse mortgage exceeds the value of the property transferred. *Crane* ultimately does not rest on its limited theory of economic benefit; instead, we read *Crane* to have approved the Commissioner's decision to treat a nonrecourse mortgage in this context as a true loan. This approval underlies *Crane*'s holdings that the amount of the nonrecourse liability is to be included in calculating both the basis and the amount realized on disposition. That the amount of the loan exceeds the fair market value of the property thus becomes irrelevant.

When a taxpayer receives a loan, he incurs an obligation to repay that loan at some future date. Because of this obligation, the loan proceeds do not qualify as income to the taxpayer. When he fulfills the obligation, the repayment of the loan likewise has no effect on his tax liability.

Another consequence to the taxpayer from this obligation occurs when the taxpayer applies the loan proceeds to the purchase price of property used to secure the loan. Because of the obligation to repay, the taxpayer is entitled to include the amount of the loan in computing his basis in the property; the loan, under § 1012, is part of the taxpayer's cost of the property. Although a different approach might have been taken with respect to a nonrecourse mortgage loan,[5] the Commissioner has chosen to accord it the same treatment he gives to a recourse mortgage loan. The Court approved that choice in *Crane*, and the respondents do not challenge it here. The choice and its resultant benefits to the taxpayer are predicated on the assumption that the mortgage will be repaid in full.

When encumbered property is sold or otherwise disposed of and the purchaser assumes the mortgage, the associated extinguishment of the mortgagor's obligation to repay is accounted for in the computation of the amount realized. Because no difference between recourse and nonrecourse obligations is recognized in calculating basis, *Crane* teaches that the Commissioner may ignore the nonrecourse nature of the obligation in determining the amount realized upon disposition of the encumbered property. He thus may include in the amount realized the amount of the nonrecourse mortgage assumed by the purchaser. The rationale for this treatment is that the original inclusion of the amount of the mortgage in basis rested on the assumption that the mortgagor incurred an obligation to repay. Moreover, this treatment balances the fact that the mortgagor originally received the proceeds of the nonrecourse loan tax-free on the same assumption. Unless the outstanding amount of the mortgage is deemed to be realized, the mortgagor effectively will have received untaxed income at the time the loan was extended and will have received an unwarranted increase in the basis of his property. The Commissioner's interpretation of § 1001(b) in this fashion cannot be said to be unreasonable.

C

The Commissioner in fact has applied this rule even when the fair market value of the property falls below the amount of the nonrecourse obligation. Treas. Reg. § 1.1001-2(b); Rev. Rul. 76-111, 1976-1 Cum. Bull. 214. Because the theory on which the rule is based applies equally in this situation, we have no reason, after *Crane*, to question this treatment.[11]

---

[5] The Commissioner might have adopted the theory, implicit in Crane's contentions, that a nonrecourse mortgage is not true debt, but, instead, is a form of joint investment by the mortgagor and the mortgagee. On this approach, nonrecourse debt would be considered a contingent liability, under which the mortgagor's payments on the debt gradually increase his interest in the property while decreasing that of the mortgagee. Because the taxpayer's investment in the property would not include the nonrecourse debt, the taxpayer would not be permitted to include that debt in basis.

We express no view as to whether such an approach would be consistent with the statutory structure and, if so, and *Crane* were not on the books, whether that approach would be preferred over *Crane*'s analysis. We note only that the *Crane* Court's resolution of the basis issue presumed that when property is purchased with proceeds from a nonrecourse mortgage, the purchaser becomes the sole owner of the property. Under the *Crane* approach, the mortgagee is entitled to no portion of the basis. The nonrecourse mortgage is part of the mortgagor's investment in the property, and does not constitute a coinvestment by the mortgagee.

[11] Professor Wayne G. Barnett, as *amicus* in the present case, argues that the liability and property portions of the transaction should be accounted for separately. Under his view, there was a transfer of the property for $1.4 million, and there was a cancellation of the $1.85 million obligation for a payment of $1.4 million. The former resulted in a capital loss of $50,000,

Respondents received a mortgage loan with the concomitant obligation to repay by the year 2012. The only difference between that mortgage and one on which the borrower is personally liable is that the mortgagee's remedy is limited to foreclosing on the securing property. This difference does not alter the nature of the obligation; its only effect is to shift from the borrower to the lender any potential loss caused by devaluation of the property. If the fair market value of the property falls below the amount of the outstanding obligation, the mortgagee's ability to protect its interests is impaired, for the mortgagor is free to abandon the property to the mortgagee and be relieved of his obligation.

This, however, does not erase the fact that the mortgagor received the loan proceeds tax-free and included them in his basis on the understanding that he had an obligation to repay the full amount. When the obligation is canceled, the mortgagor is relieved of his responsibility to repay the sum he originally received and thus realizes value to that extent within the meaning of § 1001(b). From the mortgagor's point of view, when his obligation is assumed by a third party who purchases the encumbered property, it is as if the mortgagor first had been paid with cash borrowed by the third party from the mortgagee on a nonrecourse basis, and then had used the cash to satisfy his obligation to the mortgagee.

Moreover, this approach avoids the absurdity the Court recognized in *Crane*. Because of the remedy accompanying the mortgage in the nonrecourse situation, the depreciation in the fair market value of the property is relevant economically only to the mortgagee, who by lending on a nonrecourse basis remains at risk. To permit the taxpayer to limit his realization to the fair market value of the property would be to recognize a tax loss for which he has suffered no corresponding economic loss. Such

---

and the latter in the realization of $450,000 of ordinary income. Taxation of the ordinary income might be deferred under § 108 by a reduction of respondents' bases in their partnership interests.

Although this indeed could be a justifiable mode of analysis, it has not been adopted by the Commissioner. Nor is there anything to indicate that the Code requires the Commissioner to adopt it. We note that Professor Barnett's approach does assume that recourse and nonrecourse debt may be treated identically.

The Commissioner also has chosen not to characterize the transaction as cancellation of indebtedness. We are not presented with and do not decide the contours of the cancellation-of-indebtedness doctrine. We note only that our approach does not fall within certain prior interpretations of that doctrine. In one view, the doctrine rests on the same initial premise as our analysis here—an obligation to repay—but the doctrine relies on a freeing-of-assets theory to attribute ordinary income to the debtor upon cancellation. According to that view, when nonrecourse debt is forgiven, the debtor's basis in the securing property is reduced by the amount of debt canceled, and realization of income is deferred until the sale of the property. Because that interpretation attributes income only when assets are freed, however, an insolvent debtor realizes income just to the extent his assets exceed his liabilities after the cancellation. Similarly, if the nonrecourse indebtedness exceeds the value of the securing property, the taxpayer never realizes the full amount of the obligation canceled because the tax law has not recognized negative basis.

Although the economic benefit prong of *Crane* also relies on a freeing-of-assets theory, that theory is irrelevant to our broader approach. In the context of a sale or disposition of property under § 1001, the extinguishment of the obligation to repay is not ordinary income; instead, the amount of the canceled debt is included in the amount *realized*, and enters into the computation of gain or loss on the disposition of property. According to *Crane*, this treatment is no different when the obligation is nonrecourse: the basis is not reduced as in the cancellation-of-indebtedness context, and the full value of the outstanding liability is included in the amount realized. Thus, the problem of negative basis is avoided.

a result would be to construe "one section of the Act . . . so as . . . to defeat the intention of another or to frustrate the Act as a whole."

In the specific circumstances of *Crane*, the economic benefit theory did support the Commissioner's treatment of the nonrecourse mortgage as a personal obligation. The footnote in *Crane* acknowledged the limitations of that theory when applied to a different set of facts. *Crane* also stands for the broader proposition, however, that a nonrecourse loan should be treated as a true loan. We therefore hold that a taxpayer must account for the proceeds of obligations he has received tax-free and included in basis. Nothing in either § 1001(b) or in the Court's prior decisions requires the Commissioner to permit a taxpayer to treat a sale of encumbered property asymmetrically, by including the proceeds of the nonrecourse obligation in basis but not accounting for the proceeds upon transfer of the encumbered property.

III

Relying on the Code's § 752(c), 26 U.S.C. § 752(c), however, respondents argue that Congress has provided for precisely this type of asymmetrical treatment in the sale or disposition of partnership property. Section 752 prescribes the tax treatment of certain partnership transactions, and § 752(c) provides that "[f]or purposes of this section, a liability to which property is subject shall, to the extent of the fair market value of such property, be considered as a liability of the owner of the property." Section 752(c) could be read to apply to a sale or disposition of partnership property, and thus to limit the amount realized to the fair market value of the property transferred. Inconsistent with this interpretation, however, is the language of § 752(d), which specifically mandates that partnership liabilities be treated "in the same manner as liabilities in connection with the sale or exchange of property not associated with partnerships." The apparent conflict of these subsections renders the facial meaning of the statute ambiguous, and therefore we must look to the statute's structure and legislative history.

Subsections (a) and (b) of § 752 prescribe rules for the treatment of liabilities in transactions between a partner and his partnership, and thus for determining the partner's adjusted basis in his partnership interest. Under § 704(d), a partner's distributive share of partnership losses is limited to the adjusted basis of his partnership interest. When partnership liabilities are increased or when a partner takes on the liabilities of the partnership, § 752(a) treats the amount of the increase or the amount assumed as a contribution by the partner to the partnership. This treatment results in an increase in the adjusted basis of the partner's interest and a concomitant increase in the § 704(d) limit on his distributive share of any partnership loss. Conversely, under § 752(b), a decrease in partnership liabilities or the assumption of a partner's liabilities by the partnership has the effect of a distribution, thereby reducing the limit on the partner's distributive share of the partnership's losses. When property encumbered by liabilities is contributed to or distributed from the partnership, § 752(c) prescribes that the liability shall be considered to be assumed by the transferee only to the extent of the property's fair market value.

The legislative history indicates that Congress contemplated this application of § 752(c). Mention of the fair market value limitation occurs only in the context of transactions under subsections (a) and (b). The sole reference to subsection (d) does not discuss the limitation. While the legislative history is certainly not conclusive, it indicates that the fair market value limitation of § 752(c) was directed to transactions between a partner and his partnership. 1 A. Willis, J. Pennell, & P. Postlewaite, Partnership Taxation § 44.03, p. 44-3 (3d ed. 1981); Simmons, *Tufts* v. *Commissioner: Amount Realized Limited to Fair Market Value*, 15 U.C.D.L. Rev. 577, 611-613 (1982).

By placing a fair market value limitation on liabilities connected with property contributions to and distributions from partnerships under subsections (a) and (b), Congress apparently intended § 752(c) to prevent a partner from inflating the basis of his partnership interest. Otherwise, a partner with no additional capital at risk in the partnership could raise the § 704(d) limit on his distributive share of partnership losses or could reduce his taxable gain upon disposition of his partnership interest. There is no potential for similar abuse in the context of § 752(d) sales of partnership interests to unrelated third parties. In light of the above, we interpret subsection (c) to apply only to § 752(a) and (b) transactions, and not to limit the amount realized in a sale or exchange of a partnership interest under § 752(d).

IV

When a taxpayer sells or disposes of property encumbered by a nonrecourse obligation, the Commissioner properly requires him to include among the assets realized the outstanding amount of the obligation. The fair market value of the property is irrelevant to this calculation. We find this interpretation to be consistent with *Crane* v. *Commissioner*, 331 U.S. 1 (1947), and to implement the statutory mandate in a reasonable manner.

The judgment of the Court of Appeals is therefore reversed.

It is so ordered.

Revenue Ruling 75-194
1975-1 CB 80

Advice has been requested concerning the Federal income tax consequences of the contribution of an interest in a limited partnership to a charitable organization in the situation described below.

L became a limited partner in a partnership on its formation in 1971. In 1974, L contributed his entire limited partnership interest to a charitable organization described in section 170(c) of the Internal Revenue Code of 1954. On that date all of the partnership liabilities were liabilities on which neither L, the other partners, nor the partnership had assumed any personal liability. Also on that date, L's proportionate share of the value of the partnership assets was greater than his proportionate share of the partnership liabilities and because of partnership losses L's adjusted basis for his partnership interest was less than his proportionate share of the partnership liabilities. At the time of the contribution the partnership had no unrealized receivables or inventory items described in section 751.

Section 170(a) of the Code provides the general rule that there shall be allowed as a deduction any "charitable contribution" (as defined in section 170(c)) payment of which is made within the taxable year.

Section 1.170A-1(c) of the Income Tax Regulations provides, in part, that if a contribution is made in property other than money, the amount of the contribution is the fair market value of the property at the time of the contribution reduced as provided in section 170(e)(1) of the Code.

Section 741 of the Code provides, in pertinent part, that in the case of a sale or exchange of an interest in a partnership, gain or loss shall be recognized to the transferor partner and shall be considered gain or loss from the sale or exchange of a capital asset, except as otherwise provided in section 751.

Section 752(c) of the Code provides that for purposes of section 752, a liability to which property is subject shall, to the extent of the fair market value of such property, be considered as a liability of the owner of the property.

Section 1.752-1(e) of the Regulations provides, in part, that where none of the partners have any personal liability with respect to a partnership liability (as in the case of a mortgage on real estate acquired by the partnership without assumption by the partnership or any of the partners of any liability on the mortgage), then all partners, including limited partners, shall be considered as sharing such liability under section 752(c) of the Code in the same proportion as they share the profits.

Section 752(d) of the Code and section 1.752-1(d) of the Regulations provide that where there is a sale or exchange of an interest in a partnership, liabilities shall be treated in the same manner as liabilities in connection with the sale or exchange of property not associated with partnerships. For example, if a partner sells his interest in a partnership for $750 cash and at the same time transfers to the purchaser his share of partnership liabilities amounting to $250, the amount realized by the seller on the transaction is $1,000. See also Rev. Rul. 74-40, 1974-1 C.B. 159.

Section 1011(b) of the Code provides the rules for allocating adjusted basis in the case of a "bargain sale" to a charitable organization where a deduction is allowable under section 170 by reason of such sale. Section 1.170A-4(c)(2)(iii) of the Regulations defines a "bargain sale" as a transfer of property which is in part a sale or exchange of the property and in part a charitable contribution, as defined in section 170(c), of the property. Sections 1.170A-4(c) and 1.1011-2 contain rules and examples with respect to the computation of gain and the amount of the charitable contribution in the case of a "bargain sale."

Section 1.1011-2(a)(3) of the Regulations provides that if property is transferred subject to an indebtedness, the amount of the indebtedness must be treated as an amount realized for purposes of determining whether there is a sale or exchange to which section 1011(b) of the Code and section 1.1011-2 apply, even though the transferee does not agree to assume or pay the indebtedness.

Since the value of L's share of the partnership assets at the time he transferred his partnership interest exceeded his share of partnership liabilities at that time, a charitable contribution deduction is allowable under section 170 of the Code, subject to the reductions and limitations set forth therein. At the same time, pursuant to sections 752(d) and 1011(b), the amount of L's share of partnership liabilities at the time of the transfer constitutes an amount realized by L. Based on the foregoing, a bargain sale within the meaning of sections 170 and 1011(b) has occurred.

Accordingly, in the instant case, L has a recognized gain on the transfer equal to the excess of the amount realized by L over that portion of the adjusted basis of L's partnership interest (at the time of the transfer) allocable to the sale under section 1011(b) of the Code. Since the partnership had no unrealized receivables or appreciated inventory items described in section 751, the gain is considered a gain from the sale of a capital asset under section 741.

CHAPTER 11

Transfers of Partnership Interests—Sales of Interests in Partnerships Holding Tainted Assets

PROBLEM AREA 11

INTRODUCTION

As discussed in Problem Area 10, a partner's gain or loss on the sale or exchange of a partnership interest is characterized under § 741, which provides for capital-asset status. Although this entity approach produces some alterations of the characterization of income or loss compared to an aggregate approach, such alterations are not dramatic when the partnership does not possess significant ordinary-income assets. For example, if a partnership holds two appreciated assets which would produce a short-term capital gain and a § 1231 gain if sold by the partnership, a long-term capital gain characterization under § 741 on the sale of the partnership interest is not particularly offensive from a tax-policy standpoint. However, if the sale of the partnership assets would produce ordinary income, the conversion potential of § 741 would be considerable. Congress enacted § 751(a), which overrides § 741, in order to preserve the aggregate approach when certain ordinary-income assets are present.

The ordinary-income assets identified by § 751 are "unrealized receivables" (the partnership's rights to payments which would produce ordinary income and have not been taken into account previously, as well as most recapture amounts) and "inventory" (partnership assets which would produce ordinary income if sold by the partnership or the transferor partner). These assets are often referred to collectively as the partnership's "tainted assets" or "hot assets." The presence of any of these assets, however small, mandates the application of § 751(a) on the sale of an interest in the partnership that holds them.

A selling partner's share of the ordinary income or loss attributable to unrealized receivables and inventory is the amount that would have been allocated to the partner (with respect to the interest sold) if the partnership has sold all of its assets in a fully taxable transaction. Thus, for example, if a 25 percent partner sells her partnership interest and the partnership's § 751 assets have a total value of $200 and an aggregate adjusted basis of $80, the partner has $30 ordinary income ($50 − $20) under § 751(a). The difference between the partner's overall gain or loss on the sale and the ordinary income or loss determined under this method is capital gain or loss under § 741. Thus, for example, if the partner's overall gain is $100 and $20 is ordinary under § 751(a), the partner has $80 of capital gain. If, however, the partner's ordinary income were $120, she would have $20 of capital loss.

PROBLEM 11

QUESTIONS

1. A, B, C, and D formed the calendar-year ABCD partnership, each with a one-fourth interest in the capital, profits, and losses of the partnership. The original contributions to ABCD were $10 in cash from each partner. The partnership has neither earned any income nor received additional contributions. The partnership uses an accrual method for the purchase and sale of inventory and the cash method for all other purposes. In addition to producing inventory assets for sale, the partnership renders consulting services to some of its customers. None of A, B, C, or D has activities outside of the partnership that could cause any of the partnership's assets to be considered inventory under § 751(d)(3). The balance sheet of ABCD is as follows:

	Adjusted Basis	Fair Market Value
Assets		
Cash	$ 20	$ 20
Accounts Receivable (from services)	0	25
Inventory	20	25
Stock (investment)	160	160
Land (investment)	20	70
Total	$220	$300
Liabilities and Capital		
Liabilities		
Mortgage	$180	$180
Capital		
A	10	30
B	10	30
C	10	30
D	10	30
Total Liabilities and Capital	$220	$300

a. E offers A $30 cash for A's interest in ABCD. If A accepts E's offer, what is the amount and character of A's gain or loss?

b. How would your answer in a. above change if ABCD were an accrual-method taxpayer for all items?

c. How would your answer in a. above change if the partnership's adjusted basis in the inventory were $22? $30? What if the partnership's adjusted bases in the accounts receivable and the inventory were $25 and $40, respectively?

d. How would your answer in a. above change if A were a dealer in real estate?

2. ABCD, a partnership formed on January 1, Year 1, runs a ski shop. It has a calendar year and uses the cash method of accounting. The partnership's business is

renting and selling ski equipment and providing ski lessons. ABCD owns the lot and building where the shop is located. The building was built by ABCD at a cost of $186 and was first ready for use on January 1, Year 2. As of December 31, Year 3, ABCD has taken depreciation on a straight-line basis of $5.50.

The ski equipment that ABCD holds for sale to its customers has been purchased as needed. The ski equipment used for rental purposes was purchased for $65 on January 1, Year 2, and the depreciation taken as of December 31, Year 3, is $42.

A, B, C, and D each owns a one-fourth interest in capital, profits, and losses of ABCD. Independently, A sells unimproved real estate as a full-time career. Other than his personal residence, A does not own any real estate for purposes of investment. In order to devote more time to his real estate business, A decides to sell his partnership interest in ABCD to E for $155 on January 1, Year 4. A's basis in his partnership interest is $110 resulting from his contributions, distributive share of partnership income, and partnership distributions to him. ABCD has no liabilities at the time of the sale of A's interest.

All parties agree that A's interest in each asset is one-fourth of the fair market value of that asset. The purchase price of the partnership interest is allocated in that manner.

The assets of ABCD as of December 31, Year 3, are as follows:

	Adjusted Basis	Fair Market Value	Face
Receivables			
• Sale of skis and other equipment prior to December 31, Year 3.	$ 0.00	$ 20.00	$50.00
• Ski lessons given prior to December 31, Year 3.	0.00	20.00	50.00
• Signed contracts for lessons to be given in January, Year 4 (one-half of the lessons are terminable at will). Estimated cost to complete the contracts is $10 which has been taken into account in arriving at the fair market value.	0.00	30.00	50.00
• Sale of common stock of XYW, Inc. which had been held for less than one year and was a capital asset at the time of sale, payable in Year 4. The basis is equal to the stock's basis prior to sale.	4.00	8.00	
Inventory			
• Skis for sale	20.00	26.00	
• Boots for sale	15.00	12.00	
• Bindings for sale	10.00	16.00	
• Poles for sale	5.00	14.00	
• Ski jackets, sweaters, goggles, and other equipment for sale	30.00	40.00	
Rental Equipment			
• Skis, boots, bindings, poles, and other equipment held only for rental purposes	23.00	32.00	

	Adjusted Basis	Fair Market Value	Face
Land			
• Investment lots	36.00	40.00	
• Lot where the shop is located	20.00	17.50	
• Building where the shop is located	180.50	194.50	
Investment stock	96.50	150.00	
Total	$440.00	$620.00	

    a. Which assets constitute § 751(c) property?

    b. Which assets constitute § 751(d) property?

MATERIALS

Ledoux v. Commissioner
77 TC 293 (1981)

STERRETT, Judge.

. . . The sole issue presented is whether a portion of the amount received by petitioner on the sale of his 25-percent partnership interest is taxable as ordinary income and not as capital gain. More specifically, we must decide whether any portion of the sales price is attributable to "unrealized receivables" of the partnership.

Generally, gain or loss on the sale or exchange of a partnership interest is treated as capital gain or loss. Sec. 741. Prior to 1954, a partner could escape ordinary income tax treatment on his portion of the partnership's unrealized receivables by selling or exchanging his interest in the partnership and treating the gain or loss therefrom as capital gain or loss. To curb such abuses, section 751 was enacted to deal with the problem of the so-called "collapsible partnership."

Petitioner contends that the dog track agreement gave the Collins-Ledoux partnership the right to manage and operate the dog track. According to petitioner, the agreement did not give the partnership any contractual rights to receive future payments and did not impose any obligation on the partnership to perform services. Rather, the agreement merely gave the partnership the right to occupy and use all of the corporation's properties (including the racetrack facilities and the racing permit) in operating its dog track business; if the partnership exercised such right, it would be obligated to make annual payments to the corporation based upon specified percentages of the annual mutuel handle. Thus, because the dog track agreement was in the nature of a leasehold agreement rather than an employment contract, it did not create the type of "unrealized receivables" referred to in section 751.

Respondent, on the other hand, contends that the partnership operated the racetrack for the corporation and was paid a portion of the profits for its efforts. As such, the agreement was in the nature of a management employment contract. When petitioner sold his partnership interest to the Collinses in 1972, the main right that he sold was a contract right to receive income in the future for yet-to-be-rendered personal services. This, respondent asserts, is supported by the fact that petitioner determined the sales price for his partnership interest by capitalizing his 1972 annual income (approximately $160,000) by a factor of 5. Therefore, respondent contends that the portion of the gain realized by petitioner that is attributable to the management contract should be characterized as an amount received for unrealized receivables of the partnership. Consequently, such gain should be characterized as ordinary income under section 751.

The legislative history is not wholly clear with respect to the types of assets that Congress intended to place under the umbrella of "unrealized receivables." The House report states:

> The term "unrealized receivables or fees" is used to apply to any rights to income which have not been included in gross income under the method of accounting employed by the partnership. The provision is applicable mainly to cash basis

partnerships which have acquired a contractual or other legal right to income for goods or services. . . .

Essentially the same language appears in the report of the Senate committee. In addition, the regulations elaborate on the meaning of "unrealized receivables" as used in section 751. Section 1.751-1(c), Income Tax Regs., provides:

Sec. 1.751-1(c) *Unrealized receivables.* (1) The term "unrealized receivables", . . . means any rights (contractual or otherwise) to payment for—

(i) Goods delivered or to be delivered (to the extent that such payment would be treated as received for property other than a capital asset), or

(ii) Services rendered or to be rendered, to the extent that income arising from such rights to payment was not previously includible in income under the method of accounting employed by the partnership. Such rights must have arisen under contracts or agreements in existence at the time of sale or distribution, although the partnership may not be able to enforce payment until a later time. For example, the term includes trade accounts receivable of a cash method taxpayer, and rights to payment for work or goods begun but incomplete at the time of the sale or distribution . . . .

(3) In determining the amount of the sale price attributable to such unrealized receivables, or their value in a distribution treated as a sale or exchange, any arm's length agreement between the buyer and the seller, or between the partnership and the distributee partner, will generally establish the amount or value. In the absence of such an agreement, full account shall be taken not only of the estimated cost of completing performance of the contract or agreement, but also of the time between the sale or distribution and the time of payment.

The language of the legislative history and the regulations indicates that the term "unrealized receivables" includes any contractual or other right to payment for goods delivered or to be delivered or services rendered or to be rendered. Therefore, an analysis of the nature of the rights under the dog track agreement, in the context of the aforementioned legal framework, becomes appropriate. A number of cases have dealt with the meaning of "unrealized receivables" and thereby have helped to define the scope of the term. Courts that have considered the term "unrealized receivables" generally have said that it should be given a broad interpretation. For instance, in *Logan v. Commissioner*, 51 T.C. 482, 486 (1968), we held that a partnership's right in quantum meruit to payment for work in progress constituted an unrealized receivable even though there was no express agreement between the partnership and its clients requiring payment.

In *Roth v. Commissioner*, 321 F.2d 607 (9th Cir. 1963), the Ninth Circuit dealt with the sale of an interest in a partnership which produced a movie and then gave a 10-year distribution right to Paramount Pictures Corp. in return for a percentage of the gross receipts. The selling partner claimed that his right to a portion of the payments expected under the partnership's contract with Paramount did not constitute an unrealized receivable. The court rejected this view, however, reasoning that Congress "meant to exclude from capital gains treatment any receipts which would have been treated as ordinary income to the partner if no transfer of the partnership interest had

occurred." Therefore, the partnership's right to payments under the distribution contract was in the nature of an unrealized receivable.

A third example of the broad interpretation given to the term "unrealized receivable" is *United States v. Eidson*, 310 F.2d 111 (5th Cir. 1962). The court there
considered the nature of a management contract which was similar to the one at issue
in the instant case. The case arose in the context of a sale by a partnership of all of its
rights to operate and manage a mutual insurance company. The selling partnership
received $170,000 for the rights it held under the management contract, and the
Government asserted that the total amount should be treated as ordinary income. The
Court of Appeals agreed with the Government's view on the ground that what was
being assigned was not a capital asset whose value had accrued over a period of
years; rather, the right to operate the company and receive profits therefrom during the
remaining life of the contract was the real subject of the assignment. The Fifth Circuit
found the Supreme Court's holding in *Commissioner v. P. G. Lake, Inc.*, 356 U.S. 260
(1958), to be conclusive:

> The substance of what was assigned was the right to receive future income.
> The substance of what was received was the present value of income which the
> recipient would otherwise obtain in the future. In short, consideration was paid for
> the right to receive future income, not for an increase in the value of the
> income-producing property.

In *United States v. Woolsey*, 326 F.2d 287 (5th Cir. 1963), the Fifth Circuit again
faced a situation similar to the one that we face herein. The Fifth Circuit considered
whether proceeds received by taxpayers on the sale of their partnership interests were
to be treated as ordinary income or capital gain. There, the court was faced with the
sale of interests in a partnership which held, as one of its assets, a 25-year contract to
manage a mutual insurance company. As in the instant case, the contract gave the
partners the right to render services for the term of the contract and to earn ordinary
income in the future. In holding that the partnership's management contract constituted an unrealized receivable, the court stated:

> When we look at the underlying right assigned in this case, we cannot
> escape the conclusion that so much of the consideration which relates to the right
> to earn ordinary income in the future under the "management contract," taxable
> to the assignee as ordinary income, is likewise taxable to the assignor as
> ordinary income although such income must be earned. Section 751 has defined
> "unrealized receivables" to include any rights, contractual or otherwise, to ordi-
> nary income from "services rendered, *or to be rendered*," (emphasis added) to
> the extent that the same were not previously includable in income by the
> partnership, with the result that capital gains rates cannot be applied to the rights
> to income under the facts of this case, which would constitute ordinary income
> had the same been received in due course by the partnership . . . . It is our
> conclusion that such portion of the consideration received by the taxpayers in this
> case as properly should be allocated to the present value of their right to earn
> ordinary income in the future under the "management contract" is subject to
> taxation as ordinary income . . . .

Petitioner attempts to distinguish *United States v. Woolsey*, supra, and *United States v. Eidson*, supra, from the instant case by arguing that those cases involved a sale or termination of contracts to manage mutual insurance companies in Texas and that the management contracts therein were in the nature of employment agreements. After closely scrutinizing the facts in those cases, we conclude that petitioner's position has no merit. The fact that the *Woolsey* case involved sale of 100 percent of the partnership interests, as opposed to a sale of only a 25-percent partnership interest herein, is of no consequence. In addition, the fact that *Eidson* involved the surrender of the partnership's contract right to manage the insurance company, as opposed to the continued partnership operation in the instant case, also is not a material factual distinction.

The dog track agreement at issue in the instant case is similar to the management contract considered by the Fifth Circuit in *Woolsey*. Each gives the respective partnership the right to operate a business for a period of years and to earn ordinary income in return for payments of specified amounts to the corporation that holds the State charter. Therefore, based on our analysis of the statutory language, the legislative history, and the regulations and relevant case law, we are compelled to find that the dog track agreement gave the petitioner an interest that amounted to an "unrealized receivable" within the meaning of section 751(c).

Petitioner further contends that the dog track agreement does not represent an unrealized receivable because it does not require or obligate the partnership to perform personal services in the future. The agreement only gives, the argument continues, the Collins-Ledoux partnership the right to engage in a business.

We find this argument to be unpersuasive. The words of section 751(c), providing that the term "unrealized receivable" includes the right to payment for "services rendered, or to be rendered," do not preclude that section's application to a situation where, as here, the performance of services is not required by the agreement. As the Fifth Circuit said in *United States v. Eidson*, supra:

> The fact that . . . income would not be received by the [partnership] unless they performed the services which the contract required of them, that is, actively managed the affairs of the insurance company in a manner that would produce a profit after all of the necessary expenditures, does not, it seems clear, affect the nature of this payment. It affects only the amount. That is, the fact that the taxpayers would have to spend their time and energies in performing services for which the compensation would be received merely affects the price at which they would be willing to assign or transfer the contract. . . .

Consequently, a portion of the consideration received by Ledoux on the sale of his partnership interest is subject to taxation as ordinary income.

Having established that the dog track agreement qualifies as an unrealized receivable, we next consider whether all or only part of petitioner's gain in excess of the amount attributable to his share of tangible partnership assets should be treated as ordinary income. Petitioner argues that this excess gain was attributable to goodwill or the value of a going concern.

With respect to goodwill, we note that petitioner's attorney drafted, and petitioner signed, the agreement for sale of partnership interest, dated October 17, 1972, which contains the following statement in paragraph 7:

7. In the determination of the purchase price set forth in this agreement, the parties acknowledge no consideration has been given to any item of goodwill.

The meaning of the words "no consideration" is not entirely free from doubt. They could mean that no thought was given to an allocation of any of the sales price to goodwill, or they could indicate that the parties agreed that no part of the purchase price was allocated to goodwill. The testimony of the attorney who prepared the document indicates, however, that he did consider the implications of the sale of goodwill and even did research on the subject. He testified that he believed, albeit incorrectly, that, if goodwill were part of the purchase price, his client would not be entitled to capital gains treatment.

. . . We find as a fact that petitioner agreed at arm's length with the purchasers of his partnership interest that no part of the purchase price should be attributable to goodwill. . . .

We next turn to petitioner's contention that part or all of the purchase price received in excess of the value of tangible assets is attributable to value of a going concern. In *VGS Corp. v. Commissioner*, 68 T.C. 563 (1977), we stated that—

Going-concern value is, in essence, the additional element of value which attaches to property by reason of its existence as an integral part of a going concern. . . . [T]he ability of a business to continue to function and generate income without interruption as a consequence of the change in ownership, is a vital part of the value of a going concern. . . .

However, in the instant case, the ability of the dogracing track to continue to function after the sale of Ledoux's partnership interest was due to the remaining partners' retention of rights to operate under the dog track agreement. Without such agreement, there would have been no continuing right to operate a business and no right to continue to earn income. Thus, the amount paid in excess of the value of Ledoux's share of the tangible assets was not for the intangible value of the business as a going concern but rather for Ledoux's rights under the dog track agreement.

Finally, we turn to petitioner's claim that a determination of the value of rights arising from the dog track agreement has never been made and no evidence of the value of such rights was submitted in this case. We note that the $800,000 purchase price was proposed by petitioner and was accepted by Jack Collins and Jerry Collins in an arm's-length agreement of sale evidenced in the memorandum of agreement of July 19, 1972, and the agreement for sale of partnership interest of October 17, 1972. In addition, the October 17, 1972, sales agreement, written by petitioner's attorney, provided in paragraph 1 that the "Seller [Ledoux] sells to buyer [Jerry Collins and Jack Collins] all of his interest in [the partnership] . . . including but not limited to, *the seller's right to income* and to acquire the capital stock of The Sanford-Orlando Kennel Club, Inc." (Emphasis added.) Section 1.751-1(c)(3), Income Tax Regs., provides that an arm's-length agreement between the buyer and the seller generally will establish the value attributable to unrealized receivables.

Based on the provision in the agreement that no part of the consideration was attributable to goodwill, it is clear to us that the parties were aware that they could, if they so desired, have provided that no part of the consideration was attributable to the dog track agreement. No such provision was made. Furthermore, the agreement clearly stated that one of the assets purchased was Ledoux's rights to future income.

Considering that petitioner calculated the purchase price by capitalizing future earnings expected under the dog track agreement, we conclude that the portion of Ledoux's gain in excess of the amount attributable to tangible assets was attributable to an unrealized receivable as reflected by the dog track agreement.

Decision will be entered for the respondent.

CHAPTER 12

Partnership Distributions— Liquidating Distributions That Do Not Change Partners' Interests in Tainted Assets

PROBLEM AREA 12

INTRODUCTION

The focus of Problem Area 9 was *current* distributions (including partial liquidations) not subject to § 751(b). This Problem Area 12 concerns *liquidating* distributions not subject to § 751(b). Under § 731, the gain-recognition rules applicable to distributions of cash apply equally to current distributions and to liquidating distributions. The rules for recognizing losses, however, are different for liquidating distributions than for current distributions. In contrast to the rules for current distributions which preclude loss recognition, loss can be recognized on a liquidating distribution if *only* money, unrealized receivables, and/or inventory is distributed. The amount of the loss is the excess of the basis of the distributee's partnership interest over the amount of money distributed and the § 732 basis for the distributed property. The loss is treated as arising from the sale or exchange of the partner's interest in the partnership and is therefore a capital loss.

The justification for this rule, found in § 731(a)(2), depends on the nature of the loss-producing distribution. If the partnership distributes only money, then the partner's entire interest has been "cashed out" in the liquidation, and there is no reason (not to mention no practical way) to defer loss recognition beyond that point. If the partnership distributes inventory or receivables, it would be possible to defer loss recognition until the partner sells or collects the distributed property. In such event, however, all of the loss on the disposition of the property generally would be ordinary under § 735 and, to the extent that the adjusted basis of the distributee partner's interest were greater than the aggregate basis of the distributed property, capital loss would be converted into ordinary loss. Section 731(a)(2)(B) prevents this from happening.

Thus, for example, if a partner whose adjusted basis in the partnership interest is $120 receives a liquidating distribution of partnership inventory with an adjusted basis of $100 and a value of $75, the partner will recognize an immediate capital loss of $20. The partner's basis in the distributed inventory will be $100, and he will recognize a $25 ordinary loss on its subsequent disposition. If, in contrast, this partner took a basis of $120 in the inventory, he would be entitled to an ordinary loss of $45 on such disposition.

Regardless whether loss is recognized on a property distribution in liquidation of the partner's interest, the distributee partner's adjusted basis in the distributed property is determined under §§ 732(b) and 732(c). Unlike § 732(a), which applies to current rather than liquidating distributions and generally provides that the basis of distributed property in the hands of the distributee partner equals the partnership's adjusted basis for such property, § 732(b) accords the distributed property the basis of the partner's partnership interest. Thus, for example, in a liquidating distribution to which § 751(b) does not apply, if the partnership distributes a single asset to a partner who has a basis of $100 for his partnership interest, the asset generally will take a $100 basis regardless of whether its basis to the partnership is $200 or $50. This rule has the effect of preserving the partner's basis, thus ensuring that the partner is subject to tax on the correct amount upon ultimate disposition of the distributed asset.

Section 732(c) provides for the allocation of the partner's basis in the liquidated partnership interest among the distributed assets. The basis for the partnership interest is allocated first to unrealized receivables and inventory in amounts equal to the bases of these assets to the partnership. If the aggregate basis for these assets is less than the partner's basis in the partnership interest, the remaining basis for the partnership interest is allocated first to the extent of the adjusted basis to the partnership of the other distributed properties. If any basis remains, it is allocated among the other distributed properties (not to unrealized receivables and inventory) in proportion to unrealized appreciation and then according to their fair market values.

The approach comports with economic reality. The example used in the legislative history is that of a liquidating distribution of two properties (neither unrealized receivables nor inventory) with adjusted bases and values of $5 and $40 (property A) and $10 and $10 (property B) to a partner with a basis of $55 in his partnership interest. The first $15 of the partner's basis in his partnership interest goes to the distributed assets in amounts equal to their adjusted bases in the hands of the partnership, $5 to property A and $10 to property B. The remaining basis in the partnership interest of $40 ($55 − $10 − $5) is allocated first according to relative appreciation ($35 to property A, $0 to property B). The final $5 is allocated in proportion to the fair market values of the distributed properties ($40/$50 × $5 = $4 to property A; $10/$50 × $5 = $1 to property B), yielding bases in property A and property B of $44 and $11, respectively. The result of this allocation scheme is that the bases of the distributed properties equal their fair market values, with the excess ($5 in this example) being allocated in proportion to their respective fair market values. The purpose and effect of this approach is to limit the extent to which distributed assets have non-uniform amounts of built-in gain or loss, which could produce unexpected results for the ill-informed and planning opportunities for others.

The converse approach is utilized if the basis of the distributee's partnership interest is less than the aggregate basis of the distributed assets to the partnership. In this case, the decrease in basis is allocated among the assets in proportion to unrealized depreciation and then according to relative adjusted bases. The example employed in the legislative history involves a liquidation of a partner's interest for two assets (neither unrealized receivables nor inventory) distributed to a partner with a basis of $20 in his partnership interest. The assets have adjusted bases and values of $15 and $15 (property C) and $15 and $5 (property D). Allocating first by basis of the assets to the partnership would yield a $30 asset basis in the aggregate, but such is limited to $20, the basis of the partner's partnership interest. Thus, a downward adjustment of $10 ($30 − $20) is required. The adjustment is allocated to property D, lowering its basis from $15 to $5. The basis for property C remains at $15. As in the case of positive adjustments, the effect of the allocation rules for negative adjustments is to reduce or eliminate the disparities between the fair market values and the bases of distributed assets.

PROBLEM 12

QUESTIONS

A and B are equal partners in the AB partnership. AB has the following assets:

	Adjusted Basis	Fair Market Value
Cash	$ 60	$ 60
Accounts Receivable	0	30
Inventory	30	30
Land (investment)	120	60
Total	$210	$180

A's basis in his partnership interest is $100. B's basis is $75. A and B purchased their interests from C and D in separate transactions spanning a three-year period without precipitating a termination of the partnership. The partnership has never made an election under § 754. What is each partner's gain or loss and basis in the distributed assets if the partnership is liquidated as follows?

1. A and B each receives one-half of each asset.

2. A receives the land, one-half of the inventory, and one-half of the accounts receivable, and B receives the cash, one-half of the inventory, and one-half of the accounts receivable.

3. A receives the cash, one-half of the inventory, and one-half of the accounts receivable, and B receives the land, one-half of the inventory, and one-half of the accounts receivable.

4. A receives one-half of the land, one-half of the cash, and all of the accounts receivable, and B receives one-half of the land, one-half of the cash, and all of the inventory.

5. A receives the land and the accounts receivable, and B receives the cash and the inventory.

MATERIALS

Revenue Ruling 74-40
1974-1 CB 159

Advice has been requested concerning the Federal income tax consequences to a limited partner in the situations described below.

Situation 1: *L* is a limited partner in partnership *GL* to which he contributed $10,000 in cash on its formation. His distributive share of partnership items of income and loss is 10 percent and he is not entitled to receive any guaranteed payments. The adjusted basis of his partnership interest at the end of the current year is $20,000. His proportionate share of partnership liabilities, on which neither he, the other partners nor the partnership have assumed any personal liability, is $15,000. The partnership has no other liabilities. *L* sells his interest in the partnership to *M*, an unrelated taxpayer, for $10,000 in cash. At the time of the transaction the partnership had no unrealized receivables or inventory items described in section 751 of the Code nor any goodwill and *L* had been paid his distributive share of partnership income.

Section 752(c) of the Code provides that for purposes of section 752, a liability to which property is subject shall, to the extent of the fair market value of such property, be considered as a liability of the owner of the property.

Section 1.752-1(e) of the Regulations provides, in part, that where none of the partners have any personal liability with respect to a partnership liability (as in the case of a mortgage on real estate acquired by the partnership without the assumption by the partnership or any of the partners of any liability on the mortgage), then all partners, including limited partners, shall be considered as sharing such liability under section 752(c) of the Code in the same proportion as they share the profits.

Section 1.752-1(d) of the Regulations provides that where there is a sale or exchange of an interest in a partnership, liabilities shall be treated in the same manner as liabilities in connection with the sale or exchange of property not associated with partnerships. For example, if a partner sells his interest in a partnership for $750 cash and at the same time transfers to the purchaser his share of partnership liabilities amounting to $250, the amount realized by the seller on the transaction is $1,000.

Section 741 of the Code provides, in pertinent part, that in the case of a sale or exchange of an interest in a partnership, gain or loss shall be recognized to the transferor partner and shall be considered gain or loss from the sale or exchange of a capital asset, except as otherwise provided in section 751 of the Code (relating to unrealized receivables and inventory items which have appreciated substantially in value).

Accordingly, in the instant situation, the amount realized by *L* from the sale of his partnership interest is $25,000, consisting of cash in the amount of $10,000 and release from his share of partnership liabilities in the amount of $15,000. Since the adjusted basis of *L*'s interest in the partnership is $20,000, he realized a gain of $5,000 determined under the provisions of section 741 of the Code.

Situation 2: The facts are the same as in situation 1, except that *L* withdraws from the partnership and the partnership distributes $10,000 to him in cash in complete liquidation of his interest in the partnership.

Section 752(b) of the Code provides that any decrease in a partner's share of the liabilities of a partnership, or any decrease in a partner's individual liabilities by reason of the assumption by the partnership of such individual liabilities, shall be considered as a distribution of money to the partner by the partnership.

Section 731(a) of the Code provides, in pertinent part, that in the case of a distribution by a partnership to a partner, gain shall not be recognized to such partner, except to the extent that any money distributed exceeds the adjusted basis of such partner's interest in the partnership immediately before the distribution. Any gain recognized under section 731(a) shall be considered as a gain from the sale or exchange of the partnership interest of the distributee partner.

Section 731(c) of the Code provides, in part, that section 731 shall not apply to the extent otherwise provided by section 736 (relating to payments to a retiring partner or a deceased partner's successor in interest) and section 751 of the Code (relating to unrealized receivables and inventory items).

Section 736(b) of the Code provides, in pertinent part, that payments made in liquidation of the interest of a retiring partner or a deceased partner shall, to the extent such payments are determined to be made in exchange for the interest of such partner in partnership property, be considered as a distribution by the partnership and not as a distributive share of partnership income or guaranteed payment.

Section 1.736-1(b)(1) of the Regulations provides, in pertinent part, that gain or loss with respect to distributions under section 736(b) of the Code will be recognized to the distributee to the extent provided in section 731 of the Code.

Accordingly, in the instant situation, distributions to L with respect to his partnership interest total $25,000 and consist of cash in the amount of $10,000 and a decrease in his share of the partnership liabilities in the amount of $15,000 that is considered under section 752(b) of the Code as a distribution of money to L by the partnership.

Furthermore, since the money distributed ($25,000) exceeds the adjusted basis of L's interest in the partnership immediately before the distribution ($20,000), he realizes a gain of $5,000 determined under the provisions of section 731(a) of the Code.

Situation 3: Instead of selling his interest L withdraws from the partnership at a time when the adjusted basis of his interest in the partnership is zero and his proportionate share of partnership liabilities, all of which consist of liabilities on which neither he, the other partners nor the partnership have assumed any personal liability, is $15,000.

Accordingly, L is considered to have received a distribution of money from the partnership of $15,000 and realizes a gain of $15,000 determined under the provisions of section 731(a) of the Code.

Spector v. Commissioner
641 F2d 376 (5th Cir. 1981)

JOHNSON, Circuit Judge.

In this suit brought against the Commissioner of Internal Revenue for redetermination of tax deficiencies for the years 1972 and 1973, the principal issue is whether a transaction in which taxpayer surrendered his partnership interest in an accounting firm in exchange for a specified sum constitutes a "sale" of his partnership interest, thus creating long term capital gain under section 741 of the Internal Revenue Code of 1954, or whether the transaction was a "liquidation" of taxpayer's interest under section 707(c), thus producing ordinary income gain under section 736(a)(2). The Commissioner determined on audit that taxpayer was bound to the transaction as structured by the parties, and that it therefore was a liquidation of taxpayer's interest, producing ordinary income gain. The Tax Court, 71 T.C. 1017, reversed the Commissioner's determination, and held that the transaction was a sale, although it was structured and consumated by all of the parties as a liquidation. For reasons that follow, the decision of the Tax Court is reversed, and the case remanded for further proceedings.

I

Prior to 1969, taxpayer was a partner in the accounting firm of Spector, Wilson & Co. (Spector partnership). Taxpayer decided to divest himself of his practice with that firm, and to work exclusively for a single client. Consequently, in the early part of 1969 he approached a business acquaintance, who was a partner in another accounting firm, Bielstein, LaHourcade & Lewis (Bielstein partnership), in an effort to dispose of his practice. Negotiations proceeded over a six week period, and culminated in a written agreement dated February 24, 1969, which provided for the sale of the Spector partnership's accounts receivable to the Bielstein partnership, for the merger of the Spector and Bielstein partnerships, and for the withdrawal of taxpayer from the merged partnership, with payments to him by the merged partnership of amounts designated as "guaranteed payments to a retiring partner." Taxpayer negotiated the details of the agreement with Lewis, the tax partner of the Bielstein partnership. Paragraph 7 of the agreement provided:

> 7. In the agreement for withdrawal, Bielstein agrees to pay the $96,000 as guaranteed payments to a retiring partner with one-half explicitly allocated to an agreement not to compete for the term of the payout.

On May 2, 1969, two agreements were signed to implement the plan outlined in the February 24 agreement. The first agreement, called the "Merger Agreement," provided that the Bielstein firm would merge with the Spector firm on May 3, 1969. The second agreement, called the "Withdrawal Agreement," provided that taxpayer would withdraw from the merged partnership on May 5, 1969, and would receive the agreed upon consideration from the new firm:

> In consideration of for [sic] Spector's withdrawal, Spector will be entitled to receive from the partnership for services or for the use of capital a "guaranteed payment" of $96,000. . . .
> Furthermore, none of the guaranteed payments provided for in this agreement are for partnership property within the meaning of Section 736 IRC of 1954.
> The meaning attributed to the words "guaranteed payments" provided for in this contract is the definition provided for such term in Section 707 of the Internal Revenue Code of 1954 and Regulation Section 1.707-1(c).

The amount of $96,000 to be paid to taxpayer was determined by valuing his practice at one hundred percent of its average gross annual fees.

Before the bargain was struck, the tax consequences flowing from the transaction to taxpayer and to the continuing partners was a point of intense negotiation. As practicing public accountants, all of the parties to the transaction were fully aware that the tax consequences to each would depend upon how the transaction was structured. The Tax Court found that the parties structured the transaction as a merger of the two partnerships followed by taxpayer's withdrawal from the merged firm for the sole purpose of allowing the continuing partners a deduction for income tax purposes, under section 736(a)(2) of the Code, of the amounts paid to taxpayer. Indeed, the record clearly reflects that the transaction would not have been consummated absent taxpayer's written agreement on this issue; the Tax Court found that the continuing partners would not have agreed to pay to taxpayer the total compensation of $96,000 unless the transaction were structured as a deductible "liquidation" of taxpayer's interest pursuant to section 736(a)(2).

Under the agreement, taxpayer was nominally a partner in the Bielstein-Spector partnership for only three days. He never actually performed any services for the partnership. He had no desk or office. He contributed no additional capital to the merged firm. At no time did any party to the transaction intend or expect taxpayer to actually engage in the practice of accounting with the members of the Bielstein-Spector partnership. Simply stated, the transaction was carefully structured as a merger followed by a liquidation of taxpayer's interest for the express purpose of assuming a bargained-for tax posture, and thereby of allocating the tax consequences flowing therefrom in an agreed-upon manner.

Pursuant to the agreement, taxpayer received installments of $23,500 from the Bielstein-Spector partnership in 1972 and 1973. He did not, however, report either sum as a "guaranteed payment" in liquidation of his partnership interest. On audit, the Commissioner determined that the entire amount received by taxpayer in each year should have been reported as a "guaranteed payment" to a retiring partner under section 736(a)(2) and, therefore, as ordinary income. Taxpayer thereupon brought this action in the Tax Court, seeking review of the Commissioner's deficiency determination.

In attempting to avoid the tax consequences flowing from the agreement as structured by the parties, taxpayer argued before the Tax Court that the form of the transaction should be disregarded, and that the true substance of the transaction was a sale, rather than a liquidation, of taxpayer's interest. The Tax Court found that taxpayer had presented "strong proof that the agreements which he signed did not reflect reality insofar as his status as a partner in the Bielstein partnership is concerned." Because taxpayer never became a real partner in the merged firm, the court concluded that "in essence the Bielstein partnership purchased [taxpayer's] share of the goodwill of Spector, Wilson & Company," and that the payments were not a "liquidation" of taxpayer's interest in the new partnership. The Tax Court therefore concluded that except to the extent the payments to taxpayer were allocated to the covenant not to compete, the transaction created long term capital gain pursuant to section 741 of the Code rather than ordinary income gain pursuant to section 736(a)(2), as the Commissioner had determined, and set aside the Commissioner's deficiency determination to that extent. In so holding, the Tax Court found it unnecessary to address taxpayer's alternative argument, i.e., that the payments made to taxpayer were for goodwill as provided in section 736(b)(2)(B) of the Code.

On appeal, the Commissioner argues that the Tax Court erred in allowing taxpayer to disavow the form of the transaction as agreed to by the parties on the mere showing that it did not comport with "economic reality." The Commissioner further argues that the Tax Court's holding is inconsistent with the policy underlying sections 736 and 741 of the Code. As an alternative to the Tax Court's approach, the Commissioner urges this Court to adopt the rule set forth in *Commissioner of Internal Revenue v. Danielson*, 378 F.2d 771 (3d Cir. 1967).

II

Prior to the enactment of the 1954 Code, there existed no comprehensive guidelines concerning the tax consequences resulting from a partner's withdrawal from a partnership. Subchapter K of the 1954 Code, of which sections 736 and 741 are a part, attempted to set forth the "first comprehensive statutory treatment of partners and partnerships in the history of the income tax laws." The principal objectives of the 1954 changes were "simplicity, flexibility, and equity as between the partners."

Under Subchapter K, there are at least two ways in which withdrawing partners may characterize the disposition of their partnership interests: the transaction may be structured either as a "sale" of the partnership interest pursuant to section 741 of the Code, or as a "liquidation" of that interest pursuant to section 736. The net economic result is the same under either approach: The withdrawing partner relinquishes his or her interest in exchange for a specified payment or payments. Depending upon which approach is selected, however, the tax consequences to the withdrawing and continuing partners vary greatly. If characterized as a section 741 "sale," any tax benefits flow to the withdrawing partner, who may be permitted to report any gain that results therefrom as capital, rather than ordinary income gain. Under this selection, the payments are not deductible by the continuing partners, but simply are capitalized as the purchase price of the withdrawing partner's interest and, as such, become the cost basis of the interest so acquired. By comparison, if the transaction is structured as a section 736 "liquidation" of the withdrawing partner's interest, with the payments denominated as "guaranteed payments," the tax benefit flows to the continuing partners, who are able to deduct from partnership income the payments so made. Under this selection the withdrawing partner must report the payments as ordinary income.

From the foregoing, it is readily apparent that the withdrawing and continuing partners will have adverse tax interests. Because a partner's withdrawal generally can be structured either as a section 741 sale or as a section 736 liquidation, the form of the transaction may become a major negotiating point between the parties. Indeed, in *David A. Foxman*, 41 T.C. 535 (1964), aff'd, 352 F.2d 466 (3d Cir. 1965), the Tax Court, after examining the legislative history underlying Subchapter K, noted that:

> one of the underlying philosophic objectives of the 1954 Code was to permit partners themselves to determine their tax burdens *inter sese* to a certain extent, and this is what the committee reports meant when they referred to "flexibility." The theory was that the partners would take their prospective tax liabilities into account in bargaining with one another.

Relying upon these principles, the Tax Court in *Foxman* concluded:

> [T]his policy of "flexibility" is particularly pertinent in determining the tax

consequences of the withdrawal of a partner. Where the practical differences between a "sale" and a "liquidation" are, at most, slight, if they exist at all, and where the tax consequences to the partners can vary greatly, it is in accord with the purpose of the statutory provisions to allow the partners themselves, through arm's length negotiations, to determine whether to take the "sale" route or the "liquidation" route, thereby allocating the tax burdens among themselves.

Unlike the section 741 "sale," the section 736 "liquidation" may occur only in transactions between a partner and his or her own partnership. In the case *sub judice* the Tax Court, after reviewing the evidence, and applying the test set forth in *Commissioner v. Culbertson*, 337 U.S. 733, 742 (1949) for determining the existence of a partnership, held that:

> [t]he merger of partnerships, followed by [taxpayer's] withdrawal from a "merged" partnership, as described in the agreements, never actually occurred. What did occur was a sale by [taxpayer] of his share of the goodwill of [the Spector partnership], not to his partnership or to continuing partners, but to outsiders, the Bielstein partnership. Section 736 is, therefore, inapplicable because it applies to payments made by a partnership to one of its own partners.

The Commissioner does not challenge the Tax Court's finding of fact that taxpayer was not a "bona fide" partner in the Bielstein-Spector partnership. Rather, the Commissioner argues that the Tax Court erred in allowing taxpayer to avoid the tax consequences of the form of the transaction as bargained for and agreed to by the parties merely by adducing "strong proof" that it did not comport with "economic reality," and that taxpayer, having knowingly and voluntarily agreed to structure the transaction as a section 736 liquidation, should be bound by his bargain.

III

Just as the Commissioner in determining income tax liabilities may look through the form of a transaction to its substance, *Commissioner of Internal Revenue v. Court Holding Co.*, 324 U.S. 331 (1945); *Gregory v. Helvering*, 293 U.S. 465 (1935), so, as a general rule, may he bind a taxpayer to the form in which the taxpayer has cast a transaction. . . .

Courts have recognized an exception to the foregoing principle, however, and will allow a taxpayer to challenge the form of a transaction when necessary to avoid unjust results. . . .

As the foregoing cases indicate, when determining whether a taxpayer has adduced strong proof that a contractual allocation to a covenant not to compete in reality was in payment for something else, a major inquiry is whether the covenant bears "economic reality" to the circumstances surrounding the transaction, i.e., whether the allocation to the covenant bears some relationship to its actual value. In the case *sub judice* the Tax Court limited its inquiry to this single factor and concluded that because taxpayer could not have liquidated his interest in a partnership of which he never became a member, the form of the transaction as agreed to by the parties lacked economic reality.

One difficulty with the Tax Court's approach is the aforementioned absence of any substantial difference in terms of "economic reality" between a section 736 liquidation and a section 741 sale of a partnership interest. In a particular case, a covenant not to compete indeed may be so without value as to be devoid of "economic reality." As noted in *Foxman*, however, the fundamental theory underlying Subchapter K is that, given the substantial, if not total, identity in terms of economic net result between a sale and liquidation, the withdrawing and continuing partners should be allowed to allocate the resulting tax benefits and burdens as they see fit. Notwithstanding the fact that a section 736 liquidation may occur only in transactions between a partner and his or her own partnership, once the parties have agreed to structure the transaction in such a way as to comply with that requirement, "economic reality" does not provide a ground upon which that form can be set aside.

Moreover, in contrast to the Tax Court's application of the "strong proof" rule in the present case, the prior decisions of this Court reveal a concern for the type of equitable considerations that traditionally have been invoked when determining whether a party to a transaction may, in fairness, be held to its obligations arising thereunder. Whereas *Balthrope* refers to the situation in which one party, at the expense of the other, tax-ignorant, party slips a covenant into the contract, 356 F.2d at 31, 33–34, *Dixie Finance*, 474 F.2d at 504–05 and *Sonnleitner*, 598 F.2d at 467–68, place emphasis upon whether the covenants involved therein were given for value and were bargained for at arms length. Although, under the approach adopted in the foregoing cases, the absence of any relationship between "economic reality" and the agreement indeed may be strong evidence of mistake, fraud, overreaching, duress, or perhaps some other ground for equitable recission, such as inadequacy of consideration, those decisions simply do not elevate the "economic reality" inquiry to that of a talisman, and require the Commissioner to blind himself to other relevant factors. In none of those decisions did this Court allow a taxpayer, having voluntarily and at arms length bargained for a particular form of transaction, with complete foreknowledge of the tax consequences flowing therefrom, and having represented to the Commissioner that the chosen form reflected the true nature of the transaction, to disavow that form as a sham designed for the sole purpose of misleading the Commissioner, and, having already received substantial nontax benefits therefrom, adopt one with more favorable present tax consequences.

Indeed, this Court in an analogous factual situation has strongly rejected the notion that a taxpayer may bind the Commissioner to a secret understanding as to the effect of an agreement. In *Winn-Dixie Montgomery, Inc. v. United States*, 444 F2d 677 (5th Cir. 1971), taxpayer argued that because it did not intend to allocate any portion of the purchase price to goodwill, the Commissioner should be bound by that determination, absent a contrary expression in the agreement. This Court responded:

> No decision holds or suggests that such a one-sided, uncommunicated apportionment of a sales price is conclusive on the taxing authorities, and it is obvious that it would be dangerous and unfair to lay down that categorical rule. The whole trend of the law in this area is against binding the Revenue Service by such a secret, unilateral, subjective allocation which is not carried over into the agreement.

The above-quoted admonition is particularly appropriate in the present case, and we adhere to the principle expressed therein. . . .

CHAPTER 13

Partnership Distributions— Liquidating Distributions That Change Partners' Interests in Tainted Assets

PROBLEM AREA 13

INTRODUCTION

As discussed in Problem Area 11, § 751(a) serves to prevent the potential conversion of ordinary income into capital gain under § 741 by the means of sale of a partnership interest. At first glance, a similar safeguard would appear unnecessary in the distribution context, because § 735 generally ensures ordinary income characterization on the subsequent sale of distributed unrealized receivables or inventory. However, § 751(b) acts as an additional safeguard by preventing the trading of such income potential with another partner. For example, in a two-person partnership, if an inventory asset were distributed to one partner in a low-tax bracket or with loss carryovers, while a capital asset of equal value were distributed to the other, high-bracket partner, a shifting of net tax benefits between partners would be possible. Section 751(b) acts as a safeguard and applies in the distribution context if a partner receives a disproportionate amount (more or less than the partner's share) of the aggregate value of the partnership's unrealized receivables or substantially appreciated inventory (*i.e.*, inventory items, the fair market value of which exceeds 120 percent of their adjusted basis).

In determining the applicability of § 751(b), initially the amount of the partner's share of the § 751 assets must be determined and then compared to the amount the partner actually receives in a distribution plus the partner's remaining share of those assets still owned by the partnership. Thus, if a partner's partnership interest is worth $100, of which $30 is attributable to the partnership's § 751 assets, and the partner's interest is liquidated for $100 in cash, the partner is considered to have relinquished $30 worth of § 751 assets for $30 of cash.

To the extent that the distribution is disproportionate, the distributee is treated as receiving proportionate interests in the partnership's § 751 property and other property in a current distribution. The distributee is then deemed to engage in a taxable exchange with the partnership, in which the distributee transfers back to the partnership the items of property deemed received in the hypothetical proportional distribution that are not actually received, in exchange for a like amount of the property actually received by the distributee.

Thus, in the above example, the distributee is deemed to receive $30 of § 751 assets and $70 of other property in the hypothetical current distribution. Because the actual distribution consists entirely of cash, the distributee is deemed to transfer the $30 of § 751 assets back to the partnership in exchange for $30 of additional cash. In this fully taxable exchange, the distributee's basis in the § 751 assets deemed sold is determined under the rules of § 732 generally applicable to current distributions of property. The character of the distributee's gain is determined by the nature of the relinquished property, in this case ordinary. A converse setting could arise if the distributee *actually* received a greater amount of § 751 property than his proportionate share, in which case the gain, if any, would be characterized accordingly as capital gain or § 1231 gain.

In the constructive sale or exchange of § 751(b), it is possible for the partnership to recognize tax consequences as well. No gain or loss is recognized in the above example because the partnership is viewed as having purchased the $30 of § 751 assets for $30 cash. A basis adjustment to the partnership for the inventory is appropriate. However, if the partnership relinquishes any asset other than cash in the taxable exchange, it will recognize gain or loss as well as adjust the basis of the partnership assets.

The remainder of the distribution to the distributee partner is governed by the traditional rules of §§ 731 and 732, after taking into account the reduction of the basis of the distributee's partnership interest by the basis of the constructively distributed property deemed sold in the § 751(b) exchange. In the above example, this amount is $70 cash which will produce capital gain under § 731(a) if it exceeds the distributee's remaining basis in the partnership interest, but not otherwise. Although the distributee is deemed to have received a proportionate interest in all of the partnership's assets (whether or not they are § 751 assets) in the hypothetical current distribution, § 751(b) does not treat the distributee as having sold a proportionate interest in any assets other than § 751 assets. In other words, § 751(b) does not disturb the general rule of partnership distributions that a partner may exchange one type of non-§ 751 asset for another type of non-§751 asset without tax consequences.

Section 751(b) applies to current (i.e., non-liquidating) distributions, as well as to liquidating distributions, in any case in which the distributee's interest in the partnership's § 751 property is changed by the distribution. In addition to the complexities that can arise with liquidating distributions, current distributions raise additional issues involving the effect of the property revaluations and "reverse § 704(c)" allocations that usually accompany distributions where the distributee retains a (diminished) interest in the partnership. It is not clear whether the current § 751(b) Regulations take § 704(c) principles into account in determining the partners' respective interests in the partnership's properties, although it appears that they should do so.

The current § 751(b) Regulations were promulgated in 1956 and have been heavily criticized in recent years. Chief among the complaints against them is their fearsome complexity in all but the simplest cases. In addition, they seem to be both over-inclusive (for example, causing the recognition of capital gain in some cases, although this does not seem required by the legislative purpose in enacting § 751(b)) and under-inclusive (for example, by focusing on the value, rather than the income potential, in distributed § 751 assets, thereby permitting the shifting of ordinary income between partners, although this is clearly contrary to legislative intent). The current Regulations also do not take into account developments in partnership taxation subsequent to their promulgation, notably the enhanced role of § 704(c). In Notice 2006-14,

2006-1 CB 498, the Service requested public comments on a thorough over-
haul of the current Regulations.

PROBLEM 13

QUESTIONS

1. The ABCD partnership has the following balance sheet:

	Adjusted Basis	Fair Market Value
Assets		
Cash	$240	$240
Inventory	60	100
Capital Asset X	100	260
Total	$400	$600
Capital		
A	$100	$150
B	100	150
C	100	150
D	100	150
Total	$400	$600

The partnership has made no election under § 754. A's interest is terminated when the partnership distributes $150 cash to him.

a. What is A's taxable gain on the distribution? What is the character of this gain?

b. What is the gain to the partnership on this distribution? What is the character of this gain?

c. What is the partnership's adjusted basis in the inventory and Capital Asset X following the distribution?

d. What is the balance sheet of the partnership following the distribution?

2. The ABC partnership has the following balance sheet:

	Adjusted Basis	Fair Market Value
Assets		
Cash	$ 36	$ 36
Inventory	204	204
Depreciable Equipment Recomputed Basis $350	180	300
Capital Asset Y	120	270
Total	$540	$810

	Adjusted Basis	**Fair Market Value**
Capital		
A	$180	$270
B	180	270
C	180	270
Total	$540	$810

The partnership has made no election under § 754. A's interest is terminated when the partnership distributes Capital Asset Y to him.

a. What is A's taxable gain on the distribution? What is the character of this gain?

b. What is the gain to the partnership on this distribution? What is the character of this gain?

c. What is the partnership's adjusted basis in the inventory and the equipment following the distribution?

d. What is the balance sheet of the partnership following the distribution?

3. Assume that the ABC partnership in question 2. above liquidates A's interest by distributing to him $32 cash, $108 of inventory, and a $130 interest in Capital Asset Y. Does § 751(b) apply to this distribution? Should it?

MATERIALS

Revenue Ruling 77-412
1977-2 CB 223

Advice has been requested concerning the Federal income tax consequences upon the complete liquidation of a two person partnership involving the non-pro rata distribution of "section 751 property" to the partners.

Section 751 of the Internal Revenue Code of 1954 governs the treatment of unrealized receivables of the partnership (as defined in section 751(c)) and inventory items of the partnership that have appreciated substantially in value (as defined in section 751(d)), insofar as they affect sales or exchanges of partnership interests and certain distributions by a partnership. Unrealized receivables and substantially appreciated inventory items are referred to as "section 751 property."

Under section 751(a) of the Code, the amount of any money, or the fair market value of any property, received by a transferor partner in exchange for all or a part of such partner's interest in the partnership attributable to section 751 property, is considered an amount realized from the sale or exchange of property other than a capital asset. Thus, any gain or loss attributable to the sale or exchange of section 751 property would be ordinary income or loss.

Section 751(b)(1) of the Code provides that where a partner receives, in a distribution, partnership section 751 property in exchange for all or a part of such partner's interest in other partnership property (including money), or receives other partnership property (including money) in exchange for all or a part of an interest in partnership section 751 property, such transaction shall be considered as a sale or exchange of such property between the distributee and the partnership (as constituted after the distribution). Consequently, section 751(b) of the Code applies to that part of the distribution to a partner that consists of the non-pro rata distribution of the partnership section 751 property in exchange for other property, or the non-pro rata distribution of other partnership property in exchange for section 751 property.

In *Yourman v. United States*, 277 F. Supp. 818 (S.D. Calif. 1967), the court held that section 751 of the Code applied to a non-pro rata distribution of section 751 property of a partnership even though the partnership did not continue in existence after the distribution.

Accordingly in the case of a two person partnership, to the extent that a partner either receives section 751 property in exchange for relinquishing any part of such partner's interest in other property, or receives other property in exchange for relinquishing any part of the interest in section 751 property, the distribution is treated as a sale or exchange of such properties between the distributee partner and the partnership (as constituted after the distribution), even though after the distribution the partnership consists of a single individual.

For example, the non-pro rata distribution by a two person partnership of section 751 property to its partners, A and B, as part of a distribution resulting in a complete liquidation of the partnership, can be viewed in two ways, both of which result in the same tax consequences to each party to the transaction. In the non-pro rata distribution, partner A receives more partnership section 751 property than A's underlying interest in such property, while partner B receives more partnership other property than B's interest in such property. Partner A may be treated as the distributee partner who has exchanged part of an interest in partnership property other than section 751 property with the partnership as constituted after the distribution (partner *B*) for section 751 property. Partner *A* would be treated as realizing gain or loss on a sale or exchange of the property other than section 751 property, and the partnership as constituted after the distribution would realize ordinary income or loss on the exchange of the section 751 property.

Partner *B* may be treated as the distributee partner who has exchanged part of an interest in the partnership section 751 property with the partnership as constituted after the distribution (partner *A*) for other property. Partner *B* would be treated as realizing ordinary income or loss on the exchange of the section 751 property, and the partnership as constituted after the distribution would realize gain or loss on a sale or exchange of the other property. However, regardless of which partner is considered to be the distributee and which is considered to be the remaining partner, the Federal income tax consequences are the same to each partner.

Revenue Ruling 84-102
1984-2 CB 119

ISSUE

What are the consequences to the partners under section 751(b) of the Internal Revenue Code when a new partner joins the partnership under the circumstances described below?

FACTS

A, B, and C were equal partners in partnership P. At the time of the transaction described below, the value of each partner's interest was 25*x* dollars. *D* acquired a 25 percent interest in P by contributing 25*x* dollars to P. Prior to *D*'s contribution, the liabilities of P totaled 100*x* dollars, and each partner's share of the liabilities was approximately 33.3*x* dollars. In addition, the unrealized receivables of P (as defined in section 751(c) of the Code) were 40*x* dollars, and each partner's share of the unrealized receivables was approximately 13.3*x* dollars. After the contribution by D, each partner's share of the liabilities of P was 25*x* dollars; A, B, and C's share of P's liabilities each decreased by approximately 8.3*x* dollars. Furthermore, each partner's share of *P*'s unrealized receivables was 10*x* dollars; A, B, and C's share of the unrealized receivables each decreased by approximately 3.3*x* dollars.

LAW AND ANALYSIS

Section 721(a) of the Internal Revenue Code provides that no gain or loss shall be recognized to a partnership or to any of its partners in the case of a contribution of property to the partnership in exchange for an interest in the partnership.

Section 722 of the Code provides that the basis of an interest in a partnership acquired by a contribution of property, including money, to the partnership shall be the amount of such money and the adjusted basis of such property to the contributing partner.

Section 752(a) of the Code provides that any increase in a partner's share of the liabilities of a partnership shall be considered as a contribution of money by such partner to the partnership.

Section 752(b) of the Code provides that any decrease in a partner's share of the liabilities of a partnership shall be considered as a distribution of money to the partner by the partnership.

Pursuant to sections 733 and 731(a)(1) of the Code, a distribution of money by a partnership to a partner results in a reduction of the partner's basis in the partnership interest and, to the extent the distribution exceeds basis, capital gain to the partner. However, section 731(c) provides that section 731 shall not apply to the extent otherwise provided by section 751. See also sections 1.731-1(a)(1) and 1.751-1(b) of the Income Tax Regulations.

Section 751(b)(1)(B) of the Code provides that, to the extent a partner receives a distribution of partnership property (including money) other than property described in section 751(a)(1) or (2) in exchange for all or part of the partner's interest in partnership property described in section 751(a)(1) or (2), such transaction shall be considered a sale or exchange of such property between the distributee partner and the partnership. Section 751(a)(1) of the Code refers to the "unrealized receivables" of a partnership as defined in section 751(c) of the Code.

In the instant case, A, B, and C are each treated as having received a cash distribution from P of $8.3x$ dollars in accordance with section 752(b) of the Code. Of this amount, $3.3x$ dollars is treated under sections 731(c) and 751(b)(1)(B) as being received by each partner in exchange for the interest in unrealized receivables given up. The remaining $5x$ dollars is treated in accordance with section 731(a) of the Code.

Although D has a $10x$ dollar interest in the unrealized receivables of P upon becoming a partner, section 751(b) of the Code has no application with respect to D. There is no actual or deemed distribution of property from P to D as required by 751(b). Further, D has an "increased" interest in the unrealized receivables of P as a result of becoming a partner. Any distribution of property (other than property described in section 751(a)(1) or (2)) from P to D would have to result in a decreased interest in the unrealized receivables for 751(b)(1)(B) to apply.

HOLDING

The tax consequences to D of becoming a partner are determined under sections 721, 722 and 752(a) of the Code. D is treated as having contributed $50x$ dollars, the actual contribution of $25x$ dollars plus the deemed contribution of $25x$ dollars under section 752(a), in exchange for the partnership interest. D's basis in the partnership interest is $50x$ dollars in accordance with section 722 of the Code. Section 751(b) does not apply to new partner D because there is no actual or deemed distribution of property from P to D.

Partners A, B, and C are each treated as having received a distribution of $8.3x$ dollars under section 752(b) of the Code. Of this amount, $3.3x$ dollars is treated under section 751(b)(1)(B) as being received by each partner in exchange for the interest in unrealized receivables given up.

Notice 2006-14
2006-1 CB 498

Section 1. PURPOSE

This notice invites public comments on certain distributions treated as sales or exchanges under § 751(b) of the Internal Revenue Code.

Section 2. BACKGROUND

Section 751 was enacted to prevent the conversion of ordinary income into capital gain and the shifting of ordinary income among partners. . . . Section 751(a) provides for recharacterization of capital gain or loss when an interest in a partnership is sold or exchanged to the extent of the selling partner's share of unrealized receivables and inventory items of the partnership. Section 751(b) overrides the nonrecognition scheme of § 731 for certain current and liquidating partnership distributions that alter a partner's share of unrealized receivables and substantially appreciated inventory items (disproportionate distributions). . . .

The legislative history of § 751 demonstrates that Congress was primarily concerned with unrealized appreciation in unrealized receivables and inventory items of a partnership.

> The provisions relating to unrealized receivables and appreciated inventory items are necessary to prevent the use of the partnership as a device for obtaining capital-gain treatment on fees or other rights to income and on appreciated inventory. Amounts attributable to such rights would be treated as ordinary income if realized in normal course by the partnership. The sale of a partnership interest or distributions to partners should not be permitted to change the character of this income. *The statutory treatment proposed, in general, regards the income rights as severable from the partnership interest and as subject to the same tax consequences which would be accorded an individual entrepreneur.*

S. Rep. No. 1622, at 99 (1954) . . . (emphasis added).

The current Regulations under § 751(b) require the identification of two classes of assets: (1) hot assets (unrealized receivables as defined in § 751(c) and substantially appreciated inventory as defined in § 751(b)(3) and (d)); and (2) cold assets (assets other than unrealized receivables and substantially appreciated inventory). In computing the distributee partner's income under § 751(b), the current regulations provide that the distributee partner's share of the partnership's hot assets and cold assets before and after the distribution must be compared. For purposes of this comparison, each partner's share of the partnership's hot and cold assets is determined by reference to the gross value of the assets. If the distribution results in an exchange of all or a portion of the distributee partner's share of one class of assets (relinquished assets) for assets in the other class (acquired assets), it is necessary to construct a deemed exchange by identifying which relinquished assets are treated as exchanged for which acquired assets.

For example, if a partner receives more than the partner's share of the partnership's hot assets in a distribution, that partner is treated as exchanging a portion of the partner's interest in certain cold assets of the partnership for the other partners' shares of the acquired hot assets. In order to accomplish the exchange, the distributee partner is treated as (1) receiving the relinquished assets (the cold assets) in a non-liquidating distribution and (2) engaging in a taxable exchange (with the partnership) of those assets for the acquired assets (the hot assets). Both the distributee partner and the other partners may recognize income or loss on the exchange. The distributee partner and the partnership then hold the exchanged assets (or portions thereof) with a cost basis under § 1012. The rest of the actual distribution (the part that is not subject to § 751(b)) is characterized under the general rules for partnership distributions prescribed in §§ 731 through 736.

The current Regulations under § 751(b) were published in 1956 and have not been amended to reflect significant changes in subchapter K and in the operations of contemporary partnerships. Moreover, the current § 751(b) Regulations have been widely criticized as being extraordinarily complex and burdensome and as not achieving the objectives of the statute. As a result, a distribution may reduce a partner's pro rata share of the unrealized appreciation in the partnership's hot assets without triggering § 751(b), and a distribution can trigger § 751(b) even if the partner's pro rata share of the unrealized appreciation is not reduced.

The Treasury Department and the Service are considering several possible methods, discussed below, for addressing the issues associated with the current § 751(b) Regulations.

Section 3. DISCUSSION

(a) *Determining the partners' shares of partnership property*

The current Regulations under § 751(b) provide little guidance on how each partner's share of partnership property is determined. Two economic rights are inherent in most partnership interests: a right to partnership capital, and a right to partnership profits and losses. A partner may have a different interest in each of these rights, and those interests may vary over time. Moreover, a partner's share of unrealized partnership items may be affected by both the economic arrangement of the partners and certain requirements of subchapter K, such as § 704(c).

The legislative history of § 751(b) emphasizes "income rights" of the partners and suggests that these rights may be treated as severable and subject to the same tax consequences as those of an individual entrepreneur. . . . Consistent with this legislative history, in order to determine whether a distribution may be subject to § 751(b), commentators have suggested that new Regulations could require partnerships and their partners to compare the amounts of ordinary income that would be recognized by the partners if the partnership's hot assets (including distributed assets) were sold or exchanged for fair market value in a taxable transaction both before and after the distribution (hypothetical sale approach). If the amount of ordinary income that would be allocated to any partner (including the distributee) as a result of such a sale or exchange is reduced as a result of a distribution from the partnership, an analysis under § 751(b) would be required. The hypothetical sale approach, combined with the application of § 704(c) principles, could provide rules that achieve the objective of the statute in a less burdensome manner.

Under § 704(c), if partnership property is sold or exchanged, the built-in gain or loss in contributed or revalued partnership property must be allocated to the contributing or appropriate historic partner (§ 704(c) principles). See § 704(c)(1)(A) and §§ 1.704-1(b)(4)(i), 1.704-3(a)(2), and 1.704-3(a)(6). As a result of the application of § 704(c) principles, there can be layers of appreciation in partnership assets (due to successive revaluations), each of which may be allocable separately. Moreover, distributed § 704(c) property and § 704(c) property with a substantial built-in loss must be analyzed separately to determine each partner's appropriate share of the unrealized gain or loss. See, e.g., § 704(c)(1)(B) and (C). As a result, § 704(c) generally operates to preserve each partner's share of the built-in appreciation and depreciation in partnership assets. If the Regulations under § 751(b) were amended to specify that § 704(c) principles are taken into account for purposes of determining whether a partner's share of partnership hot assets has been altered by a distribution, significantly fewer distributions would trigger § 751(b).

Example 1. Assume that A, B, and C each contribute $120 to partnership ABC. ABC purchases land for $210, which appreciates in value to $300. At a time when the partnership also has $90 of zero-basis unrealized receivables and cash of $150, ABC distributes $90 to C, reducing C's interest in ABC from 1/3 to 1/5. If, immediately before the distribution, the partnership's assets are revalued and the partners' capital accounts are increased to reflect each partner's share of the unrealized appreciation in the partnership's assets, C's entire pre-distribution share of the partnership's unrealized income in the accounts receivable (1/3 of $90, or $30) is preserved in C's capital account after the distribution. ABC will have the following post-distribution balance sheet (before the application of § 751(b)):

Assets	Basis	Value	Capital	Basis	Value
Cash	$ 60	$ 60	A	$120	$180
Unrealized Receivables	0	90	B	120	180
Land	210	300	C	30	90
Total	$270	$450		$270	$450

If § 704(c) principles were applicable for purposes of § 751(b), the distribution to C would not trigger § 751(b), as C's pre-distribution share of the unrealized income in the receivables ($30) is fully preserved in its capital account after the distribution. Section 704(c) principles would require the partnership to allocate that share of appreciation to C when it is recognized.

Special rules may be necessary to address distributions of hot assets to a partner where the adjusted basis of the distributed assets (and the unrealized appreciation in those assets) is different in the hands of the distributee partner than it was in the hands of the partnership. Under §§ 732(a)(2) and (b), the adjusted basis of distributed hot assets is reduced (and the unrealized appreciation in those hot assets is increased) if the distributee partner's basis in its partnership interest is insufficient to absorb the partnership's adjusted basis in the distributed hot asset. If the partnership has a § 754 election in effect at the time of the distribution, § 734(b)(1)(B) permits the partnership to increase the adjusted basis of the partnership's retained hot assets to the extent of the reduction in the basis of the distributed hot assets under §§ 732(a)(2) or (b). Under these circumstances, the hot asset appreciation remaining in the partnership is reduced. As such, one of the issues raised by use of a hypothetical sale to measure changes in a partner's interest in hot asset appreciation is the extent to which basis adjustments under §§ 732 and 734(b) should be taken into account.

Moreover, a hypothetical sale at any one point in time does not take into account future allocations that are planned or expected. For example, a partner's allocations with respect to a particular asset may vary over time. Measuring income or loss on a hypothetical sale of that asset at a particular time may not accurately reflect that partner's income rights with respect to that asset over the life of the partnership.

Once it is determined that a partner's share of the income rights in the partnership's hot assets has been reduced by a distribution, the tax consequences of the distribution under § 751(b) must be determined.

(b) *Determining the tax consequences of disproportionate distributions*

The current § 751(b) Regulations impose a complex deemed distribution/exchange approach for determining the tax consequences of a disproportionate distribution. One possible way to simplify this determination would be to treat a disproportionate distribution as triggering a taxable sale of the partners' shares of relinquished hot assets to the partnership immediately before the distribution (hot asset sale approach). The hot asset sale approach would apply §751(b) in a fully aggregate manner that is arguably consistent with its legislative history (under which each partner's tax treatment should be that of an individual entrepreneur).

This approach could be combined with the hypothetical sale approach. Thus, new Regulations could provide that § 751(b) applies if any partner's share of the net unrealized appreciation in hot assets of the partnership is reduced as a result of a distribution from the partnership. Under the hot asset sale approach, for any partner whose share of hot assets is reduced (selling partner), whether or not the selling partner is the distributee, the selling partner would be treated as receiving the relinquished hot assets in a deemed distribution and selling to the partnership the relinquished share of the hot assets immediately before the actual distribution. The selling partner would recognize ordinary income from the deemed sale, and the partner's basis in the partnership interest and the partner's capital account would be adjusted to reflect the consideration treated as contributed to the partnership. The assets deemed sold to the partnership would have a cost basis under § 1012. Under the hot asset sale approach, there would be no deemed exchange for cold assets, thereby eliminating the need to identify cold assets to be exchanged and to construct a deemed distribution of those assets.

The hot asset sale approach can be straightforward if the distributee partner's share of hot asset appreciation is reduced by the distribution. In this situation, the partnership would be treated as distributing the relinquished share of hot assets to the distributee who sells the hot assets back to the partnership, recognizing ordinary income, with appropriate adjustments to the distributee partner's basis in the partnership interest and capital account. The asset deemed sold would take a cost basis, and the distribution would be governed by §§ 731 through 736.

Example 2. Assume A, B and C are each 1/3 partners in a partnership that holds one hot asset and one cold asset, each with a basis of $0 and a fair market value of $150. A, B, and C each have an adjusted basis in the partnership interest of $0, and a $50 share of hot asset appreciation. A is fully redeemed by a distribution of 2/3 of the cold asset ($100). Immediately before the distribution, the partnership's assets are revalued and the partners' capital accounts are increased to $100 to reflect each partner's share of the unrealized appreciation in the partnership's assets. Because the entire $150 of hot asset appreciation remains in the partnership after the distribution, A's share of that appreciation has been reduced by $50. Under the hot asset sale approach, PRS would be treated as distributing the relinquished share of the hot asset ($50) to A and then purchasing that share for $50. A would recognize income of $50 and would be treated as contributing the $50 to PRS. A's basis in the partnership interest would increase to $50 and A's capital account would be restored to $100. The portion of the hot asset deemed sold would take a cost basis, increasing the partnership's basis in the hot asset to $50.

In this example, because A's basis in its partnership interest is $50, the basis of the distributed cold asset would be increased under § 732(b) to $50 in A's hands. The cold asset remaining in the partnership has a $0 basis and would not be subject to a basis reduction under § 734(b) even if the partnership had a § 754 election in effect. In these circumstances, $50 of capital gain is potentially eliminated from the system, however.

The hot asset sale approach also raises certain complications where the distributee partner has insufficient basis in its partnership interest to absorb the partnership's adjusted basis in the distributed hot assets. This can lead to results inconsistent with the intent of § 751(b).

Example 3. Assume the same facts as Example 2, except that instead of distributing 2/3 of the cold asset to A, the partnership fully redeems A by a distribution of 2/3 of the hot asset ($100). Because only $50 of hot asset appreciation remains in the partnership after the distribution, B's and C's shares of that appreciation have been reduced by $25 each. Under the hot asset sale approach, PRS would be deemed to distribute the relinquished share of the hot asset ($50) equally to B and C and each would be treated as selling $25 worth of the hot asset to the partnership. B and C would each recognize $25 of ordinary income and would be treated as contributing $25 to the partnership. The portion of the hot asset deemed sold would take a cost basis, increasing the partnership's basis in the distributed portion of the distributed hot asset to $50. Because A's basis in its partnership interest is $0, however, the basis of the distributed hot asset would be reduced under § 732(b) to $0 in A's hands. If the partnership had a § 754 election in effect, the partnership would increase the basis of the retained hot asset under § 734(b) by $50. After the distribution, A's share of unrealized income in hot assets would still be $100, and B and C, who each recognized $25 of ordinary income, would recognize no additional ordinary income.

Commentators have suggested that, in these situations, it may be appropriate to permit or require the distributee partner to recognize capital gain to the extent the adjusted basis of the distributed hot assets exceeds that partner's basis in the partnership interest. In Example 3, A could elect, or be required, to recognize capital gain equal to the amount by which the adjusted basis of the distributed hot assets exceeds that partner's basis in the partnership interest ($50), thereby increasing A's basis to $50. The distributed hot asset would take a $50 basis in A's hands under § 732(b), and no § 734(b) adjustment would be made to the retained hot asset. If A recognizes capital gain on the distribution, future Regulations could permit an equivalent increase to the basis of the partnership's retained cold assets.

Section 4. REQUEST FOR COMMENTS

The Treasury Department and the Service are conducting a study of the current § 751(b) Regulations and are considering alternative approaches to achieving the purpose of the statute that would provide greater simplicity. For example, it may be possible to provide safe harbor methods for calculating the share of ordinary income or capital gain that should be recognized as a result of a disproportionate distribution that may reduce some administrative burden but still serve the purpose of the statute. In this regard, the Treasury Department and the Service request comments on the approaches discussed in this Notice (as well as other possible approaches) to determining a partner's share of hot assets and to prescribing the tax consequences of a disproportionate distribution. Comments are requested concerning the following issues:

A. For purposes of determining each partner's share of partnership assets before and after a distribution that may be subject to § 751(b),

(1) Whether the hypothetical sale approach (combined with the application of § 704(c) principles) for determining each partner's share of partnership assets provides an accurate and appropriate measure for purposes of § 751(b). In particular,

a. Whether special rules would be necessary to address situations in which the distributee partner's interest in unrealized appreciation in hot assets prior to the distribution exceeds the partner's interest in partnership capital after the distribution;

b. Whether the hypothetical sale approach should be modified to take into account changes in allocations that are planned or may occur in the future or changes in the partner's interest in anticipated future appreciation and depreciation in partnership assets;

c. The extent to which Regulations adopting the hypothetical sale approach should take into account the distributee partner's basis in the partnership interest and basis adjustments under §§ 734(b) and 743(b), including basis adjustments resulting from the distribution;

d. Whether the partners' shares of partnership liabilities should be considered in determining the partners' shares of partnership assets, and how the rules of § 752 should be coordinated with those of § 751(b).

(2) Whether § 751(b) should be limited to transactions that change the partners' shares of unrealized appreciation in hot assets or should also apply to transactions that change the partners' shares of unrealized depreciation in hot assets.

(3) Whether other approaches to determining a partner's share of partnership hot and cold assets should be considered.

B. For purposes of simplifying the tax consequences of a distribution that is subject to § 751(b), whether the hot asset sale approach is an appropriate method of applying § 751(b) or whether other approaches should be considered. Comments are specifically requested on the following:

(1) Whether the Regulations should provide a simple safe harbor that approximates the appropriate taxation of a disproportionate distribution and, if so, the appropriate parameters and availability of such a safe harbor.

(2) Whether the current § 751(b) Regulations should be generally retained or retained in combination with a safe harbor, or whether the current § 751(b) Regulations should be completely revised to adopt a new paradigm such as the hot asset sale approach.

(3) Whether mandatory or elective capital gain recognition should be included in the hot asset sale approach. . . .

CHAPTER 14

Death or Retirement of a Partner—Payments in Liquidation of the Interest of a Retired Partner

PROBLEM AREA 14

INTRODUCTION

Upon first encounter with § 736, it appears to be one of the more significant provisions of Subchapter K, applicable to all payments in liquidation of a partnership interest. However, appearances can be deceiving. Subsequent to its amendment in 1993, § 736 is a modest provision, which is of practical interest mainly to personal-services businesses such as law and accounting firms.

Today, § 736 functions primarily to direct traffic. If the interest of a retiring partner or of his successor by reason of death is retired by complete liquidation, § 736 dictates the tax consequences to the recipient and to the partnership, albeit in some cases with reference to other sections of the Code previously considered. Section 736 is not applicable to a sale or exchange of a partnership interest or to a partial liquidation of a partner's interest or to a current distribution.

Where applicable, § 736 forces a bifurcation of the distribution into two categories—§ 736(b) payments, those made for a partner's interest in partnership property, and § 736(a) payments, all other payments made by the partnership. Section 736 applies only to liquidating distributions, and therefore not to the proceeds of the sale or exchange of a partnership interest, to payments in partial liquidation of a partner's interest, or to current distributions.

The tax treatment of § 736(b) payments has been discussed previously, as such payments are subject to the general rules of §§ 731 and 751(b). Section 736(a) payments fall into either of two categories—a guaranteed payment or a distributive share of partnership income—depending upon whether they are computed with regard to partnership income. Once classified, they are taxed and characterized according to the general rules governing guaranteed payments and distributive shares. Thus, both the distributee and the partnership may be affected by the classification of the payments, since § 736(a) treatment frequently generates ordinary income to the recipient and a deduction (or its equivalent) to the partnership, while § 736(b) often results in capital characterization to the partner and nondeductibility to the partnership.

As § 736 payments may span a number of years, the Regulations provide numerous timing and allocation rules for determining the taxable year in which the § 736(a) or § 736(b) payments are deemed received by the distributee partner.

Section 736 would be a significant provision indeed if it provided a vehicle for the diversion of liquidating distributions that ordinarily would be governed by the rules of §§ 731 and 751(b) into the rules that govern guaranteed payments and partners' distributive shares. This would be particularly true if the amount so diverted could be chosen at the behest of the taxpayer, so that some significant amount of a liquidating distribution electively could be either (i) taxable to the retiring partner and deductible (or its equivalent) by the partnership or (ii) non-taxable to both the retiring partner and the partnership. Indeed, this is precisely what § 736 did prior to its 1993 amendment with respect to payments for goodwill.

In that year, however, Congressional concern with the operation of § 736 led to the addition of § 736(b)(3) to the Code. With respect to payments for goodwill, the electivity formerly provided by § 736 is limited by this amendment to retirement payments to a general partner of a partnership for which capital is not a material income-producing factor. As acknowledged in the legislative history, such partnerships (such as law and accounting firms) seldom make retirement payments based on their partners' shares of goodwill. Thus, electivity is now limited to partnerships that generally will not make use of it.

Since 1993, many states have enacted statutes authorizing the practice of law and other professions through limited liability partnerships and other vehicles offering liability protection to their partners. The existence of limited liability presents the question of whether such individuals are "general partners" within the meaning of § 736(b)(3), to whom deductible retirement payments may be made. Consistent with the purpose of § 736 to distinguish deductible payments of compensation (governed by § 736(a)) from non-deductible payments in liquidation of a partner's interest (governed by § 736(b)), it appears that such individuals should be treated as "general partners" if they actively participate in the partnership's business, irrespective of whether they are liable for the partnership's debts. To date, however, no case or Ruling has confirmed this result.

PROBLEM 14

QUESTIONS

1. A, B, C, and D are members of ABCD, a calendar-year, cash-method, general partnership. Each has a one-fourth interest in capital, profits, and losses, which each received on an initial contribution of $20,000 to ABCD. Unless otherwise stated, assume that the partnership does not revalue its property in connection with partner retirements and has not made a § 754 election. ABCD's balance sheet is as follows:

ABCD Balance Sheet

	Adjusted Basis	Fair Market Value
Assets		
Cash	$30,000	$ 30,000
Accounts Receivable	0	20,000
Real Property	58,000	62,000
Total	$88,000	$112,000
Liabilities and Capital		
Liabilities		
Mortgage (recourse)	$ 8,000	$ 8,000
Capital Accounts		
A	20,000	26,000
B	20,000	26,000
C	20,000	26,000
D	20,000	26,000
Total	$88,000	$112,000

A retires and, pursuant to the partnership agreement, receives a lump-sum payment of $30,000 in complete liquidation of his partnership interest.

a. What are the tax consequences to A and to ABCD if capital is a material income-producing factor for ABCD?

b. What are the tax consequences to A and to ABCD if capital is not a material income-producing factor for ABCD?

c. Same as b. above, except that the partnership agreement provides that all payments in excess of the fair market value of the retiring partner's share of partnership assets are a "premium."

d. Same as b. above, except that the partnership agreement provides that all payments in excess of the fair market value of the retiring partner's share of partnership assets are either a guaranteed payment or goodwill.

e. Same as b. above, except that the partnership agreement provides that all payments in excess of the fair market value of the retiring partner's share of partnership assets are considered received in exchange for goodwill.

f. Same as b. above, except that the partnership agreement provides that the partnership will revalue its property (including intangible assets such as goodwill) and adjust the capital accounts accordingly in connection with the retirement of any partner. Such revaluation causes goodwill in the amount of $16,000 to be placed on the partnership's books immediately prior to A's retirement.

g. Same as b. above, except that the partnership agreement provides that A will receive a lump-sum distribution of $25,000, plus 20 percent of the gross income of ABCD for the year. ABCD's gross income for the year, irrespective of any payments to A, is $80,000.

h. Same as a. above, except that ABCD has no goodwill.

i. Same as b. above, except that ABCD has no goodwill.

j. Same as a. above, except that ABCD has made a § 754 election.

k. Same as b. above, except that ABCD has made a § 754 election.

2. Assume that the ABCD partnership in question 1. above is established as a limited liability partnership (LLP) under state law, and that ABCD is a service partnership for which capital is not a material income-producing factor. ABCD's balance sheet is the same as in question 1. above and its agreement does not provide for the revaluation of partnership property in connection with partner retirements. A retires on December 31, Year 1, and pursuant to the partnership agreement receives a lump-sum payment of $21,000 on that date. A is also entitled to receive a cash payment of $1,000 on December 31 in each of Years 2 through 6, representing his share of the value of ABCD's accounts receivable on A's retirement date. These deferred payments bear interest at five percent. What are the tax consequences to A and to ABCD?

3. X, Y, and Z are members of the XYZ general partnership, a calendar-year, cash-method partnership. XYZ is a service partnership for which capital is not a material income-producing factor. X, Y, and Z each has a one-third interest in capital, profits, and losses. XYZ's balance sheet as of December 31, Year 1 is as follows:

Assets	Adjusted Basis	Fair Market Value
Cash	$12,000	$12,000
Equipment	48,000	15,000
Accounts Receivable	0	15,000
Total	$60,000	$42,000

	Adjusted Basis	Fair Market Value
Liabilities and Capital		
Liabilities		
Mortgage (recourse)	$15,000	$15,000
Capital Accounts		
X	15,000	9,000
Y	15,000	9,000
Z	15,000	9,000
Total Liabilities and Capital	$60,000	$42,000

a. Y retires from the partnership as of December 31, Year 1. Under the terms of the partnership agreement, Y receives a payment of $5,000 on December 31, Year 1 and is entitled to 20 percent of the partnership's net income for each of the next two years. In Year 2, net income is $3,000; in Year 3, net income is $17,000 (irrespective of any distributions to Y). What are the tax consequences to the parties?

b. (1) Same as a. above, except that the partnership agreement provides that after the initial $5,000 payment on December 31, Year 1, Y is entitled to the greater of $3,000 or 20 percent of the partnership's net income for each of the next two years.

(2) In Year 2, due to a poor year, the partnership experiences a cash-flow problem. The partnership pays Y only $1,000 with a promise to make up the difference in Year 3. In Year 3, the partnership pays $5,400 to Y.

c. Same as a. above, except that the partners wish to allocate two-thirds of each payment to § 736(b) payments and one-third to § 736(a) payments until such time as Y has received all the § 736(b) payments to which she is entitled. Thereafter, all payments are to be § 736(a) payments.

MATERIALS

The Revenue Reconciliation Act of 1993, P.L. No. 103-66, § 13262(a), 107 Stat. 541 (1993)

Sec. 13262. Treatment of Certain Payments to Retired or Deceased Partner.
(a) SECTION 736(B) NOT TO APPLY IN CERTAIN CASES. – Subsection (b) of section 736 (relating to payments for interest in partnership) is amended by adding at the end thereof the following new paragraph:
   "(3) LIMITATION ON APPLICATION OF PARAGRAPH (2). – Paragraph (2) shall apply only if –
   "(A) capital is not a material income-producing factor for the partnership, and
   "(B) the retiring or deceased partner was a general partner in the partnership."

H.R. Rep. No. 103-111, 103d Cong., 1st Sess. 781-83 (1993)

Present Law

Payments for purchase of goodwill and accounts receivable. A current deduction generally is not allowed for a capital expenditure (i.e., and expenditure that yields benefits beyond the current taxable year). The cost of goodwill acquired in connection with the assets of a going concern normally is a capital expenditure, as is the cost of acquiring accounts receivable. The cost of acquiring goodwill is recovered only when the goodwill is disposed of, while the cost of acquiring accounts receivable is taken into account only when the receivable is disposed of or becomes worthless.

Payments made in liquidation of partnership interest. The tax treatment of a payment made in liquidation of the interest of a retiring or deceased partner depends upon whether the payment is made in exchange for the partner's interest in partnership property. A liquidating payment made in exchange for such property is treated as a distribution by the partnership (sec. 736(b)). Such distribution generally results in gain to the retiring partner only to the extent that the cash distributed exceeds such partner's adjusted basis in the partnership interest.

A liquidating payment not made in exchange for the partner's interest in partnership property receives either of two possible treatments. If the amount of the payment is determined without reference to partnership income, it is treated as a guaranteed payment and is generally deductible (sec. 736(a)(2)). If the amount of payment is determined by reference to partnership income, the payment is treated as a distributive share of partnership income, thereby reducing the distributive shares of other partners (which is equivalent to a deduction) (sec. 736(a)(1)).

A special rule treats amounts paid for goodwill of the partnership (except to the extent provided in the partnership agreement) and unrealized receivables as not made in exchange for an interest in partnership property (sec. 736(b)(2)(B)). Thus, such amounts may be deductible. . . .

Reasons for Change

In general. By treating a payment for unstated goodwill and unrealized receivables as a guaranteed payment or distributive share, present law in effect permits a deduction for an amount that would otherwise constitute a capital expenditure. This treatment does not measure partnership income properly. It also threatens to erode the rule requiring capitalization of such payments generally. . . .

Section 736 was intended to simplify the taxation of payments in liquidation. Instead, it has created confusion as to whether a particular payment is a payment in liquidation or is made pursuant to a sale of the partnership interest to the continuing partners. The proposal reduces this confusion by eliminating a primary difference between sales and liquidations.

The special treatment of goodwill was apparently predicated on the assumption that the adverse positions of the taxpayers will result in a stated price equal to the true value of the goodwill. That assumption is false. If the value of the preferential rate (if any) and the income deflection are not equal, the stated goodwill and total retirement payments will likely be set so as to maximize the combined tax savings for both retiring and continuing partners.

It is recognized, however, that general partners in service partnerships do not ordinarily value goodwill in liquidating partners. Accordingly, such partners may continue to receive the special rule of present law. . . .

Explanation of Provision

In general. The bill generally repeals the special treatment of liquidation payments made for goodwill and unrealized receivables. Thus, such payments would be treated as made in exchange for the partner's interest in partnership property, and not as a distributive share or guaranteed payment that could give rise to a deduction or its equivalent. The bill does not change present law with respect to payments made to a general partner in a partnership in which capital is not a material income-producing factor. The determination of whether capital is a material income-producing factor would be made under principles of present and prior law. For purposes of this provision, capital is not a material income-producing factor where substantially all the gross income of the business consists of fees, commissions, or other compensation for personal services performed by an individual. The practice of his or her profession by a doctor, dentist, lawyer, architect, or accountant will not, as such, be treated as a trade or business in which capital is a material income-producing factor even though the practitioner may have a substantial capital investment in professional equipment or in the physical plant constituting the office from which such individual conducts his or her practice so long as such capital investment is merely incidental to such professional practice. In addition, the bill does not affect the deductibility of compensation paid to a retiring partner for past services. . . .

CHAPTER 15

Adjustment to the Bases of Partnership Assets— Adjustments When Partnership Interests Are Transferred

PROBLEM AREA 15

INTRODUCTION

Many Code provisions treat the partnership as an entity separate and distinct from its members. For example, when a partner contributes property to a partnership, he is considered to have contributed the entire property to an entity, the partnership, which is considered to become the owner of that property. The partner no longer has a direct interest in any part of the contributed asset, and thus has no tax basis in it. Instead, the partnership takes a basis in the asset that it now owns (the "inside basis"), and the partner takes a basis in the partner's interest in the partnership (the "outside basis").

Upon formation of a partnership, the aggregate of the partners' bases in their partnership interests will equal the aggregate of the partnership's bases in its assets due to the operation of §§ 722, 723, and 752. However, following the sale or exchange of a partnership interest, inside and outside basis generally will no longer run in tandem. The purchaser of the interest is paying fair market value for the interest, which becomes the purchaser's outside basis under § 742, but § 743(a) prohibits corresponding adjustments to the basis of any partnership property. Upon the subsequent disposition by the partnership of an asset, the purchaser of the partnership interest will be required to recognize his share of the pre-acquisition gain or loss with respect to the asset, even though he paid full and adequate consideration for the interest. While ultimately (assuming no further fluctuation in the value of the partnership's assets) any gain or loss will be offset by an equivalent amount of loss or gain upon the sale or liquidation of the partnership interest, mismatches of timing and character will occur.

In order to prevent such mismatching, § 743(b) provides for an adjustment (for the benefit of the purchaser of the partnership interest only) to the basis of the assets of the partnership to reflect the disparity between inside and outside basis. Typically, a prerequisite to such treatment is a partnership election under § 754 which is binding for all subsequent transfers of partnership interests and distributions of partnership assets. The election may be revoked with the consent of the Service. Ignoring the additional recordkeeping burden, it might be expected that a partnership would make a § 754 election if its assets were appreciated (thereby reducing the gain taken into account by transferees on the sale of partnership assets or affording them greater depreciation or amortization), but would avoid making the election if its assets were depreciated (thereby preserving a larger tax loss for transferees on the sale of partnership assets or unreduced depreciation or amortization deductions). Concerned with this tax-planning opportunity, Congress in 2004 amended § 743(b) to make its application mandatory in settings in which the partnership possesses a "substantial built-in loss," *i.e.*, where the aggregate basis of the partnership's property exceeds its value by more than $250,000.

The amount of the § 743(b) special basis adjustment is the difference between the transferee's basis for the partnership interest and the transferee's share of the basis of the partnership's property. Under the Regulations, the transferee's share of the basis of the partnership's assets is the sum of the transferee's share of the partnership's liabilities and "previously taxed capital." The latter term refers to the portion of the basis of the partnership's assets that has been funded by the partners' capital. The transferee's share of this amount is the cash that the transferee would receive if the partnership sold all of its assets at their fair market values and liquidated, decreased by the amount of gain (or increased by the amount of loss) that the transferee would be allocated as a result of such a sale.

Under § 743(c), the allocation rules of § 755 control the determination of the special basis adjustment for each particular partnership asset. Section 755 provides that the overall adjustment is allocated between two classes of assets, (i) capital and §1231 assets and (ii) all other assets, based on relative appreciation or depreciation. Thereafter, a similar allocation is made within each class.

The special basis adjustment comes into play for the benefit (or detriment) of the purchasing partner in determining the partner's share of depreciation, amortization, and gain or loss on the disposition of partnership assets. It can also affect the determination of the basis of assets upon their distribution or by the partnership. Thus, a partner receiving a current distribution of property from a partnership increases (or decreases) the basis of the distributed property by any special basis adjustment the partner may have with respect to the distributed property. A distribution of property to a partner with no special basis adjustment, by contrast, involves no adjustment of the basis of the distributed property, but does require the special basis adjustments of any other partners to be reallocated among the remaining partnership properties.

PROBLEM 15

FACTS

ABC Factory Company is a calendar-year, accrual-method partnership in which each partner has a one-third interest in capital and profits.

A sells his partnership interest to D for $95,000 in cash. Immediately prior to the sale, the balance sheet of the partnership is as follows:

	Adjusted Basis	Fair Market Value
Assets		
Cash	$ 75,000	$ 75,000
Accounts Receivable	30,000	30,000
Inventory	10,000	15,000
Building (assume no recapture potential)	55,000	70,000
Investment Land—Parcel X	40,000	90,000
Investment Land—Parcel Y	10,000	45,000
Total	$220,000	$325,000
Liabilities and Capital		
Liabilities	$ 40,000	$ 40,000
Capital		
A	60,000	95,000
B	60,000	95,000
C	60,000	95,000
Total	$220,000	$325,000

QUESTIONS

1. What are the tax consequences to D if the partnership does not make a § 754 election?

2. Same as question 1. above, except that the partnership makes an election under § 754. What is D's special basis adjustment?

3. Allocate the special basis adjustment determined in question 2. above to the various partnership assets.

4. Same as question 3. above, except that, for purposes of this question only, assume that the building has a fair market value of $30,000 and that Parcel X has a fair market value of $130,000. Assume alternatively that the fair market value of Parcel X remains at $90,000 and the building has a fair market value of $30,000. However, the purchaser, D, still pays $95,000 for the partnership interest in an arm's-length transaction.

5. In questions 2. and 3. above, what are the tax consequences to D if the partnership makes a non-liquidating distribution of Parcel X to D?

6. In questions 2. and 3. above, what are the tax consequences to D if the partnership makes a non-liquidating distribution of Parcel X to B?

MATERIALS

Revenue Ruling 87-115
1987-2 CB 163

ISSUES

Under section 743(b) of the Internal Revenue Code, does a sale of an interest in an upper-tier partnership (*UTP*) result in an adjustment to the basis of the property of a lower-tier partnership (*LTP*) in which *UTP* has an interest if:

(1) both *UTP* and *LTP* have made an election under section 754?

(2) only *UTP* has made the election under section 754?

(3) only *LTP* has made the election under section 754?

FACTS

UTP is a partnership in which *A*, *B*, *C*, and *D* are equal partners. *UTP* is a partnership in which *A*, *B*, *C*, and *D* each contributed 30x dollars of cash to *UTP* upon its formation, and they each have a 30x interest in partnership capital and surplus. *A*'s share of the adjusted basis of partnership property is 30x dollars, the sum of *A*'s interest as a partner in partnership capital and surplus, plus *A*'s share of partnership liabilities (neither *UTP* nor *LTP* have any liabilities). *UTP* is an equal partner in *LTP*, along with *X* and *Y*. *LTP* was formed by *X*, *Y*, and *Z*, who each contributed 110x dollars of cash to *LTP* upon its formation. *UTP* purchased its interest in *LTP* from *Z* for 80x dollars in a taxable year for which *LTP* did not have an election under section 754 in effect. *UTP*, *X*, and *Y* each have a 110x dollar interest in partnership capital and surplus.

UTP has an adjusted basis of 120x dollars in its property as follows: an adjusted basis of 80x dollars in its partnership interest in *LTP* and an adjusted basis of 40x dollars in inventory. *UTP*'s partnership interest in *LTP* has a fair market value of 120x dollars, and *UTP*'s inventory has a fair market value of 80x dollars. *LTP* has only one asset, a capital asset that is not a section 751 asset. *LTP*'s asset has an adjusted basis of 330x dollars and a fair market value of 360x dollars.

In 1985, *A* sold *A*'s entire interest in *UTP* to *E* for 50x dollars.

Situation 1

Both *UTP* and *LTP* have valid section 754 elections in effect.

Situation 2

UTP has a section 754 election in effect, but *LTP* does not.

Situation 3

UTP does not have a section 754 election in effect, but *LTP* does.

LAW AND ANALYSIS

Section 742 of the Code provides that the basis of an interest in a partnership acquired other than by contribution shall be determined under part II of subchapter O of Chapter 1 (sections 1011 through 1015).

Section 1012 of the Code provides, with certain exceptions, that the basis of property shall be the cost of such property.

Section 754 of the Code provides that if a partnership files an election, in accordance with Regulations prescribed by the Secretary, the basis of partnership property shall be adjusted, in the case of a transfer of a partnership interest, in the manner provided in section 743(b). Such election shall apply with respect to all transfers of interests in the partnership during the taxable year with respect to which such election was filed and all subsequent years.

Section 743(a) of the Code provides the general rule that the basis of partnership property shall not be adjusted as the result of a transfer of an interest in a partnership by sale or exchange or on the death of a partner unless the election provided by section 754 is in effect with respect to such partnership.

Section 743(b) of the Code provides that, in the case of a transfer of an interest in a partnership by sale or exchange or upon the death of a partner, a partnership with respect to which the election provided in section 754 is in effect shall (1) increase the adjusted basis of partnership property by the excess of the basis to the transferee partner of such partner's interest in the partnership over the partner's proportionate share of the adjusted basis of partnership property; or (2) decrease the adjusted basis of partnership property by the excess of the transferee partner's proportionate share of the adjusted basis of partnership property over the basis of such partner's interest in the partnership. Section 743(b) further provides that the increase or decrease shall be an adjustment to the basis of partnership property with respect to the transferee partner only. . . .

Section 741 of the Code provides that, except as provided in section 751, the gain or loss on the exchange of an interest in a partnership shall be considered as a gain or loss from the sale of a capital asset.

Rev. Rul. 78-2, 1978-1 C.B. 202, concerns the transfer of an interest in an investment partnership, *X*, which is a partner of an operating partnership, *Y*. The ruling concludes that if elections under section 754 of the Code are in effect for *X* and *Y*, the adjustment to the basis of partnership property under section 743(b) includes (a) an adjustment to *X*'s partnership interest in *Y* and (b) a corresponding basis adjustment to *Y*'s property with respect to *X* and the transferee partner of *X* only.

In essence, if an election under section 754 is not in effect, the partnership is treated as an independent entity, separate from its partners. Thus, absent a section 754 election, even though the transferee receives a cost basis for the acquired partnership interest, the partnership does not adjust the transferee's share of the adjusted basis of partnership property. If, however, an election under section 754 is in effect, the partnership is treated more like an aggregate of its partners, and the transferee's overall basis in the assets of the partnership is generally the same as it would have been had the transferee acquired a direct interest in its share of those assets. . . .

HOLDINGS

Situation 1

Upon the sale of *A*'s partnership interest in *UTP*, the transferee's (*E*'s) share of *UTP*'s adjusted basis in its assets is adjusted by the amount by which the basis in *E*'s partnership interest differs from *E*'s share of *UTP*'s adjusted basis in its assets. In addition, *E*'s share of *LTP*'s adjusted basis in its assets is adjusted by the amount by which *E*'s share of *UTP*'s adjusted basis in *LTP* differs from *E*'s share of the adjusted basis of *LTP*'s property.

Situation 2

Upon the sale of *A*'s partnership interest in *UTP*, *E*'s share of *UTP*'s adjusted basis in its assets is adjusted by the amount by which the basis in *E*'s partnership interest differs from *E*'s share of *UTP*'s adjusted basis in its assets. However, because *LTP* did not make a section 754 election, the transfer does not affect *LTP*'s adjusted basis in its property.

Situation 3

The sale of *A*'s partnership interest in *UTP* does not affect either *UTP*'s adjusted basis in its property or *LTP*'s adjusted basis in its property.

CHAPTER 16

Adjustments to the Bases of Partnership Assets— Adjustments in Connection With Distributions

PROBLEM AREA 16

INTRODUCTION

As discussed in Problem Area 15, the § 743(b) adjustment attempts to ensure that inside and outside basis run in tandem and that a purchaser or other successor in interest of a partnership interest does not realize gain or loss accruing prior to his acquisition and for which he paid, or was considered to have paid, full value. Its companion adjustment, provided by § 734(b), attempts to ensure that the remaining partners in a partnership that has made a distribution of money or property to a partner will recognize neither more nor less gain on the partnership's subsequent dispositions of the remaining assets than they would have had the distribution not taken place. Indeed, § 734(b) achieves this goal in situations where aggregate inside and outside bases are equal prior to the distribution. It is less successful in other situations, an advanced topic taken up in Problem Area 24.

Although the goal of § 734(b) bears a resemblance to that of § 743(b), its effect is not always the same. Section 743(b) has the effect of eliminating disparities between inside and outside basis. Section 734(b), on the other hand, has the effect of preserving the aggregate basis of a partnership's assets, taking into account both the basis of the assets remaining in the partnership and the basis of any of the partnership's assets that are distributed to the partners. Thus, for example, if the basis of a distributed asset is reduced in the hands of the distributee partner by the operation of § 732(a)(2) or § 732(b), § 734(b) requires an increase in the basis of the partnership's remaining assets by an equal amount. If the basis of a distributed asset is increased by the operation of § 732(b), § 734(b) requires a reduction in the basis of the partnership's remaining assets by an equal amount. If aggregate inside basis equals aggregate outside basis prior to the distribution, these § 734(b) adjustments will maintain that equality. If, on the other hand, aggregate inside basis is either higher or lower than aggregate outside basis prior to the distribution, § 734(b) will maintain that disparity. In contrast to the § 743(b) adjustment, which is personal to the new partner who acquires an interest by purchase, bequest, or devise, the § 734(b) adjustment applies to the partnership as a whole.

A distribution of partnership assets, unless pro rata among the members, necessarily involves an acquision of some share of the non-distributed assets by the remaining partners in exchange for the relinquishment of their share of the distributed assets (similar to the treatment of § 751(b) distributions discussed in Problem Area 13). The § 734(b) adjustment attempts to treat such a transaction accordingly. Thus, if a three-person equal partnership holds two assets, cash of $11,000 and a capital asset with a basis of $19,000 and value of $22,000, a complete liquidation for cash of a partner's interest in the partnership which has a basis of $10,000 and a value of $11,000 will produce a $1,000 gain to the distributee. A partnership with a § 754 election will be entitled to a $1,000 increase in the basis of the capital asset, which will then be $20,000. Consequently, only $2,000 of gain would be recognized by the partnership on a subsequent disposition of the asset. In essence, the adjustment remedies the fact that the partnership did not distribute the distributee's pro rata share of each asset ($3,667 cash and one-third of the capital asset with a basis of $6,333 and value of $7,333), which would have preserved the $1,000 gain potential for the distributee and retained for the partnership only a $2,000 gain (basis for the remaining two-thirds interest in the asset of $12,667 and a value of $14,667). The § 734(b) adjustment is mandatory if the adjustment results in a substantial basis reduction (greater than $250,000) for the assets of the partnership. IRC § 734(d).

Section 734(b) also makes adjustments to the basis of the partnership's remaining assets if the distributee partner recognizes a loss on the distribution under § 731(a)(2) and in any case in which the distributed asset or assets take a basis in the hands of the distributee partner that is either greater than or less than their pre-distribution basis in the hands of the partnership. The § 734(b) adjustment is allocated to the same class of retained assets as the class of distributed assets generating the increase or decrease in basis. The Regulations dictate that gain or loss arising from the distribution of cash constitutes an adjustment attributable solely to the class of assets consisting of capital and § 1231 assets. Allocations of the adjustment in the case of multiple undistributed assets of the partnership are governed by § 755 and Regulation § 1.755-1(c).

PROBLEM 16

QUESTIONS

1. Each partner has a basis of $30,000 for his one-third interest in partnership PQR, which has a § 754 election in effect. Calculate the basis adjustment under § 734(b) to the partnership's property if the partnership liquidates P's entire partnership interest in each of the following circumstances.

a. The partnership has assets consisting of cash of $33,000 and property with a basis of $57,000 and a value of $66,000 and no liabilities. P receives $33,000 in cash for his interest.

b. The partnership has assets consisting of cash of $27,000 and property with a basis of $63,000 and a value of $54,000 and no liabilities. P receives $27,000 in cash for his interest.

c. The partnership has cash of $12,000 and two pieces of property with bases of $33,000 and $45,000 and values of $33,000 and $54,000, respectively. P receives the property valued at $33,000 in liquidation of his interest.

d. The partnership has cash of $12,000 and two pieces of property with bases of $27,000 and $51,000 and values of $27,000 and $42,000, respectively. P receives the property valued at $27,000 in liquidation of his interest.

↳ FMV 27000, Basis 27000

2. The ABC partnership is a cash-method, calendar-year partnership which has made a § 754 election. The profit and loss ratios of the partners are not equal. ABC has the following balance sheet:

	Adjusted Basis	Fair Market Value
Assets		
Cash	$18,000	$18,000
Parcel X	23,000	22,000
Parcel Y	19,000	29,000
Total	$60,000	$69,000
Capital		
A	$20,000	$18,000
B	20,000	22,000
C	20,000	29,000
Total	$60,000	$69,000

What are the tax consequences to the partners and the partnership under the following alternative circumstances?

a. Partner A receives the cash in complete liquidation of his partnership interest.

b. Partner B receives Parcel X in complete liquidation of her partnership interest.

c. Partner C receives Parcel Y in complete liquidation of his partnership interest.

3. D purchases a one-third interest in the ABC partnership for $50,000 in cash. The partnership does not have a § 754 election in effect. Immediately following D's purchase, the balance sheet of the partnership is as follows:

Assets	Adjusted Basis	Fair Market Value
Cash	$ 30,000	$ 30,000
Parcel X	60,000	90,000
Parcel Y	15,000	30,000
Total	$105,000	$150,000
Capital		
A	$ 35,000	$ 50,000
B	35,000	50,000
D	50,000	50,000
Total	$120,000	$150,000

The following year, the partnership makes a current distribution of Parcel Y to D. What is D's basis in Parcel Y and in her remaining partnership interest following this distribution?

MATERIALS

Revenue Ruling 92-15
1992-1 CB 215

ISSUES

(1) An upper-tier partnership (*UTP*), has an interest in a lower-tier partnership (*LTP*), and both partnerships have elections in effect under section 754 of the Internal Revenue Code. If *UTP* distributes property to a partner and, as a consequence of the distribution, adjusts the basis of its interest in *LTP* under section 734(b), does *LTP* also adjust the basis of its property under section 734(b). . . ?

FACTS

A and *B* are partners in partnership *UTP*, each with a 50 percent interest in the capital, profits and losses of the partnership. *A's* partnership interest in *UTP* has an adjusted basis of zero and a fair market value of 160*x* dollars. *UTP* has no liabilities and only two properties, capital asset *X* and a 10 percent interest in the capital, profits and losses of partnership *LTP*. Asset *X* has an adjusted basis to *UTP* of 140*x* dollars and a fair market value of 240*x* dollars. *UTP's* interest in *LTP* has an adjusted basis to *UTP* of 30*x* dollars and a fair market value of 80*x* dollars.

LTP has no liabilities and only two properties, capital asset *Y* and noncapital asset *Z*. Asset *Y* has an adjusted basis of 200*x* dollars and a fair market value of 700*x* dollars. Asset *Z* has an adjusted basis of zero and a fair market value of 100*x* dollars. *UTP's* share of the adjusted basis of *LTP's* properties is 20*x* dollars.

For the taxable year in which the events described in Situations 1 and 2 occur, *UTP* and *LTP* make valid elections under section 754 of the Code. Capital assets *X* and *Y*, and noncapital asset *Z*, are not assets described in section 751. Section 732(d) does not apply to *A*.

Situation 1

UTP distributes one-half of capital asset *X* to partner *A*, in order to reduce *A's* 50 percent interest in *UTP* to 20 percent, and increase *B's* interest to 80 percent. The distribution reduces the value of *A's* partnership interest in *UTP* to 40*x* dollars. . . .

LAW AND ANALYSIS

Section 734(a) of the Code provides that the basis of partnership property is not adjusted as the result of a distribution of property to a partner unless the partnership has an election in effect under section 754 of the Code.

Section 743(a) of the Code provides that the basis of partnership property is not adjusted as the result of a transfer of an interest in a partnership unless the partnership has an election in effect under section 754 of the Code.

Section 754 of the Code provides that if a partnership files an election in accordance with regulations prescribed by the Secretary, the basis of partnership property is adjusted, in the case of a distribution of property, in the manner provided in section 734(b), and, in the case of a transfer of a partnership interest, in the manner provided in section 743(b).

Section 734(b) of the Code provides that, in the case of a distribution of property to a partner, a partnership that has a section 754 election in effect increases or decreases the adjusted basis of partnership property under specified circumstances. Under section 734(b)(1)(A), the amount of increase is the amount of any gain recognized to the distributee partner with respect to the distribution. Under section 734(b)(1)(B), in the case of distributed property to which section 732(a)(2) applies, the amount of increase also includes the excess of the adjusted basis of the distributed property immediately before the distribution over the basis of the distributed property to the distributee. The partnership does not make the adjustment described in the preceding sentence if the distributed property is an interest in another partnership that does not have an election in effect under section 754 of the Code.

Section 732(a)(1) of the Code provides that the basis of property (other than money) distributed by a partnership to a partner other than in liquidation of the partner's interest is generally equal to the property's adjusted basis to the partnership immediately before the distribution. Section 732(a)(2), however, limits the basis of the property to the distributee partner to the adjusted basis of the partner's interest in the partnership reduced by any money distributed in the same transaction.

Section 734(c) of the Code requires the allocation of any basis adjustment among partnership properties in accordance with section 755 of the Code.

Section 743(b) of the Code provides that, in the case of a transfer of an interest in a partnership by sale or exchange or upon the death of a partner, a partnership that has a section 754 election in effect increases or decreases the adjusted basis of partnership property under specified circumstances.

Section 743(c) of the Code requires the allocation of any basis adjustment among partnership properties in accordance with section 755 of the Code.

Section 755(a)(1) of the Code provides that the basis adjustment is allocated among partnership properties . . . .

Section 741 of the Code provides that, except as provided in section 751, the gain or loss from the sale or exchange of an interest in a partnership is considered to be a gain or loss from the sale or exchange of a capital asset. . . .

Situation 1

UTP distributes one-half of capital asset *X* to partner *A*, reducing the value of *A*'s partnership interest to 40*x* dollars. Under section 732(a)(1) of the Code, *A*'s basis in the distributed half of asset *X* would be equal to the basis of the distributed half of asset *X* to *UTP* immediately before the distribution, or 70*x* dollars. Section 732(a)(2), however, limits *A*'s basis in the distributed half of asset *X* to *A*'s basis in its *UTP* partnership interest, or zero. Because *UTP* has a section 754 election in effect, under section 734(b)(1)(B), *UTP* increases the adjusted basis of its remaining property by 70*x* dollars, the excess of the adjusted basis of the distributed property to *UTP* immediately before the distribution (70*x* dollars) over the basis of the distributed property to *A* (zero). . . .

Because both *UTP* and *LTP* have made elections under section 754 of the Code, it is appropriate to treat *UTP*'s distribution of one-half of asset *X* to *A* and the subsequent 35*x* dollar increase to *UTP*'s basis in *LTP* as an event that triggers a section 734(b) basis increase of 35*x* dollars to *UTP*'s share of *LTP*'s assets. Under section 755(b) of the Code and section 1.755-1(b)(1) of the Regulations, the basis adjustment to undistributed partnership property under section 734(b)(1)(B) is allocated to remaining partnership property of a character similar to that of the distributed property. Accordingly, *LTP* increases its basis in *UTP*'s share of asset *Y* from 20*x* dollars to 55*x* dollars. This adjustment to basis is for *UTP* only and does not affect the basis in *LTP* property of other partners of *LTP*. No adjustment is made to *UTP*'s share of *LTP*'s basis in noncapital asset *Z*. . . .

HOLDINGS

(1) If partnership *UTP* and partnership *LTP* have elections in effect under section 754 of the Code, if *UTP* distributes property to a partner and one of *UTP*'s undistributed properties is an interest in partnership *LTP*, and if *UTP* adjusts the basis of its interest in *LTP* under section 734(b), then this adjustment is an event that is deemed to require *LTP* to adjust the basis of its property under section 734(b) by the same amount. This adjustment to basis is for *UTP* only and does not affect the basis in *LTP* property of other partners of *LTP*. . . .

CHAPTER **17**

Taxing Partnership Operations—Termination of a Partnership Other Than By Division or Merger

PROBLEM AREA 17

INTRODUCTION

Earlier discussions in this book have addressed the tax consequences to particular partners of the disposition (sale, exchange, or liquidation) of partnership interests, but the effects on the partnership and its other members generally have not been considered. This topic is addressed by § 708, which prescribes the governing rules as to when a partnership terminates for tax purposes. The two most obvious circumstances are when an enterprise ceases to conduct operations or continues to conduct operations but not in a partnership mode (*e.g.*, as a sole proprietorship). In either case, § 708 mandates a termination of the partnership and a determination of the tax consequences based upon an assumption that a distribution in complete liquidation of the members' interests occurs. In such a case, gain or loss may be recognized and basis must be determined for any distributed assets.

The other event under § 708 precipitating a termination is the sale or exchange during a 12-month period of 50 percent or more of the partnership interests. Not all ownership changes are taken into account in applying this provision. For example, transfers of interests by gift or bequest are exempted by the Regulations as are ownership shifts through the admission of a new partner or the withdrawal of an old partner. Under § 761(e)(1), a distribution (whether by a partnership or by a corporation) of an interest in a partnership is treated as a sale or exchange of that interest for purposes of § 708. Thus, for example, a distribution by one partnership of an interest in a second partnership is treated as a sale or exchange for purposes of determining the change in ownership of the second partnership, but not of the first.

Once the 50-percent ownership shift described in § 708(b)(1)(B) (a "constructive termination") has occurred, the Regulations dictate that the transaction be viewed as a contribution of all of the partnership's assets and liabilities to a new partnership, followed immediately by a liquidating distribution of the partnership interests in the new partnership to the partners (including the member who acquired the interest which precipitated the termination). This treatment can produce various tax consequences, including a bunching of income or loss and termination of the old partnership's elections, but it does not generally involve either the recognition of gain or loss or any redistribution of basis among the partnership's assets.

In addition to the above-described terminating events, § 708 prescribes termination rules for partnership mergers and divisions. These rules, which have been expanded in scope and complexity by the issuance of detailed Regulations, are reserved for separate discussion in Problem Area 25.

PROBLEM 17

QUESTIONS

1. A is a 50 percent partner and B and C are equal 25 percent partners in the ABC partnership. Determine if and when the partnership terminates in the following alternative circumstances.

a. A gives his partnership interest to his daughter, C, on July 15, Year 1.

b. A sells one-half of his partnership interest to C on June 30, Year 1. C sells this interest to D on May 30, Year 2. B sells her partnership interest to E on October 31, Year 2.

c. A is a corporation which liquidates on June 30, Year 1, distributing its partnership interest to its shareholders, D and E.

d. A dies on June 30, Year 1, at which time his estate becomes the owner of his partnership interest. On March 10, Year 2, the estate distributes the partnership interest to a named legatee.

e. A's partnership interest is liquidated. Shortly thereafter, D acquires from the partnership a 50 percent interest in the partnership.

2. A and B are equal partners in the AB partnership. B forms a new partnership BC with C. B's contribution to BC is her interest in the AB partnership. Does this contribution terminate the AB partnership?

3. A and B are equal partners in the AB partnership. Do either of the following transactions terminate the AB partnership?

a. C is admitted as a partner with a fully vested 50 percent interest in capital and profits in consideration for his agreement to render services to the partnership.

b. C is admitted as a partner with a fully vested 50 percent interest in capital and profits as compensation for services that he has rendered in the past to A and B.

4. D and F are partners in partnership DF, holding 51 percent and 49 percent, respectively, of the total interests in capital and profits. DF holds a 60 percent interest in partnership QTZ. D sells her DF partnership interest to A. Is QTZ terminated? What result if instead D owned a 40 percent interest in DF and DF owned 90 percent of QTZ?

5. On August 31, Year 1, the AB partnership, which has a June 30 tax year, sells all of its operating assets for cash, recognizing a substantial taxable gain. A and B, the sole partners, are calendar-year taxpayers. The proceeds of sale are placed in a high-yield money market account in the name of the partnership. The partnership makes a single distribution of all of the funds in this account on January 1, Year 2. When does the AB partnership terminate?

6. A, an equal partner in the AB partnership, dies on June 30, Year 1. The partnership agreement provides that A's estate will continue to own his partnership interest, which will be liquidated through distributions over a six-month period. When does the partnership terminate? What if the agreement provided instead for the immediate retirement of the partnership interest with payment by the partnership over a period of time?

7. A is a 50 percent partner and B and C are equal 25 percent partners in the ABC partnership. All are calendar-year taxpayers. The ABC partnership has a June 30 tax year. Describe the tax consequences to the partnership and all partners if A sells his interest to B on September 30, Year 1.

8. A and B, calendar-year taxpayers, are equal partners in the AB partnership, which has a June 30 tax year. Describe the tax consequences to the partnership and both partners if A sells his interest to B on September 30, Year 1.

MATERIALS

Revenue Ruling 87-51
1987-1 CB 158

ISSUE

In a multi-tiered partnership arrangement, if a partner of an upper-tier partnership sells a partnership interest of less than 50 percent of the capital and profits of the upper-tier partnership, then, for purposes of section 708(b)(1)(B) of the Internal Revenue Code, is that sale also considered a sale of the partner's proportionate share of the upper-tier partnership's interest in a lower-tier partnership?

FACTS

AB is a partnership that holds a 50 percent interest in the capital and profits of *XYZ*, another partnership. *A*, a partner in *AB*, sold *A*'s 40 percent interest in the capital and profits of *AB*, and, within twelve months of the sale by *A*, *X*, a partner in *XYZ*, sold all of *X*'s 30 percent interest in the capital and profits of *XYZ*. There were no other sales of interests in either *AB* or *XYZ* during the same twelve month period.

LAW AND ANALYSIS

Section 708(b)(1)(B) of the Code provides that a partnership will be considered terminated if within a 12-month period there is a sale or exchange of 50 percent or more of the total interest in partnership capital and profits.

Section 741 of the Code provides that, in the case of a sale or exchange of an interest in a partnership, gain or loss shall be recognized to the transferor partner. Such gain or loss shall be considered as gain or loss from the sale or exchange of a capital asset, except as otherwise provided in section 751 (relating to unrealized receivables and inventory items which have appreciated substantially in value).

In the present situation, *A* sold a 40 percent partnership interest in *AB*, which held a 50 percent partnership interest in the partnership *XYZ*. In addition, within twelve months of the sale by *A*, *X* sold a 30 percent interest in *XYZ*. If *A*'s sale of a 40 percent partnership interest in *AB* is also considered a sale of a 20 percent (40 percent of 50 percent) interest in *XYZ*, then *A*'s sale of the 20 percent interest combined with *X*'s sale of a 30 percent interest in *XYZ* within twelve months would result in the termination of *XYZ* under section 708(b)(1)(B) of the Code.

Under the provisions of subchapter K of the Code, a partnership is considered for various purposes to be either an aggregate of its partners or an entity, transactionally independent of its partners. Generally, subchapter K adopts an entity approach with respect to transactions involving partnership interests. *See* Rev. Rul. 75-62, 1975-1 C.B. 188. Whether an aggregate or entity theory of partnerships should be applied to a particular Code section depends upon which theory is more appropriate to such section. *See* S. Rep. No. 1622, 83d Cong., 2d Sess. 89 (1954), and H.R. Rep. No. 2543, 83d Cong., 2d Sess. 59 (1954); *Casel v. Commissioner*, 79 T.C. 424 (1982). The termination of a partnership under section 708(b)(1)(B) depends on whether there was a sale or exchange of a partnership interest and on whether there was a transfer of at least 50 percent of the total interest in partnership capital and profits. Because section 708(b)(1)(B) is an entity-oriented provision, an entity approach is more appropriate for that section.

Thus, in a multi-tiered partnership arrangement, the sale of a partner's interest in the capital and profits of an upper-tier partnership that is itself a partner in a lower-tier partnership is not a sale of the partner's proportionate share of the underlying assets of the upper-tier partnership for purposes of section 708(b)(1)(B). Rather, under section 741, the sale of A's interest in AB is considered the sale of a single capital asset, the interest in AB. Accordingly, only X's sale of a 30 percent partnership interest in XYZ qualifies for the determination of whether there has been a sale or exchange of 50 percent or more of the total interest in the partnership capital and profits of XYZ.

HOLDING

In a multi-tiered partnership arrangement, the sale of a partner's interest in an upper-tier partnership that does not trigger a termination of the upper tier partnership is not considered a sale of that partner's proportionate share of the upper-tier partnership's interest in a lower-tier partnership for purposes of the termination provisions of section 708(b)(1)(B) of the Code. . . .

Revenue Ruling 99-6
1999-1 CB 432

ISSUE

What are the federal income tax consequences if one person purchases all of the ownership interests in a domestic limited liability company (LLC) that is classified as a partnership under section 301.7701-3 of the Regulations, causing the LLC's status as a partnership to terminate under section 708(b)(1)(A) of the Code?

FACTS

In each of the following situations, an LLC is formed and operates in a state which permits an LLC to have a single owner. Each LLC is classified as a partnership under section 301.7701-3. Neither of the LLCs holds any unrealized receivables or substantially appreciated inventory for purposes of section 751(b). For the sake of simplicity, it is assumed that neither LLC is liable for any indebtedness, nor are the assets of the LLCs subject to any indebtedness.

Situation 1. A and B are equal partners in AB, an LLC. A sells A's entire interest in AB to B for $10,000. After the sale, the business is continued by the LLC, which is owned solely by B.

Situation 2. C and D are equal partners in CD, an LLC. C and D sell their entire interests in CD to E, an unrelated person, in exchange for $10,000 each. After the sale, the business is continued by the LLC, which is owned solely by E.

After the sale, in both situations, no entity classification election is made under section 301.7701-3(c) to treat the LLC as an association for federal tax purposes.

LAW

Section 708(b)(1)(A) and section 1.708-1(b)(1) of the Regulations provide that a partnership shall terminate when the operations of the partnership are discontinued and no part of any business, financial operation, or venture of the partnership continues to be carried on by any of its partners in a partnership.

Section 731(a)(1) provides that, in the case of a distribution by a partnership to a partner, gain is not recognized to the partner except to the extent that any money distributed exceeds the adjusted basis of the partner's interest in the partnership immediately before the distribution.

Section 731(a)(2) provides that, in the case of a distribution by a partnership in liquidation of a partner's interest in a partnership where no property other than money, unrealized receivables (as defined in section 751(c)), and inventory (as defined in section 751(d)(2)) is distributed to the partner, loss is recognized to the extent of the excess of the adjusted basis of the partner's interest in the partnership over the sum of (A) any money distributed, and (B) the basis to the distributee, as determined under section 732, of any unrealized receivables and inventory.

Section 732(b) provides that the basis of property (other than money) distributed by a partnership to a partner in liquidation of the partner's interest shall be an amount equal to the adjusted basis of the partner's interest in the partnership, reduced by any money distributed in the same transaction.

Section 735(b) provides that, in determining the period for which a partner has held property received in a distribution from a partnership (other than for purposes of section 735(a)(2)), there shall be included the holding period of the partnership, as determined under section 1223, with respect to the property.

Section 741 provides that gain or loss resulting from the sale or exchange of an interest in a partnership shall be recognized by the transferor partner, and that the gain or loss shall be considered as gain or loss from a capital asset, except as provided in section 751 (relating to unrealized receivables and inventory items).

Section 1.741-1(b) provides that section 741 applies to the transferor partner in a two-person partnership when one partner sells a partnership interest to the other partner, and to all the members of a partnership when they sell their interests to one or more persons outside the partnership.

Section 301.7701-2(c)(1) provides that, for federal tax purposes, the term "partnership" means a business entity (as the term is defined in section 301.7701-2(a)) that is not a corporation and that has at least two members.

In *Edwin E. McCauslen v. Commissioner*, 45 TC 588 (1966), one partner in an equal, two-person partnership died, and his partnership interest was purchased from his estate by the remaining partner. The purchase caused a termination of the partnership under section 708(b)(1)(A). The Tax Court held that the surviving partner did not purchase the deceased partner's interest in the partnership, but that the surviving partner purchased the partnership assets attributable to the interest. As a result, the surviving partner was not permitted to succeed to the partnership's holding period with respect to these assets.

Rev. Rul. 67-65, 1967-1 CB 168, also considered the purchase of a deceased partner's interest by the other partner in a two-person partnership. The Service ruled that, for the purpose of determining the purchaser's holding period in the assets attributable to the deceased partner's interest, the purchaser should treat the transaction as a purchase of the assets attributable to the interest. Accordingly, the purchaser was not permitted to succeed to the partnership's holding period with respect to these assets.

ANALYSIS AND HOLDINGS

Situation 1. The AB partnership terminates under section 708(b)(1)(A) when B purchases A's entire interest in AB. Accordingly, A must treat the transaction as the sale of a partnership interest. Reg. section 1.741-1(b). A must report gain or loss, if any, resulting from the sale of A's partnership interest in accordance with section 741.

Under the analysis of *McCauslen* and Rev. Rul. 67-65, for purposes of determining the tax treatment of B, the AB partnership is deemed to make a liquidating distribution of all of its assets to A and B, and following this distribution, B is treated as acquiring the assets deemed to have been distributed to A in liquidation of A's partnership interest.

B's basis in the assets attributable to A's one-half interest in the partnership is $10,000, the purchase price for A's partnership interest. Section 1012. Section 735(b) does not apply with respect to the assets B is deemed to have purchased from A. Therefore, B's holding period for these assets begins on the day immediately following the date of the sale. See Rev. Rul. 66-7, 1966-1 CB 188, which provides that the holding period of an asset is computed by excluding the date on which the asset is acquired.

Upon the termination of AB, B is considered to receive a distribution of those assets attributable to B's former interest in AB. B must recognize gain or loss, if any, on the deemed distribution of the assets to the extent required by section 731(a). B's basis in the assets received in the deemed liquidation of B's partnership interest is determined under section 732(b). Under section 735(b), B's holding period for the assets attributable to B's one-half interest in AB includes the partnership's holding period for such assets (except for purposes of section 735(a)(2)).

Situation 2. The CD partnership terminates under section 708(b)(1)(A) when E purchases the entire interests of C and D in CD. C and D must report gain or loss, if any, resulting from the sale of their partnership interests in accordance with section 741.

For purposes of classifying the acquisition by E, the CD partnership is deemed to make a liquidating distribution of its assets to C and D. Immediately following this distribution, E is deemed to acquire, by purchase, all of the former partnership's assets. Compare Rev. Rul. 84-111, 1984-2 CB 88 (Situation 3), which determines the tax consequences to a corporate transferee of all interests in a partnership in a manner consistent with *McCauslen*, and holds that the transferee's basis in the assets received equals the basis of the partnership interests, allocated among the assets in accordance with section 732(c).

E's basis in the assets is $20,000 under section 1012. E's holding period for the assets begins on the day immediately following the date of sale.

McCauslen v. Commissioner
45 TC 588 (1966)

MULRONEY, Judge.

Respondent determined a deficiency in petitioners' income tax for 1959 in the amount of $20,738.86. The only issue is whether the gain realized by petitioners from a sale of certain partnership properties acquired by them under a buy-sell agreement is taxable as a long-term or short-term capital gain, which turns upon whether petitioners are entitled to use the partnership's holding period with respect to such properties.

All of the facts were stipulated and they are so found.

Edwin E. and Frances E. McCauslen, husband and wife, are residents of Steubenville, Ohio. They filed their joint Federal income tax return for 1959 with the district director of internal revenue at Cleveland, Ohio.

In 1946 petitioner Edwin E. McCauslen and his brother, William T. McCauslen, formed a two-man partnership to engage in the nursery, greenhouse, wholesale, and retail flower business. Both men were equal, active partners in the business until William died on March 7, 1959, and after William's death the floral business was continued by the petitioner. The partnership had a fiscal year ending May 31 for tax and accounting purposes.

On October 17, 1956, petitioner and William (together with their wives) executed an agreement which provided, in part, as follows:

> WHEREAS, Edwin E. McCauslen and William T. McCauslen are partners operating at Steubenville, Ohio, under the firm name of McCauslen Florists;
>
> WHEREAS, the parties mutually desire to enter into an agreement by which, on the event of the death of one of them, the survivor shall purchase and the decedent's estate shall sell the share of the latter in the partnership at a price determinable by such agreement;
>
> WHEREAS, the parties mutually desire that life insurance be used as a means of providing all or a portion of the funds with which to finance the obligations arising under such sale and purchase agreement;
>
> NOW, THEREFORE, IT IS MUTUALLY AGREED by and between the parties hereto, and on behalf of their eventual heirs and personal representatives, as follows:
>
> 1. On the death of a partner, the surviving partner shall purchase and the decedent's estate shall sell the share of the latter in the partnership for a consideration equal to 80% of the book value of each share as shown by the books of the partnership as of the close of the fiscal year next preceding the date of death, after the books have been closed and adjusted by a certified public accountant in accordance with good accounting practice to include all known assets and liabilities of the partnership but before any provision for income tax liability of the individual partners and with no valuation recorded for good will or other intangibles, whether or not same exists . . . .
>
> 4. The surviving partner shall be under obligation to save and protect the decedent's estate from all legitimate claims and demands on account of the obligations and debts of the partnership. As a means of assuring the

fulfillment of this obligation, the decedent's estate may condition the convey-
ance of its share in the partnership upon the procurement and submission by
the surviving partner of releases or agreements by the partnership creditors
effectively exonerating the decedent's estate from such debts or claims. Any
such claims or demands may, however, if satisfied by the surviving partners,
be used to recompute the book value of the shares and the consideration
provided in paragraph No. 2 above, in accordance with the partnership
participation existing just prior to the death of a partner . . . .

10. This agreement does not purport to be an agreement of partnership, its purpose being merely to establish a basis and means as between
the partners of effecting a sale and purchase of the share of a partner on his
death. Any partnership agreement existing between the partners shall continue in effect unchanged as it may relate to the subject matter of this
agreement, in which respect it shall be regarded as amended or superseded.

William died on March 7, 1959, and pursuant to the agreement of October 17,
1956, petitioner acquired William's partnership interest. On May 28, 1959, petitioner
sold for $200,000 a greenhouse and greenhouse equipment which had previously
been owned by the partnership for a period of longer than 6 months.

Petitioner and his wife reported the sale on their 1959 return as follows:

SALE OF GREENHOUSE BUSINESS

Sold to Dieckmann Bros., May 28, 1959			$200,000.00
Less commission to broker			8,000.00
Net sale price			$192,000.00
Less cost of assets sold:			
Land		$ 35,172.75	
Greenhouse and equipment	$185,388.32		
Less depreciation to date	155,316.16	30,072.16	65,244.91
Long-term capital gain			$126,755.09

Respondent in his statutory notice of deficiency increased petitioners' taxable
income for 1959 and explained the adjustment as follows:

During the taxable year ended December 31, 1959 you sold a greenhouse and
equipment for $200,000.00. You reported the gain realized of $126,755.09 as a
long-term capital gain on Schedule D of your income tax return. Since one-half of
your interest in these assets was acquired by you within 6 months before their
sale, it is held that under Section 1222 of the Internal Revenue Code, the gain on
this portion is a short-term capital gain . . . .

Section 741 of the Internal Revenue Code of 1954 recognizes a partnership interest
as a capital asset which may be sold or exchanged with capital gain or loss treatment.
When petitioner purchased the decedent's interest in the partnership from the estate
pursuant to the October 17, 1956, agreement, the partnership was terminated. Sec.
708(b). At that point petitioner owned all of the partnership assets, i.e., the assets
attributable to his own one-half partnership interest since 1946 in the two-man
partnership, as well as the assets attributable to the decedent's partnership interest
acquired by petitioner in 1959.

There does not now appear to be any dispute between the parties as to the proper bases to be applied to the partnership assets in petitioner's hands after the termination of the partnership. Moreover, as to the proper holding period of these assets, respondent recognizes that petitioner acquired by distribution that portion of the partnership assets relating to his own partnership interest and that with respect to such assets the petitioner is entitled to include the partnership's holding period. Therefore, when petitioner in May 1959 (less than 6 months after decedent's death) sold some of the former partnership assets which had previously been held by the partnership for more than 6 months, the partnership's holding period could be tacked on to petitioner's holding period for that portion of the assets attributable to his own partnership interest, entitling him to long-term capital gains treatment of a portion of the gain realized.

Petitioner argues that he is also entitled to tack on the holding period of the partnership to the portion of the partnership assets he acquired when he purchased the partnership interest of the decedent partner from the estate. Petitioner relies upon section 735, the pertinent portions of which we have set forth in a footnote, and which in section 735(b) provides that in determining the period for which a partner has held property received in a distribution from a partnership (excluding certain inventory items), there shall be included the holding period of the partnership with respect to such property.

We believe that petitioner's reliance upon section 735(b) is misplaced. Sections 731 through 735 represent an attempt to deal comprehensively with the whole problem of partnership distributions of property. Generally, the statutory sections allow tax-free distributions of property by a partnership, with provisions for a carryover basis or a substituted basis, depending upon the type of distribution, and for adjustments to the basis of a distributee partner's interest in the partnership. Section 735 merely follows the distributed partnership property into the hands of the partner and describes the character of the gain or loss when the partner disposes of such distributed property, and in section 735(b) provides that the holding period of the partnership for the distributed property may be tacked on to the holding period in the hands of the partner. The emphasis throughout these sections is upon distributions to a partner in connection with an existing partnership interest.

Much of the complexity of the partnership provisions in the 1954 Code arises because they are based upon conflicting concepts of the nature of a partnership, i.e., the entity approach and the aggregate approach, as well as from Congress' desire to introduce a certain amount of flexibility in this area of partnership taxation. Thus, as we indicated in the *Foxman* case, drastic tax differences can result depending upon the categorization of a transaction (for example, as a "sale" of a partnership interest rather than a "liquidation" of such interest), even though the ultimate economic effect is much the same. Therefore, it would seem that concepts which might be meaningful under one section might prove misleading under another section.

The provision for tacking on the partnership's holding period is entirely consistent with the general statutory scheme of postponing recognition of gain or loss until the distributee partner finally disposes of the distributed partnership property. But where, as here, a partner acquires another partner's share by purchase and, as a conse-quence of the termination of the partnership resulting from such purchase, acquires the partnership assets relating to such purchased interest, the statute has no applica-tion. The statute cannot be construed as permitting the purchaser to tack on the partnership's holding period of such assets. In effect, petitioner is contending that he purchased assets belonging to another with a built-in holding period. Neither logic nor necessity supports such an argument and we do not believe that section 735(b) calls for such a result.

Since petitioner's purchase of the decedent's partnership interest resulted in a termination of the partnership under section 708(b), it is our view that petitioner acquired the partnership assets relating to such interest by purchase, rather than by any distribution from the partnership, and that petitioner's holding period for such assets begins from the date of such purchase. Consequently, we agree with respondent's determination that petitioner's holding period for the assets attributable to the purchased interest was less than 6 months at the time of their sale by petitioner on May 28, 1959, with the result that the portion of the gain attributable to such assets is taxable as short-term capital gain.

Reviewed by the Court.

Decision will be entered under Rule 50.

Harbor Cove Marina Partners Partnership v. Commissioner
123 TC 64 (2004)

LARO, Judge: . . . Collins indicated on the Form 8082 that he was filing inconsistently with those positions because they reflected HCMP's erroneous belief that it had terminated during 1998. According to Collins, HCMP continues to exist today pending the final outcome of his lawsuit (lawsuit) against HCMP's managing general partner and others. The lawsuit, which is currently before the California Court of Appeal for the Fourth Appellate District (court of appeal), seeks enforcement of a provision in HCMP's partnership agreement (and a directive of the court of appeal) that requires that HCMP sell its assets in the public market rather than distribute those assets to its managing general partner (or to an affiliate of that partner), as was done at the time of HCMP's reported termination.

. . . We are left to decide whether HCMP terminated during 1998. We hold it did not.

Background

. . .

HCMP was formed on April 8, 1985, under the Uniform Partnership Act of California. It is governed by a written partnership agreement (partnership agreement) executed on that date and entitled "Restated Partnership Agreement of Harbor Cove Marina Partners". Among its purposes under the partnership agreement are to acquire, own, commercially develop, and hold for investment and the production of income a leasehold interest in certain real property owned by the San Diego Unified Port District (Port District). Another purpose is to develop a marina (marina) on that leasehold and to hold that marina for investment. Its term as stated in the partnership agreement expires no later than December 31, 2020.

HCMP's partnership agreement was signed by (or, in the case of a corporation, on behalf of) its initial partners; namely, Collins, Charles B. Hope (Hope), Frank L. Hope, Jr. (Hope Jr.), and a California corporation named Sunroad Marina, Inc. (Sunroad corporation). The partnership agreement stated that Sunroad corporation was HCMP's managing general partner and tax matters partner, that Sunroad corporation owned a 70-percent interest in HCMP, and that the other three partners each owned a 10-percent interest in HCMP. The partnership agreement stated that the partners shared in each item of income, expense, gain, loss, and credit in accordance with their ownership interests and that, on liquidation and distribution, the shares of Collins, Hope, Hope Jr., and Sunroad corporation were 12, 12, 12, and 64 percent, respectively. The partnership agreement also stated as to the partners' business relationship extensive details on, among other things, the manner in which HCMP shall acquire its capital, the manner in which HCMP shall allocate its profits and losses, the manner in which HCMP shall be dissolved, and the manner in which HCMP shall be liquidated following its dissolution.

On or about January 30, 1987, HCMP agreed to lease from the Port District 1,315,440 square feet of tideland area located on Harbor Island Drive in San Diego, upon which HCMP would construct the marina. The underlying lease (marina lease) was signed by each HCMP partner and stated that the tideland area was let for a 40-year period beginning February 1, 1987. On or about March 16, 1988, the Mutual

Life Insurance Company of New York (MONY) lent $13.5 million to HCMP (MONY loan) to acquire and develop the marina. The MONY loan was nonrecourse, and it was secured by an interest in the marina lease granted to MONY by HCMP. Each HCMP partner signed and executed in favor of MONY a single $13.5 million promissory note ($13.5 million promissory note), the terms of which were governed and construed by California law.

The partnership agreement provided that the managing general partner had the sole right to manage HCMP's business. During HCMP's existence, Collins vigorously challenged many of the decisions made by Sunroad corporation as to that business. This animosity led to Sunroad corporation's suing Collins in San Diego Superior Court in an attempt to compel a buyout of his HCMP interest. This litigation ended unfavorably to Sunroad corporation.

On or about November 19, 1996, Sunroad corporation assigned its interest in HCMP to Sunroad Real Estate Holding Corporation (Sunroad Real Estate) to reflect a change in name from the former to the latter. Approximately 8 months later, in or about August 1997, Hope and Hope Jr. sold their interests in HCMP to Marina Holdings Partners, L.P. (Marina Holdings), a California limited partnership that was formed on May 29, 1997. On or about December 31, 1997, Sunroad Real Estate was liquidated, and its HCMP interest was assigned to Sunroad Asset Management, Inc. (Sunroad Asset), the general partner of Marina Holdings. Contemporaneous with the liquidation of Sunroad Real Estate, HCMP's partnership agreement was amended to reflect the aforementioned assignment and sales and to reflect the fact that (1) Marina Holdings as part of the sales assumed all HCMP obligations of Hope and Hope Jr. and accepted the partnership agreement, and (2) Sunroad Asset as part of the assignment assumed all HCMP obligations of Sunroad Real Estate and accepted the partnership agreement. As of the end of December 31, 1997, HCMP's partners were Sunroad Asset, Marina Holdings, and Collins, and their ownership interests were 70, 20, and 10 percent, respectively. Sunroad Asset was at that time HCMP's managing general partner.

On May 26, 1998, Sunroad Asset, in its capacity as HCMP's managing general partner, notified Collins that it had decided to dissolve HCMP pursuant to paragraph 11 of the partnership agreement. Paragraph 11 stated in relevant part that HCMP "shall be dissolved upon the . . . decision of the MGP [managing general partner] . . . .[or] . . . The sale of all or substantially all of the Partnership assets and collection of all monies due therefrom". The notification also stated that paragraph 12 of the partnership agreement directed Sunroad Asset, as HCMP's managing general partner, to wind up and liquidate HCMP by selling its property and by applying and distributing those proceeds in the manner described in the partnership agreement. Paragraph 12, entitled *"LIQUIDATION"*, stated in relevant part:

12.1   In the event of a dissolution as hereinabove provided, the Partnership shall forthwith be dissolved and terminated, and any certificates or notices thereof required by law shall be filed or published by the Liquidator (as defined below). The MGP . . . shall wind up and liquidate the Partnership by selling the Partnership property. The proceeds of liquidation and any other assets of the Partnership shall be applied and distributed in the following order of priority:

12.1.1   To the extent of debts and liabilities of the Partnership . . . and the expense of liquidation;

12.1.2   To the setting up of any reserves that the Liquidator may deem reasonably necessary for any contingent or unforeseen liabilities or obligations of the Partnership . . .;

12.1.3   To the payment of any loans or advances (including interest thereon) that may have been made by any of the Partners;

12.1.4   To the Partners in accordance with their respective capital accounts; and

12.1.5   Any balance then remaining shall be distributed to the Partners in proportion to their respective interest in the Partnership.

Sunroad Asset later informed Collins that it intended to distribute to him in connection with HCMP's dissolution the cash value of his HCMP interest as ascertained using the marina's July 31, 1998, appraised value of $16.5 million. That approach was consistent with the partnership agreement's "buyout provisions," discussed infra, but inconsistent with the applicable provisions of paragraph 12 of the partnership agreement. Collins also knew at or about that time that Sunroad Asset intended to distribute the marina to itself or to its affiliate. That approach also was inconsistent with the applicable provisions of paragraph 12 of the partnership agreement.

On October 7, 1998, Collins commenced the lawsuit in the Superior Court of California, San Diego County (trial court), under the caption "Collins v. Feldman, et al., Case No. 724762". . . .

Collins alleged in the lawsuit that the "buyout provisions" of the partnership agreement, which allowed for a liquidation of a partner's interest on the basis of the appraised values of HCMP's assets, were not applicable but that the applicable provisions were those in paragraph 12 of the partnership agreement. Collins also alleged that Sunroad Asset was not allowed by the partnership agreement to distribute the marina to itself or to an entity under its control but had to sell the marina in the public market and divide the net proceeds among the partners in accordance with their applicable percentages as set forth in the partnership agreement.

On November 18, 1998, Sunroad Asset, in its capacity as a general partner of HCMP and Sunroad limited partnership, formally assigned the rights, title, and interest in the marina lease from HCMP to Sunroad limited partnership. The document underlying this assignment was not executed by either Collins or the Port District. Approximately 3 weeks later, on December 8, 1998, Sunroad Asset sent to Collins a check for $389,662; i.e., the amount that Sunroad Asset maintained was the value of Collins's interest in HCMP as ascertained using the aforementioned appraised value of the marina. Collins did not cash this check upon receipt but deposited it with the trial court pending resolution of the lawsuit.

On April 15, 1999, HCMP filed its 1998 partnership return for the period from January 1 to December 7, 1998. In addition to reporting that it was a "final" return, the return reported that as of the end of December 7, 1998, (1) HCMP had terminated and had no assets or liabilities, (2) HCMP had liquidated Collins's interest in it through a cash distribution of $389,662, (3) each HCMP partner's share of partnership liabilities was zero, and (4) each HCMP partner's capital account had a zero balance. HCMP's partners as of December 7, 1998 were Collins, Marina Holdings, and Sunroad general partnership. HCMP reported on its 1998 partnership return that these partners had received . . . distributions during 1998 . . . .

Marina Holdings and Sunroad general partnership each filed a "final" 1998 partnership return for the period from January 1, to December 7, 1998 . . . .

. . . HCMP reported on Collins's 1998 Schedule K-1 that his withdrawals and distributions for that year totaled $389,662, or more specifically, the amount listed on that return as a cash distribution made to him during that year. Collins reported on the Form 8082 that he had not received any distribution or withdrawal during 1998 in that the "CHECK RECEIVED BY TAXPAYER WAS TRANSFERRED TO THE CLERK OF THE SUPERIOR COURT OF SAN DIEGO PENDING FINAL SETTLEMENT OF THE CASE".

The lawsuit was tried on April 4, 5, 6, and 26, 2000, and the trial court filed its Statement of Decision and entered its related judgment on October 17, 2000. The judgment stated in relevant part that:

IT IS ORDERED, ADJUDGED AND DECREED THAT:

1.   Pursuant to the Court's August 11, 1999, Order on Plaintiff's Fourth Cause of Action for Declaratory Relief, plaintiff is entitled to and has a judicial declaration that Harbor Cove Marina Partners dissolved as of May 26, 1998, and that the applicable Partnership Agreement required a public sale of the partnership assets upon dissolution;

2.   Notwithstanding the foregoing, plaintiff shall have and recover nothing against defendants, or any of them, except the plaintiff may withdraw the sum of $389,662 deposited with the Court, plus interest accrued thereon; . . .

Collins appealed to the court of appeal the portion of the trial court's judgment that denied him specific performance of the provision in the partnership agreement that required the liquidation and sale of HCMP's assets upon its dissolution . . . .

On March 29, 2002, 3 days after the FPAA was issued, the court of appeal affirmed the holding for Collins on the fourth cause of action and reversed the trial court's holding against Collins on the sixth cause of action concerning specific performance. The court of appeal directed the trial court to grant to Collins specific performance of that provision of the partnership agreement and awarded to him his costs of appeal. The court of appeal noted that the trial court's denial of Collins's request for specific performance allowed Sunroad Asset to do expressly what the partnership agreement and the trial court had stated that it could not do; i.e., operate under the buyout provisions of the partnership agreement rather than the applicable liquidation provisions. . . .

Discussion

. . .

The linchpin of the four items is the parties' dispute as to whether HCMP terminated in 1998 for Federal tax purposes. Section 708(a) provides that a partnership continues to exist until terminated. Section 708(b) provides that a termination requires the happening of one of two events. First, under section 708(b)(1)(A), a partnership terminates when "no part of any business, financial operation, or venture of the partnership continues to be carried on by any of its partners in a partnership". Second, under section 708(b)(1)(B), a partnership terminates when "within a 12-month period there is a sale or exchange of 50 percent or more of the total interest in partnership capital and profits."

The parties focus on the first of these events. So do we. While the dissolution of a partnership is governed by State law, the termination of a partnership for Federal tax purposes is controlled by Federal law. A termination of a partnership for Federal tax purposes may be different from its termination, dissolution, or winding-up under State law, and a partnership may continue to exist for Federal tax purposes even though State law provides that the partnership has terminated, dissolved, or wound-up. When a partnership terminates under Federal law, its taxable year closes on the same date.

For purposes of Federal tax law or, more specifically, section 708(b)(1)(A), the date of termination is the date on which the partnership winds up its affairs in cessation of its business operation. Whether a partnership has done so is a factual determination that generally rests on an analysis of the various subsidiary elements of proof. The regulations interpreting section 708(b)(1)(A) establish a liberal approach to a finding of a business nexus sufficient not to terminate a partnership. In accordance with those regulations, a partnership continues to exist even when its operations are substantially changed or reduced in a period of winding up, and even when its sole asset during that period is cash. A termination under section 708(b)(1)(A) occurs only when "the operations of the partnership are discontinued and no part of any business, financial operation, or venture of the partnership continues to be carried on by any of its partners in a partnership." In other words, the Regulations indicate, a partnership is terminated under section 708(b)(1)(A) only when the winding up of its business affairs is completed and "all remaining assets, consisting only of cash, are distributed to the partners".

The decided cases apply the statute similarly. Those cases indicate that a nominal amount of continuing business or financial activity precludes a partnership from terminating for Federal tax purposes even when the partnership has abandoned or discontinued its primary business activity. In Foxman v. Commissioner, 41 T.C. 535 (1964), affd. 352 F.2d 466 (3d Cir. 1965), for example, a partnership sold its assets to a corporation in which the partners were shareholders and received in exchange two promissory notes. The Court held that the partnership continued to exist after its asset sale in that it held the notes received in the sale, collected interest on those notes, and made minor purchases. In Baker Commodities, Inc. v. Commissioner, 415 F.2d 519 (9th Cir. 1969), affg. 48 T.C. 374 (1967), the Court of Appeals for the Ninth Circuit reached a similar result. There, the partnership's principal asset was a convalescent hospital that was closed and then sold 9 months later in exchange for a note. The court cited Foxman and held that the partnership's sale of its asset did not result in its termination. Respondent argued in *Baker Commodities, Inc.* that the partnership had terminated upon its sale of the hospital because it then ceased engaging in its principal business activity. The court disagreed. The court held that the cessation of a partnership's primary purpose is not necessarily a termination under section 708 but what is required by the statute is a complete cessation of all partnership activity, inclusive of a distribution to the partners of all of the partnership's assets. The court noted that a partnership whose sole operation is the winding up of its affairs terminates only upon the cessation of all activity and the distribution of its remaining asset, cash.

In *Baker Commodities, Inc.* the court also relied upon Ginsburg v. United States, 184 Ct. Cl. 444, 396 F.2d 983 (1968). There, the partnership discontinued its primary business activity, the development of land, but continued to cultivate the land. The Court of Claims declined to find that the partnership had terminated through a cessation of its primary business. The Court of Claims rejected the Government's argument that a partnership terminates upon the abandonment of its primary purpose, stating:

> Subparagraph (A) of Section 708(b)(1) provides that a partnership is terminated if '*no part of any* business, financial operation, or venture of the partnership continues to be carried on by any of its partners in a partnership' (emphasis added). There is nothing to indicate that this provision requires less than what it says—a complete cessation of all partnership business—and therefore we cannot accept the Government's contention that a partnership is terminated if it abandons just its 'primary purpose.'

The Court of Claims also stated that "the fact that the partnership continued to hold the property for a business purpose—investment—might well be an adequate showing that it was not sufficiently inoperative to evoke the termination provision of Section 708(b)(1)(A)."

Turning to the facts at hand, we are unaware of any decided case that directly answers the question at hand; to wit, whether a partnership terminates for Federal tax purposes when (1) its controlling partner purportedly winds up the affairs of the partnership's business operation by using procedures apparently contrary to those stated in the partnership agreement, (2) another partner has filed a lawsuit to compel the use of the procedures stated in the agreement, and (3) a resolution of that lawsuit could reasonably lead to the partnership's reporting in a subsequent year of significant income, credit, gain, loss, or deduction. With our understanding of the statute, Regulations, and judicial jurisprudence in mind, however, it is evident to us that we must answer this question in the negative and hold that HCMP was not terminated during 1998. HCMP's affairs as to its business operations were not completed as of the end of that year in that an HCMP partner, Collins, was at that time legitimately challenging the procedures used by the managing general partner in winding up the partnership's business, and a resolution of Collins's lawsuit could reasonably lead to HCMP's reporting in a subsequent year of significant income, credit, gain, loss, or deduction (e.g., from a public sale of the marina).[1] While HCMP's managing general partner may have subjectively intended to terminate HCMP for Federal tax purposes during 1998, the fact of the matter is that it failed to wind up HCMP's business operation in accordance with the procedures which the HCMP partners as a whole

---

[1] We also do not believe that Collins' HCMP partnership interest was effectively liquidated as of the end of 1998 in that (1) he had filed the lawsuit challenging as inconsistent with the partnership agreement his right to keep the $389,662 check sent to him as a liquidation distribution and (2) he had delivered that check to the trial court pending resolution of the lawsuit.

had agreed would be applied in such a situation. The agreed-upon procedures of paragraph 12 state clearly and unequivocally that the managing general partner of HCMP shall in the case of HCMP's dissolution wind up and liquidate the partnership by "selling the Partnership property".

For Federal tax purposes, Congress has given the partners of a partnership broad authority to negotiate the terms of their business relationship, including the terms governing their business's formation, operation, and dissolution, so as to achieve simplicity, flexibility, and equity as between the partners. Given this broad grant of authority, the legislative intent for simplicity, flexibility, and equity as between the partners, and the fact that each partner's distributive share of income, gain, loss, deduction, or credit generally turns on the partnership agreement, sec. 704(a), it seems to us that the winding up of HCMP (and hence its termination) for Federal tax purposes must also be in accordance with the partnership agreement. In fact, but for a procedural violation that the trial court stated was committed by Collins as to the lawsuit, and which the trial court believed made void all judicial action taken in the lawsuit after October 17, 2000, even the trial court has concluded that HCMP continues to exist for State law purposes. The trial court concluded in 2003 that HCMP was not then wound up, that Collins remained an HCMP partner, and that Collins, as a partner, was entitled to his share of HCMP income from November 18, 1998, through the time that the marina was publicly sold. As the Treasury Regulations on the termination of partnerships are careful to note, a partnership's termination under section 708(b)(1)(A) does not occur until the winding up of its business operations is completed.

Respondent seeks a contrary holding focusing on the fact that HCMP and its partners other than Collins filed tax returns reporting that HCMP had been terminated during 1998 and that Sunroad limited partnership filed a tax return for a period thereafter reporting that it had acquired HCMP's business, assets, and liabilities. According to respondent, Collins may not unilaterally disavow his other partners' view that HCMP had terminated during 1998, nor the fact that HCMP's business operation is now being reported by another taxpayer. We find respondent's focus misplaced. Simply because a managing partner acts unilaterally to dissolve a partnership, to zero out the partnership assets and liabilities, and to report to the Commissioner that the partnership has been terminated does not mean that the partnership has terminated for Federal tax purposes. Nor is it critical to our decision that HCMP is no longer reporting the marina business as its own. What is important to us is that the parties to the HCMP partnership agreement had agreed that the marina would be sold by HCMP in the case of a dissolution, that basic tax principles establish that any income or loss on such a sale must be reported by HCMP, and that such a sale by or on behalf of HCMP may reasonably occur in a year after 1998.

We hold that HCMP was not terminated during 1998 as reported by its managing general partner and as determined by respondent. All arguments for a contrary holding have been considered, and those arguments not discussed herein have been found to be without merit. Accordingly,

Decision will be entered under Rule 155.

CHAPTER **18**

Hybrid Entities

PROBLEM AREA 18

INTRODUCTION

A "hybrid" entity is one that is treated as a conduit entity ("fiscally transparent") by one jurisdiction but as a taxable entity ("fiscally opaque") by another. For example, a limited liability company with more than one member may be treated as a partnership by the United States but as a taxable corporation by Japan. As to the types of hybrid entities, there are four logical possibilities. An entity treated as fiscally transparent by the United States but fiscally opaque by another jurisdiction is commonly referred to as a "regular" hybrid; such an entity may be formed either under the laws of the United States or under foreign law (a "domestic regular hybrid" or a "foreign regular hybrid," respectively). Similarly, a "reverse" hybrid, which is treated as a taxable entity by the United States but as a conduit by the foreign jurisdiction, may be formed under either United States or foreign law, resulting in a "domestic reverse hybrid" or a "foreign reverse hybrid," respectively.

Although it was possible for hybrids to exist under earlier law, the promulgation of the "check the box" Regulations in the mid-1990s created a proliferation of hybrids that would not have occurred otherwise. This, in turn, presented numerous challenges to the tax system. For example, a foreign partnership with foreign partners that has elected to be taxed as a corporation for United States tax purposes will likely still be treated as a partnership under the tax laws of most foreign jurisdictions. If this foreign reverse hybrid can use its status as a corporation (a fiscally opaque entity) under United States law to claim the benefits of an income tax treaty between the United States and hybrid's home jurisdiction, it can reduce or eliminate its United States tax liability on United States-source income while paying no foreign tax on such income to its home jurisdiction, thereby achieving double non-taxation.

Every income tax treaty to which the United States is a party contains a definition of "resident," identifying the persons who are entitled to claim the benefits of that treaty. One approach to solving the problems of double non-taxation (as well as double taxation) presented by hybrids would be to amend these treaty definitions as necessary to reach appropriate results. While this effort is ongoing, it is time-consuming and uncertain.

In the meantime, the Treasury Department has issued Regulations under § 894 to address this issue. The central tenet of these Regulations is that a foreign person's entitlement to treaty benefits with respect to an item of United States-source income depends on whether that person is subject to tax on the item in his or its home jurisdiction. Thus, a foreign entity that is fiscally transparent in its home jurisdiction cannot claim treaty benefits, even if it is treated as fiscally opaque for United States tax purposes. The owners of such an entity may, however, be entitled to treaty benefits, if they are not fiscally transparent themselves. These results follow from the purpose of income tax treaties to reduce or eliminate double taxation: if the foreign entity is not subject to tax in its home jurisdiction, United States taxation of the entity will not create double taxation of the entity.

The § 894 Regulations have not rendered treaty language irrelevant, because the Regulations provide that an explicit agreement in the text of an income tax treaty will override any inconsistent provision of the Regulations. Accordingly, one must consult any applicable income tax treaty in addition to the Regulations; in many cases, the two sources will reach perfectly consistent results.

The § 894 Regulations apply to passive income like dividends and interest, not to business profits, where § 875(1) dictates that the partners of an entity treated as a partnership for United States tax purposes are treated as engaged in the business of the partnership directly, apparently even if the entity is treated as fiscally opaque under foreign law. Importantly, the § 894 Regulations apply not only to hybrid entities, but also to entities that are treated as fiscally transparent in all relevant jurisdictions. These issues are explored in the questions that follow.

PROBLEM 18

QUESTIONS

1. The ABC partnership, formed in Austria and treated by Austria and the United States as a partnership, receives a $9,000 dividend from Z Inc., a United States corporation. ABC owns less than ten percent of the stock of Z Inc. A, B, and C are individuals who are residents of Austria. Which persons, if any, are entitled to tax treaty benefits?

2. Same as question 1. above, except that A is a resident of Argentina, which treats ABC as a partnership.

3. Same as question 1. above, except that A, B, and C are residents of Argentina, which treats ABC as a partnership.

4. Same as question 1. above, except that A is a resident of France, which treats ABC as a partnership.

5. Same as question 1. above, except that Austria treats ABC as a corporation even though the United States considers it to be a partnership.

6. The ABC partnership, formed in Austria and treated as a corporation by Austria and as a partnership by the United States, receives a $9,000 dividend from Z Inc., a United States corporation. ABC owns less than ten percent of the stock of Z Inc. A is an individual resident of France, which considers ABC to be a partnership. B and C are individual residents of Austria. Which persons, if any, are entitled to tax treaty benefits?

7. The ABC partnership, formed in Austria and treated as a partnership by Austria and the United States, receives a $9,000 dividend from Z Inc., a United States corporation. ABC owns less than ten percent of the stock of Z Inc. A and B are individual residents of Ireland, which considers ABC to be a corporation. C is an individual resident of France, which also considers ABC to be a corporation. Which persons, if any, are entitled to tax treaty benefits?

8. Same as question 6. above, except that the income derived by ABC is profits from carrying on a trade or business in the United States.

9. Same as question 6. above, except that the United States treats ABC as a corporation, while Austria and France treat ABC as a partnership.

MATERIALS

Convention Between the Republic of Austria and the United States of America for the Avoidance of Double Taxation and the Prevention of Fiscal Evasion with Respect to Taxes on Income (1996)

The Republic of Austria and the United States of America, desiring to conclude a convention for the avoidance of double taxation and the prevention of fiscal evasion with respect to taxes on income, have agreed as follows:

ARTICLE 1
Personal Scope

1. Except as otherwise provided in this Convention, this Convention shall apply to persons who are residents of one or both of the Contracting States. . . .

ARTICLE 3
General Definitions

1. For the purposes of this Convention:

a) the term "person" includes an individual, an estate, a trust, a company and any other body of persons;

b) the term "company" means any body corporate or any entity which is treated as a body corporate for tax purposes;

c) the terms "enterprise of a Contracting State" and "enterprise of the other Contracting State" mean respectively an enterprise carried on by a resident of a Contracting State and an enterprise carried on by a resident of the other Contracting State; . . .

ARTICLE 4
Resident

1. For the purposes of this Convention, the term "resident of a Contracting State" means any person who, under the laws of that State, is liable to tax therein by reason of the person's domicile, residence, citizenship, place of management, place of incorporation, or any other criterion of a similar nature, provided, however, that:

a) this term does not include any person who is liable to tax in that State in respect only of income from sources in that State;

b) in the case of income derived or paid by a partnership, estate, or trust, this term applies only to the extent that the income derived by such partnership, estate, or trust is subject to tax in that State as the income of a resident, either in its hands or in the hands of its partners, beneficiaries or grantor; . . .

ARTICLE 5
Permanent Establishment

1. For the purposes of this Convention, the term "permanent establishment" means a fixed place of business through which the business of an enterprise is wholly or partly carried on.

2. The term "permanent establishment" shall include especially:

a) a place of management;

b) a branch;

c) an office;

d) a factory;

e) a workshop; and

f) a mine, an oil or gas well, a quarry, or any other place of extraction of natural resources. . . .

4. Notwithstanding the preceding provisions of this Article, the term "permanent establishment" shall be deemed not to include:

a) the use of facilities solely for the purpose of storage, display, or delivery of goods or merchandise belonging to the enterprise;

b) the maintenance of a stock of goods or merchandise belonging to the enterprise solely for the purpose of storage, display or delivery;

c) the maintenance of a stock of goods or merchandise belonging to the enterprise solely for the purpose of processing by another enterprise;

d) the maintenance of a fixed place of business solely for the purpose of purchasing goods or merchandise, or of collecting information, for the enterprise;

e) the maintenance of a fixed place of business solely for the purpose of carrying on, for the enterprise, any other activity of a preparatory or auxiliary character;

f) the maintenance of a fixed place of business solely for any combination of the activities mentioned in subparagraphs a) to e) of this paragraph. . . .

ARTICLE 7
Business Profits

1. The business profits of an enterprise of a Contracting State shall be taxable only in that State unless the enterprise carries on business in the other Contracting State through a permanent establishment situated therein. If the enterprise carries on business as aforesaid, the business profits of the enterprise may be taxed in the other State but only so much of them as is attributable to that permanent establishment.

2. Subject to the provisions of paragraph 3, where an enterprise of a Contracting State carries on business in the other Contracting State through a permanent establishment situated therein, there shall in each Contracting State be attributed to that permanent establishment the business profits which it might be expected to make if it were a distinct and independent enterprise engaged in the same or similar activities under the same or similar conditions.

3. In determining the business profits of a permanent establishment, there shall be allowed as deductions expenses which are incurred for the purposes of the permanent establishment, including a reasonable allocation of executive and general administrative expenses, research and development expenses, interest, and other expenses incurred for the purposes of the enterprise as a whole (or the part thereof which includes the permanent establishment), whether incurred in the State in which the permanent establishment is situated or elsewhere. . . .

ARTICLE 10
Dividends

1. Dividends paid by a company which is a resident of a Contracting State to a resident of the other Contracting State may be taxed in that other State.

2. However, such dividends may also be taxed in the Contracting State of which the company paying the dividends is a resident, and according to the laws of that State, but if the beneficial owner of the dividends is a resident of the other Contracting State, the tax so charged shall not exceed:

a) 5 percent of the gross amount of the dividends if the beneficial owner is a company (other than a partnership) which owns directly at least 10 percent of the voting stock of the company paying the dividends;

b) 15 percent of the gross amount of the dividends in all other cases. . . .

3. The term "dividends" as used in this Article means income from shares or other rights, not being debt-claims, participating in profits, as well as income from other corporate rights which is subjected to the same taxation treatment as income from shares by the laws of the State of which the company making the distribution is a resident; and income from arrangements, including debt obligations, carrying the right to participate in, or determined with reference to, profits, to the extent so characterized under the law of the Contracting State in which the income arises.

4. The provisions of paragraphs 1 and 2 shall not apply if the recipient of the dividends, being a resident of a Contracting State, carries on business in the other Contracting State, of which the company paying the dividends is a resident, through a permanent establishment situated therein . . . and the holding in respect of which the dividends are paid is effectively connected with such permanent establishment . . . . In such a case, the provisions of Article 7 (Business Profits) . . . shall apply. . . .

ARTICLE 16
Limitation on Benefits

1. A person which is a resident of a Contracting State and derives income from the other Contracting State shall be entitled, in that other Contracting State, to benefits of this Convention only if such person is:

    a) an individual;

    b) a Contracting State or a political subdivision or local authority thereof;

    c) engaged in the active conduct of a trade or business in the first-mentioned Contracting State (other than the business of making or managing investments, unless these activities are banking or insurance activities carried on by a bank or insurance company), the income derived from the other Contracting State is derived in connection with, or is incidental to, that trade or business, and, with respect to income derived in connection with that trade or business, the trade or business is substantial in relation to the activity carried on in the other Contracting State giving rise to the income in respect of which treaty benefits are being claimed in that other Contracting State;

    d) a person, if:

        (i) more than 50 percent of the beneficial interest in such person (or in the case of a company, more than 50 percent of the number of shares of each class of the company's shares) is owned, directly or indirectly, by persons entitled to benefits of this Convention under subparagraphs (a), (b), (e), [or] (f) . . . of this paragraph or who are citizens of the United States; and

        (ii) not more than 50 percent of the gross income of such person is used, directly or indirectly, to meet liabilities (including liabilities for interest or royalties) to persons who are not entitled to benefits of this Convention under subparagraph (a), (b), (e), [or] (f) . . . of this paragraph and are not citizens of the United States;

    e) a company in whose principal class of shares there is substantial and regular trading on a recognized stock exchange;

    f) a company that is at least 90 percent owned, directly or indirectly, by not more than five companies referred to in subparagraph e), provided that each person in the chain of ownership is a resident of a Contracting State, and provided further that the owner of any remaining portion of the company is an individual resident of a Contracting State; . . . .

Convention Between the Government of the United States of America and the Government of the French Republic for the Avoidance of Double Taxation and the Prevention of Fiscal Evasion with Respect to Taxes on Income and Capital (1994, as amended by Protocols signed December 2004, and January 13, 2009)

The Government of the United States of America and the Government of the French Republic, desiring to conclude a new convention for the avoidance of double taxation and the prevention of fiscal evasion with respect to taxes on income and capital, have agreed as follows:

ARTICLE 1
Personal Scope

This Convention shall apply only to persons who are residents of one or both of the Contracting States, except as otherwise provided in the Convention. . . .

ARTICLE 3
General Definitions

1. For the purposes of this Convention: . . .

d) the term "person" includes, but is not limited to, an individual and a company;

e) the term "company" means any body corporate or any entity which is treated as a body corporate for tax purposes;

f) the terms "enterprise of a Contracting State" and "enterprise of the other Contracting State" mean, respectively, an enterprise carried on by a resident of a Contracting State and an enterprise carried on by a resident of the other Contracting State; . . .

ARTICLE 4
Resident

1. For the purposes of this Convention, the term "resident of a Contracting State" means any person who, under the laws of that State, is liable to tax therein by reason of his domicile, residence, place of management, place of incorporation, or any other criterion of a similar nature. But this term does not include any person who is liable to tax in that State in respect only of income from sources in that State, or of capital situated therein.

2. . . .

c) An item of income paid from the United States to a French qualified partnership shall be considered derived by a resident of France only to the extent that such income is included currently in the taxable income of a shareholder, associate, or other member that is otherwise treated as a resident of France under the provisions of this Convention. A French qualified partnership means a partnership:

(i) that has its place of effective management in France,

(ii) that has not elected to be taxed in France as a corporation,

(iii) the tax base of which is computed at the partnership level for French tax purposes, and

(iv) all of the shareholders, associates or other members of which, pursuant to the tax laws of France, are liable to tax therein in respect of their share of the profits of that partnership.

3. For purposes of applying this Convention, an item of income, profit, or gain derived through an entity that is fiscally transparent under the laws of either Contracting State, and that is formed or organized:

a) in either Contracting State, or;

b) in a state that has concluded an agreement containing a provision for the exchange of information with a view to the prevention of tax evasion with the Contracting State from which the income, profit, or gain is derived,

shall be considered to be derived by a resident of a Contracting State to the extent that the item is treated for purposes of the taxation law of such Contracting State as the income, profit, or gain of a resident. . . .

ARTICLE 5
Permanent Establishment

1. For the purposes of this Convention, the term "permanent establishment" means a fixed place of business through which the business of an enterprise is wholly or partly carried on.

2. The term "permanent establishment" includes especially:

a) a place of management;

b) a branch;

c) an office;

d) a factory;

e) a workshop; and

f) a mine, an oil or gas well, a quarry, or any other place of extraction of natural resources. . . .

4. Notwithstanding the preceding provisions of this Article, the term "permanent establishment" shall be deemed not to include:

a) the use of facilities solely for the purpose of storage, display, or delivery of goods or merchandise belonging to the enterprise;

b) the maintenance of a stock of goods or merchandise belonging to the enterprise solely for the purpose of storage, display, or delivery;

c) the maintenance of a stock of goods or merchandise belonging to the enterprise solely for the purpose of processing by another enterprise;

d) the maintenance of a fixed place of business solely for the purpose of purchasing goods or merchandise, or of collecting information, for the enterprise;

e) the maintenance of a fixed place of business solely for the purpose of carrying on, for the enterprise, any other activity of a preparatory or auxiliary character;

f) the maintenance of a fixed place of business solely for any combination of the activities mentioned in subparagraphs (a) to (e), provided that the overall activity of the fixed place of business resulting from this combination is of a preparatory or auxiliary character. . . .

ARTICLE 7
Business Profits

1. The profits of an enterprise of a Contracting State shall be taxable only in that State unless the enterprise carries on business in the other Contracting State through a permanent establishment situated therein. If the enterprise carries on business as aforesaid, the profits of the enterprise may be taxed in the other State but only so much of them as is attributable to that permanent establishment.

2. Subject to the provisions of paragraph 3, where an enterprise of a Contracting State carries on business in the other Contracting State through a permanent establishment situated therein, there shall in each Contracting State be attributed to that permanent establishment the profits which it might be expected to make if it were a distinct and independent enterprise engaged in the same or similar activities under the same or similar conditions.

3. In determining the profits of a permanent establishment, there shall be allowed as deductions expenses which are reasonably connected with such profits, including executive and general administrative expenses, whether incurred in the State in which the permanent establishment is situated or elsewhere.

4. A partner shall be considered to have realized income or incurred deductions to the extent of his share of the profits or losses of a partnership, as provided in the partnership agreement (provided that any special allocations of profits or losses have substantial economic effect). For this purpose, the character (including source and attribution to a permanent establishment) of any item of income or deduction accruing to a partner shall be determined as if it were realized or incurred by the partner in the same manner as realized or incurred by the partnership. . . .

ARTICLE 10
Dividends

1. Dividends paid by a company that is a resident of a Contracting State to a resident of the other Contracting State may be taxed in that other State.

2. However, such dividends may also be taxed in the Contracting State of which the company paying the dividends is a resident and according to the laws of that State, but if the beneficial owner of the dividends is a resident of the other Contracting State, the tax so charged shall not exceed:

a) 5 percent of the gross amount of the dividends if the beneficial owner is a company that owns:

(i) directly at least 10 percent of the voting stock of the company paying the dividends, if such company is a resident of the United States; or

(ii) directly or indirectly at least 10 percent of the capital of the company paying the dividends, if such company is a resident of France;

b) 15 percent of the gross amount of the dividends in all other cases . . . .

CHAPTER 19

Section 704(c)

PROBLEM AREA 19

INTRODUCTION

The purpose of § 704(c), as set forth in Regulation § 1.704-3(a)(1), is "to prevent the shifting of tax consequences among partners with respect to precontribution gain or loss." When property is contributed to a partnership with built-in gain or loss, there is a difference between its book carrying value and its adjusted tax basis to the partnership, and a corresponding difference between the book capital and the tax capital of the contributing partner. (A partner's "tax capital" is his share of the partnership's basis in its assets, exclusive of any portion of such basis that is attributable to debt.) The goal of allocations under § 704(c) is to eliminate such "book/tax disparities" by allocating pre-contribution gain or loss, when realized by the partnership, to the contributing partner, and thereby to prevent the shifting of such gain or loss to any other partner. Both in this case and in the case of depreciation or amortization, § 704(c) achieves its goal by allocating tax items equal to book items to the non-contributing partners.

The development of § 704(c) as a tool to prevent gain-shifting and loss-shifting is the most important development in partnership taxation over the past 25 years. The rising prominence of § 704(c) is attributable to the growing number and importance of low-taxed or non-taxed entities with which United States taxpayers may partner, including pension funds, university endowments and, significantly, non-United States entities. These potential partners present ripe opportunities for the shifting of gains (generally to such tax-advantaged partners) and losses (generally away from such partners). In addition, resistance to the computational complexities of § 704(c) in practice has diminished as a result of the increasing sophistication of taxpayers and the availability of personal computers.

Prior to 1984, application of the statute was wholly voluntary. Today, the principles of § 704(c) must be applied whenever a partnership depreciates, amortizes, or makes a taxable disposition of any property that a partner contributed to the partnership with built-in gain or loss. Without more, however, there would be boundless opportunities for the shifting of gains and losses through the use of partnerships. Some of these opportunities have been largely foreclosed, while others remain.

If, for example, a partnership using the "traditional" method under § 704(c) recognizes less than the amount of pre-contribution gain on its disposition of contributed property, the allocation of gain to the contributing partner will be limited to the amount recognized by the partnership by operation of the "ceiling rule." Consider, for example, an equal partnership between A and B, to which A contributes property with a value of $10,000 and an adjusted basis for tax purposes of $4,000, while B contributes $10,000 in cash. If the partnership thereafter sells the contributed property for $6,000, each of A and B will have realized an economic loss of $2,000. If the ceiling rule applies, however,

B will be allocated no tax loss, and A will be allocated only $2,000 of tax gain.

While it may seem that no gain has been shifted in this case, in fact B has realized a book (economic) loss but no tax loss, and A's tax gain is correspondingly smaller than it would be if B were allowed to claim the $2,000 tax loss. Thus, in effect, the operation of the ceiling rule shifts tax gain from the contributing partner to the non-contributing partners. Regulations finalized in 1993 and 1994 authorize partnerships to use "curative" or "remedial" allocations to correct this effect, but the use of these allocations is voluntary, except in cases of abuse. Thus, the potential imbalance of book consequences and tax consequences illustrated by this simple example continues to be present in many cases.

Despite the statement in Regulation § 1.704-3(a)(1) that the focus of § 704(c) is pre-contribution gain or loss, there has been considerable development of § 704(c) as a tool to prevent the shifting of gain or loss economically accrued while property is held by a partnership. The concern here arises from a change in the composition of the partnership by, for example, the entry or exit of a partner or simply by a change in the percentages of ownership. Absent a mechanism to route such gain or loss back to the original partners, gain or loss could be shifted away from them. The revaluation of the partnership's property and of the partners' capital accounts at the time of such an ownership change provides this mechanism. If the values of the partnership's assets have changed, a revaluation will create book/tax disparities upon which § 704(c) can operate.

Assume, for example, that an equal partnership formed with cash contributions from A and B is considering the admission of a new partner, C. Prior to admitting C, the partnership revalues its assets from their original book carrying value of $20,000 to their new value of $30,000. This revaluation, in turn, increases the book capital of A and B by $5,000 each, but does not increase their tax capital. Thus, each of A and B has a book/tax disparity of $5,000 as a result of the revaluation.

The approach of the Regulations is to require § 704(c) allocations (confusingly called "reverse" § 704(c) allocations in this context) to be made in any such case, but generally not to require revaluations. Regulation § 1.704-1(b)(2)(iv)(f) cautions, however, that a partnership's failure to revalue its assets may be scrutinized. Moreover, Proposed Regulation § 1.704-1(b)(2)(iv)(s), which would require revaluation upon exercise of a non-compensatory option, may point toward a less permissive approach in the future.

The shifting of gain or loss through partnership distributions is a topic that to date has been incompletely addressed by either Congress or the Treasury Department. Sections 704(c)(1)(B) and 737, considered in Problem Area 24, represent statutory responses to taxpayers' attempts to shift pre-contribution gain or loss through coordinated partnership contributions and distributions. A more pervasive issue, perhaps, is a partnership's ability to shift through property distributions gain or loss that has accumulated while the distributed property (or other property) has been held by the partnership. There is as yet no analogue to the reverse § 704(c) allocation to address this issue.

PROBLEM 19

QUESTIONS

1. A and B form equal partnership AB on January 1, Year 1. B contributes $50,000 cash. A contributes non-depreciable Property 1 with a basis of $30,000 and a value of $50,000.

    a. On January 1, Year 3, the partnership sells Property 1 for $90,000. What are the results to the parties if the partnership uses the traditional method for purposes of § 704(c)? What if Property 1 were sold for $40,000? What if it were sold for $20,000?

    b. On January 1, Year 3, the partnership sells Property 1 for $20,000. What are the results to the parties if the partnership uses the traditional method with curative allocations for purposes of § 704(c)? In this and following examples, feel free to assume the existence of additional partnership income, gain, or loss as needed.

    c. On January 1, Year 3, the partnership sells Property 1 for $20,000. What are the results to the parties if the partnership uses the remedial method for purposes of § 704(c)?

2. A and B form equal partnership AB on January 1, Year 1. B contributes $50,000 cash. A contributes non-depreciable Property 1 with a basis of $30,000 and a value of $50,000. C joins the partnership as a one-third partner on January 1, Year 2, when Property 1 has appreciated to $110,000 and the partnership continues to hold the initial amount of cash and no other assets. On that date, the partnership invests all of its cash in Property 2. On December 31, Year 4, the partnership sells Property 1 for $125,000, sells Property 2 for $160,000, and liquidates. What are the results to the parties if C acquires the partnership interest by making a cash contribution of $80,000?

3. Using the facts of question 2. above, assume that the partnership sells Property 1 for $95,000, rather than $125,000. What are the results to the parties if the partnership uses:

    a. The traditional method?

    b. The traditional method with curative allocations?

    c. The remedial method?

4. A and B form equal partnership AB on July 1, Year 1. B contributes $50,000 cash. A contributes Property 1 with a basis of $20,000, a value of $50,000, and a 15-year depreciable life for book and tax purposes with ten years remaining. (In this and following questions, assume that Property 1 is depreciated on a straight-line basis.) The partnership sells Property 1 on June 30, Year 3, for $45,000. What are the results to the parties if the partnership uses:

    a. The traditional method?

b. The traditional method with curative allocations?

c. The remedial method?

5. A and B form equal partnership AB on July 1, Year 1. B contributes $50,000 cash. A contributes Property 1 with a basis of $5,000, a value of $50,000, and a 15-year depreciable life for book and tax purposes with two years remaining. The partnership sells Property 1 on June 30, Year 3, for $40,000. What are the results to the parties if the partnership uses:

   a. The traditional method?

   b. The traditional method with curative allocations?

   c. The remedial method?

6. A and B form partnership AB on July 1, Year 1. B contributes $50,000 cash. A contributes Property 1 with a basis of zero, a value of $50,000, and a 15-year depreciable life for book and tax purposes with five years remaining. Each year, the partnership generates $10,000 of operating cash flow, $8,000 from Property 1 and $2,000 from the cash, $10,000 of taxable income, and zero book income. The partnership agreement provides that income will be allocated 20 percent to A and 80 percent to B, and gain or loss on the disposition of Property 1 will be allocated 80 percent to A and 20 percent to B. The partnership dissolves on June 30,Year 5, distributing Property 1, the value of which remains $50,000, and cash to A and the remaining cash to B. What are the results to the parties if the partnership utilizes the traditional method?

7. A, B, and C form equal partnership ABC on January 1, Year 1. B and C contribute $50,000 in cash. A contributes non-depreciable Property 1 with a basis of $70,000 and a value of $50,000. In Year 2, A sells the partnership interest to D for $50,000 and the partnership makes no election under § 754. In Year 3, the partnership sells Property 1 for $50,000. What are the results to the parties?

8. A and B form equal partnership AB on July 1, Year 1. B contributes $50,000 in cash. A contributes Property 1 with a basis of $70,000, a value of $50,000, and a 15-year depreciable life for both book and tax purposes with ten years remaining.

   a. On June 30, Year 3, the partnership sells Property 1 for $25,000. What are the results to the parties if the partnership uses the traditional method for purposes of § 704(c)? What if Property 1 were sold for $45,000?

   b. On June 30, Year 3, the partnership sells Property 1 for $45,000. What are the results to the parties if the partnership uses the traditional method with curative allocations for purposes of § 704(c)?

   c. On June 30, Year 3, the partnership sells Property 1 for $45,000. What are the results to the parties if the partnership uses the remedial method for purposes of § 704(c)?

MATERIALS

Rev. Rul. 2004-49
2004-1 C.B. 939

ISSUE

If, pursuant to § 1.704-1(b)(2)(iv)(*f*) of the Regulations, a partnership revalues a section 197 intangible, may the partnership allocate amortization with respect to the section 197 intangible so as to take into account the built-in gain or loss from the revaluation?

FACTS

Situation 1. A and B are partners in the AB partnership. C contributes money (more than a de minimis amount) to the partnership in exchange for a partnership interest. The partnership revalues the assets of the partnership under § 1.704-1(b)(2)(iv)(*f*). The AB partnership owns several assets, including Asset 1, a section 197 intangible. Asset 1 is amortizable in the hands of the partnership. A, B, and C are not related.

Situation 2. Situation 2 is the same as Situation 1 except that Asset 1 is not amortizable in the hands of the partnership [i.e., is subject to the anti-churning rules of § 197(f)(9)].

LAW

Section 197(a) provides that a taxpayer is entitled to an amortization deduction with respect to any amortizable section 197 intangible. The amount of the deduction is determined by amortizing the adjusted basis (for purposes of determining gain) of the intangible ratably over the 15-year period beginning with the month in which the intangible was acquired. Section 197(c)(1) provides that, with certain exceptions, the term "amortizable section 197 intangible" means any section 197 intangible, (A) that is acquired by the taxpayer after the date of the enactment of § 197, and (B) that is held in connection with the conduct of a trade or business or an activity described in § 212.

Section 197(d)(1) provides that the term "section 197 intangible" means (A) goodwill; (B) going concern value; (C) any of the following intangible items: (i) workforce in place including its composition and terms and conditions (contractual or otherwise) of its employment, (ii) business books and records, operating systems, or any other information base (including lists or other information with respect to current or prospective customers), (iii) any patent, copyright, formula, process, design, pattern, knowhow, format, or other similar items, (iv) any customer-based intangible, (v) any supplier-based intangible, and (vi) any other similar item; (D) any license, permit, or other right granted by a governmental unit or an agency or instrumentality thereof; (E) any covenant not to compete (or other arrangement to the extent the arrangement has substantially the same effect as a covenant not to compete) entered into in connection with an acquisition (directly or indirectly) of an interest in a trade or business or substantial portion thereof; and (F) any franchise, trademark, or trade name.

Under § 197(f)(9)(A), the term "amortizable section 197 intangible" does not include any section 197 intangible that is goodwill or going concern value (or for which depreciation or amortization would not have been allowable but for § 197) and that is acquired by the taxpayer after the date of the enactment of § 197, if (i) the intangible was held or used at any time on or after July 25, 1991, and on or before such date of enactment by the taxpayer or a related person, (ii) the intangible was acquired from a person who held such intangible at any time on or after July 25, 1991, and on or before such date of enactment, and, as part of the transaction, the user of such intangible does not change, or (iii) the taxpayer grants the right to use such intangible to a person (or a person related to such person) who held or used such intangible at any time on or after July 25, 1991, and on or before such date of enactment.

An intangible described in § 197(f)(9) (a section 197(f)(9) intangible) is treated as an amortizable section 197 intangible only to the extent permitted under § 1.197-2(h). The purpose of the anti-churning rules of §§ 197(f)(9) and 1.197-2(h) is to prevent the amortization of section 197(f)(9) intangibles unless they are transferred after the applicable effective date in a transaction giving rise to a significant change in owner-ship or use. Section 1.197-2(h)(1)(ii). Section 1.197-2(h)(12) provides special rules that apply for purposes of determining whether transactions involving partnerships give rise to a significant change in ownership or use.

Under § 1.197-2(h)(5), a section 197(f)(9) intangible may be amortized by the acquirer of the intangible if the intangible was an amortizable section 197 intangible in the hands of the seller (or transferor), but only if the acquisition transaction and the transaction in which the seller (or transferor) acquired the intangible or interest therein are not part of a series of related transactions.

Under § 704(b), a partner's distributive share of income, gain, loss, deduction, or credit (or item thereof) is determined in accordance with the partnership agreement provided that those allocations have substantial economic effect. If the allocations under the partnership agreement do not have substantial economic effect or the partnership agreement does not provide as to a partner's distributive shares of partnership items, then the partner's distributive share of such items is determined in accordance with the partner's interest in the partnership (determined by taking into account all facts and circumstances).

Section 1.704-1(b) describes various requirements that must be met for partner-ship allocations to have substantial economic effect. Among these requirements is that (except as otherwise provided in § 1.704-1(b)) the partnership agreement must provide for the determination and maintenance of capital accounts in accordance with the rules of § 1.704-1(b)(2)(iv).

Section 1.704-1(b)(2)(iv)(f) provides that, if certain criteria are met, the capital account maintenance rules of § 1.704-1(b)(2)(iv) will not be violated if a partnership agreement, upon the occurrence of certain events, increases or decreases the capital accounts of the partners to reflect a revaluation of partnership property (including intangibles such as goodwill) on the partnership's books.

Section 704(c)(1)(A) provides that, under Regulations prescribed by the Secre-tary, income, gain, loss, and deduction with respect to property contributed to the partnership by a partner shall be shared among the partners so as to take account of the variation between the basis of the property to the partnership and its fair market value at the time of contribution.

Section 1.704-3 provides rules applicable to partnership allocations under § 704(c)(1)(A). Section 1.704-3(a)(1) provides that allocations under § 704(c)(1)(A) must be made using a reasonable method that is consistent with the purpose of § 704(c). Section 1.704-3 describes three allocation methods that are generally reasonable: the traditional method, the traditional method with curative allocations, and the remedial allocation method.

Section 1.704-3(a)(6)(i) provides that the principles of § 1.704-3 apply to allocations with respect to property for which differences between book value and adjusted tax basis are created when a partnership revalues partnership property pursuant to § 1.704-1(b)(2)(iv)(f) (reverse § 704(c) allocations). Partnerships are not required to use the same allocation method for reverse § 704(c) allocations as for contributed property, even if at the time of revaluation the property is already subject to §§ 704(c)(1)(A) and 1.704-3.

Section 1.197-2(g)(4)(i) provides that, to the extent that an intangible was an amortizable section 197 intangible in the hands of the contributing partner, a partnership may make allocations of amortization deductions with respect to the intangible to all of its partners under any of the permissible methods described in the Regulations under § 704(c). Section 1.197-2(g)(4)(ii) provides that, to the extent that an intangible was not an amortizable section 197 intangible in the hands of the contributing partner, the intangible is not amortizable by the partnership. However, if a partner contributes a section 197 intangible to a partnership and the partnership adopts the remedial allocation method for making § 704(c) allocations of amortization deductions, the partnership generally may make remedial allocations of amortization deductions with respect to the contributed section 197 intangible in accordance with § 1.704-3(d).

Section 1.197-2(h)(12)(vii)(A) provides that the anti-churning rules do not apply to curative or remedial allocations of amortization with respect to a section 197(f)(9) intangible if the intangible was an amortizable section 197 intangible in the hands of the contributing partner (unless § 1.197-2(h)(10) causes the intangible to cease to be an amortizable section 197 intangible in the hands of the partnership).

Section 1.197-2(h)(12)(vii)(B) provides that, if a section 197(f)(9) intangible was not amortizable in the hands of the contributing partner, a non-contributing partner generally may receive remedial allocations of amortization under § 704(c) that are deductible for federal income tax purposes. However, such a partner may not receive remedial allocations of amortization under § 704(c) if that partner is related to the partner that contributed the intangible or if, as part of a series of related transactions that includes the contribution of the section 197(f)(9) intangible to the partnership, the contributing partner or related person (other than the partnership) becomes (or remains) a direct user of the contributed intangible. Under § 1.197-2(h)(12)(vii)(B), taxpayers may use any reasonable method to determine amortization of the asset for book purposes, provided that the method used does not contravene the purposes of the anti-churning rules.

ANALYSIS

If, under § 1.704-1(b)(2)(iv)(f), a partnership revalues a section 197 intangible that is amortizable in the hands of the partnership, then the partnership may make allocations of amortization deductions with respect to the built-in gain or loss from the revaluation (i.e., the increase or decrease, respectively, in the book value of the intangible as a result of the revaluation) to all of its partners under any of the permissible methods described in § 1.704-3. If the revalued section 197 intangible is not amortizable in the hands of the partnership, then §§ 1.197-2(g)(4)(ii) and 1.197-2(h)(12)(vii) generally prevent the partnership from allocating amortization with respect to the intangible under § 1.704-3(a)(6)(i), but do not prevent the partnership from making remedial allocations of amortization with respect to the intangible. However, remedial allocations of amortization with respect to built-in gain or loss from the revaluation of a section 197(f)(9) intangible are not allowed to the extent that such allocations are, in substance, the equivalent of a remedial allocation of amortization to a partner that is related to the "contributing partner" (with respect to the revaluation). Also, under § 1.197-2(h)(12)(vii)(B), remedial allocations of amortization with respect to the built-in gain or loss from the revaluation of a section 197(f)(9) intangible are not allowed if, as part of a series of related transaction that includes the revaluation, the "contributing partners" (with respect to the revaluation) or related persons (other than the partnership) become (or remain) direct users of the intangible.

In Situation 1, the partnership may make traditional, curative, or remedial allocations of amortization under § 1.704-3 to take into account the built-in gain or loss from the revaluation of Asset 1. Section 1.197-2(g)(4)(i). Because Asset 1 is amortizable in the hands of the AB partnership, the anti-churning rules do not apply to reverse § 704(c) allocations of amortization from Asset 1.

In Situation 2, because Asset 1 is not amortizable in the hands of AB, the anti-churning rules apply. Under §§ 197-2(g)(4)(ii) and (h)(12)(vii)(B), the partnership may make deductible remedial, but not traditional or curative, allocations of amortization to take into account the built-in gain or loss from the revaluation of Asset 1, provided that such allocations are not limited by § 1.197- 2(h)(12)(vii)(B).

HOLDING

If, pursuant to § 1.704-1(b)(2)(iv)(f), a partnership revalues a section 197 intangible that was amortizable in the hands of the partnership, then the § 197 anti-churning rules do not apply and the partnership may make reverse § 704(c) allocations (including curative and remedial allocations) of amortization to take into account the built-in gain or loss from the revaluation of the intangible. If the revalued section 197 intangible was not amortizable in the hands of the partnership, then the partnership may make remedial, but not traditional or curative, allocations of amortization to take into account the built-in gain or loss from the revaluation of the intangible, provided that such allocations are not limited by § 1.197-2(h)(12)(vii)(B).

CHAPTER 20

Property Contributions: Non-Compensatory Options and Disguised Sales

PROBLEM AREA 20

INTRODUCTION

Section 707(a)(2)(B) was added to the Code in 1984 in response to what Congress believed to be an overly permissive approach by courts to transactions that are commonly referred to as "disguised sales." The statue authorizes (and the accompanying legislative history directs) the Service to issue Regulations to reign in these transactions, and the Service responded to this directive with Regulations issued in final form in 1992.

In one such transaction, a partner transfers appreciated property to the partnership and the partnership makes a related transfer of cash to the partner. Assume, for example, that a partner has a basis of $2,500 in his 20 percent interest in a partnership. He transfers to the partnership an asset valued at $1,000 with an adjusted basis of $400 and shortly thereafter the partnership transfers $1,000 in cash to him. There is no change in the partner's interest in the partnership as a result of this transaction.

If one applies the ordinary rules relating to contributions to and distributions from a partnership, the partner's outside basis is increased by $400, the partner's basis in the transferred property, to $2,900 under § 722. The cash distribution of $1,000 is not taxable under § 731(a)(1), because it does not exceed the partner's $2,900 outside basis, although the distribution reduces such basis to $1,900. Under § 723, the partnership takes a $400 basis in the transferred property, equal to the partner's former basis.

If, on the other hand, the transaction is treated as a sale of the transferred property, the partner calculates taxable gain by applying the $400 basis of the property sold against the $1,000 cash received from the partnership, thereby producing a taxable gain of $600 for the partner. The partnership takes a $1,000 cost basis in the transferred asset under § 1012. The $600 difference from the non-sale setting reflects the $600 gain realized by the partner.

Instead of distributing cash to the contributing partner, the partnership could duplicate the economic effect of the foregoing transaction by assuming indebtedness incurred by the contributing partner prior to making the contribution. Accordingly, the Regulations treat such a transaction as a disguised sale in certain cases.

It is possible for a partnership to make a disguised sale of its own property to one of its partners, for example by transferring appreciated (or depreciated) property to a partner in exchange for cash. Alternatively, a disguised sale may involve a transfer of non-cash consideration by both the partnership and the partner, in which case both the partner and the partnership are engaged in taxable transactions. (To the extent that such transactions are not re-characterized under § 707(a)(2)(B), they must still run the gauntlet of § 737.)

Finally, it is possible for partners to undertake a disguised sale of partnership interests by using the partnership as a "conduit" through which to flow the transfers of property and cash between the selling partner and the buying partner. Proposed Regulations on this topic were withdrawn amid great controversy in early 2009. Absent Regulations, the Service is left to challenge such transactions under judicial principles such as the step-transaction doctrine, as informed by the legislative history of § 707(a)(2)(B) itself.

Options issued by partnerships for consideration other than services rendered, *i.e.*, so-called "non-compensatory options," are most commonly found in the form of convertible debt (debt that gives the holder an option to exchange it for an equity stake in the partnership) or warrants issued to a lender as part of an investment unit that includes debt. In 2003, the Service issued Proposed Regulations to address a number of lingering concerns relating to the taxation of the issuance, exercise, and lapse of such options.

Although not at the heart of these Proposed Regulations, their treatment of § 704(c) issues is perhaps their most interesting contribution. Under the Proposed Regulations, a partnership must revalue its assets immediately after the exercise of a non-compensatory option and adjust the capital account of the exercising partner to reflect his claim on the partnership's assets. This process captures in the exercising partner's capital account the value that he has obtained through the option exercise and, to the extent that such value exceeds the amount paid (in option premium and exercise price), it creates a book/tax disparity to be addressed by future reverse § 704(c) allocations.

PROBLEM 20

QUESTIONS

1. The AB Partnership is a general partnership that has the following balance sheet.

	Adjusted Basis	Book Value	Fair Market Value
Assets			
Cash	$ 70,000	$ 70,000	$ 70,000
Land	100,000	100,000	200,000
Total	$170,000	$170,000	$270,000
Capital			
A	$ 85,000	$ 85,000	$135,000
B	85,000	85,000	135,000
Total	$170,000	$170,000	$270,000

C pays $10,000 for an option to acquire a one-third interest in the partnership at any time within the next three years for $125,000. What is the result to the parties upon the grant of the option? What is the result if the option price is $200,000? What is the result if the option price is $30,000?

2. The AB Partnership has the same balance sheet as in question 1. above. C transfers property with a basis of $2,000 and a value of $10,000 to the partnership in return for the option. What are the results to the parties?

3. Subsequent to the issuance to C of the option described in question 1. above, the AB Partnership has the following balance sheet.

	Adjusted Basis	Book Value	Fair Market Value
Assets			
Cash	$ 80,000	$ 80,000	$ 80,000
Land	100,000	100,000	200,000
Total	$180,000	$180,000	$280,000
Liabilities			
Option	$ 10,000	$ 10,000	$ 10,000
Capital			
A	$ 85,000	$ 85,000	$135,000
B	85,000	85,000	135,000
Total Liabilities & Capital	$180,000	$180,000	$280,000

The value of the partnership's land appreciates to $600,000, and C exercises the option through the payment of $125,000 to the partnership. What are the results to the parties? How is this transaction reflected on the partnership's books? Assume alternatively that the value of the partnership's land is $100,000 and C exercises the option through the payment of $60,000 to the partnership. What is the effect of this alternative transaction on the partnership's books?

4. The AB Partnership has the same balance sheet as in question 3. above. The value of the partnership's land appreciates to $600,000, and C exercises the option through the payment of $100,000 cash and stock worth $25,000 with a basis of $10,000, leaving the partnership with land worth $600,000, cash of $180,000, and stock worth $25,000. What are the results to the parties? The land thereafter appreciates to $700,000 and the partnership sells it. How are the book gain and the tax gain on this sale allocated among the partners?

5. The AB Partnership has the same balance sheet as in question 1. above. C contributes property with a value of $135,000 and a basis of $20,000 in return for a 20 percent interest in the partnership, followed immediately by a distribution of $67,500 to C. What are the results to the parties?

6. The AB Partnership has the same balance sheet as in question 1. above. C contributes property with a value of $135,000 and a basis of $20,000, subject to an encumbrance of $67,500, which C incurred 60 days before the contribution, for a 20 percent interest in the partnership. What is the result? Does it matter whether the encumbrance is recourse or nonrecourse?

7. The AB Partnership has the same balance sheet as in question 1. above. C transfers property worth $150,000 with a basis of $20,000, encumbered by a $67,500 recourse liability incurred three years ago, for a 20 percent interest in the partnership and a distribution of $15,000. What is the result to C?

8. AB, an LLC treated as a partnership for tax purposes, has assets valued at $100,000. C contributes unencumbered property worth $60,000 to AB in exchange for a one-third interest in capital and profits. In connection with this contribution, the LLC borrows $10,000 and distributes the proceeds of this borrowing to C. C guarantees repayment of the $10,000 liability to the lender. What is the result to C?

9. The AB Partnership has the same balance sheet as in question 1. above. C contributes $135,000 for a partnership interest and $67,500 is distributed to A immediately thereafter in reduction of his partnership interest. What are the results to the parties?

10. The AB Partnership has the same balance sheet as in question 1. above. C contributes property with a value of $135,000 and a basis of $20,000 in exchange for an interest in the partnership, followed by a distribution of $67,500 to A. What are the results to the parties?

MATERIALS

Rev. Rul. 58-234
1958-1 C.B. 279

. . .

Section 61 of the Internal Revenue Code of 1954 provides, generally, that, except as otherwise provided, gross income means all income from whatever source derived, including (but not limited to) certain specified items. . . .

An optionor, by the mere granting of an option to sell ("put"), or buy ("call"), certain property, may not have parted with any physical or tangible assets; but, just as the optionee thereby acquires a right to sell, or buy, certain property at a fixed price during a specified future period or on or before a specified future date, so does the optionor become obligated to accept, or deliver, such property at that price, if the option is exercised. Since the optionor assumes such obligation, which may be burdensome and is continuing until the option is terminated, without exercise, or otherwise, there is no closed transaction nor ascertainable income or gain realized by an optionor upon mere receipt of a premium for granting such an option. The open, rather than closed, status of an unexercised and otherwise unterminated option to buy (in effect a "call") was recognized, for Federal income tax purposes, in *A. E. Hollingsworth v. Commissioner*, 27 B.T.A. 621 (1933). It is manifest, from the nature and consequences of "put" or "call" option premiums and obligations, that there is no Federal income tax incidence on account of either the receipt or the payment of such option premiums, i.e., from the standpoint of either the optionor or the optionee, unless and until the options have been terminated, by failure to exercise, or otherwise, with resultant gain or loss. The optionor, seeking to minimize or conclude the eventual burden of his option obligation, might pay the optionee, as consideration for cancellation of the option, an amount equal to or greater than the premium. Hence, no income, gain, profits, or earnings are derived from the receipt of either a "put" or "call" option premium unless and until the option expires without being exercised, or is terminated upon payment by the optionor of an amount less than the premium. Therefore, it is considered that the principle of the decision in *North American Oil Consolidated v. Burnet*, 286 U.S. 417 (1932), which involved the receipt of "earnings," is not applicable to receipts of premiums on outstanding options. . . .

REG – 103580-02

Preamble: Proposed Regulations on the Tax Treatment of Partnership Non-Compensatory Options (January 22, 2003)

. . .

Explanation of Provisions
1. Scope of Proposed Regulations

The Proposed Regulations describe certain of the income tax consequences of issuing, transferring, and exercising non-compensatory options. These Proposed Regulations apply only if the call option, warrant, or conversion right entitles the holder to the right to acquire an interest in the issuer (or to cash or property having a value equal to the value of such an interest). The Proposed Regulations generally provide that the exercise of a non-compensatory option does not cause recognition of gain or loss to either the issuing partnership or the option holder. In addition, the Proposed Regulations modify the Regulations under section 704(b) regarding the maintenance of the partners' capital accounts and the determination of the partners' distributive shares of partnership items. Finally, the Proposed Regulations contain a characterization rule providing that the holder of a call option, warrant, convertible debt, or convertible preferred equity issued by a partnership (or an eligible entity, as defined in § 301.7701-3(a), that would become a partnership if the option holder were treated as a partner) is treated as a partner under certain circumstances.

The rule providing for non-recognition of gain or loss on the exercise of a non-compensatory option does not apply to any call option, warrant, or convertible debt issued by an eligible entity, as defined in § 301.7701-3(a), that would become a partnership under § 301.7701-3(f)(2) if the option, warrant, or conversion right were exercised. Treasury and the IRS request comments on whether the non-recognition rule should be extended to such instruments.

2. Issuance, Exercise, and Lapse of Non-Compensatory Options

Section 721(a) and § 1.721-1 provide that, with certain exceptions, no gain or loss is recognized to a partnership or any of its partners on the contribution of property to a partnership in exchange for an interest in the partnership. However, § 1.721-1 does not provide clear guidance as to the tax consequences to the holder of a non-compensatory option and the partnership upon the issuance, lapse, and exercise of a non-compensatory option to acquire a partnership interest. Many taxpayers have requested guidance clarifying the tax consequences of these transactions.

Generally, the Proposed Regulations do not treat the issuance of a non-compensatory option as a transaction described in section 721. Therefore, the issuance of a non-compensatory option is taxed under general tax principles. Under these principles, the issuance of a non-compensatory call option or warrant (stand-alone option) is generally an open transaction for the issuer. The issuer's income or loss from the non-compensatory stand-alone option does not become fixed and determinable until the lapse, exercise, repurchase, or other termination of the option. For the holder of the non-compensatory stand-alone option, the purchase of the option is merely an investment in the option—a capital expenditure that is neither taxable to nor deductible by the holder. See Rev. Rul. 78-182, 1978-1 CB 265. However, if the holder uses appreciated or depreciated property (property with a value greater or less than the holder's basis in the property) to acquire the non-compensatory stand-alone option, then the holder recognizes gain or loss in accordance with the provisions of section 1001, subject to the generally applicable rules governing the allowance of losses, such as section 707(b).

The Proposed Regulations do not change the rules relating to the issuance of convertible debt or convertible equity. Under general tax principles, the conversion right embedded in convertible debt or convertible equity typically is taken into account for tax purposes as part of the underlying instrument.

The Proposed Regulations also provide guidance on the tax consequences resulting from the exercise of a non-compensatory option. Section 1.721-1(b) provides that, to the extent that a partner gives up his right to be repaid all or a portion of his capital contribution in favor of another partner "as compensation for services (or in satisfaction of an obligation)," section 721 does not apply. Some commentators have expressed a concern that this regulation could be read to exclude from the application of section 721 a shift in partnership capital from the historic partners to the holder of the non-compensatory option in satisfaction of the partnership's option obligation upon exercise of the option. If this were the case, the partnership could be deemed to have sold a portion of each of its assets to the holder in a taxable exchange. Alternatively, the partnership could be deemed to have sold a partnership interest with a $0 basis to the option holder in a taxable exchange.

Despite these concerns, most commentators believe that § 1.721-1(b)(1) should not cause the issuance of a partnership interest upon exercise of a non-compensatory option to be taxable. They assert that the exercise of such an option should be nontaxable to the holder and the partnership, both under general tax principles applicable to non-compensatory options and under the policy of section 721 to facilitate business combinations through the pooling of capital.

Treasury and the IRS agree that, in general, the issuance of a partnership interest to the holder of a non-compensatory option should not be taxable to the holder or the partnership. Upon exercise, the option holder may be viewed as contributing property in the form of the premium, the exercise price, and the option privilege to the partnership in exchange for the partnership interest. Generally, this is a transaction to which section 721 should apply—a transaction through which persons join together in order to conduct a business or make investments. Accordingly, the Proposed Regulations generally provide that section 721 applies to the holder and the partnership upon the exercise of a non-compensatory option issued by the partnership. . . .

The Proposed Regulations also clarify that section 721 does not apply to the lapse of a non-compensatory option. If a non-compensatory option lapses, the former option holder does not contribute property to the partnership in exchange for an interest in the partnership. Accordingly, consistent with general tax principles, the lapse of a non-compensatory option generally results in the recognition of income by the partnership and the recognition of loss by the former option holder.

3. Accounting for Non-Compensatory Options

The Proposed Regulations also contain rules to assist partnerships in properly accounting for any shifts in capital that may result from the exercise of non-compensatory options.

Generally, upon the exercise of a non-compensatory option, the option holder receives a partnership interest with a value that is greater or less than the aggregate value of the premium and exercise price that the option holder contributes to the partnership. In other words, the option privilege represents an asset with built-in gain or loss, i.e., an asset to which section 704(c) would apply. However, because the option privilege terminates upon its contribution to the partnership, the partnership cannot allocate gain or loss from the option privilege to the option holder under section 704(c)(1)(A). To address this problem, the Proposed Regulations generally allow partnerships to substitute built-in gain or loss in the partnership's assets for the built-in gain or loss in the option.

The Proposed Regulations achieve this result by providing that a non-compensatory option holder's initial capital account is equal to the consideration paid to the partnership to acquire the non-compensatory option and the fair market value of any property (other than the option) contributed to the partnership on the exercise of the non-compensatory option. The Proposed Regulations then require the partnership to revalue its property immediately following the exercise of the non-compensatory option, when the holder has become a partner. Under the Proposed Regulations, the partnership must allocate the unrealized income, gain, loss, and deduction from this revaluation, first, to the non-compensatory option holder, to the extent necessary to reflect the holder's right to share in partnership capital under the partnership agreement, and, then, to the historic partners, to reflect the manner in which the unrealized income, gain, loss, or deduction in partnership property would be allocated among those partners if there were a taxable disposition of such property for its fair market value on that date. To the extent that unrealized appreciation or depreciation in the partnership's assets has been allocated to the capital account of the non-compensatory option holder, the holder will, under section 704(c) principles, recognize any income or loss attributable to that appreciation or depreciation as the underlying assets are sold, depreciated, or amortized.

In some cases, the built-in gain or loss in the option will exceed the unrealized appreciation or depreciation in the partnership's assets (that has not been reflected in the partners' capital accounts previously). In those cases, even after all of the unrealized appreciation or depreciation in the partnership's assets has been allocated to the option holder, a disparity may remain between the non-compensatory option holder's right to share in partnership capital and the value of money and other property contributed by the partner. Most commentators have recommended and Treasury and the IRS agree that the partnership nevertheless should be allowed to shift capital between the historic partners and the non-compensatory option holder on the exercise of the non-compensatory option.

Some commentators also have suggested that the historic partners and the non-compensatory option holder should be allocated notional tax items over the recovery period for partnership assets similar to the remedial allocations that are permitted, but not required, under the Regulations issued under section 704(c)(1)(A). Although the use of section 704(c) notional tax items would ensure that the non-compensatory option holder and the historic partners receive the proper amount of income and loss over time, Treasury and the IRS believe that implementing such a system would be unduly complex where the built-in gain or loss to be allocated to the non-compensatory option holder exceeds the built-in gain or loss in the partnership's assets.

Instead, the Proposed Regulations require that the partnership make corrective allocations of gross income or loss to the partners in the year in which the option is exercised so as to take into account any shift in the partners' capital accounts that occurs as a result of the exercise of a non-compensatory option. These corrective allocations are allocations of tax items that differ from the partnership's allocations of book items. If there are not sufficient actual partnership items in the year of exercise to conform the partnership's tax allocations to the capital shift, additional corrective allocations are required in succeeding taxable years until the capital shift has been fully taken into account.

The Proposed Regulations also provide rules for revaluing the partners' capital accounts while a non-compensatory option is outstanding. Section 1.704-1(b)(2)(iv) contains rules for maintaining a partnership's capital accounts. Section 1.704-1(b)(2)(iv)(f) provides that a partnership may, upon the occurrence of certain events (including the contribution of money to the partnership by a new or existing partner), increase or decrease the partners' capital accounts to reflect a revaluation of partnership property. If one or more options are outstanding when a revaluation occurs, and the revaluation does not account for the value associated with the outstanding options, the partners' capital accounts will not reflect the true economic value of their interests. For example, in partnerships with appreciated property, the historic partners' capital accounts often would overstate the distributions that would be made to the partners if the partnership were liquidated, because a portion of the partnership's assets may ultimately be paid to the option holder. Therefore, the Proposed Regulations modify § 1.704-1(b)(2)(iv)(f) and 1.704-1(b)(2)(iv)(h) to provide that any revaluation during the period in which there are outstanding non-compensatory options generally must take into account the fair market value, if any, of outstanding options.

4. Characterization Rule

Under section 704(b), a partner's distributive share of income, gain, loss, deduction, or credit (or item thereof) is determined under the partnership agreement if the allocation under the agreement has substantial economic effect. If the allocation does not have substantial economic effect, or the partnership agreement does not provide for the allocation, then the allocation must be made in accordance with the partner's interest in the partnership (determined by taking into account all facts and circumstances). Section 1.704-1(b)(2)(ii)(h) provides in part that, for this purpose, the partnership agreement includes all agreements among the partners, or between one or more partners and the partnership, concerning affairs of the partnership and responsibilities of partners, whether oral or written, and whether or not embodied in a document referred to by the partners as the partnership agreement, including puts, options, and buy-sell agreements. Currently, there is some uncertainty about the extent to which these rules require a partnership to take into account a non-compensatory option to acquire an interest in a partnership when making its annual allocations.

Treasury and the IRS believe that it is appropriate to clarify these rules with respect to non-compensatory options addressed in this project. As these Proposed Regulations are limited to non-compensatory options, nothing in these Proposed Regulations provides any inference as to the operation of this rule for compensatory options or other types of agreements.

Given the uncertainty of the exercise of most non-compensatory options, Treasury and the IRS believe that non-compensatory options generally should not be treated as entitling the holder to a fixed right to share in partnership income until the option is exercised. However, if a non-compensatory option provides the holder with rights that are substantially similar to the rights afforded to a partner, then the holder should be treated as a partner and the option should be taken into account in allocating partnership income. At the same time, Treasury and the IRS recognize that treating a non-compensatory option holder as a partner may, in some circumstances, frustrate the intent of the parties without substantially altering their aggregate tax liabilities.

For these reasons, the Proposed Regulations generally respect non-compensatory options as such and do not characterize them as partnership equity. However, the Proposed Regulations contain a rule that characterizes the holder of a non-compensatory option as a partner if the option holder's rights are substantially similar to the rights afforded to a partner. This rule applies only if, as of the date that the non-compensatory option is issued, transferred, or modified, there is a strong likelihood that the failure to treat the option holder as a partner would result in a substantial reduction in the present value of the partners' and the option holder's aggregate tax liabilities.

The Proposed Regulations use a facts and circumstances test to determine whether a non-compensatory option holder's rights are substantially similar to the rights afforded to a partner, including whether the option is reasonably certain to be exercised and whether the option holder has partner attributes. The Proposed Regulations list a number of factors that are used to determine whether a non-compensatory option is reasonably certain to be exercised, including the premium paid for the option, the exercise price of the option, the term of the option, the predictability and stability of the value of the underlying partnership interest, and whether the partnership is expected to make distributions during the term of the option. If a non-compensatory option is reasonably certain to be exercised, then the holder of the option ordinarily has rights that are substantially similar to the rights afforded to a partner. Partner attributes include the extent to which the option holder shares in the economic benefit and detriment of partnership income and loss and the extent to which the option holder has the right to participate in the management of the partnership.

If the holder of a non-compensatory option is treated as a partner under the Proposed Regulations, then the holder's distributive share of the partnership's income, gain, loss, deduction, or credit (or items thereof) generally must be determined in accordance with such partner's interest in the partnership (taking into account all facts and circumstances) as determined under § 1.704-1(b)(3). For this purpose, the partner's interest in the partnership generally must reflect the economic differences between holding an option to acquire a partnership interest and holding the partnership interest itself. For example, unlike a partner, a non-compensatory option holder is not required initially to contribute to the partnership the full amount of the purchase price for the partnership interest. Instead, the non-compensatory option holder generally pays an option premium that is considerably smaller than the purchase price and may wait until the option is about to expire to decide whether to exercise the option and pay the exercise price. The computation of the non-compensatory option holder's share of partnership items should reflect this lesser amount of capital investment to the extent appropriate in a particular case. In addition, a non-compensatory option holder's cumulative distributive share of partnership losses and deductions may be limited under sections 704(b) and 704(d) to the amount paid by the holder to the partnership for the option.

Technical Advice Memorandum 200037005 (May 18, 2000)

ISSUE(S)

Whether the transactions resulting in the Reconfiguration of P1 into an umbrella partnership real estate investment trust effectuated a disguised sale of a portion of the Original Partners interests in P1 to P3 and REIT? . . .

CONCLUSION(S)

The transactions resulting in the Reconfiguration of P1 into an umbrella partnership real estate investment trust effectuated a disguised sale of a portion of the Original Partners' interests in P1 to P3 and REIT. . . .

LAW AND ANALYSIS
ISSUE ONE: DISGUISED SALE OF A PARTNERSHIP INTEREST
BACKGROUND OF SECTION 707(a)(2)(B)

Section 707(a)(2)(B) provides that if (i) there is a direct or indirect transfer of money or other property by a partner to a partnership, (ii) there is a related direct or indirect transfer of money or other property by the partnership to such partner (or another partner), and (iii) the transfers described in clauses (i) and (ii), when viewed together, are properly characterized as a sale or exchange of property, such transfers shall be treated either as occurring between the partnership and one who is not a partner, or as a transaction between two or more partners acting other than in their capacity as members of the partnership.

The legislative history of section 707(a)(2)(B) indicates that the provision was adopted as a result of Congress' concern that taxpayers were deferring or avoiding tax on sales of partnership property, including sales of partnership interests, by characterizing sales as contributions of property, including money, followed or preceded by a related partnership distribution. See S. Prt. No. 169, (Vol. I), 98th Cong., 2d Sess. 225 (1984)(hereinafter "S. Prt."); H.R. Rep. No. 432, (Pt. 2) 98th Cong., 2d Sess. 1218 (1984) (hereinafter "H.R. Rep."). Specifically, Congress was concerned about court decisions that allowed tax-free treatment in cases which were economically indistinguishable from sales of property to a partnership or another partner. See S. Prt. at 225; H.R. Rep. at 1218 (discussing *Jupiter Corp. v. United States*, No. 83-842 (Ct. Cl. 1983), and *Communications Satellite Corp. v. United States*, 223 Ct. Cl. 253 (1980), both of which involved the disguised sale of a partnership interest). Congress believed that these transactions should be treated for tax purposes in a manner consistent with their underlying economic substance.

In the legislative history to section 707(a)(2)(B), Congress explained that pursuant to section 721, gain or loss is generally not recognized on the contribution of property to a partnership in return for a partnership interest, and pursuant to section 731 distributions of money from a partnership to a partner are generally tax-free to the extent of the adjusted basis of the recipient partner's interest in the partnership. Congress referred to Treasury Regulations issued under section 721 and section 731 in its discussion of disguised sales. The section 721 Regulations provide that, if the transfer of property by a partner to a partnership results in the receipt by the partner of money or other consideration, including a promissory obligation fixed in amount and time for payment, the transaction will be treated as a sale or exchange rather than a contribution (Reg. Sec. 1.721-1(a)). These Regulations require that the substance of the transaction, rather than its form, will govern in such cases. The Regulations issued under section 731 provide that if a contribution of property is made to a partnership and (1) within a short time before or after such contribution other property is distributed to the contributing partner and the contributed property is retained by the partnership, or (2) within a short time after such contribution to the partnership, contributed property is distributed to another partner, tax free distribution treatment may not apply (Reg. Sec. 1.731-1(c)(3)). The Regulations deny tax-free treatment if a purported distribution was, in fact, made to effect an exchange of property between two or more of the partners or between the partnership and a partner.

Congress expressed its concern that the Regulations issued under section 721 and 731 may not always prevent de facto sales of property to a partnership or another partner from being structured as a contribution to the partnership, followed or preceded by a tax-free distribution from the partnership. Congress specifically discussed case law that permitted results which were economically indistinguishable from a sale of all or part of the property despite the Regulations described above and enacted section 707(a)(2)(B) to expressly prohibit such transactions. . . .

LEGAL ANALYSIS

The Reconfiguration can be viewed as a disguised sale of a partnership interest in either of two ways. As discussed below, P2's ownership of the Loans and interest in P1 lacked economic substance and should be disregarded for Federal income tax purposes. Accordingly, the true economic substance of the Reconfiguration is a disguised sale by the Original Partners of interests in P1 to P3 and REIT. . . .

P2's OWNERSHIP OF THE LOANS AND P1 INTERESTS
SHOULD BE DISREGARDED

To be respected, a transaction must have economic substance separate and distinct from the economic benefit achieved solely by tax reduction. If a taxpayer seeks to claim tax benefits which were not intended by Congress, by means of transactions that serve no economic purpose other than tax savings, the doctrine of economic substance is applicable. . . . Whether a transaction has economic substance is a factual determination. . . . This determination turns on whether the transaction is rationally related to a useful nontax purpose that is plausible in light of the taxpayer's conduct and useful in light of the taxpayers economic situation and intentions. The utility of the stated purpose and the rationality of the means chosen to effectuate it must be evaluated in accordance with commercial practices in the relevant industry. . . .

In determining whether a transaction has economic substance so as to be respected for tax purposes, both the objective economic substance of the transaction and the subjective business motivation must be determined. . . . The two inquiries are not separate prongs, but are interrelated factors used to analyze whether the transaction had sufficient substance, apart from its tax consequences, to be respected for tax purposes. . . .

ABSENCE OF REGULATIONS REGARDING DISGUISED SALES
OF PARTNERSHIP INTERESTS

Although the Service has not promulgated Regulations for disguised sales of partnership interests under section 707(a)(2)(B) (Regulation Section 1.707-7 is reserved), it may enforce section 707(a)(2)(B) in the context of a disguised sale of a partnership interest in the absence of Regulations. See *Pittway Corp. v. United States*, 102 F.3d 932 (7th Cir. 1996) (although the statute provided "to the extent provided in regulations" the plain language of the statue [sic] directs a single conclusion); *Estate of Neuman*, 106 T.C. 216 (1996) (Regulations contemplated under section 2663(2) are not a necessary precondition to the imposition of the generation-skipping transfer tax on transfers involved in the case); Rev. Rul. 91-47 (Service enforced section 108(e)(4), which applies "to the extent provided in regulations" before the Regulations were issued). The plain language of the statute, as confirmed by the legislative history, imposes liability on the taxpayer in this case. . . .

CHAPTER 21

Acquisition of a Partnership Interest in Exchange for Services: Profits Interests, Capital Accounting, and Forfeiture Allocations

PROBLEM AREA 21

INTRODUCTION

In common parlance, a "capital interest" is an interest in a partnership that would give the holder thereof a right to receive a distribution if the assets of the partnership were sold for their fair market value and the proceeds were distributed to the partners in complete liquidation of the partnership. The transfer of a capital interest to a partner in exchange for rendering services to the partnership is an event producing income for the service partner and a deduction or capital expenditure for the partnership. A "profits interest" is a partnership interest other than a capital interest and encompasses the right to an allocation of future income, gains, and (less frequently) losses if and when realized by the partnership. Although only one reported case has held the transfer of a profits interest to be a taxable event, *Sol Diamond v. Commissioner*, 56 TC 530 (1971), *aff'd*, 492 F2d 286 (7th Cir. 1974), this issue has attracted more than its share of attention from academics, the Internal Revenue Service, and, more recently, Congress.

Historically, profits interests have played a significant role in the compensation of service partners in certain industries, notably real estate, oil and gas, and, more recently, investment management, including hedge funds and private equity funds. By causing the service partner's compensation to depend on the profits generated by the partnership, this mode of incentive compensation aligns the interests of the service partner more closely with those of the partners who have furnished capital to the partnership. Yet it cannot be denied that the favorable tax treatment of profits interests has also played a role in their popularity.

This favorable treatment takes two forms. The first, which is relevant in all cases, is the postponement of taxation until the partnership actually earns and allocates profits to the service partner—a "timing" benefit. The second, which is relevant in some cases more than others, arises from the fact that the profits allocated to the service provider retain their capital or ordinary character in the partner's hands under the general rule of § 702(b). Thus, if the partnership happens to generate mostly capital gains (as is the case, for example, for private equity and real estate funds, but not for most hedge funds), the service provider receives compensation mostly in the form of capital gains, not ordinary income—a "character" benefit.

The former benefit has been justified in various ways over the years, including (i) that there is no realization event when a partnership issues an interest to a partner, (ii) that a profits interest is akin to an unsecured and unfunded promise to pay, (iii) that profits interests are typically very difficult to value, and (iv) that taxing profits interests on receipt would subject the service partner to double taxation, because he would be taxed again when the profits (if any) are allocated to him. At least some of these rationales underlay General Counsel Memorandum 36346 (July 23, 1977), which was issued in the aftermath of the Seventh Circuit's decision in *Sol Diamond* and settled the waters on this issue for more than a decade. The Tax Court's decision in *Campbell* broke this truce, following *Sol Diamond* in finding current taxation on the receipt of a profits interest. This decision, however, was reversed on appeal. *Campbell v. Commissioner*, TC Memo 1990-162, 59 TCM 236, *rev'd*, 943 F2d 815 (8th Cir. 1991). The Service followed *Campbell* with two Revenue Procedures confirming non-taxation on the receipt of a profits interest, whether or not subject to a substantial risk of forfeiture, provided that certain conditions are met. Rev. Proc. 93-27, 1993-2 CB 343; Rev. Proc. 2001-43, 2001-2 CB 191. For now, the "timing" benefit of profits interests seems secure.

In recent years, the "character" benefit of profits interests has attracted Congressional scrutiny. At least four times since 2007, the House of Representatives has passed legislation that generally would require service partners in the investment management business to report their allocable shares of partnership profits as ordinary income, except to the extent attributable to capital invested in the partnership by the service partner.

Meanwhile, in 2005, the Service issued Proposed Regulations on exchanges of partnership interests for services. The Proposed Regulations abandon the practice of providing separate rules for the taxation of capital interests and profits interests by prescribing a single tax regime that would apply to both. If finalized, these Regulations would clearly establish that all partnership interests, profits interests as well as capital interests, are property for purposes of § 83. Thus, a service partner would be required to include the value of a capital interest or profits interest as gross income under the rules of that section. While this might appear to challenge, and indeed terminate, the "timing" benefit for profits interests, the Proposed Regulations contain a "safe harbor" election pursuant to which the value of a partnership interest would be determined by its liquidation value, which in the case of a profits interest would be zero. The Proposed Regulations also would not alter the "character" benefit currently enjoyed by profits interests – a change that in all events would seem to require legislation to override the application of § 702(b).

PROBLEM 21

QUESTIONS

1. The AB Partnership has the following balance sheet:

	Adjusted Basis	Book Value	Fair Market Value
Assets			
Cash	$ 70,000	$ 70,000	$ 70,000
Land	100,000	100,000	200,000
Total	$170,000	$170,000	$270,000
Capital			
A	$ 85,000	$ 85,000	$135,000
B	85,000	85,000	135,000
Total	$170,000	$170,000	$270,000

C agrees to join the partnership, receiving a one-third interest in capital, profits, and losses in return for the rendition of services to the partnership. What adjustments are made to the partnership's books to reflect this transaction? What are the tax consequences to the partnership and to A, B, and C?

2. Assume the same facts as in question 1. above, except that the AB Partnership grants C an option to acquire a one-third interest in capital, profits, and losses in return for services to be rendered. The exercise price of the option is $60,000. C exercises this option when the value of the partnership's assets is $450,000, taking into account the partnership's receipt of C's $60,000 exercise price, and the value of a one-third partnership interest is $150,000. What adjustments are made to the partnership's books to reflect these transactions? What are the tax consequences to the partnership and to A, B, and C?

3. Assume the same facts as in question 1. above, except that C must remain with the partnership for five years before his ownership vests. The partnership leases its land and generates $18,000 net income annually, which it retains for future growth. C ceases to perform services for the partnership after three years. What are the results to C and to the partnership if:

    a. C does not make a § 83(b) election, or
    b. C makes a timely election under § 83(b), valuing his partnership interest at $90,000?

Do these results change if the partnership distributes its $18,000 net income annually instead of retaining it?

4. Assume the same facts as in question 1. above, except that C receives a one-third interest in all future profits and losses of the partnership, but no interest in partnership capital as of the date of C's admission. What adjustments are made to the partnership's books to reflect this transaction? What are the tax consequences to the partnership and to A, B, and C?

5. Assume the same facts as in question 4. above, except that C must remain with the partnership for five years before his ownership vests. What are the results to C and to the partnership if:

    a. C does not make a § 83(b) election, or
    b. C makes a timely election under § 83(b), valuing his partnership interest at zero?

6. Assume that the AB Partnership in question 1. above intends to construct an office building, which is expected to generate $100,000 of rental income per year. C is an architect and is admitted as a one-fourth partner in return for a contribution of $90,000 cash. The partnership agreement provides that C will receive a one-fourth interest in net profits and losses as well as an allocation of 15 percent of the gross income of the partnership for the first two years after his admission. What are the tax consequences to C and to the partnership?

MATERIALS

General Counsel Memorandum 36346
July 23, 1977

Your memorandum of April 18, 1975 referred a Proposed Revenue Ruling for our concurrence or comment. The proposed Ruling concludes that the fair market value of an interest in the profits and losses of a partnership is includible in the gross income of the recipient if it was received as compensation for services he had performed for another individual, citing *Sol Diamond*, 56 T.C. 530 (1971), *aff'd*, 492 F.2d 286 (7th Cir. 1974).

The proposed Revenue Ruling is being returned to you without comment pursuant to the agreement reached by representatives of our respective offices at our July 21, 1975 meeting. It was the consensus of opinion that publication of the proposed Ruling should be deferred pending further discussion of the alternative positions available to the Service in resolving the issue involved. Such alternatives are to be set forth in a memorandum to be prepared by this office. . . .

As you may be aware this Office has been considering the proper treatment of the receipt of a profits interest in a partnership as compensation for services. This consideration stems from the decision in *Diamond*, holding that the fair market value of an interest in partnership profits received as compensation for services is taxable under § 61(a)(1). This decision has been widely criticized as being contrary to Regulation § 1.721-1, as creating severe valuation problems and as resulting in double taxation to the recipient partner. *See, e.g.*, A. Willis, Partnership Taxation, § 11.04 (2d ed. 1976). Previously it has been proposed that the Service not follow *Diamond* when a profits interest is received as compensation for services rendered in a capacity as partner. . . . This approach was found unacceptable because it seemed to place a premium on whether the partnership is formed before or after the services are rendered.

The position of this Office is set forth in the attached proposed Revenue Ruling which states that the Service will not follow *Diamond* to the extent that it holds that the receipt of an interest in future partnership profits as compensation for services results in taxable income. Having conceded this question, the Ruling generally preserves the result in *Diamond* by concluding that most of the interest the taxpayer received was an interest in capital, as distinguished from an interest in future profits. In addition the Ruling seeks to limit the conversion of compensation into capital gain upon the receipt and sale of a profits interest by emphasizing that the renderer of services must be a partner rather than an employee or independent contractor. Whether an interest is a capital interest or an interest in future profits and whether the recipient is a partner rather than an employee or independent contractor are primarily factual questions.

Arguably the only rationale for not taxing a profits interest received as compensation is that Regulation § 1.721-1(b) was apparently designed to reach such a result. *See* A. Willis, supra at § 11.01. It is difficult to quarrel with the Tax Court's finding that such an interest is property under Regulation § 1.61-2(d)(1). When a profits interest is defined to preclude any interest in partnership assets, as is done in the proposed Revenue Ruling, such an interest becomes analogous to an unfunded, unsecured promise to pay deferred compensation. Such a promise is not taxable upon receipt and, in fact, is not considered to be property. *See* Reg. § 1.83-3(e). An analogy of a partnership profits interest to an unfunded, unsecured promise to pay deferred compensation is imperfect, however, because amounts received pursuant to or upon assignment of such a promise are taxable as compensation whereas the character of partnership profits or the character of the gain on a sale of a profits interest is determined under Code § 702(b) and Code § 741.

It must be emphasized that in holding that the receipt of a "profits" interest is not taxable, the proposed Revenue Ruling is limited to interests that give the holder no rights to existing partnership assets upon the liquidation of his interest. Correspondingly, a "capital" interest, which is taxable, includes an interest in earned but unrealized gains. This broad definition of a capital interest is simply an extension of the rule in Regulation § 1.61-2(d)(1) that property received as compensation is taxed at its fair market value. This rule is reflected in both Regulation § 1.704-1(e) and Regulation § 1.721-1(b)(1). . . .

PROPOSED REVENUE RULING

Advice has been requested concerning the treatment, for Federal income tax purposes, of the receipt of an interest in a partnership as compensation for services under the circumstances described below.

On May 15, 1976, X entered into a contract to purchase an apartment building on June 15, 1976 for $300,000. On June 1, 1976 A, an individual, purchased X's interest in the contract for $10,000.

At the time A was negotiating with X, A asked B, a mortgage broker, if B could obtain financing for the entire $300,000 purchase price. In return, A offered to give B an interest in the building. B agreed to obtain the financing in exchange for a 25 percent interest in a partnership to be formed by A and B to own and operate the building.

On June 10, 1976, A and B entered into a partnership agreement under which B was to receive, as compensation for services rendered in arranging the financing, 25 percent of the operating profits from the apartment building. B was also chargeable with 25 percent of the losses. When the building was sold, the proceeds of the sale were to be used first to satisfy any mortgages and to repay A the $10,000 A had paid to X for the right to purchase the property and the remaining proceeds were to be distributed 75 percent to A and 25 percent to B. A was to manage the building for the partnership and was to receive compensation in addition to a 75 percent distributive share of profits and losses for such managerial services. B was to render no services in connection with the building other than to arrange the financing and such services were performed both before and after formation of the partnership. The approval of both A and B was required for a sale of the property.

On June 15 the building was purchased in the names of A and B for $300,000 and contributed to the partnership. The entire purchase price was financed by the lender. An independent appraisal concluded that with 100 percent financing the fair market value of the property on June 15 was $360,000. On July 1, 1977 B sold his interest in the partnership to an unrelated third party for $15,000.

Under section 61 . . . gross income means all income from whatever source derived, unless specifically excluded from gross income by law.

Section 1.61-2(d)(1) of the Regulations provides, in part, that if services are paid for other than in money, the fair market value of the property or services taken in payment must be included in income.

Section 721 of the Code provides that no gain or loss shall be recognized to a partnership or to any of its partners in the case of a contribution of property to the partnership in exchange for an interest in the partnership.

Section 1.721-1(b)(1) of the Regulations provides, in part, that normally under local law, each partner is entitled to be repaid his contributions of money or other property to the partnership (at the value placed upon such property by the partnership at the time of the contribution) whether made at the formation of the partnership or subsequent thereto. To the extent that any of the partners gives up any part of his right to be repaid his contributions (as distinguished from a share in partnership profits) in favor of another partner as compensation for services (or in satisfaction of an obligation), section 721 of the Code does not apply.

For purposes of section 1.721-1(b)(1) a partner's right to be repaid his contributions consists of the value of any property that would be distributable to him on liquidation of his interest. Thus, under the Regulations the value of an interest in such partnership capital so transferred to a partner as compensation for services constitutes income to the partner under section 61.

Correspondingly, a partner who receives a partnership interest as compensation for services is treated as receiving a capital interest to the extent of the fair market value of partnership assets that would be distributable to such partner if the partner withdrew from the partnership or if the partner's interest were liquidated immediately after it was acquired. For example, an interest in any unrealized appreciation of partnership assets is a capital interest. A service partner who receives only an interest in the appreciation occurring subsequent to such partner's admission receives an interest the value of which is attributable to the right to participate in the partnership's future profits. Whether an interest in a partnership is a capital interest as distinguished from an interest in future partnership profits, must be determined on the facts and circumstances of each case.

Section 741 of the Code provides that gain or loss on the sale or exchange of an interest in a partnership shall be considered as gain or loss from the sale of a capital asset, except as otherwise provided in section 751 (relating to unrealized receivables and inventory items . . .).

In the case of *Sol Diamond*, the court held the receipt of an interest in a partnership as compensation for services results in taxable income without regard to whether the interest represented an interest in capital as distinguished from an interest in future partnership profits. The Internal Revenue Service will not follow the decision in *Sol Diamond* to the extent that it holds that the receipt by a partner of an interest in future partnership profits as compensation for services results in taxable income.

However, the fact that a person holds the right to a share of the future profits of a venture does not necessarily mean that such person is a joint venturer or partner for Federal income tax purposes. An examination of the facts and circumstances of each case is necessary in order to determine whether an interest in the future profits of a venture was acquired as compensation for services rendered by a partner as distinguished from an employee or an independent contractor. *See* Rev. Rul. 75-43, 1975-1 C.B. 383, for a discussion of some of the factors considered in determining whether a person who has a right to a share of profits is a partner.

In addition to the factors in Rev. Rul. 75-43, a person who acquires an interest in the future profits of a venture as compensation for services rendered or to be rendered will not be treated as a partner unless there is an intent to invest his services in the enterprise. In other words, it must be intended that the return for the services be contingent upon the future success of the venture. The fact that a future profits interest acquired as compensation for services is sold shortly after it is acquired may be evidence that the seller of the interest intended to receive a fixed amount for the services rather than investing the services in the enterprise and that, therefore, it was not intended that the seller become a partner.

When an interest in the future profits of an enterprise is acquired as compensation for services by someone other than a partner, such interest is not considered property for purposes of section 61 of the Code and Regulation § 1.61-2(d)(1). *See* Reg. § 1.83-3(e); Rev. Rul. 60-31, 1960-1 C.B. 174. Any profits subsequently received and any gain on the sale of the profits interest is taxable as compensation for services.

In the instant case, A and B referred to the venture as a partnership in their agreement. Since title to the building was in the names of A and B, a sale of the building would have required B's approval. B had a proprietary interest in any profits and had an obligation to share any losses. Although B sold his interest after acquiring it, the sale was not prearranged. B did not intend to sell his interest upon receiving it but instead contemplated an investment of his services the return on which would be contingent upon the future success of the venture. Thus, based on all the facts and circumstances, B acquired his interest in the venture as a joint venturer or partner, rather than as an employee or independent contractor.

In the instant case, B's interest in the venture entitled B to 25 percent of the value of the building in excess of $310,000, its basis on the date B received the interest. Because the building was in fact worth $360,000 on the date B received the 25 percent interest as compensation, B acquired a capital interest having a value of $12,500 ($360,000–310,000 × 25%).

Accordingly, for 1976 B must recognize $12,500 of compensation income under Code § 61 and Regulation § 1.721-1(b)(1). Upon the sale of B's interest for $15,000 in 1977, B also must recognize gain to the extent the amount realized exceeds B's adjusted basis in the partnership interest (which includes the $12,500 compensation taxed to him in 1976). This gain will be considered as gain from the sale of an interest in a partnership and, therefore, is treated as capital gain under Code § 741 except as provided in Code § 751.

Rev. Proc. 93-27
1993-2 CB 343

SECTION 1
PURPOSE

This Revenue Procedure provides guidance on the treatment of the receipt of a partnership profits interest for services provided to or for the benefit of the partnership.

SECTION 2
DEFINITIONS

The following definitions apply for purposes of this Revenue Procedure:

.01 A capital interest is an interest that would give the holder a share of the proceeds if the partnership's assets were sold at fair market value and then the proceeds were distributed in a complete liquidation of the partnership. This determination generally is made at the time of receipt of the partnership interest.

.02 A profits interest is a partnership interest other than a capital interest.

SECTION 3
BACKGROUND

Under section 1.721-1(b)(1) of the Regulations, the receipt of a partnership capital interest for services provided to or for the benefit of the partnership is taxable as compensation. On the other hand, the issue of whether the receipt of a partnership profits interest for services is taxable has been the subject of litigation. Most recently, in *Campbell v. Commissioner*, 943 F.2d 815 (8th Cir. 1991), the Eighth Circuit in dictum suggested that the taxpayer's receipt of a partnership profits interest received for services was not taxable, but decided the case on valuation. Other courts have determined that in certain circumstances the receipt of a partnership profits interest for services is a taxable event under section 83 of the Internal Revenue Code. *See, e.g.,* *Campbell v. Commissioner*, T.C.M. 1990-236, *rev'd*, 943 F.2d 815 (8th Cir. 1991); *St. John v. United States*, No. 82-1134 (C.D. Ill. Nov. 16, 1983). The courts have also found that typically the profits interest received has speculative or no determinable value at the time of receipt. In *Diamond v. Commissioner*, 56 T.C. 530 (1971), *aff'd,* 492 F.2d 286 (7th Cir. 1974), however, the court assumed that the interest received by the taxpayer was a partnership profits interest and found the value of the interest was readily determinable. In that case, the interest was sold soon after receipt.

SECTION 4
APPLICATION

.01 Other than as provided below, if a person receives a profits interest for the provision of services to or for the benefit of a partnership in a partner capacity or in anticipation of being a partner, the Internal Revenue Service will not treat the receipt of such an interest as a taxable event for the partner or the partnership.

.02 This Revenue Procedure does not apply:

(1) If the profits interest relates to a substantially certain and predictable stream of income from partnership assets, such as income from high-quality debt securities or a high-quality net lease;

(2) If within two years of receipt, the partner disposes of the profits interest; or

(3) If the profits interest is a limited partnership interest in a "publicly traded partnership" within the meaning of section 7704(b) of the Internal Revenue Code.

Rev. Proc. 2001-43
2001-2 CB 191

SECTION 1
PURPOSE

This Revenue Procedure clarifies Rev. Proc. 93-27, 1993-2 C.B. 343, by providing guidance on the treatment of the grant of a partnership profits interest that is substantially nonvested for the provision of services to or for the benefit of the partnership.

SECTION 2
BACKGROUND

Rev. Proc. 93-27 provides that (except as otherwise provided in section 4.02 of the revenue procedure), if a person receives a profits interest for the provision of services to or for the benefit of a partnership in a partner capacity or in anticipation of being a partner, the Internal Revenue Service will not treat the receipt of the interest as a taxable event for the partner or the partnership. For this purpose, section 2.02 of Rev. Proc. 93-27 defines a profits interest as a partnership interest other than a capital interest. Section 2.01 of Rev. Proc. 93-27 defines a capital interest as an interest that would give the holder a share of the proceeds if the partnership's assets were sold at fair market value and then the proceeds were distributed in a complete liquidation of the partnership. Section 2.01 of Rev. Proc. 93-27 provides that the determination as to whether an interest is a capital interest generally is made at the time of receipt of the partnership interest.

SECTION 3
SCOPE

This Revenue Procedure clarifies Rev. Proc. 93-27 by providing that the determination under Rev. Proc. 93-27 of whether an interest granted to a service provider is a profits interest is, under the circumstances described below, tested at the time the interest is granted, even if, at that time, the interest is substantially nonvested (within the meaning of section 1.83-3(b) of the Regulations). Accordingly, where a partnership grants a profits interest to a service provider in a transaction meeting the requirements of this revenue procedure and Rev. Proc. 93-27, the Internal Revenue Service will not treat the grant of the interest or the event that causes the interest to become substantially vested (within the meaning of section 1.83-3(b) of the Regulations) as a taxable event for the partner or the partnership. Taxpayers to which this Revenue Procedure applies need not file an election under section 83(b) of the Code.

SECTION 4
APPLICATION

This Revenue Procedure clarifies that, for purposes of Rev. Proc. 93-27, where a partnership grants an interest in the partnership that is substantially nonvested to a service provider, the service provider will be treated as receiving the interest on the date of its grant, provided that:

.01 The partnership and the service provider treat the service provider as the owner of the partnership interest from the date of its grant and the service provider takes into account the distributive share of partnership income, gain, loss, deduction, and credit associated with that interest in computing the service provider's income tax liability for the entire period during which the service provider has the interest;

.02 Upon the grant of the interest or at the time that the interest becomes substantially vested, neither the partnership nor any of the partners deducts any amount (as wages, compensation, or otherwise) for the fair market value of the interest; and.

.03 All other conditions of Rev. Proc. 93-27 are satisfied.

SECTION 5
EFFECT ON OTHER DOCUMENTS

Rev. Proc. 93-27 is clarified.

REG – 105346-03
Preamble: Proposed Regulations on Exchanges of Partnership Interests for Services (May 24, 2005)

Background

Partnerships issue a variety of instruments in connection with the performance of services. These instruments include interests in partnership capital, interests in partnership profits, and options to acquire such interests (collectively, partnership equity). On June 5, 2000, the Treasury Department and the Service issued Notice 2000-29 (2000-1 C.B. 1241), inviting public comment on the Federal income tax treatment of the exercise of an option to acquire a partnership interest, the exchange of convertible debt for a partnership interest, and the exchange of a preferred interest in a partnership for a common interest in that partnership. On January 22, 2003, the Treasury Department and the Service published in the Federal Register . . . Proposed Regulations regarding the Federal income tax consequences of noncompensatory partnership options, convertible equity, and convertible debt. In the preamble to those Proposed Regulations, the Treasury Department and the Service requested comments on the proposed amendment to § 1.721-1(b)(1) that was published in the

Federal Register on June 3, 1971 . . . and on the Federal income tax consequences of the issuance of partnership capital interests in connection with the performance of services and options to acquire such interests. In response to the comments received, the Treasury Department and the Service are withdrawing the proposed amendment to § 1.721-1(b)(1) and issuing these Proposed Regulations, which prescribe rules on the application of section 83 to partnership interests and the Federal income tax consequences associated with the transfer, vesting, and forfeiture of partnership interests transferred in connection with the performance of services.

Explanation of Provisions
1. Application of Section 83 to Partnership Interests

Section 83 generally applies to a transfer of property by one person to another in connection with the performance of services. The courts have held that a partnership capital interest is property for this purpose. See *Schulman v. Commissioner*, 93 T.C. 623 (1989) (section 83 governs the issuance of an option to acquire a partnership interest as compensation for services provided as an employee); *Kenroy, Inc. v. Commissioner*, T.C. Memo 1984-232. Therefore, the Proposed Regulations provide that a partnership interest is property within the meaning of section 83, and that the transfer of a partnership interest in connection with the performance of services is subject to section 83.

The Proposed Regulations apply section 83 to all partnership interests, without distinguishing between partnership capital interests and partnership profits interests. Although the application of section 83 to partnership profits interests has been the subject of controversy, *see, e.g., Campbell v. Commissioner*, T.C. Memo 1990-162, 943 F.2d 815 (8th Cir. 1991); *St. John v. U.S.*, 84-1 USTC 9158 (C.D. Ill. 1983), the Treasury Department and the Service do not believe that there is a substantial basis for distinguishing among partnership interests for purposes of section 83. All partnership interests constitute personal property under state law and give the holder the right to share in future earnings from partnership capital and labor. Moreover, some commentators have suggested that the same tax rules should apply to both partnership profits interests and partnership capital interests. These commentators have suggested that taxpayers may exploit any differences in the tax treatment of partnership profits interests and partnership capital interests. The Treasury Department and the IRS agree with these comments. Therefore, all of the rules in these Proposed Regulations and the accompanying proposed Revenue Procedure (described below) apply equally to partnership capital interests and partnership profits interests. However, a right to receive allocations and distributions from a partnership that is described in section 707(a)(2)(A) is not a partnership interest. In section 707(a)(2)(A), Congress directed that such an arrangement should be characterized according to its substance, that is, as a disguised payment of compensation to the service provider. See S. Rep. No. 98-169, 98 Cong. 2d Sess., at 226 (1984).

Section 83(b) allows a person who receives substantially nonvested property in connection with the performance of services to elect to include in gross income the difference between: (A) the fair market value of the property at the time of transfer (determined without regard to a restriction other than a restriction which by its terms will never lapse); and (B) the amount paid for such property. Under section 83(b)(2), the election under section 83(b) must be made within 30 days of the date of the transfer of the property to the service provider.

Consistent with the principles of section 83, the Proposed Regulations provide that, if a partnership interest is transferred in connection with the performance of services, and if an election under section 83(b) is not made, then the holder of the partnership interest is not treated as a partner until the interest becomes substantially vested. If a section 83(b) election is made with respect to such an interest, the service provider will be treated as a partner for purposes of Subtitle A of the Code.

These principles differ from Rev. Proc. 2001-43. Under that Revenue Procedure, if a partnership profits interest is transferred in connection with the performance of services, then the holder of the partnership interest may be treated as a partner even if no section 83(b) election is made, provided that certain conditions are met.

Certain changes to the Regulations under both subchapter K and section 83 are needed to coordinate the principles of subchapter K with the principles of section 83. Among the changes that are proposed in these Regulations are: (1) conforming the subchapter K rules to the section 83 timing rules; (2) revising the section 704(b) Regulations to take into account the fact that allocations with respect to an unvested interest may be forfeited; and (3) providing that a partnership generally recognizes no gain or loss on the transfer of an interest in the partnership in connection with the performance of services for that partnership. In addition, Rev. Procs. 93-27 (1993-2 C.B. 343), and 2001-43 (2001-2 C.B. 191), which generally provide for nonrecognition by both the partnership and the service provider on the transfer of a profits interest in the partnership for services performed for that partnership, must be modified to be consistent with these Proposed Regulations. Accordingly, in conjunction with these Proposed Regulations, the Service is issuing Notice 2005-43. That Notice contains a proposed Revenue Procedure that, when finalized, will obsolete Rev. Procs. 93-27 and 2001-43. The Treasury Department and the Service intend for these Proposed Regulations and the proposed Revenue Procedure to become effective at the same time. The proposed amendments to the regulations under section 83 and subchapter K, as well as the Notice, are described in further detail below.

The proposed Revenue Procedure and certain parts of the Proposed Regulations (as described below) only apply to a transfer by a partnership of an interest in that partnership in connection with the performance of services for that partnership (compensatory partnership interests). The Treasury Department and the Service request comments on the income tax consequences of transactions involving related persons, such as, for example, the transfer of an interest in a lower-tier partnership in exchange for services provided to the upper-tier partnership.

2. Timing of Partnership's Deduction

Except as otherwise provided in § 1.83-6(a)(3), if property is transferred in connection with the performance of services, then the service recipient's deduction, if any, is allowed only for the taxable year of that person in which or with which ends the taxable year of the service provider in which the amount is included as compensation. See section 83(h). In contrast, under section 706(a) and § 1.707-1(c), guaranteed payments described in section 707(c) are included in the partner's income in the partner's taxable year within or with which ends the partnership's taxable year in which the partnership deducted the payments. Under § 1.721-1(b)(2) of the Regulations, an interest in partnership capital issued by the partnership as compensation for services rendered to the partnership is treated as a guaranteed payment under section 707(c). Some commentators suggested that the Proposed Regulations should resolve the potential conflict between the timing rules of section 83 and the timing rules of section 707(c).

Under the Proposed Regulations, partnership interests issued to partners for services rendered to the partnership are treated as guaranteed payments. Also, the Proposed Regulations provide that the section 83 timing rules override the timing rules of section 706(a) and § 1.707-1(c) to the extent they are inconsistent. Accordingly, if a partnership transfers property to a partner in connection with the performance of services, the timing and the amount of the related income inclusion and deduction is determined by section 83 and the Regulations thereunder.

In drafting these Regulations, the Treasury Department and the Service considered alternative approaches for resolving the timing inconsistency between section 83 and section 707(c). One alternative approach considered was to provide that the transfer of property in connection with the performance of services is not treated as a guaranteed payment within the meaning of section 707(c). This approach was not adopted in the Proposed Regulations due to, among other things, concern that such a characterization of these transfers could have unintended consequences on the application of provisions of the Code outside of subchapter K that refer to guaranteed payments. The Treasury Department and the Service request comments on alternative approaches for resolving the timing inconsistency between section 83 and section 707(c).

3. Allocation of Partnership's Deduction

The Proposed Regulations provide guidance regarding the allocation of the partnership's deduction for the transfer of property in connection with the performance of services. Some commentators suggested that the Proposed Regulations require that the partnership's deduction be allocated among the partners in accordance with their interests in the partnership prior to the transfer.

Section 706(d)(1) provides generally that, if, during any taxable year of a partnership, there is a change in any partner's interest in the partnership, each partner's distributive share of any item of income, gain, loss, deduction, or credit of the partnership for such taxable year shall be determined by the use of any method prescribed by regulations which takes into account the varying interests of the partners in the partnership during the taxable year. Regulations have not yet been issued describing the rules for taking into account the varying interests of the partners in the partnership during a taxable year. Section 1.706-1(c)(2)(ii) provides that, in the case of a sale, exchange, or liquidation of a partner's entire interest in a partnership, the partner's share of partnership items for the taxable year may be determined by either: (1) closing the partnership's books as of the date of the transfer (closing of the books method); or (2) allocating to the departing partner that partner's pro rata part of partnership items that the partner would have included in the partner's taxable income had the partner remained a partner until the end of the partnership taxable year (proration method). The Treasury Department and the Service believe that section 706(d)(1) adequately ensures that partnership deductions that are attributable to the portion of the partnership's taxable year prior to a new partner's entry into the partnership are allocated to the historic partners.

Section 706(d)(2), however, places additional limits on how partnerships may allocate these deductions. Under section 706(d)(2)(B), payments for services by a partnership using the cash receipts and disbursements method of accounting are allocable cash basis items. Under section 706(d)(2)(A), if during any taxable year of a partnership there is a change in any partner's interest in the partnership, then (except to the extent provided in regulations) each partner's distributive share of any allocable cash basis item must be determined under the proration method. To allow partnerships to allocate deductions with respect to property transferred in connection with the performance of services under a closing of the books method, the Proposed Regulations provide that section 706(d)(2)(A) does not apply to such a transfer.

4. Accounting for Compensatory Partnership Interests
A. Transfer of compensatory partnership interest

Under the Proposed Regulations, the service provider's capital account is increased by the amount the service provider takes into income under section 83 as a result of receiving the interest, plus any amounts paid for the interest. Some commentators suggested that the amount included in the service provider's income under section 83, plus the amount paid for the interest, may differ from the amount of capital that the partnership has agreed to assign to the service provider. These commentators contend that the substantial economic effect safe harbor in the section 704(b) Regulations should be amended to allow partnerships to reallocate capital between the historic partners and the service provider to accord with the economic agreement of the parties.

The reallocation of partnership capital in these circumstances is not consistent with the policies underlying the substantial economic effect safe harbor and the capital account maintenance rules. The purpose of the substantial economic effect safe harbor is to ensure that, to the extent that there is an economic benefit or burden associated with a partnership allocation, the partner to whom the allocation is made receives the economic benefit or bears the economic burden. Under section 83, the economic benefit of receiving a partnership interest in connection with the performance of services is the amount that is included in the compensation income of the service provider, plus the amount paid for the interest. This is the amount by which the service partner's capital account should be increased.

As explained in section 6 below, a proposed Revenue Procedure issued concurrently with these Proposed Regulations would allow a partnership, its partners, and the service provider to elect to treat the fair market value of a partnership interest as equal to the liquidation value of that interest. If such an election is made, the capital account of a service provider receiving a partnership interest in connection with the performance of services is increased by the liquidation value of the partnership interest received.

B. Forfeiture of certain compensatory partnership interests

If an election under section 83(b) has been made with respect to a substantially nonvested interest, the holder of the nonvested interest may be allocated partnership items that may later be forfeited. For this reason, allocations of partnership items while the interest is substantially nonvested cannot have economic effect. Under the Proposed Regulations, such allocations will be treated as being in accordance with the partners' interests in the partnership if: (a) the partnership agreement requires that the partnership make forfeiture allocations if the interest for which the section 83(b) election is made is later forfeited; and (b) all material allocations and capital account adjustments under the partnership agreement not pertaining to substantially nonvested partnership interests for which a section 83(b) election has been made are recognized under section 704(b). This safe harbor does not apply if, at the time of the section 83(b) election, there is a plan that a substantially nonvested interest will be forfeited. All of the facts and circumstances (including the tax status of the holder of the substantially nonvested interest) will be considered in determining whether there is a plan that the interest will be forfeited. In such a case, the partners' distributive shares of partnership items shall be determined in accordance with the partners' interests in the partnership under § 1.704-1(b)(3).

Generally, forfeiture allocations are allocations to the service provider of partnership gross income and gain or gross deduction and loss (to the extent such items are available) that offset prior distributions and allocations of partnership items with respect to the forfeited partnership interest. These rules are designed to ensure that any partnership income (or loss) that was allocated to the service provider prior to the forfeiture is offset by allocations on the forfeiture of the interest. Also, to carry out the prohibition under section 83(b)(1) on deductions with respect to amounts included in income under section 83(b), these rules generally cause a forfeiting partner to be allocated partnership income to offset any distributions to the partner that reduced the partner's basis in the partnership below the amount included in income under section 83(b).

Forfeiture allocations may be made out of the partnership's items for the entire taxable year. In determining the gross income of the partnership in the taxable year of the forfeiture, the rules of § 1.83-6(c) apply. As a result, the partnership generally will have gross income in the taxable year of the forfeiture equal to the amount of the allowable deduction to the service recipient partnership upon the transfer of the interest as a result of the making of the section 83(b) election, regardless of the fair market value of the partnership's assets at the time of forfeiture.

In certain circumstances, the partnership will not have enough income and gain to fully offset prior allocations of loss to the forfeiting service provider. The proposed Revenue Procedure includes a rule that requires the recapture of losses taken by the service provider prior to the forfeiture of the interest to the extent that those losses are not recaptured through forfeiture allocations of income and gain to the service provider. This rule does not provide the other partners in the partnership with the opportunity to increase their shares of partnership loss (or reduce their shares of partnership income) for the year of the forfeiture by the amount of loss that was previously allocated to the forfeiting service provider.

In other circumstances, the partnership will not have enough deductions and loss to fully offset prior allocations of income to the forfeiting service provider. It appears that, in such a case, section 83(b)(1) may prohibit the service provider from claiming a loss with respect to partnership income that was previously allocated to the service provider. However, a forfeiting partner is entitled to a loss for any basis in a partnership that is attributable to contributions of money or property to the partnership (including amounts paid for the interest) remaining after the forfeiture allocations have been made. See § 1.83-2(a).

Comments are requested as to whether the Regulations should require or allow partnerships to create notional tax items to make forfeiture allocations where the partnership does not have enough actual tax items to make such allocations. Comments are also requested as to whether section 83(b)(1) should be read to allow a forfeiting service provider to claim a loss with respect to partnership income that was previously allocated to the service provider and not offset by forfeiture allocations of loss and deduction and, if so, whether it is appropriate to require the other partners in the partnership to recognize income in the year of the forfeiture equal to the amount of the loss claimed by the service provider. In particular, comments are requested as to whether section 83 or another section of the Code provides authority for such a rule.

5. Valuation of Compensatory Partnership Interests

Commentators requested guidance regarding the valuation of partnership interests transferred in connection with the performance of services. Section 83 generally provides that the recipient of property transferred in connection with the performance of services recognizes income equal to the fair market value of the property, disregarding lapse restrictions. *See Schulman v. Commissioner*, 93 T.C. 623 (1989). However, some authorities have concluded that, under the particular facts and circumstances of the case, a partnership profits interest had only a speculative value or that the fair market value of a partnership interest should be determined by reference to the liquidation value of that interest. *See* § 1.704-1(e)(1)(v); *Campbell v. Commissioner*, 943 F.2d 815 (8th Cir. 1991); *St. John v. U.S.*, 1984-1 USTC 9158 (C.D. Ill. 1983). *But see Diamond v. Commissioner*, 492 F.2d 286 (7th Cir. 1974) (holding under pre-section 83 law that the receipt of a profits interest with a determinable value at the time of receipt resulted in immediate taxation); *Campbell v. Commissioner*, T.C. Memo 1990-162, *aff'd in part and rev'd in part*, 943 F.2d 815 (8th Cir. 1991).

The Treasury Department and the Service have determined that, provided certain requirements are satisfied, it is appropriate to allow partnerships and service providers to value partnership interests based on liquidation value. This approach ensures consistency in the treatment of partnership profits interests and partnership capital interests, and accords with other Regulations issued under subchapter K, such as the Regulations under section 704(b).

In accordance with these Proposed Regulations, the Revenue Procedure proposed in Notice 2005-43 will, when finalized, provide additional rules that partnerships, partners, and persons providing services to the partnership in exchange for interests in that partnership would be required to follow when electing under § 1.83-3(l) of these Proposed Regulations to treat the fair market value of those interests as being equal to the liquidation value of those interests. For this purpose, the liquidation value of a partnership interest is the amount of cash that the holder of that interest would receive with respect to the interest if, immediately after the transfer of the interest, the partnership sold all of its assets (including goodwill, going concern value, and any other intangibles associated with the partnership's operations) for cash equal to the fair market value of those assets, and then liquidated.

6. Application of Section 721 to Partnership on Transfer

There is a dispute among commentators as to whether a partnership should recognize gain or loss on the transfer of a compensatory partnership interest. Some commentators believe that, on the transfer of such an interest, the partnership should be treated as satisfying its compensation obligation with a fractional interest in each asset of the partnership. Under this deemed sale of assets theory, the partnership would recognize gain or loss equal to the excess of the fair market value of each partial asset deemed transferred to the service provider over the partnership's adjusted basis in that partial asset. Other commentators believe that a partnership should not recognize gain or loss on the transfer of a compensatory partnership interest. They argue, among other things, that the transfer of such an interest is not properly treated as a realization event for the partnership because no property owned by the partnership has changed hands. They also argue that taxing a partnership on the transfer of such an interest would result in inappropriate gain acceleration, would be difficult to administer, and would cause economically similar transactions to be taxed differently.

Generally, when appreciated property is used to pay an obligation, gain on the property is recognized. The Treasury Department and the Service are still analyzing whether an exception to this general rule is appropriate on the transfer of an interest in the capital or profits of a partnership to satisfy certain partnership obligations (such as the obligations to pay interest or rent). However, the Treasury Department and the Service believe that partnerships should not be required to recognize gain on the transfer of a compensatory partnership interest. Such a rule is more consistent with the policies underlying section 721—to defer recognition of gain and loss when persons join together to conduct a business—than would be a rule requiring the partnership to recognize gain on the transfer of these types of interests. Therefore, the Proposed Regulations provide that partnerships are not taxed on the transfer or substantial vesting of a compensatory partnership interest. Under § 1.704-1(b)(4)(i) (reverse section 704(c) principles), the historic partners generally will be required to recognize any income or loss attributable to the partnership's assets as those assets are sold, depreciated, or amortized.

The rule providing for nonrecognition of gain or loss does not apply to the transfer or substantial vesting of an interest in an eligible entity, as defined in § 301.7701-3(a) of the Regulations, that becomes a partnership under § 301.7701-3(f)(2) as a result of the transfer or substantial vesting of the interest. See *McDougal v. Commissioner*, 62 T.C. 720 (1974) (holding that the service recipient recognized gain on the transfer of a one-half interest in appreciated property to the service provider, immediately prior to the contribution by the service recipient and the service provider of their respective interests in the property to a newly formed partnership). . . .

Proposed Effective Date

These Regulations are proposed to apply to transfers of property on or after the date final Regulations are published in the Federal Register.

Notice 2005-43
2005-1 CB 1221

Proposed Revenue Procedure Regarding Partnership Interests Transferred in Connection with the Performance of Services

June 13, 2005

SECTION 1
PURPOSE

This Notice addresses the taxation of a transfer of a partnership interest in connection with the performance of services. In conjunction with this Notice, the Treasury Department and the Internal Revenue Service are proposing Regulations under § 83 of the Internal Revenue Code. The Proposed Regulations grant the Commissioner authority to issue guidance of general applicability related to the taxation of the transfer of a partnership interest in connection with the performance of services. This Notice includes a proposed Revenue Procedure under that authority. The proposed Revenue Procedure provides additional rules for the elective safe harbor under Proposed § 1.83-3(l) for a partnership's transfers of interests in the partnership in connection with the performance of services for that partnership. The safe harbor is intended to simplify the application of § 83 to partnership interests and to coordinate the provisions of § 83 with the principles of partnership taxation. Upon the finalization of the proposed Revenue Procedure, Rev. Proc. 93-27, 1993-2 C.B. 343, and Rev. Proc. 2001-43, 2001-2 C.B. 191, (described below) will be obsoleted. Until that occurs, taxpayers may not rely upon the safe harbor set forth in the proposed Revenue Procedure, but taxpayers may continue to rely upon current law, including Rev. Proc. 93-27 and Rev. Proc. 2001-43.

PROPOSED REVENUE PROCEDURE

SECTION 1
PURPOSE

Proposed § 1.83-3(l) of the Regulations allows taxpayers to elect to apply special rules (the Safe Harbor) to a partnership's transfers of interests in the partnership in connection with the performance of services for the partnership. The Treasury Department and the Internal Revenue Service intend for the Safe Harbor to simplify the application of § 83 of the Internal Revenue Code to partnership interests transferred in connection with the performance of services and to coordinate the principles of § 83 with the principles of partnership taxation. This Revenue Procedure sets forth additional rules for the elective safe harbor under Proposed § 1.83-3(l) for a partnership's transfer of interests in the partnership in connection with the performance of services for that partnership.

SECTION 2
LAW AND DISCUSSION

Section 83(a) provides that if, in connection with the performance of services, property is transferred to any person other than the person for whom such services are performed, the excess of (1) the fair market value of such property (determined without regard to any restriction other than a restriction which by its terms will never lapse) at the first time the rights of the person having the beneficial interest in such property are transferable or are not subject to a substantial risk of forfeiture, whichever occurs earlier, over (2) the amount (if any) paid for such property, is included in the gross income of the person who performed such services in the first taxable year in which the rights of the person having the beneficial interest in such property are transferable or are not subject to a substantial risk of forfeiture, whichever is applicable.

Section 1.83-3(e) provides that, for purposes of § 83 and the Regulations thereunder, the term property includes real and personal property other than either money or an unfunded and unsecured promise to pay money or property in the future. For these purposes, under Proposed § 1.83-3(e) property includes a partnership interest. Generally, a mere right to allocations or distributions described in § 707(a)(2)(A) is not a partnership interest. Proposed § 1.83-3(e) also provides that, in the case of a transfer of a partnership interest in connection with the performance of services, the Commissioner may prescribe generally applicable administrative rules to address the application of § 83 to the transfer.

Section 83(b) provides that a service provider may elect to include in his or her gross income, for the taxable year in which substantially nonvested property is transferred, the excess of (1) the fair market value of the property at the time of the transfer (determined without regard to any restriction other than a restriction which by its terms will never lapse), over (2) the amount (if any) paid for the property. If such an election is made, § 83(a) does not apply with respect to the transfer of the property upon vesting and, if the property is subsequently forfeited, no deduction is allowed to the service provider in respect of the forfeiture.

Section 1.83-2(b) provides that an election under § 83(b) must be filed not later than 30 days after the date the property was transferred and may be filed prior to the date of the transfer. . . .

Section 1.83-1(a) provides that, unless an election under § 83(b) is made, the transferor is regarded as the owner of substantially nonvested property transferred in connection with the performance of services until such property becomes substantially vested, and any income from such property received by the service provider (or beneficiary thereof), or the right to the use of such property by the service provider, constitutes additional compensation and is included in the gross income of the service provider for the taxable year in which the income is received or the use is made available. Under this rule, a partnership must treat as unissued any substantially nonvested partnership interest transferred in connection with the performance of services for which an election under § 83(b) has not been made. If the service provider who holds such an interest receives distributions from the partnership with respect to that interest while the interest is substantially nonvested, the distributions are treated as compensation in the capacity in which the service provider performed the services. For example, if a service provider that is not a pre-existing partner holds a substantially nonvested partnership interest that the service provider received in connection with the performance of services and the service provider did not make an election under § 83(b) with respect to that interest, then any distributions made to the service provider on account of such interest are treated as additional compensation and not partnership distributions. If, instead, the service provider who receives a substantially nonvested partnership interest in connection with the performance of services makes a valid election under § 83(b), then the service provider is treated as the owner of the property. The service provider is treated as a partner with respect to such an interest, and the partnership must allocate partnership items to the service provider as if the partnership interest were substantially vested.

Section 1.83-3(b) provides that property is substantially nonvested for § 83 purposes when it is subject to a substantial risk of forfeiture and is nontransferable. Property is substantially vested for § 83 purposes when it is either transferable or not subject to a substantial risk of forfeiture.

Section 1.83-3(c) provides that, for § 83 purposes, whether a risk of forfeiture is substantial or not depends upon the facts and circumstances. A substantial risk of forfeiture exists where rights in property that are transferred are conditioned, directly or indirectly, upon the future performance (or refraining from performance) of substantial services by any person, or the occurrence of a condition related to a purpose of the transfer, and the possibility of forfeiture is substantial if such condition is not satisfied.

Section 1.83-3(d) provides that, for § 83 purposes, the rights of a person in property are transferable if such person can transfer any interest in the property to any person other than the transferor of the property, but only if the rights in such property of such transferee are not subject to a substantial risk of forfeiture.

Proposed § 1.83-3(l) provides that, subject to such additional conditions, rules, and procedures that the Commissioner may prescribe in Regulations, Revenue Rulings, Notices, or other guidance published in the Internal Revenue Bulletin, a partnership and all of its partners may elect a safe harbor under which the fair market value of a partnership interest that is transferred in connection with the performance of services is treated as being equal to the liquidation value of that interest for transfers on or after the date final Regulations are published in the Federal Register if the following conditions are satisfied: (1) the partnership must prepare a document, executed by a partner who has responsibility for federal income tax reporting by the partnership, stating that the partnership is electing, on behalf of the partnership and each of its partners, to have the safe harbor apply irrevocably as of the stated effective date with respect to all partnership interests transferred in connection with the performance of services while the safe harbor election remains in effect and attach the document to the tax return for the partnership for the taxable year that includes the effective date of the election; (2) except as provided below, the partnership agreement must contain provisions that are legally binding on all of the partners stating that (a) the partnership is authorized and directed to elect the safe harbor, and (b) the partnership and each of its partners (including any person to whom a partnership interest is transferred in connection with the performance of services) agrees to comply with all requirements of the safe harbor with respect to all partnership interests transferred in connection with the performance of services while the election remains effective; and (3) if the partnership agreement does not contain the provisions described in clause (2) of this sentence, or the provisions are not legally binding on all of the partners of the partnership, then each partner in a partnership that transfers a partnership interest in connection with the performance of services must execute a document containing provisions that are legally binding on that partner stating that (a) the partnership is authorized and directed to elect the safe harbor, and (b) the partner agrees to comply with all requirements of the safe harbor with respect to all partnership interests transferred in connection with the performance of services while the election remains effective....

Section 83(h) provides that, in the case of a transfer of property in connection with the performance of services or a cancellation of a restriction described in § 83(d), there is allowed as a deduction under § 162, to the person for whom the services were performed (the service recipient), an amount equal to the amount included under § 83(a), (b), or (d)(2) in the gross income of the service provider. The deduction is allowed for the taxable year of the service recipient in which or with which ends the taxable year in which such amount is included in the gross income of the service provider. Under § 1.83-6(a)(3), if property is substantially vested upon the transfer, the deduction is allowed to the service recipient in accordance with its method of accounting (in conformity with §§ 446 and 461).

Section 1.83-6(c) provides that if, under § 83(h) and § 1.83-6(a), a deduction, an increase in basis, or a reduction of gross income was allowable (disregarding the reasonableness of the amount of compensation) in respect of a transfer of property and such property is subsequently forfeited, the amount of such deduction, increase in basis, or reduction of gross income shall be includable in the gross income of the person to whom it was allowable for the taxable year of the forfeiture. The basis of such property in the hands of the person to whom it is forfeited shall include any such amount includable in the gross income of such person, as well as any amount such person pays upon forfeiture.

Section 704(b) requires that a partner's distributive share of income, gain, loss, deduction, or credit (or item thereof) be determined in accordance with the partner's interest in the partnership, determined by taking into account all facts and circumstances, if (1) the partnership agreement does not provide otherwise as to the partner's distributive share, or (2) the allocation to a partner under the agreement does not have substantial economic effect.

Proposed § 1.704-1(b)(2)(iv)(b)(1) provides that a partner's capital account includes the amount contributed by that partner to the partnership, and, in the case of a compensatory partnership interest that is transferred on or after the date final Regulations are published in the Federal Register, the amount included on or after that date as the partner's compensation income under § 83(a), (b), or (d)(2). For these purposes, a compensatory partnership interest is an interest in the transferring partnership that is transferred in connection with the performance of services for that partnership (either before or after the formation of the partnership), including an interest that is transferred on the exercise of a compensatory partnership option. A compensatory partnership option is an option to acquire an interest in the issuing partnership that is granted in connection with the performance of services for that partnership (either before or after the formation of the partnership).

Proposed § 1.704-1(b)(4)(xii)(a) provides that if a § 83(b) election has been made with respect to a substantially nonvested interest, allocations of partnership items while the interest is substantially nonvested cannot have economic effect.

Proposed § 1.704-1(b)(4)(xii)(b) provides that allocations of partnership items to a holder of a nonvested interest for which a § 83(b) election has been made will be deemed to be in accordance with the partners' interests in the partnership if the partnership agreement requires that: (1) in the event that the interest for which the § 83(b) election is made is later forfeited, the partnership shall make forfeiture allocations in the year of the forfeiture; and (2) all material allocations and capital account adjustments under the partnership agreement not pertaining to substantially nonvested partnership interests for which a § 83(b) election has been made are recognized under § 704(b). Proposed § 1.704-1(b)(4)(xii)(e) provides that proposed § 1.704-1(b)(4)(xii)(b) does not apply to allocations of partnership items made with respect to a substantially nonvested interest for which the holder has made a § 83(b) election if, at the time of the § 83(b) election, there is a plan that the interest will be forfeited. In determining whether there is a plan that the interest will be forfeited, the Commissioner will consider all of the facts and circumstances (including the tax status of the holder of the forfeitable compensatory partnership interest).

Proposed § 1.704-1(b)(4)(xii)(c) defines forfeiture allocations as allocations to the service provider (consisting of a pro rata portion of each item) of gross income and gain or gross deduction and loss (to the extent such items are available) for the taxable year of the forfeiture in a positive or negative amount equal to (1) the excess (not less than zero) of (a) the amount of the distributions (including deemed distributions under § 752(b) and the adjusted tax basis of any property so distributed) to the partner with respect to the forfeited partnership interest (to the extent such distributions are not taxable under § 731), over (b) the amounts paid for the interest and the adjusted tax basis of property contributed by the partner (including deemed contributions under § 752(a)) to the partnership with respect to the forfeited partnership interest, minus (2) the cumulative net income (or loss) allocated to the partner with respect to the forfeited partnership interest. Proposed § 1.704-1(b)(4)(xii)(d) provides that for purposes of Proposed § 1.704-1(b)(4)(xii)(c), items of income and gain are reflected as positive amounts, and items of deduction and loss are reflected as negative amounts.

Section 721(a) provides that no gain or loss is recognized to a partnership or to any of its partners in the case of a contribution of property to the partnership in exchange for an interest in the partnership.

Proposed § 1.721-1(b)(1) provides that § 721 generally does not apply to the transfer of a partnership interest in connection with the performance of services. Such a transfer constitutes a transfer of property to which § 83 and the Regulations thereunder apply. However, under Proposed § 1.721-1(b)(2), except as provided in § 83(h) or § 1.83-6(c), no gain or loss is recognized by a partnership upon: (i) the transfer or substantial vesting of a compensatory partnership interest, or (ii) the forfeiture of a compensatory partnership interest.

Proposed § 1.761-1(b) provides that if a partnership interest is transferred in connection with the performance of services, and that partnership interest is substantially nonvested (within the meaning of § 1.83-3(b)), then the holder of the partnership interest is not treated as a partner solely by reason of holding the interest, unless the holder makes an election with respect to the interest under § 83(b) . . . .

SECTION 3
SCOPE

.01 In General. The Safe Harbor in section 4 of this Revenue Procedure applies to any Safe Harbor Partnership Interest transferred by a partnership if the transfer is made during the period in which the Safe Harbor Election is in effect (whether or not the Safe Harbor Partnership Interest is substantially vested on the date of transfer). Thus, for example, sections 4.02 through 4.04 of this Revenue Procedure apply to a Safe Harbor Partnership Interest that is transferred during the period in which the Safe Harbor Election is in effect, even if that Safe Harbor Partnership Interest does not become substantially vested until after the Safe Harbor Election is terminated, a § 83(b) election is made after the Safe Harbor Election is terminated, or that Safe Harbor Partnership Interest is forfeited after the Safe Harbor Election is terminated. Further, a Safe Harbor Election is binding on the partnership, all of its partners, and the service provider. The Safe Harbor includes all of the rules set forth in section 4 of this Revenue Procedure, and a partnership, its partners, and the service provider may not choose to apply only certain of the rules in section 4 of this Revenue Procedure or to apply the Safe Harbor only to certain partners, service providers, or partnership interests.

.02 **Safe Harbor Partnership Interest.** (1) Except as otherwise provided in section 3.02(2) of this revenue procedure, a Safe Harbor Partnership Interest is any interest in a partnership that is transferred to a service provider by such partnership in connection with services provided to the partnership (either before or after the formation of the partnership), provided that the interest is not (a) related to a substantially certain and predictable stream of income from partnership assets, such as income from high-quality debt securities or a high-quality net lease, (b) transferred in anticipation of a subsequent disposition, or (c) an interest in a publicly traded partnership within the meaning of § 7704(b). Unless it is established by clear and convincing evidence that the partnership interest was not transferred in anticipation of a subsequent disposition, a partnership interest is presumed to be transferred in anticipation of a subsequent disposition for purposes of the preceding clause (b) if the partnership interest is sold or disposed of within two years of the date of receipt of the partnership interest (other than a sale or disposition by reason of death or disability of the service provider) or is the subject, at any time within two years of the date of receipt, of a right to buy or sell regardless of when the right is exercisable (other than a right to buy or sell arising by reason of the death or disability of the service provider). For the purposes of this revenue procedure, "disability" means a condition which causes a service provider to be unable to engage in any substantial gainful activity by reason of a medically determinable physical or mental impairment expected to result in death or to last for a continuous period of not less than 12 months.

(2) An interest in a partnership is not a Safe Harbor Partnership Interest unless at the date of transfer the requirements of section 3.03 of this Revenue Procedure are satisfied and a Safe Harbor Election has not terminated pursuant to section 3.04 of this Revenue Procedure. For the first taxable year that a partnership is subject to a Safe Harbor Election, a partnership interest may be a Safe Harbor Partnership Interest if a Safe Harbor Election is attached to the partnership tax return for the taxable year including the date of transfer, provided that the other requirements of section 3.03 of this Revenue Procedure are satisfied on or before the date of such transfer.

.03 **Required Conditions for Safe Harbor Election.** In order to effect and maintain a valid Safe Harbor Election the following conditions must be satisfied:

(1) The partnership must prepare a document, executed by a partner who has responsibility for federal income tax reporting by the partnership, stating that the partnership is electing, on behalf of the partnership and each of its partners, to

have the Safe Harbor described in Rev. Proc. 200X-XX apply irrevocably with respect to all partnership interests transferred in connection with the performance of services while the Safe Harbor Election remains in effect . . . .

(2) Except as provided in section 3.03(3) of this Revenue Procedure, the partnership agreement must contain provisions that are legally binding on all of the partners stating that (a) the partnership is authorized and directed to elect the Safe Harbor described in this Revenue Procedure, and (b) the partnership and each of its partners (including any person to whom a partnership interest is transferred in connection with the performance of services) agrees to comply with all requirements of the Safe Harbor described in this Revenue Procedure with respect to all partnership interests transferred in connection with the performance of services while the election remains effective. If a partner that is bound by these provisions transfers a partnership interest to another person, the requirement that each partner be bound by these provisions is satisfied only if the person to whom the interest is transferred assumes the transferring partner's obligations under the partnership agreement. If an amendment to the partnership agreement is required, the amendment must be effective before the date on which a transfer occurs for the Safe Harbor to be applied to such transfer. . . .

SECTION 4
SAFE HARBOR

.01 Safe Harbor. For purposes of § 83, the rules in sections 4.02 through 4.04 of this Revenue Procedure apply to any Safe Harbor Partnership Interest for which a Safe Harbor Election is in effect.

.02 Liquidation Value. Under the Safe Harbor, the fair market value of a Safe Harbor Partnership Interest is treated as being equal to the liquidation value of that interest. For this purpose, liquidation value is determined without regard to any lapse restriction (as defined at § 1.83-3(i)) and means the amount of cash that the recipient of the Safe Harbor Partnership Interest would receive if, immediately after the transfer, the partnership sold all of its assets (including goodwill, going concern value, and any other intangibles associated with the partnership's operations) for cash equal to the fair market value of those assets and then liquidated.

.03 Vesting. Under the Safe Harbor, a Safe Harbor Partnership Interest is treated as substantially vested if the right to the associated capital account balance equivalent is not subject to a substantial risk of forfeiture or the interest is transferable. A Safe Harbor Partnership Interest is treated as substantially nonvested only if, under the terms of the interest at the time of the transfer, the interest terminates and the holder may be required to forfeit the capital account balance equivalent credited to the holder under conditions that would constitute a substantial risk of forfeiture, and the interest is not transferable. For these purposes, the capital account balance equivalent is the amount of cash that the recipient of the Safe Harbor Partnership Interest would receive if, immediately prior to the forfeiture, the interest vested and the partnership sold all of its assets (including goodwill, going concern value, or any other intangibles associated with the partnership's operations) for cash equal to the fair market value of those assets and then liquidated. Notwithstanding the previous sentence, a Safe Harbor Partnership Interest will not be considered substantially nonvested if the sole portion of the capital account balance equivalent forfeited is the excess of the capital account balance equivalent at the date of termination of services over the capital account balance equivalent at the end of the prior partnership tax year or any later date before the date of termination of services.

.04 Forfeiture Subsequent to § 83(b) Election. If a Safe Harbor Partnership Interest with respect to which a § 83(b) election has been made is forfeited, the service provider must include as ordinary income in the taxable year of the forfeiture an amount equal to the excess, if any, of (1) the amount of income or gain that the partnership would be required to allocate to the service provider under Proposed § 1.704-1(b)(4)(xii) if the partnership had unlimited items of gross income and gain, over (2) the amount of income or gain that the partnership actually allocated to the service provider under Proposed § 1.704-1(b)(4)(xii).

SECTION 5
APPLICATION OF SAFE HARBOR TO SERVICE PROVIDER AND SERVICE RECIPIENT

.01 Application of Safe Harbor to the Service Provider. Under the Safe Harbor, the service provider recognizes compensation income upon the transfer of a substantially vested Safe Harbor Partnership Interest in an amount equal to the liquidation value of the interest, less any amount paid for the interest. If the service provider receives a Safe Harbor Partnership Interest that is substantially nonvested, does not make an election under § 83(b), and holds the interest until it substantially vests, the service provider recognizes compensation income in an amount equal to the liquidation value of the interest on the date the interest substantially vests, less any amount paid for the interest. If the service provider receives a Safe Harbor Partnership Interest that is substantially nonvested and makes an election under § 83(b), the service provider recognizes compensation income on the date of transfer equal to the liquidation value of the interest, determined as if the interest were substantially vested, pursuant to the rules of § 83(b) and § 1.83-2, less any amount paid for the interest.

.02 Application of Safe Harbor to the Service Recipient. Under § 83(h), the service recipient generally is entitled to a deduction equal to the amount included as compensation in the gross income of the service provider under § 83(a), (b), or (d)(2), but only to the extent the amount meets the requirements of § 162 or § 212. Under the Safe Harbor, the amount included in the service provider's gross income in accordance with section 4.02 of this Revenue Procedure is considered the amount included as compensation in the gross income of the service provider under § 83(a) or (b) for purposes of § 83(h). The deduction generally is allowed for the taxable year of the partnership in which or with which ends the taxable year of the service provider in which the amount is included in gross income as compensation. However, in accordance with § 1.83-6(a)(3), where the deduction relates to the transfer of substantially vested property, the deduction is available in accordance with the service recipient's method of accounting.

SECTION 6
EXAMPLES

The following facts apply for all of the examples below:

SP is an individual with a calendar year taxable year. PRS is a partnership with a calendar year taxable year. Except as otherwise stated, PRS's partnership agreement provides for all partnership items to be allocated to the partners in proportion to the partners' interests in the partnership. PRS's partnership agreement provides that the partners' capital accounts will be determined and maintained in accordance with § 1.704-1(b)(2)(iv), that liquidation proceeds will be distributed in accordance with the partners' positive capital account balances, and that any partner with a deficit balance in the partner's capital account following the liquidation of the partner's interest must restore that deficit to the partnership. All allocations and distributions to all parties are not recast under § 707(a)(2), and § 751(b) does not apply to any distribution. The partnership, its members, and the service providers elect the Safe Harbor provided in section 4 of this Revenue Procedure and file all affected returns consistent with the Safe Harbor, and each partnership interest transferred constitutes a Safe Harbor Partnership Interest under section 3.02 of this Revenue Procedure. The issuance of the partnership interest in each example is not required to be capitalized under the rules of § 263 or other applicable provision of the Code. In examples in which the partnership interest transferred to the service provider is not substantially vested, there is not a plan that the service provider will forfeit the partnership interest.

(1) Example 1: Substantially Vested Profits Interest

Facts: PRS has two partners, A and B, each with a 50% interest in PRS. On March 1, 2005, SP agrees to perform services for the partnership in exchange for a partnership interest. Under the terms of the partnership agreement, SP is entitled to 10% of the future profits and losses of PRS, but is not entitled to any of the partnership's capital as of the date of transfer. Although SP must surrender the partnership interest upon termination of services to the partnership, SP will not surrender any share of the profits accumulated through the end of the partnership taxable year preceding the partnership taxable year in which SP terminates services.

Conclusion: Under section 4.03 of this Revenue Procedure, SP's interest in PRS is treated as substantially vested at the time of transfer. Under section 4.02 of this Revenue Procedure, the fair market value of the interest for purposes of § 83 is treated as being equal to its liquidation value (zero). Therefore, SP does not recognize compensation income under § 83(a) as a result of the transfer, PRS is not entitled to a deduction, and SP is not entitled to a capital account balance.

(2) Example 2: Substantially Vested Interest

Facts: PRS has two partners, A and B, each with a 50% interest in PRS. On March 1, 2005, SP pays the partnership $10 and agrees to perform services for the partnership in exchange for a 10% partnership interest that is treated as substantially vested under section 4.03 of this revenue procedure. Immediately before SP's $10 payment to PRS and the transfer of the partnership interest to SP in connection with the performance of services, the value of the partnership's assets (including goodwill, going concern value, and any other intangibles associated with the partnership's operations) is $990.

Conclusion: Under section 4.02 of this Revenue Procedure, the fair market value of SP's interest in PRS at the time the interest becomes substantially vested is treated as being equal to its liquidation value at that time for purposes of § 83. Therefore, in 2005, SP includes $90 ($100 liquidation value less $10 amount paid for the interest) as compensation income under § 83(a), PRS is entitled to a deduction of $90 under § 83(h), and SP's initial capital account is $100 ($90 included in income plus $10 amount paid for the interest).

(3) Example 3: Substantially Nonvested Interest; No § 83(b) Election; Pre-Existing Partner

Facts: PRS has two partners, A and SP, each with a 50% interest in PRS. On December 31, 2004, SP agrees to perform services for the partnership in exchange for a 10% increase in SP's interest in the partnership from 50% to 60%. SP is not required to pay any amount in exchange for the additional 10% interest. Under the terms of the partnership agreement, if SP terminates services on or before January 1, 2008, SP forfeits any right to any share of accumulated, undistributed profits with respect to the additional 10% interest. The partnership interest transferred to SP is not transferable and no election is made under § 83(b). SP continues performing services through January 1, 2008. PRS has taxable income of $500 in 2005 and $1,000 in each of 2006 and 2007. No distributions are made to A or SP during such period. On January 1, 2008, the value of the partnership's assets (including goodwill, going concern value, and any other intangibles associated with the partnership's operations) is $3,500.

Conclusion: Under section 4.03 of this Revenue Procedure, the 10% partnership interest transferred to SP on December 31, 2004, is treated as substantially nonvested at the time of transfer. Because a § 83(b) election is not made, SP does not include any amount as compensation income attributable to the transfer, and correspondingly, PRS is not entitled to a deduction under § 83(h).

In accordance with the partnership agreement, PRS's taxable income for 2005 is allocated $250 to A and $250 to SP, and PRS's taxable income for each of 2006 and 2007 is allocated $500 to A and $500 to SP.

On January 1, 2008, SP's additional 10% interest in PRS is treated as becoming substantially vested under section 4.03 of this Revenue Procedure. At that time, the additional 10% interest in the partnership has a liquidation value of $350 (10% of $3,500). Under section 4.02 of this Revenue Procedure, the fair market value of the interest at the time it becomes substantially vested is treated as being equal to its liquidation value at that time for purposes of § 83. Therefore, in 2008, SP includes $350 as compensation income under § 83(a), PRS is entitled to a deduction of $350 under § 83(h), and SP's capital account is increased by $350.

(4) Example 4: Substantially Nonvested Interest; No § 83(b) Election

Facts: PRS has two partners, A and B, each with a 50% interest in PRS. On December 31, 2004, SP pays the partnership $10 and agrees to perform services for the partnership in exchange for a 10% partnership interest. Under the terms of the partnership agreement, if SP terminates services on or before January 1, 2008, SP forfeits any rights to any share of accumulated, undistributed profits, but is entitled to a return of SP's $10 initial contribution. SP's partnership interest is not transferable and no election is made under § 83(b). SP continues performing services through January 1, 2008. PRS earns $500 of taxable income in 2005, and $1,000 in each of 2006 and 2007. A and B each receive distributions of $225 in 2005, but neither A nor B receive distributions in 2006 and 2007. PRS transfers $50 to SP in 2005, but does not make any transfers to SP in 2006 or 2007. On January 1, 2008, SP's partnership interest has a liquidation value of $300 (taking into account   the unpaid partnership income credited to SP through that date).

Conclusion: Under section 4.03 of this Revenue Procedure, SP's partnership interest is treated as substantially nonvested at the time of transfer. Because a § 83(b) election is not made, SP does not include any amount as compensation income attributable to the transfer and, correspondingly, PRS is not entitled to a deduction under § 83(h). Under Proposed § 1.761-1(b), SP is not a partner in PRS; therefore, none of PRS's taxable income for the years in which SP's interest is substantially nonvested may be allocated to SP. Rather, PRS's taxable income is allocated exclusively to A and B. In addition, the $50 paid by PRS to SP in 2005 is compensation income to SP, and PRS is entitled to a deduction of $50 under § 162 in accordance with its method of accounting.

On January 1, 2008, SP's interest in PRS is treated as becoming substantially vested under section 4.03 of this Revenue Procedure. Under section 4.02 of this Revenue Procedure, the fair market value of the interest at the time the interest becomes substantially vested is treated as being equal to its liquidation value at that time for § 83 purposes. Therefore, in 2008, SP includes $290 ($300 liquidation value less $10 amount paid for the interest) as compensation income under § 83(a), PRS is entitled to a $290 deduction, and SP's capital account is increased to $300 ($290 included in income plus $10 amount paid for the interest).

(5) Example 5: Substantially Nonvested Interest; § 83(b) Election

Facts: The facts are the same as in Example 4, except that SP makes an election under § 83(b) with respect to SP's interest in PRS. The liquidation value of the interest is $100 at the time the interest in PRS is transferred to SP. SP continues performing services through January 1, 2008.

Conclusion: Under section 4.02 of this Revenue Procedure, the fair market value (disregarding lapse restrictions) of SP's interest in PRS at the time of transfer is treated as being equal to its liquidation value (disregarding lapse restrictions) at that time for § 83 purposes. Because a § 83(b) election is made, in 2004 SP includes $90 ($100 liquidation value less $10 amount paid for the interest) as compensation income, PRS is entitled to a $90 deduction, and SP's initial capital account is $100 ($90 included in SP's income plus $10 amount paid for the interest). Under Proposed § 1.761-1(b), as a result of SP's election under § 83(b), SP is treated as a partner starting from the date of the transfer of the interest to SP. Accordingly, SP includes in 2005 taxable income SP's $50 distributive share of PRS income, and the $50 payment to SP by PRS in 2005 is a partnership distribution under § 731. SP includes in 2006 and 2007 taxable income SP's $100 distributive shares of PRS income for those years.

(6) Example 6: Substantially Nonvested Interest; § 83(b) Election; Forfeiture; Net Profit

Facts: The facts are the same as in Example 5, except that SP terminates services on September 30, 2007, and is repaid the $10 that SP paid for the PRS interest in 2004. The partnership agreement provides that if SP's partnership interest is forfeited, SP's distributive share of all partnership items (other than forfeiture allocations) will be zero with respect to the interest for the taxable year of the partnership in which the interest is forfeited.

Conclusion: The tax consequences for 2004 through 2006 are the same as in Example (5). As a result of the forfeiture in 2007, PRS is required under § 1.83-6(c) to include in gross income $90 (the amount of the allowable deduction on the transfer of the interest to SP). In accordance with the partnership agreement, PRS also makes forfeiture allocations in 2007 to offset partnership income and loss that was allocated to SP and partnership distributions to SP prior to the forfeiture. Cumulative net income of $150 was allocated to SP prior to the forfeiture ($50 in 2005 and $100 in 2006) and SP received a total of $60 of distributions from PRS ($50 in 2005 and $10 in 2007 (the repayment of SP's initial contribution to PRS)). Under Proposed § 1.704-1(b)(4)(xii), the total forfeiture allocations to SP is $100 of partnership loss and deduction, the difference between $50 ($60 of distributions to SP less $10 of contributions to PRS by SP) and $150 (cumulative net income allocated to SP). Pursuant to the partnership agreement, none of the partnership income for the year 2007 is allocated to SP. In accordance with § 83(b)(1) (last sentence), SP does not receive a deduction or capital loss for the amount ($90) that was included as SP's compensation income as a result of the election under § 83(b).

(7) Example 7: Substantially Nonvested Interest; § 83(b) Election; Forfeiture; Net Loss

Facts: PRS has two partners, A and B, each with a 50% interest in PRS. On December 31, 2004, SP pays the partnership $10 and agrees to perform services for the partnership in exchange for a 10% partnership interest. Under the terms of the partnership agreement, if SP terminates services before January 1, 2008, SP forfeits any right to any share of accumulated, undistributed profits, but is entitled to a return of SP's $10 initial contribution. SP's partnership interest is not transferable. The partnership agreement provides that if SP's partnership interest is forfeited, SP's distributive share of all partnership items (other than forfeiture allocations) will be zero with respect to the interest for the taxable year of the partnership in which the interest is forfeited. At the time of the transfer, the liquidation value of the 10% partnership interest is $100, and SP makes an election under § 83(b) with respect to the interest. In 2005, PRS earns $500 of taxable income, which is allocated and distributed $225 to each of A and B and $50 to SP. In 2006, PRS has net taxable loss of $1,000, $100 of which is allocated to SP. PRS does not make any distributions in 2006. PRS has no items of income, gain, loss, or deduction in 2007, other than gross income recognized under § 1.83-6(c). SP terminates services on September 30, 2007, and is repaid the $10 that SP paid for the PRS interest in 2004. PRS does not make any distributions in 2007, other than the return of SP's $10 contribution.

Conclusion: Under section 4.02 of this Revenue Procedure, the fair market value (disregarding lapse restrictions) of SP's interest in PRS at the time of transfer is treated as being equal to its liquidation value (disregarding lapse restrictions) at that time for purposes of § 83. Because a § 83(b) election is made, SP includes as compensation income in 2004 $90 ($100 liquidation value less $10 amount paid for the interest), PRS is entitled to a $90 deduction under § 83(h), and SP's initial capital account is $100 ($90 compensation income plus $10 amount paid for the interest). Under Proposed § 1.761-1(b), as a result of SP's election under § 83(b), SP is treated as a partner starting from the date of the transfer of the interest to SP. Accordingly, SP includes in 2005 taxable income SP's $50 distributive share of PRS's income, and the

$50 payment to SP in 2005 is a partnership distribution under § 731. SP includes in computing 2006 taxable income SP's $100 distributive share of PRS's loss.

As a result of the forfeiture in 2007, PRS is required under § 1.83-6(c) to include in gross income $90 (the amount of the allowable deduction on the transfer of the interest to SP). In accordance with the partnership agreement, PRS also makes forfeiture allocations in 2007 to offset partnership income and loss that was allocated to SP and partnership distributions to SP prior to the forfeiture. Cumulative net loss of $50 was allocated to SP prior to the forfeiture ($50 of income in 2005 and $100 of loss in 2006) and SP received a total of $60 of partnership distributions ($50 in 2005 and $10 in 2007 (the repayment of SP's initial contribution to PRS)). If PRS had unlimited items of gross income and gain, the total forfeiture allocations to SP under Proposed § 1.704-1(b)(4)(xii) would be $100 of partnership income and gain, the difference between $50 ($60 distributions to SP less $10 of contributions to PRS by SP) and – $50 (cumulative net loss allocated to SP). However, PRS's only income in 2007 is the $90 of income recognized by PRS under § 1.83-6(c), all of which must be used to make forfeiture allocations to SP. Under section 4.04 of this Revenue Procedure, in 2007, SP must include in ordinary income $10 (the difference between the forfeiture allocations that would be required under Proposed § 1.704-1(b)(4)(xii) if PRS had an unlimited amount of gross income and gain, $100, and the actual forfeiture allocations to SP, $90). PRS is not entitled to a deduction for the amount ($10) that SP is required to include in income under section 4.04 of this revenue procedure....

CHAPTER 22

Allocation of Partnership Debt and Debt-Financed Losses and Deductions

PROBLEM AREA 22

INTRODUCTION

The allocation of partnership debt under the rules of § 752 and the allocation of the losses and deductions funded by that debt under the rules of § 704(b) are closely related topics, but must be understood separately before their interrelationship can be appreciated fully. Problem Area 4 considers debt allocation; Problem Area 7, the allocation of profits, losses, and deductions. Problem Area 22 provides the opportunity to examine these topics together.

In addition, the questions in this Problem Area highlight special liability topics, including the treatment of contingent liabilities under Regulations finalized in 2005, the allocation and possible exclusion from income of cancellation of debt income arising from the discharge of partnership debt, and the effect of disregarded entities on allocations under § 752.

PROBLEM 22

QUESTIONS

1. A and B form an equal general partnership AB, and each contributes $10,000 in cash to the capital of the partnership. Assume that the partnership agreement provides for capital-account maintenance in accordance with the Regulations and for liquidating distributions in accordance with capital-account balances. Furthermore, it contains provisions for minimum-gain chargeback and qualified-income offset but no explicit deficit-restoration obligation for either partner. Under applicable state law, each partner is obligated to restore a deficit capital account only to the extent necessary to pay creditors, but not to pay the amount of the positive balance, if any, in the capital account of the other partner. The partnership purchases personal property valued at $100,000 for $20,000 cash and $80,000 borrowed on a recourse basis. The partnership suffers a $30,000 loss attributable exclusively to depreciation on the personal property in its first year of operation. What are the partners' bases for their partnership interests at the beginning and end of this first year? Does this answer change if the liability is nonrecourse?

How much of the partnership's $30,000 loss is allowed to each partner in each of the following alternatives? What are the partners' bases for their partnership interests at the beginning and end of the year? In each case, compare the results obtained if the liability is recourse with those if the liability is nonrecourse.

a. AB is a general partnership. A and B share profits in a 40:60 ratio and losses in a 70:30 ratio.

b. AB is an equal limited partnership with B as the limited partner. B has no deficit-restoration obligation.

c. Same as b. above, except that B is obligated under the partnership agreement to contribute an additional $30,000.

d. Same as b. above, except that B has agreed to pay A up to $40,000 if A actually pays off the partnership's liability from his personal funds.

e. Same as b. above, except that B has agreed to guarantee $40,000 of the partnership's liability directly to the partnership's lender.

2. On January 1, Year 1, A contributes $150,000 and B $50,000 in cash to the AB general partnership, which applies the funds as a down payment in purchasing equipment with an $800,000 nonrecourse mortgage. The equipment has a ten-year depreciable life for book and tax purposes. Assume that the partnership agreement provides for capital-account maintenance in accordance with the Regulations, and for liquidating distributions in accordance with capital-account balances, and contains provisions for minimum-gain chargeback and qualified-income offset but no explicit deficit-restoration obligation for either partner. All partnership items, other than the minimum-gain chargeback and qualified-income offset, will be allocated 75 percent to A and 25 percent to B until overall partnership income equals previous partnership losses and deductions. Thereafter, income and loss will be allocated equally. For

Years 1, 2, and 3, the partnership, although a bona fide, profit-driven enterprise, derives no income or loss other than the depreciation deduction.

a. What are the results to the parties for Years 1-3? (In this and the following questions assume that the partnership is entitled to three full years of depreciation for Years 1-3 and is not entitled to depreciation for Year 4.)

b. What if the property falls in value to $575,000, and the partnership defaults on the obligation in Year 4?

c. What if the property appreciates in value to $1,500,000, and the partnership sells it to a third party in Year 4?

d. What result in Year 4, if A and B contribute $225,000 and $75,000, respectively, which the partnership utilizes to pay down the mortgage?

e. What is the result in a. above, if the parties allocate the nonrecourse deductions 85 percent to A and 15 percent to B?

f. What is the result in c. above, if the partnership borrows an additional $300,000 against the equipment on a nonrecourse basis and distributes the proceeds (i) equally to A and B or (ii) 75 percent to A and 25 percent to B?

3. A and B form an equal general partnership AB. A contributes depreciable property with an adjusted basis of $40,000 and a fair market value of $100,000, subject to a $60,000 nonrecourse liability incurred three years ago. B contributes $40,000 in cash. What is the tax basis of A and of B in their partnership interests? Does your answer depend on the § 704(c) method chosen by the partnership? What is the tax basis of each of A and B after the depreciable property has been fully depreciated, assuming (unrealistically) that the partnership realizes no other income, gain, or loss? What if A's adjusted basis in the contributed property is $20,000?

4. A partnership is formed by two individuals, A and B. A contributes property with a value and a basis of $20,000, subject to a contingent obligation of $15,000 for a 50 percent interest in the partnership. B contributes $5,000 in cash. What is the result to the parties? What is the result (other than a partnership termination) if A sells his partnership interest to C six months later for $5,000?

5. The equal ABC general partnership was formed with cash capital contributions of $150,000 from each of A, B, and C and incurred a recourse liability of $300,000. With these funds, it purchased land for $50,000 and depreciable property for $700,000. The adjusted bases of the land and the depreciable property are now $50,000 and $100,000, respectively, although their values are de minimis. Each partner has an adjusted basis in his partnership interest of $50,000. The partnership declares bankruptcy. A is also in bankruptcy, B is insolvent to the extent of $200,000, and C is solvent. What is the result to the parties? What is the result if the parties share capital and losses equally but profits are shared 35 percent to A, 15 percent to B, and 50 percent to C? What is the result if the creditor agrees to take a 40 percent interest in the partnership in complete satisfaction of the debt?

6. Z forms X, a single-member LLC, with $200,000 in cash, which X contributes to a limited partnership, XWY, in return for the general partner's interest (W and Y are limited partners). XWY borrows $600,000 on a recourse basis. Under the partnership agreement, X has a deficit-restoration obligation, but W and Y do not. How is the liability shared among the partners?

MATERIALS

Rev. Rul. 92-97
1992-2 CB 124

ISSUE

If a partner is allocated a share of the partnership's cancellation of indebtedness (COD) income that differs from the partner's share of the cancelled debt under section 752(b) of the Internal Revenue Code, does the allocation of COD income have substantial economic effect under section 704(b)?

FACTS

Situation 1. In Year 1, A contributes $10x and B contributes $90x to form AB, a general partnership. A and B share the partnership's losses 10 percent and 90 percent, respectively, and share the partnership's income 50 percent each (i.e., income allocations do not first restore previous losses). The partnership maintains capital accounts under the rules of section 1.704-1(b)(2)(iv) of the Regulations, and the partners agree to liquidate according to positive capital-account balances under the rules of section 1.704-1(b)(2)(ii)(*b*)(*2*).

Under applicable state law, A and B are jointly and severally liable to creditors for all partnership recourse liabilities. However, A and B do not agree to unconditional deficit-restoration obligations as described in section 1.704-1(b)(2)(ii)(*b*)(*3*) of the Regulations; they are obligated to restore deficit capital accounts only to the extent necessary to pay creditors. Thus, if AB were to liquidate after paying all creditors, and one partner had a positive capital-account balance, the other partner would not be required to restore a deficit capital account to permit a liquidating distribution to the partner with a positive capital-account balance.

Because the partners do not have unconditional deficit-restoration obligations, the economic effect test of section 1.704-1(b)(2)(ii)(*b*) of the Regulations is not met. However, A and B agree to a qualified-income offset and are treated under section 1.704-1(b)(2)(ii)(*c*) as having a limited obligation to restore deficit capital accounts by reason of their liability to PB's creditors. Accordingly, the requirements of the alternate test for economic effect of section 1.704-1(b)(2)(ii)(*d*) are met.

AB purchases property for $1000x from an unrelated seller, paying $100x in cash and borrowing the $900x balance from an unrelated bank that is not the seller of the property. The note is a general obligation of the partnership, and no partner has been relieved from personal liability. The principal of the loan is due in six years; interest is payable semi-annually at the applicable federal rate.

A and B bear an economic risk of loss equal to $90x and $810x, respectively, for the partnership's $900x recourse liability and each increases basis in the partnership interest (outside basis) accordingly. See section 1.752-2 of the Regulations.

The property generates $200x of depreciation each year for five years. All other partnership deductions and losses exactly equal the partnership's income, so that in each of its first five taxable years AB has a net loss of $200x. Under the partnership agreement, these losses are allocated 10 percent to A and 90 percent to B. The losses reduce A's capital account to negative $90x and B's capital account to negative $810x. At the beginning of year 6, after the fair market value of AB's property has substantially declined, the creditor cancels the debt as part of a work-out arrangement. Because of the cancellation of the debt, A and B are no longer treated as obligated to restore their deficit capital accounts.

Situation 2. The facts are the same as Situation 1, except that A and B agree to unconditional deficit-restoration obligations as described in section 1.704-1(b)(2)(ii)(*b*)(*3*) of the Regulations. A and B thus have an obligation to restore deficit capital accounts not only to pay creditors, but to satisfy the other partner's positive capital-account balance on liquidation.

LAW AND ANALYSIS

Section 61(a)(12) of the Code requires the amount of a taxpayer's discharged debt to be included in gross income.

Under section 108(a) of the Code, COD income is excluded from gross income if the debt is discharged in a title 11 case, if the taxpayer is insolvent, or if the debt discharged is qualified farm indebtedness. If a partnership's liability is discharged, the partnership recognizes income equal to the amount of debt cancelled and must allocate that income to the partners as a separately stated item under section 702(a). Under section 108(d)(6), the section 108(a) exclusions are applied at the partner level to the COD income.

If an allocation of a share of a partnership's COD income is made to a partner, and the allocation has substantial economic effect, the partner increases outside basis under section 705(a)(1)(A) of the Code, receives a capital-account increase under section 1.704-1(b)(2)(iv)(*b*)(*3*) of the Regulations, and must determine, based on the partner's own circumstances, if all or part of the distributive share may be excluded from gross income under section 108(a).

Under section 722 of the Code, a partner's outside basis is increased by the amount of money and the adjusted basis of property contributed to the partnership. Under section 731(a), a partner recognizes gain from the sale or exchange of a partnership interest to the extent the partner receives a distribution of money from the partnership that exceeds the partner's outside basis immediately before the distribution. Under section 733, a partner's outside basis is decreased (but not below zero) by the amount of any distribution of money from the partnership. Under section 752(a), an increase in a partner's share of partnership liabilities is treated as a contribution of money by the partner to the partnership. Under section 752(b), a decrease in a partner's share of partnership liabilities is treated as a distribution of money by the partnership to the partner.

Although section 731(a) of the Code requires gain recognition if a distribution of money exceeds the distributee partner's outside basis immediately before the distribution, section 1.731-1(a)(1)(ii) of the Regulations treats certain distributions as occurring at the end of the partnership's taxable year. Under section 1.731-1(a)(1)(ii), advances or drawings of money or property against a partner's distributive share of income are treated as current distributions made on the last day of the partnership taxable year.

Under section 704(b) of the Code and the Regulations thereunder, allocations of a partnership's items of income, gain, loss, deduction, or credit provided for in the partnership agreement will be respected if the allocations have substantial economic effect. Allocations that fail to have substantial economic effect will be reallocated according to the partners' economic interests in the partnership. The fundamental principles for establishing economic effect require an allocation to be consistent with the partners' underlying economic arrangement. A partner allocated a share of income should enjoy any corresponding economic benefit, and a partner allocated a share of losses or deductions should bear any corresponding economic burden. See section 1.704-1(b)(2)(ii)(*a*) of the Regulations.

To come within the safe harbor for establishing economic effect in section 1.704-1(b)(2)(ii) of the Regulations, partners must agree to maintain capital accounts under the rules of section 1.704-1(b)(2)(iv) and liquidate according to positive capital-account balances; in addition, any partner with a deficit capital account must either agree to an unconditional deficit-restoration obligation as described in section 1.704-1(b)(2)(ii)(*b*)(*3*) (as in Situation 2) or satisfy the requirements of the alternate test for economic effect provided in section 1.704-1(b)(2)(ii)(*d*) (as in Situation 1).

In Situations 1 and 2, the allocations of losses to A and B in Years 1 through 5 meet the economic effect requirements under sections 1.704-1(b)(2)(ii)(*d*) and 1.704-1(b)(2)(ii)(*b*) of the Regulations. These allocations are thus within the economic effect safe harbor provided by the Regulations under section 704 of the Code.

In Year 6, when the $900x recourse liability is cancelled, the partnership recognizes $900x of COD income that must be allocated to A and B as a separately stated item under section 702(a) of the Code. In both Situations 1 and 2, A and B receive a deemed distribution of money equal to $90x and $810x, respectively, because of the decrease in their shares of the liability when the debt is cancelled. See section 752(b) and section 1.752-1(c) of the Regulations. Under section 733, A and B reduce outside bases (but not below zero) by $90x and $810x, respectively, and under section 731(a), A and B recognize gain to the extent their respective distributions exceed their outside bases at the end of Year 6.

Situation 1 Analysis:

The AB partnership agreement provides for income to be allocated equally between A and B. However, in Situation 1, the allocation of the partnership's COD income $450x to A and $450x to B, which would cause A's capital account to equal $360x (negative $90x plus $450x) and B's capital account to equal negative $360x (negative $810x plus $450x), cannot have economic effect even though the partners maintain capital accounts and liquidate according to positive capital accounts. The cancellation of the debt eliminates both partners' obligations to restore a deficit capital account, and neither partner has an independent deficit-restoration obligation that could be invoked to satisfy the other partner's positive capital account. Because the partners' deficit-restoration obligations were dependent on the cancelled debt, A can neither enjoy the economic benefit of an allocation of COD income exceeding $90x nor bear the economic burden of an allocation of COD income of less than $90x. Similarly, B can neither enjoy the economic benefit of an allocation of COD income exceeding $810x nor bear the economic burden of an allocation of COD income of less than $810x. See section 1.704-1(b)(5), example 15(iii), of the Regulations. Thus, for the partnership's allocations of the COD income to have economic effect, the COD income must be allocated $90x to A and $810x to B, which is the same ratio as the decrease in A's and B's shares of partnership liability.

When the COD income is properly allocated, the outside bases of A and B are increased under section 705(a)(1)(A) of the Code by $90x and $810x, respectively, for their distributive shares of the partnership's COD income. Under section 108(d)(6), A and B individually determine if any portion of their distributive shares is excluded from gross income. Under section 705(a)(2), the outside bases of A and B are decreased by $90x and $810x, respectively, for their distributions of money under section 752(b) resulting from the cancellation of the debt. A and B recognize no gain under section 731 in Year 6 because the distributive shares of COD income provide an outside basis increase for each partner sufficient to cover the distribution of money to that partner. Because of the integral relationship between the COD income and the section 752(b) distribution of money from the cancelled debt, section 1.731-1(a)(1)(ii) of the Regulations treats the distribution of money to each partner from the cancellation of the debt as occurring at the end of AB's taxable year as an advance or drawing against that partner's distributive share of COD income.

Situation 2 Analysis:

In Situation 2, the allocation of the partnership's COD income $450x to A and $450x to B, which causes A's capital account to equal $360x and B's capital account to equal negative $360x, has economic effect and, therefore, meets the substantial economic effect safe harbor if substantiality is independently established. Because B's deficit-restoration obligation is not dependent on the cancelled debt and can be invoked to satisfy A's positive capital account, the allocation of COD income results in B incurring an obligation to contribute $360x to satisfy A's $360x positive capital account. Similarly, if the COD income were allocated so that A had a deficit capital-account balance, A would incur an obligation to contribute the amount of the deficit to satisfy B's positive capital account.

Under section 705(a)(1)(A) of the Code, the outside bases of A and B are increased by $450x each, for their distributive shares of the partnership's COD income. Under section 108(d)(6), A and B individually determine if any portion of their distributive shares is excluded from gross income. This allocation, which is not in proportion to the partners' shares of the cancelled debt under section 752(b), causes B to recognize a $360x capital gain under sections 752(b) and 731(a). Although B's outside basis is increased under section 705(a)(1)(A) for B's $450x distributive share of COD income, the $810x distribution of money resulting from the decrease in B's share of the partnership liability exceeds B's outside basis by $360x.

B recognizes gain even though the distribution of money from the cancellation of the debt is treated under section 1.731-1(a)(1)(ii) of the Regulations as occurring at the end of AB's taxable year. Because of the application of section 1.731-1(a)(1)(ii), however, A does not recognize gain in Situation 2. A's outside basis is increased by the allocation to A of $450x of the partnership's COD income, so the $90x distribution of money resulting from the decrease in A's share of the partnership liability does not exceed A's outside basis. After adjustment for the $90x distribution, A has an outside basis of $360x.

HOLDING

An allocation to a partner of a share of the partnership's cancellation of indebtedness income that differs from the partner's share of the cancelled debt under section 752(b) of the Code has substantial economic effect under section 704(b) if (1) the deficit-restoration obligations covering any negative capital-account balances resulting from the COD income allocations can be invoked to satisfy other partners' positive capital-account balances, (2) the requirements of the economic effect test are otherwise met, and (3) substantiality is independently established.

Rev. Rul. 95-41
1995-1 CB 132

ISSUE

How does section 704(c) of the Internal Revenue Code affect the allocation of nonrecourse liabilities under section 1.752-3(a) of the Regulations?

FACTS

A and B form a partnership, PRS, and agree that each will be allocated a 50 percent share of all partnership items. A contributes depreciable property subject to a nonrecourse liability of $6,000, with an adjusted tax basis of $4,000 and a fair market value of $10,000. B contributes $4,000 cash.

LAW

Section 1.752-3(a) provides that a partner's share of the nonrecourse liabilities of a partnership equals the sum of the amounts specified in section 1.752-3(a)(1)−(3).

Section 1.752-3(a)(1) provides that the partner's share of the nonrecourse liabilities of a partnership includes the partner's share of partnership minimum gain determined in accordance with the rules of section 704(b) and the Regulations thereunder. See section 1.704- 2.

Section 1.752-3(a)(2) provides that the partner's share of the nonrecourse liabilities of the partnership includes the amount of any taxable gain that would be allocated to the partner under section 704(c) (or in the same manner as section 704(c) in connection with a revaluation of partnership property) if the partnership disposed of (in a taxable transaction) all partnership property subject to one or more nonrecourse liabilities of the partnership in full satisfaction of the liabilities and for no other consideration.

Section 1.752-3(a)(3) provides that the partner's share of the nonrecourse liabilities of the partnership includes the partner's share of the excess nonrecourse liabilities (those not allocated under section 1.752-3(a)(1) and (a)(2)) of the partnership as determined in accordance with the partner's share of partnership profits. The partner's interest in partnership profits is determined by taking into account all facts and circumstances relating to the economic arrangement of the partners. The partnership agreement may specify the partners' interests in partnership profits for purposes of allocating excess nonrecourse liabilities, provided the interests so specified are reasonably consistent with allocations (that have substantial economic effect under the section 704(b) regulations) of some other significant item of partnership income or gain. Alternatively, excess nonrecourse liabilities may be allocated among the partners in accordance with the manner in which it is reasonably expected that the deductions attributable to those nonrecourse liabilities will be allocated.

Section 704(c)(1)(A) provides that income, gain, loss, and deduction with respect to property contributed to the partnership by a partner shall be shared among the partners so as to take account of the variation between the adjusted tax basis of the property to the partnership and its fair market value at the time of contribution.

Section 1.704-3(a)(3)(i) provides that the book value of contributed property is equal to its fair market value at the time of contribution and is subsequently adjusted for cost recovery and other events that affect the basis of the property.

Section 1.704-3(a)(3)(ii) provides that the built-in gain on section 704(c) property is the excess of the property's book value over the contributing partner's adjusted tax basis in the property upon contribution. The built-in gain is thereafter reduced by decreases in the difference between the property's book value and adjusted tax basis.

ANALYSIS

Upon A's contribution of the depreciable property to PRS, there is $6,000 of section 704(c) built-in gain (the excess of the book value of the property ($10,000) over A's adjusted tax basis in the property at the time of contribution ($4,000)). As a result of the contribution, A's individual liabilities decreased by $6,000 (the amount of the nonrecourse liability which PRS is treated as having assumed). A's share of the partnership's nonrecourse liabilities is determined under section 1.752-3.

(1) First-Tier Allocations:

Under section 1.752-3(a)(1), a partner's share of the nonrecourse liabilities of PRS includes the partner's share of partnership minimum gain determined in accordance with the rules of section 704(b) and the Regulations thereunder. Section 1.704-2(d)(1) provides that partnership minimum gain is determined by computing, for each partnership nonrecourse liability, any gain the partnership would realize if it disposed of the property subject to that liability for no consideration other than full satisfaction of the liability, and then aggregating the separately computed gains. Pursuant to section 1.704-2(d)(3), partnership minimum gain is determined with reference to the contributed property's book value rather than its adjusted tax basis.

In contrast, section 704(c) requires that allocations take into account the difference between the contributed property's adjusted tax basis and its fair market value. Thus, because partnership minimum gain is computed using the contributed property's book value rather than its tax basis, allocations of nonrecourse liabilities under section 1.752-3(a)(1) are not affected by section 704(c). Moreover, because the book value of the property at the time of contribution ($10,000) exceeds the amount of the nonrecourse liability ($6,000), there is no partnership minimum gain immediately after the contribution, and neither A nor B receive an allocation of nonrecourse liabilities under section 1.752-3(a)(1) immediately after the contribution.

(2) Second-Tier Allocations:

Under section 1.752-3(a)(2), a partner's share of the nonrecourse liabilities of the partnership includes the amount of taxable gain that would be allocated to the contributing partner under section 704(c) if the partnership, in a taxable transaction, disposed of the contributed property in full satisfaction of the nonrecourse liability and for no other consideration. If PRS sold the contributed property in full satisfaction of the liability and for no other consideration, PRS would recognize a taxable gain of $2,000 on the sale ($6,000 amount of the nonrecourse liability less $4,000 adjusted tax basis of the property). Under section 704(c) and section 1.704-3(b)(1), all of this taxable gain would be allocated to A. The hypothetical sale also would result in a book loss of $4,000 to PRS (excess of $10,000 book value of property over $6,000 amount of the nonrecourse liability). Under the terms of the partnership agreement, this book loss would be allocated equally between A and B. Because B would receive a $2,000 book loss but no corresponding tax loss, the hypothetical sale would result in a $2,000 disparity between B's book and tax allocations.

If PRS used the traditional method of making section 704(c) allocations de-scribed in section 1.704-3(b), A would be allocated a total of $2,000 of taxable gain from the hypothetical sale of the contributed property. Therefore, A would be allocated $2,000 of nonrecourse liabilities under section 1.752-3(a)(2) immediately after the contribution.

If PRS adopted the remedial allocation method described in section 1.704-3(d), PRS would be required to make a remedial allocation of $2,000 of tax loss to B in connection with the hypothetical sale to eliminate the $2,000 disparity between B's book and tax allocations. PRS also would be required to make an offsetting remedial allocation of tax gain to A of $2,000. Thus, A would be allocated a total of $4,000 of tax gain ($2,000 actual gain plus the $2,000 allocation of remedial gain) from the hypothetical sale of the contributed property. Therefore, if the partnership adopted the remedial allocation method, A would be allocated $4,000 of nonrecourse liabilities under section 1.752-3(a)(2) immediately after the contribution.

If PRS used the traditional method with curative allocations described in section 1.704-3(c), PRS would be permitted to make reasonable curative allocations to reduce or eliminate the difference between the book and tax allocations to B that resulted from the hypothetical sale. However, PRS's ability to make curative allocations would depend on the existence of other partnership items and could not be determined solely from the hypothetical sale of the contributed property. Because any potential curative allocations could not be determined solely from the hypothetical sale of the contributed property, curative allocations are not taken into account in allocating nonrecourse liabilities under section 1.752-3(a)(2). Therefore, if PRS used the traditional method with curative allocations, A would be allocated $2,000 of nonrecourse liabilities under section 1.752-3(a)(2) immediately after the contribution.

(3) Third-Tier Allocations:

Following the allocation under section 1.752-3(a)(2), PRS has excess nonre-course liabilities that must be allocated between A and B. Section 1.752-3(a)(3) provides several alternatives for allocating excess nonrecourse liabilities.

(a) First, PRS may choose to allocate excess nonrecourse liabilities in accordance with the partners' shares of partnership profits. The partners' interests in partnership profits are determined by taking into account all the facts and circumstances relating to the economic arrangement of the partners. The partners' agreement to share the profits of the partnership equally is one fact to be considered in making this determination. Another fact to be considered is a partner's share of section 704(c) built-in gain to the extent that the gain was not taken into account in making an allocation of nonrecourse liabilities under section 1.752-3(a)(2). This built-in gain is one factor because, under the principles of section 704(c), this excess built-in gain, if recognized, will be allocated to A. A's share of section 704(c) built-in gain that is not taken into account in making allocations under section 1.752- 3(a)(2) is, therefore, one factor, but not the only factor, to be considered in determining A's interest in partnership profits. The amount of the section 704(c) built-in gain that is not considered in making allocations under section 1.752-3(a)(2) must be given an appropriate weight in light of all other items of partnership profit. For example, if it is reasonable to expect that PRS will have items of partnership profit over the life of the partnership that will be allocated to B, PRS may not allocate all of the excess nonrecourse liabilities to A. Rather, the remaining nonrecourse liabilities must be allocated between A and B in proportion to their interests in total partnership profits.

(b) Second, the PRS partnership agreement may specify the partners' interests in partnership profits for purposes of allocating excess nonrecourse liabilities, provided that the interests specified are reasonably consistent with allocations (that have substantial economic effect under the section 704(b) Regulations) of some other significant item of partnership income or gain. The partnership agreement provides that each partner will be allocated a 50 percent share of all partnership items. Assuming that such allocations have substantial economic effect, PRS can choose to allocate the excess nonrecourse liabilities 50 percent to each partner.

Section 704(c) allocations, however, do not have substantial economic effect under the section 704(b) Regulations. See section 1.704-1(b)(2)(iv)(*d*). Accordingly, under this alternative, section 704(c) allocations cannot be used as a basis for allocating excess nonrecourse liabilities.

(c) Finally, PRS may choose to allocate the excess nonrecourse liabilities in accordance with the manner in which it is reasonably expected that the deductions attributable to the excess nonrecourse liabilities will be allocated. Because A and B have agreed to allocate all partnership items 50 percent to each partner, A and B each will be entitled to allocations of book depreciation of $5,000 over the life of the contributed property. The contributed property, however, has an adjusted tax basis of $4,000 and, regardless of the method used by the partnership under section 704(c), the entire $4,000 of tax depreciation over the life of the contributed property must be allocated to B. Therefore, PRS must allocate all of the excess nonrecourse liabilities to B if it chooses to allocate the excess nonrecourse liabilities in accordance with the manner that the deductions attributable to the excess nonrecourse liabilities will be allocated.

HOLDINGS

(1) Allocations of nonrecourse liabilities under section 1.752-3(a)(1) are not affected by section 704(c).

(2) Allocations of nonrecourse liabilities under section 1.752-3(a)(2) take into account remedial allocations of gain that would be made to the contributing partner under section 1.704-3(d). Allocations of nonrecourse liabilities under section 1.752-3(a)(2) do not take into account curative allocations under section 1.704-3(c).

(3) Allocations of nonrecourse liabilities under section 1.752-3(a)(3) are affected by section 704(c) in the following manner:

(a) If the partnership determines the partners' interests in partnership profits based on all of the facts and circumstances relating to the economic arrangement of the partners, section 704(c) built-in gain that was not taken into account under section 1.752-3(a)(2) is one factor, but not the only factor, to be considered under section 1.752-3(a)(3).

(b) If the partnership chooses to allocate excess nonrecourse liabilities in a manner reasonably consistent with allocations (that have substantial economic effect under the section 704(b) Regulations) of some other significant item of partnership income or gain, section 704(c) does not affect the allocation of nonrecourse liabilities under section 1.752-3(a)(3) because section 704(c) allocations do not have substantial economic effect.

(c) If the partnership chooses to allocate excess nonrecourse liabilities in accordance with the manner in which it is reasonably expected that the deductions attributable to the nonrecourse liabilities will be allocated, the partnership must take into account the allocations required by section 704(c) in determining the manner in which the deductions attributable to the nonrecourse liabilities will be allocated.

Rev. Rul. 97-38
1997-2 CB 69

If a partner is treated as having a limited deficit-restoration obligation under section 1.704-1(b)(2)(ii)(c) of the Regulations by reason of the partner's liability to the partnership's creditors, how is the amount of that obligation calculated?

FACTS

In year 1, GP and LP, general partner and limited partner, each contribute $100x to form limited partnership LPRS. In general, GP and LP share LPRS's income and loss 50 percent each. However, LPRS allocates to GP all depreciation deductions and gain from the sale of depreciable assets up to the amount of those deductions. LPRS maintains capital accounts according to the rules set forth in section 1.704-1(b)(2)(iv), and the partners agree to liquidate according to positive capital-account balances under the rules of section 1.704-1(b)(2)(ii)(*b*)(*2*).

Under applicable state law, GP is liable to creditors for all partnership recourse liabilities, but LP has no personal liability. GP and LP do not agree to unconditional deficit-restoration obligations as described in section 1.704-1(b)(2)(ii)(b)(3) (in general, a deficit-restoration obligation requires a partner to restore any deficit capital-account balance following the liquidation of the partner's interest in the partnership); GP is obligated to restore a deficit capital account only to the extent necessary to pay creditors. Thus, if LPRS were to liquidate after paying all creditors and LP had a positive capital-account balance, GP would not be required to restore GP's deficit capital account to permit a liquidating distribution to LP. In addition, GP and LP agree to a qualified- income offset, thus satisfying the requirements of the alternate test for economic effect of section 1.704-1(b)(2)(ii)(d). GP and LP also agree that no allocation will be made that causes or increases a deficit balance in any partner's capital account in excess of the partner's obligation to restore the deficit.

LPRS purchases depreciable property for $1,000x from an unrelated seller, paying $200x in cash and borrowing the $800x balance from an unrelated bank that is not the seller of the property. The note is recourse to LPRS. The principal of the loan is due in six years; interest is payable semi-annually at the applicable federal rate. GP bears the entire economic risk of loss for LPRS's recourse liability, and GP's basis in LPRS (outside basis) is increased by $800x. See section 1.752-2.

In each of years 1 through 5, the property generates $200x of depreciation. All other partnership deductions and losses exactly equal income, so that in each of years 1 through 5 LPRS has a net loss of $200x.

LAW AND ANALYSIS

Under section 704(b) of the Code and the Regulations thereunder, a partnership's allocations of income, gain, loss, deduction, or credit set forth in the partnership agreement are respected if they have substantial economic effect. If allocations under the partnership agreement would not have substantial economic effect, the partnership's allocations are determined according to the partners' interests in the partnership. The fundamental principles for establishing economic effect require an allocation to be consistent with the partner's underlying economic arrangement. A partner allocated a share of income should enjoy any corresponding economic benefit, and a partner allocated a share of losses or deductions should bear any corresponding economic burden. See section 1.704-1(b)(2)(ii)(a).

To come within the safe harbor for establishing economic effect in section 1.704-1(b)(2)(ii), partners must agree to maintain capital accounts under the rules of section 1.704-1(b)(2)(iv), liquidate according to positive capital-account balances, and agree to an unconditional deficit-restoration obligation for any partner with a deficit in that partner's capital account, as described in section 1.704-1(b)(2)(ii)(b)(3). Alternatively, the partnership may satisfy the requirements of the alternate test for economic effect provided in section 1.704-1(b)(2)(ii)(d). LPRS's partnership agreement complies with the alternate test for economic effect.

The alternate test for economic effect requires the partners to agree to a qualified-income offset in lieu of an unconditional deficit-restoration obligation. If the partners so agree, allocations will have economic effect to the extent that they not create a deficit capital account for any partner (in excess of any limited deficit-restoration obligation of that partner) as of the end of the partnership taxable year to which the allocation relates. Section 1.704-1(b)(2)(ii)(*d*)(*3*)(flush language).

A partner is treated as having a limited deficit-restoration obligation to the extent of: (1) the outstanding principal balance of any promissory note contributed to the partnership by the partner, and (2) the amount of any unconditional obligation of the partner (whether imposed by the partnership agreement or by state or local law) to make subsequent contributions to the partnership. Section 1.704-1(b)(2)(ii)(*c*).

LP has no obligation under the partnership agreement or state or local law to make additional contributions to the partnership and, therefore, has no defi-cit-restoration obligation. Under applicable state law, GP may have to make additional contributions to the partnership to pay creditors. However, GP's obligation only arises to the extent that the amount of LPRS's liabilities exceeds the value of LPRS's assets available to satisfy the liabilities. Thus, the amount of GP's limited deficit-restoration obligation each year is equal to the difference between the amount of the partnership's recourse liabilities at the end of the year and the value of the partnership's assets available to satisfy the liabilities at the end of the year.

To ensure consistency with the other requirements of the Regulations under section 704(b), where a partner's obligation to make additional contributions to the partnership is dependent on the value of the partnership's assets, the partner's deficit-restoration obligation must be computed by reference to the rules for determining the value of partnership property contained in the Regulations under section 704(b). Consequently, in computing GP's limited deficit-restoration obligation, the value of the partnership's assets is conclusively presumed to equal the book basis of those assets under the capital-account maintenance rules of section 1.704-1(b)(2)(iv). See section 1.704-1(b)(2)(ii)(*d*) (value equals basis presumption applies for purposes of determining expected allocations and distributions under the alternate test for economic effect); section 1.704-1(b)(2)(iii) (value equals basis presumption applies for purposes of the substantiality test); section 1.704-1(b)(3)(iii) (value equals basis presumption applies for purposes of the partner's interest in the partnership test); section 1.704-2(d) (value equals basis presumption applies in computing partnership minimum gain).

The LPRS agreement allocates all depreciation deductions and gain on the sale of depreciable property to the extent of those deductions to GP. Because LPRS's partnership agreement satisfies the alternate test for economic effect, the allocations of depreciation deductions to GP will have economic effect to the extent that they do not create a deficit capital account for GP in excess of GP's obligation to restore the deficit balance. At the end of year 1, the basis of the depreciable property has been reduced to $800x. If LPRS liquidated at the beginning of year 2, selling its depreciable property for its basis of $800x, the proceeds would be used to repay the $800x principal on LPRS's recourse liability. All of LPRS's creditors would be satisfied and GP would have no obligation to contribute to pay them. Thus, at the end of year 1, GP has no obligation to restore a deficit in its capital account.

Because GP has no obligation to restore a deficit balance in its capital account at the end of year 1, an allocation that reduces GP's capital account below $0 is not permitted under the partnership agreement and would not satisfy the alternate test for economic effect. An allocation of $200x of depreciation deductions to GP would reduce GP's capital account to negative $100x. Because the allocation would result in a deficit capital- account balance in excess of GP's obligation to restore, the allocation is not permitted under the partnership agreement, and would not satisfy the safe harbor under the alternate test for economic effect. Therefore, the deductions for year 1 must be allocated $100x each to GP and LP (which is in accordance with their interests in the partnership).

The allocation of depreciation of $200x to GP in year 2 has economic effect. Although the allocation reduces GP's capital account to negative $200x, while LP's capital account remains $0, the allocation to GP does not create a deficit capital account in excess of GP's limited deficit-restoration obligation. If LPRS liquidated at the beginning of year 3, selling the depreciable property for its basis of $600x, the proceeds would be applied toward the $800x LPRS liability. Because GP is obligated to restore a deficit capital account to the extent necessary to pay credits, GP would be required to contribute $200x to LPRS to satisfy the outstanding liability. Thus, at the end of year 2, GP has a deficit-restoration obligation of $200x, and the allocation of depreciation to GP does not reduce GP's capital account below its obligation to restore a deficit capital account.

This analysis also applies to the allocation of $200x of depreciation to GP in years 3 through 5. At the beginning of year 6, when the property is fully depreciated, the $800x principal amount of the partnership liability is due. The partners' capital accounts at the beginning of year 6 will equal negative $800x and $0, respectively, for GP and LP. Because value is conclusively presumed to equal basis, the depreciable property would be worthless and could not be used to satisfy LPRS's $800x liability. As a result, GP is deemed to be required to contribute $800x to LPRS. A contribution by GP to satisfy this limited deficit-restoration obligation would increase GP's capital-account balance to $0.

HOLDING

When a partner is treated as having a limited deficit-restoration obligation by reason of the partner's liability to the partnership's creditors, the amount of that obligation is the amount of money that the partner would be required to contribute to the partnership to satisfy partnership liabilities if all partnership property were sold for the amount of the partnership's book basis in the property.

Rev. Rul. 99-43
1999-2 CB 506

ISSUE

Do partnership allocations lack substantiality under section 1.704-1(b)(2)(iii) of the Regulations when the partners amend the partnership agreement to create offsetting special allocations of particular items after the events giving rise to the items have occurred?

FACTS

A and B, both individuals, formed a general partnership, PRS. A and B each contributed $1,000 and also agreed that each would be allocated a 50-percent share of all partnership items. The partnership agreement provides that, upon the contribution of additional capital by either partner, PRS must revalue the partnership's property and adjust the partners' capital accounts under section 1.704-1(b)(2)-(iv)(f).

PRS borrowed $8,000 from a bank and used the borrowed and contributed funds to purchase nondepreciable property for $10,000. The loan was nonrecourse to A and B and was secured only by the property. No principal payments were due for 6 years, and interest was payable semi-annually at a market rate.

After one year, the fair market value of the property fell from $10,000 to $6,000, but the principal amount of the loan remained $8,000. As part of a workout arrangement among the bank, PRS, A, and B, the bank reduced the principal amount of the loan by $2,000, and A contributed an additional $500 to PRS. A's capital account was credited with the $500, which PRS used to pay currently deductible expenses incurred in connection with the workout. All $500 of the currently deductible workout expenses were allocated to A. B made no additional contribution of capital. At the time of the workout, B was insolvent within the meaning of section 108(a) of the Code. A and B agreed that, after the workout, A would have a 60-percent interest and B would have a 40-percent interest in the profits and losses of PRS.

As a result of the property's decline in value and the workout, PRS had two items to allocate between A and B. First, the agreement to cancel $2,000 of the loan resulted in $2,000 of cancellation of indebtedness income (COD income). Second, A's contribution of $500 to PRS was an event that required PRS, under the partnership agreement, to revalue partnership property and adjust A's and B's capital accounts. Because of the decline in value of the property, the revaluation resulted in a $4,000 economic loss that must be allocated between A's and B's capital accounts.

Under the terms of the original partnership agreement, PRS would have allocated these items equally between A and B. A and B, however, amend the partnership agreement (in a timely manner) to make two special allocations. First, PRS specially allocates the entire $2,000 of COD income to B, an insolvent partner. Second, PRS specially allocates the book loss from the revaluation $1,000 to A and $3,000 to B.

While A receives a $1,000 allocation of book loss and B receives a $3,000 allocation of book loss, neither of these allocations results in a tax loss to either partner. Rather, the allocations result only in adjustments to A's and B's capital accounts. Thus, the cumulative effect of the special allocations is to reduce each partner's capital account to zero immediately following the allocations despite the fact that B is allocated $2,000 of income for tax purposes.

LAW

Section 61(a)(12) provides that gross income includes income from the discharge of indebtedness.

Revenue Ruling 91-31, 1991-1 CB 19, holds that a taxpayer realizes COD income when a creditor (who was not the seller of the underlying property) reduces the principal amount of an under-secured nonrecourse debt.

Under section 704(b) and the Regulations thereunder, allocations of a partnership's items of income, gain, loss, deduction, or credit provided for in the partnership agreement will be respected if the allocations have substantial economic effect. Allocations that fail to have substantial economic effect will be reallocated according to the partners' interests in the partnership (as defined in section 1.704-1(b)(3)).

Section 1.704-1(b)(2)(iv)(f) provides that a partnership may, upon the occurrence of certain events (including the contribution of money to the partnership by a new or existing partner), increase or decrease the partners' capital accounts to reflect a revaluation of the partnership property.

Section 1.704-1(b)(2)(iv)(g) provides that, to the extent a partnership's property is reflected on the books of the partnership at a book value that differs from the adjusted tax basis, the substantial economic effect requirements apply to the allocations of book items. Section 704(c) and section 1.704-1(b)(4)(i) govern the partners' distributive shares of tax items.

Section 1.704-1(b)(2)(i) provides that the determination of whether an allocation of income, gain, loss, or deduction (or item thereof) to a partner has substantial economic effect involves a two-part analysis that is made at the end of the partnership year to which the allocation relates. In order for an allocation to have substantial economic effect, the allocation must have both economic effect (within the meaning of section 1.704-1(b)(2)(ii)) and be substantial (within the meaning of section 1.704-1(b)(2)(iii)).

Section 1.704-1(b)(2)(iii)(a) provides that the economic effect of an allocation (or allocations) is substantial if there is a reasonable possibility that the allocation (or allocations) will substantially affect the dollar amounts to be received by the partners from the partnership independent of the tax consequences. However, the economic effect of an allocation is not substantial if, at the time the allocation becomes part of the partnership agreement (1) the after-tax economic consequences of at least one partner may, in present value terms, be enhanced compared to the consequences if the allocation (or allocations) were not contained in the partnership agreement, and (2) there is a strong likelihood that the after-tax economic consequences of no partner will, in present value terms, be substantially diminished compared to the consequences if the allocation (or allocations) were not contained in the partnership agreement. In determining the after-tax economic benefit or detriment to a partner, tax consequences that result from the interaction of the allocation with the partner's tax attributes that are unrelated to the partnership will be taken into account.

Section 1.704-1(b)(2)(iii)(b) provides that the economic effect of an allocation (or allocations) in a partnership taxable year is not substantial if the allocations result in shifting tax consequences. Shifting tax consequences result when, at the time the allocation (or allocations) becomes part of the partnership agreement, there is a strong likelihood that (1) the net increases and decreases that will be recorded in the partners' respective capital accounts for the taxable year will not differ substantially from the net increases and decreases that would be recorded in the partners' respective capital accounts for the year if the allocations were not contained in the partnership agreement, and (2) the total tax liability of the partners (for their respective tax years in which the allocations will be taken into account) will be less than if the allocations were not contained in the partnership agreement.

Section 1.704-1(b)(2)(iii)(c) provides that the economic effect of an allocation (or allocations) in a partnership taxable year is not substantial if the allocations are transitory. Allocations are considered transitory if a partnership agreement provides for the possibility that one or more allocations (the "original allocation(s)") will be largely offset by other allocations (the "offsetting allocation(s)"), and, at the time the allocations become part of the partnership agreement, there is a strong likelihood that (1) the net increases and decreases that will be recorded in the partners' capital accounts for the taxable years to which the allocations relate will not differ substantially from the net increases and decreases that would be recorded in such partners' respective capital accounts for such years if the original and offsetting allocation(s) were not contained in the partnership agreement, and (2) the total tax liability of the partners (for their respective tax years in which the allocations will be taken into account) will be less than if the allocations were not contained in the partnership agreement.

Section 761(c) provides that a partnership agreement includes any modifications made prior to, or at, the time prescribed for filing a partnership return (not including extensions) which are agreed to by all partners, or which are adopted in such other manner as may be provided by the partnership agreement.

ANALYSIS

PRS is free to allocate partnership items between A and B in accordance with the provisions of the partnership agreement if the allocations have substantial economic effect under section 1.704-1(b)(2). To the extent that the minimum gain chargeback rules do not apply,[1] COD income may be allocated in accordance with the rules under section 1.704-1(b)(2). This is true notwithstanding that the COD income arises in connection with the cancellation of a nonrecourse debt.

The economic effect of an allocation is not substantial if, at the time that the allocation becomes part of the partnership agreement, the allocation fails each of two tests. The allocation fails the first test if the after-tax consequences of at least one partner may, in present value terms, be enhanced compared to the consequences if the allocation (or allocations) were not contained in the partnership agreement. The allocation fails the second test if there is a strong likelihood that the after-tax economic consequences of no partner will, in present value terms, be substantially diminished compared to such consequences if the allocation (or allocations) were not contained in the partnership agreement.

A and B amended the PRS partnership agreement to provide for an allocation of the entire $2,000 of the COD income to B. B, an insolvent taxpayer, is eligible to exclude the income under section 108, so it is unlikely that the $2,000 of COD income would increase B's immediate tax liability. Without the special allocation, A, who is not insolvent or otherwise entitled to exclude the COD income under section 108, would pay tax immediately on the $1,000 of COD income allocated under the general ratio for sharing income. A and B also amended the PRS partnership agreement to provide for the special allocation of the book loss resulting from the revaluation. Because the two special allocations offset each other, B will not realize any economic benefit from the $2,000 income allocation, even if the property subsequently appreciates in value.

---

[1] Under certain circumstances, the COD income would be allocated between the partners in accordance with their shares of partnership minimum gain because the cancellation of the nonrecourse debt would result in a decrease in partnership minimum gain. See section 1.704-2(d). However, in this situation, there is no minimum gain because the principal amount of the debt never exceeded the property's book value. Therefore, the minimum gain chargeback requirement does not govern the manner in which the COD income is allocated between A and B, and PRS's special allocation of COD income must satisfy the substantial economic effect standard. See Rev. Rul. 92-97, 1992-2 CB 124.

The economics of PRS are unaffected by the paired special allocations. After the capital accounts of A and B are adjusted to reflect the special allocations, A and B each has a capital account of zero. Economically, the situation of both partners is identical to what it would have been had the special allocations not occurred. In addition, a strong likelihood exists that the total tax liability of A and B will be less than if PRS had allocated 50 percent of the $2,000 of COD income and 50 percent of the $4,000 book loss to each partner. Therefore, the special allocations of COD income and book loss are shifting allocations under section 1.704-1(b)(2)(iii)(b) and lack substantiality. (Alternatively, the allocations could be transitory allocations under section 1.704-1(b)(2)(iii)(c) if the allocations occur during different partnership taxable years).

This conclusion is not altered by the "value equals basis" rule that applies in determining the substantiality of an allocation. See section 1.704-1(b)(2)(iii)(c)(2). Under that rule, the adjusted tax basis (or, if different, the book value) of partnership property will be presumed to be the fair market value of the property. This presumption is appropriate in most cases because, under section 1.704-1(b)(2)(iv), property generally will be reflected on the books of the partnership at its fair market value when acquired. Thus, an allocation of gain or loss from the disposition of the property will reflect subsequent changes in the value of the property that generally cannot be predicted.

The substantiality of an allocation, however, is analyzed "at the time the allocation becomes part of the partnership agreement," not the time at which the allocation is first effective. See section 1.704-1(b)(2)(iii)(a). In the situation described above, the provisions of the PRS partnership agreement governing the allocation of gain or loss from the disposition of property are changed at a time that is after the property has been revalued on the books of the partnership, but are effective for a period that begins prior to the revaluation. See section 1.704-1(b)(2)(iv)(f).

Under these facts, the presumption that value equals basis does not apply to validate the allocations. Instead, PRS's allocations of gain or loss must be closely scrutinized in determining the appropriate tax consequences. Cf. section 1.704-1(b)-(4)(vi). In this situation, the special allocations of the $2,000 of COD income and $4,000 of book loss will not be respected and, instead, must be allocated in accordance with the A's and B's interests in the partnership under section 1.704-1(b)(3).

Close scrutiny also would be required if the changes were made at a time when the events giving rise to the allocations had not yet occurred but were likely to occur or if, under the original allocation provisions of a partnership agreement, there was a strong likelihood that a disproportionate amount of COD income earned in the future would be allocated to any partner who is insolvent at the time of the allocation and would be offset by an increased allocation of loss or a reduced allocation of income to such partner or partners.

HOLDING

Partnership special allocations lack substantiality when the partners amend the partnership agreement to specially allocate COD income and book items from a related revaluation after the events creating such items have occurred if the overall economic effect of the special allocations on the partners' capital accounts does not differ substantially from the economic effect of the original allocations in the partnership agreement. . . .

CHAPTER **23**

Transfers of Partnership Interests: Selected Topics

PROBLEM AREA 23

INTRODUCTION

In 1999, the Service published final Regulations addressing, among other things, the optional adjustments to the basis of partnership property following certain transfers of partnership interests under § 743(b), the calculation of gain or loss under § 751(a) following the sale or exchange of a partnership interest, and the allocation of basis adjustments among partnership assets under § 755. These Regulations substantially simplified the operation of prior law, eliminating traps for the unwary and planning opportunities that had existed previously. The changes wrought by these Regulations were so significant that the Service granted all partnerships with an existing § 754 election a one-time right to revoke the election, no questions asked, for the partnership taxable year which included December 15, 1999, the Regulations' effective date. The first questions in this Problem Area illustrate the basically smooth operation of the new regulatory regime.

The Service's effort to calm the troubled waters was disturbed in 2004 by the enactment of § 704(c)(1)(C), which Congress intended to combat the duplication of tax losses that had figured in some tax shelters. The general approach of this new statute is to equalize the book and tax values of property contributed to a partnership with a built-in loss for all but the contributing partner. In the case of a partnership that has made a § 754 election, the § 743(b) adjustments that take place upon a sale of the contributing partner's interest accomplish the same effect, at least with respect to the transferee partner, but in a very different manner. Against this background, later questions in this Problem Area illustrate the contrasting approaches of §§ 704(c)(1)(C) and 743(b) to the same issue, and consider the complexities when both statutes apply to the same transaction.

Finally, the application of the installment method to the sale of a partnership interest provides an opportunity to reconsider the fundamental question of whether a partnership is an entity or an aggregate for federal tax purposes, and to ponder whether the Service has ventured into uncharted waters in answering this old question in a new context.

PROBLEM 23

QUESTIONS

1. The balance sheet of equal general partnership ABC is as follows:

	Adjusted Basis	Fair Market Value
Assets		
Cash	$30,000	$ 30,000
Inventory	15,000	45,000
Investment Asset	33,000	48,000
Total	$78,000	$123,000
Capital		
A	$26,000	$ 41,000
B	26,000	41,000
C	26,000	41,000
Total	$78,000	$123,000

What are the tax consequences to A of each of the following:

a. A sells his partnership interest to D for $41,000.

b. Assume that the value and the basis of the partnership's inventory (only) are reversed, i.e., $45,000 basis and $15,000 value. Obviously, this impacts the value and basis for A's interest, which are assumed to be $31,000 and $36,000, respectively. A sells his partnership interest to D for $31,000.

c. Instead of sharing profits and losses equally among its partners, ABC partnership has agreed to share profits 40 percent, 40 percent, and 20 percent to A, B and C, respectively, and losses 35 percent, 35 percent, and 30 percent. This too impacts the value and basis for A's interest, which are assumed to be $44,000 and $26,000, respectively. A sells his interest for $44,000.

2. The balance sheet of equal general partnership ABC is as follows:

	Adjusted Basis	Fair Market Value
Assets		
Cash	$30,000	$ 30,000
Inventory	21,000	18,000
Equipment (Purchased for $60,000)	45,000	36,000
Self-Created Goodwill	0	90,000
Total	$96,000	$174,000
Capital		
A	$32,000	$ 58,000
B	32,000	58,000
C	32,000	58,000
Total	$96,000	$174,000

A sells his interest to D for $58,000 in Year 1 with a § 754 election in effect. What is the result to A and D?

3. At formation, A contributed Capital Asset # 1 (basis $30,000, value $90,000), B $90,000 in cash, and C Capital Asset # 2 (basis $90,000, value $90,000) to form equal general partnership ABC. The balance sheet of the partnership now is as follows:

	Adjusted Basis	Fair Market Value
Assets		
Cash	$ 90,000	$ 90,000
Capital Asset #1	30,000	90,000
Capital Asset #2	90,000	120,000
Total	$210,000	$300,000
Capital		
A	$ 30,000	$100,000
B	90,000	100,000
C	90,000	100,000
Total	$210,000	$300,000

A sells his interest to D for $100,000 while a § 754 election is in effect. What is the result to A and D?

4. At formation, A contributed Capital Asset # 1 (basis $90,000, value $30,000), B $30,000 in cash, and C Capital Asset # 2 (basis $30,000, value $30,000) to form equal general partnership ABC. The balance sheet of the partnership now is as follows:

	Adjusted Basis	Fair Market Value
Assets		
Cash	$ 30,000	$ 30,000
Capital Asset #1	90,000	30,000
Capital Asset #2	30,000	48,000
Total	$150,000	$108,000
Capital		
A	$ 90,000	$ 36,000
B	30,000	36,000
C	30,000	36,000
Total	$150,000	$108,000

A sells his interest to D for $36,000. What is the result to A and D upon the sale of Capital Asset #1 for $30,000? What is the effect of § 704(c)(1)(C) on these results? Does it matter whether the partnership has made a § 754 election?

5. Same as question 4. above, except that the value of Capital Asset #1 appreciates to $45,000 after A contributes it to the partnership, but before A sells his partnership interest to D for $41,000. At the time of the sale, the balance sheet of the partnership is as follows:

	Adjusted Basis	Fair Market Value
Assets		
Cash	$ 30,000	$ 30,000
Capital Asset #1	90,000	45,000
Capital Asset #2	30,000	48,000
Total	$150,000	$123,000
Capital		
A	$ 90,000	$ 41,000
B	30,000	41,000
C	30,000	41,000
Total	$150,000	$123,000

To what special basis adjustment, if any, is D entitled with respect to Capital Asset #1? Assume that the partnership uses the traditional method under § 704(c). How would this answer differ if the partnership had elected the remedial method?

6. At formation, A, B, and C each contributed $300,000 to equal general partnership ABC. The partnership used $600,000 of its cash to purchase Capital Asset #1 and Capital Asset #2. The balance sheet of the partnership is now as follows:

	Adjusted Basis	Fair Market Value
Assets		
Cash	$300,000	$300,000
Capital Asset #1	300,000	180,000
Capital Asset #2	300,000	120,000
Total	$900,000	$600,000
Capital		
A	$300,000	$200,000
B	300,000	200,000
C	300,000	200,000
Total	$900,000	$600,000

A sells his interest to D for $200,000. What is the result to the parties if there is a § 754 election in effect? What if an election is not in effect?

7. The balance sheet of equal general partnership ABC is as follows:

	Adjusted Basis	Fair Market Value
Assets		
Cash	$18,000	$ 18,000
Accounts Receivable	0	24,000
Inventory	3,000	15,000
Equipment (Purchased for $30,000)	21,000	36,000
Land	48,000	90,000
Total	$90,000	$183,000
Capital		
A	$30,000	$ 61,000
B	30,000	61,000
C	30,000	61,000
Total	$90,000	$183,000

A sells his partnership interest to D for $61,000, payable $2,000 in Year 2, $9,000 in Year 3, $20,000 in Year 4, $18,000 in Year 5, and $12,000 in Year 6. All deferred payments carry market interest rates. What are the tax consequences of this sale to A?

MATERIALS

Internal Legal Memorandum 200722027 (April 27, 2007)

This Chief Counsel Advice responds to your request for assistance dated March 15, 2007. Specifically, you asked that our office address whether a taxpayer may report income from the sale of the taxpayer's interest in a partnership under the installment method to the extent that it represents income attributable to unrealized receivables for payment for services rendered. . . . This advice may not be used or cited as precedent.

ISSUES

1. Whether a taxpayer may report income from the sale of the taxpayer's interest in a partnership under the installment method pursuant to § 453 of the Internal Revenue Code to the extent it represents income attributable to § 751(c)(2) unrealized receivables for payment for services rendered. . . .

CONCLUSIONS

1. A taxpayer may not report income from the sale of the taxpayer's interest in a partnership under the installment method pursuant to § 453 to the extent that it represents income attributable to § 751(c)(2) unrealized receivables for payment for services rendered. The taxpayer may report the balance of the income realized from the sale of the partnership interest using the installment method of reporting. . . .

FACTS

A taxpayer was a partner in a partnership that held § 751(c)(2) unrealized receivables for payment for services rendered. The taxpayer reports income on the cash method. A corporation purchased the taxpayer's interest in the partnership in exchange for a promissory note (Note) issued by the corporation.... Part of the income the taxpayer realized from the sale was attributable to the partnership's unrealized receivables for services rendered. The taxpayer did not realize any income attributable to a sale of inventory within the meaning of § 751(d).

LAW AND ANALYSIS

Section 453(a) of the Code provides that, except as otherwise provided, income from an installment sale shall be taken into account under the installment method. Section 453(b)(1) defines an installment sale as a disposition of property where at least one payment is to be received after the close of the taxable year in which the disposition occurs. Section 453(c) defines the installment method as a method under which the income recognized for any taxable year from a disposition is that proportion of the payments received in that year which the gross profit (realized or to be realized when payment is completed) bears to the total contract price.

Section 453A(e) of the Code authorizes the Secretary to prescribe Regulations . . . ., including Regulations providing that the sale of an interest in a partnership will be treated as the sale of the proportionate share of the assets of the partnership.

Section 741 of the Code provides that, in the case of a sale or exchange of a partnership interest, gain or loss recognized to the transferor partner is considered gain or loss from the sale or exchange of a capital asset, except as otherwise provided in § 751.

Section 751(a) of the Code provides that the amount received by a transferor partner in exchange for all or part of a partnership interest shall be considered as an amount realized from the sale or exchange of property other than a capital asset, to the extent such an amount is attributable to unrealized receivables or inventory items of the partnership.

Section 751(c)(2) of the Code provides that the term "unrealized receivables" includes, to the extent not previously includable in income under the method of accounting used by the partnership, any rights (contractual or otherwise) to payment for services rendered, or to be rendered.

The Service has not issued Regulations under §§ 453 or 453A to provide expressly that the sale of a partnership interest should be treated as the sale of a proportionate share of the assets of the partnership. However, there is sufficient authority to support the conclusion that a taxpayer may not report income from the sale a partnership interest under the installment method to the extent that the sale represents income attributable to § 751(c)(2) unrealized receivables for payment for services rendered.

Revenue Ruling 89-108, 1989-2 CB 100, holds that income from the sale of a partnership interest may not be reported under the installment method to the extent it represents income attributable to the partnership's substantially appreciated inventory (within the meaning of § 751(d)), which would not be eligible for the installment sale treatment if sold directly. The balance of the income realized from the sale of the partnership interest may be reported under the installment method. The ruling ex-plains:

> [B]ecause § 751 effectively treats a partner as if the partner had sold an interest in the § 751 property of the partnership, the portion of the gain that is attributable to § 751 property is reportable under the installment method only to the extent that income realized on a direct sale of the § 751 property would be reportable under such method.

The ruling further states that ". . . the installment method is not available for reporting income realized on the sale of a partnership interest to the extent attributable to the substantially appreciated inventory which constitutes inventory within the meaning of section 453(b)(2)(B)."

Based on the reasoning of Revenue Ruling 89-108, to determine if the taxpayer may use the installment method to report income from the sale of a partnership interest to the extent that the income is attributable to certain unrealized receivables, the Service must determine whether income realized on a direct sale of certain unrealized receivables would be reportable under the installment method. While § 453(b)(2)(B) precludes the use of the installment method to report the sale of inventory, judicial authority also supports a conclusion that the installment method may not be used to report the income arising from compensation for services.

The seminal case is *Sorensen v. Commissioner*, 22 TC 321 (1954), in which a cash basis taxpayer entered into an employment arrangement with Willys-Overland

Motors (Willys). Willys granted the taxpayer transferable options, exercisable on specified future dates, to purchase stock at a price that was 25 percent of the then existing market price. Mr. Sorensen continued in Willys' employment but never exercised any of the options. Instead, he sold three of the options prior to their expiration date for cash and notes payable over a number of years.

The Tax Court first determined that the options were granted to Mr. Sorensen as compensation. Mr. Sorensen then argued that he was entitled to report the income from the sale of the options on the installment method. The court disagreed, stating:

> Since the sales of the options operated to compensate petitioner for his services, what he received in the form of both cash and notes was income by way of compensation. The provisions of [§ 453] relate only to the reporting of income arising from the sale of property on the installment basis. Those provisions do not in anywise purport to relate to the reporting of income arising by way of compensation for services. Petitioner is not entitled to have them applied here.

The Tax Court held that, as the options were granted to Mr. Sorensen as compensation for services, the income from the sale of the options could not be reported as income from the sale of property under the installment method. . . .

Therefore, based on the above-cited case law and revenue ruling, a sole proprietor could not report the income realized on the sale of unrealized receivables for services rendered under the installment method. Accordingly, based on the reasoning of Revenue Ruling 89-108 and judicial decisions, a taxpayer may not report income from the sale of a partnership interest under the installment method to the extent that it represents income attributable to § 751(c)(2) unrealized receivables arising from compensation for services. The taxpayer may report the balance of the income realized from the sale of the partnership interest using the installment method of reporting.

CASE DEVELOPMENT, HAZARDS AND OTHER CONSIDERATIONS

A taxpayer may argue that the sale of a partnership interest need not be fragmented for purposes of the installment sale provisions in the absence of Regulations. However, we think that Revenue Ruling 89-108 and case law provides sufficient authority to support the conclusion that a taxpayer may not report income from the sale of the taxpayer's interest in a partnership under the installment method pursuant to § 453 to the extent that it represents income attributable to § 751(c)(2) unrealized receivables for payment for services rendered. In addition, a taxpayer might challenge the underpinnings of Revenue Ruling 89-108. Secondary authority suggests that fragmentation of partnership interests may be appropriate for purposes of applying the installment sale provisions. . . . *But compare*, Monte A. Jackel, *Installment Sale of Partnership Interests: Aggregate or Entity?* 69 Tax Notes 363 (Oct. 16, 1995).

CHAPTER 24

Distributions: Marketable Securities, Basis Shifting, and Mixing Bowls

PROBLEM AREA 24

INTRODUCTION

The rules of the Internal Revenue Code pertaining to property distributions by partnerships are essentially permissive. As a general rule, a property distribution is not taxable either to the partnership or to the distributee partner. Instead, in a current distribution, the distributee takes a basis in the distributed property equal to the partnership's prior basis in such property, so that the partnership's gain or loss in the property is preserved for taxation to the extent it is realized by the distributee on a future sale. If the distributee partner's basis in his partnership interest is less than the partnership's basis in the distributed property, the property takes the lower basis, preserving a larger amount for future taxation. In a liquidating distribution, the distributee partner takes a basis in the distributed property equal to his prior basis in the partnership interest, regardless of whether that amount is larger or smaller than the partnership's basis in the distributed property.

Every distribution that changes the distributee partner's continuing interest in the partnership (including a current distribution that results in a diminution of the partner's percentage interest) involves, conceptually, an exchange by the partner of part or all of his interest in the undistributed properties for a larger interest in the distributed property. The decision not to tax this exchange gives partners great flexibility in untangling their affairs. There are, however, limits to this flexibility. Section 751(b), discussed in Problem Area 13, taxes this exchange to the extent that the distributee partner takes more (or less) than his share of the partnership's § 751 assets. Section 731(c), discussed here, taxes the distributee partner to the extent that he takes more than his share of the net gain in the partnership's "marketable securities."

In addition, the use of a partnership to accomplish an exchange of properties is curtailed by §§ 704(c)(1)(B) and 737. The archetypical transaction that is the focus of these statutory provisions is the "mixing bowl" transaction, in which two partners each contribute appreciated property to a partnership with the intention of distributing it to the other partner. Under the usual distribution rules, this transaction would be taxable neither to the partnership nor to either of the partners, and each partner would take a basis in the property distributed to him equal to his former basis in the property he contributed. The cited statutes require the partnership to own the properties for at least seven years before the provision becomes inapplicable – a sufficient period of time to discourage most potential participants. If the partnership holds the contributed properties for less than this period of time, the pre-contribution gain (or loss) on the properties must be recognized by the contributing partner at the time of the distribution. Post-contribution gain (or loss), if any, is not triggered.

Taken together, § 731(c) and the anti-mixing-bowl rules represent a significant incursion into the traditionally tax-free treatment of partnership property distributions. Tax-free treatment still applies, however, to all property distributions that are not marketable securities, if either (i) the partnership has not received a contribution of an asset with built-in gain or loss or (ii) at least seven years have elapsed since the last such contribution. This will often be the case, a fact that leaves open fruitful avenues for tax planning.

In a liquidating distribution, for example, the distributee partner's basis in the distributed property is almost always different than the partnership's former basis in that property. If the distributed property is thereafter sold, the amount of gain realized by the distributee partner will be greater or less than the gain that would have been realized on a partnership sale due to this so-called "basis shifting." In addition, the tax gain or loss resulting from the sale will inure solely to the detriment or benefit of the distributee partner, rather than being allocated among the partners. In this manner, liquidating distributions are a ready tool for lessening the tax burden on taxable asset dispositions and for allocating such burden in ways that would be impermissible under § 704(b) or § 704(c).

Current distributions, in contrast, are less obviously useful for basis shifting for two reasons. First, unless the distributee partner's basis in the partnership interest is less than the partnership's basis in the distributed property, the partner will take the partnership's basis in the distributed property. Second, the recipient of a current distribution remains, by definition, a partner of the partnership, and therefore potentially subject to allocations under § 704(c) that could correct misallocations of gain or loss that occur as a result of the distribution. Even so, a current distribution can rearrange the tax liabilities of the partners, as explored in question 1. below.

When applicable, § 734(b) may require an adjustment to the basis of the partnership's remaining properties. Under that provision, if the distributee partner takes a lower basis in the distributed property than such property had in the hands of the partnership, the basis of the partnership's remaining properties must be increased by a like amount. Similarly, if the distributee partner's basis in the distributed asset is higher, the basis of the remaining assets must be reduced by a like amount.

The goal of § 734(b) is not to equalize inside and outside basis. If inside and outside basis are equal prior to the distribution, they will remain so after the application of § 734(b). If, however, they are different, § 734(b) will preserve that difference – with perverse results, as explored in question 8.

PROBLEM 24

QUESTIONS

1. The ABC partnership, which was formed to invest in real estate with cash contributions of $80,000 each from A, B, and C, now has the following balance sheet:

	Adjusted Basis	Book Value	Fair Market Value
Assets			
Land 1	$ 90,000	$ 90,000	$210,000
Land 2	80,000	80,000	110,000
Land 3	70,000	70,000	10,000
Total	$240,000	$240,000	$330,000
Capital			
A	$ 80,000	$ 80,000	$110,000
B	80,000	80,000	110,000
C	80,000	80,000	110,000
Total	$240,000	$240,000	$330,000

The partnership desires to sell Land 1 and Land 3 while continuing to hold Land 2 for further appreciation. At the same time, the partners wish to minimize the tax liability of Partner C arising from these sales. How can a current distribution help to achieve these goals?

2. The balance sheet of equal partnership ABC is as follows:

	Adjusted Basis	Book Value	Fair Market Value
Assets			
Cash	$ 6,000	$ 6,000	$ 6,000
Stock	18,000	18,000	108,000
Land	30,000	30,000	120,000
Total	$ 54,000	$ 54,000	$234,000
Capital			
A	$ 18,000	$ 18,000	$ 78,000
B	18,000	18,000	78,000
C	18,000	18,000	78,000
Total	$ 54,000	$ 54,000	$234,000

The partnership was formed with cash contributions and holds all of its assets for investment. The partnership distributes two-thirds of the stock to the partners as a current distribution ($24,000 of stock to each). No § 754 election is in effect. What is the result to all parties? What if the entire distribution ($72,000 of stock) is made only to C? How do these answers change if the stock is a marketable security?

3. A, B, and C form the equal ABC partnership, with A contributing stock held for investment, B contributing Land 2, and C contributing Land 1. No § 754 election is in effect. After one year of operations, the balance sheet of the partnership is as follows:

	Adjusted Basis	Book Value	Fair Market Value
Assets			
Stock	$ 21,000	$ 21,000	$ 27,000
Land 1	9,000	21,000	27,000
Land 2	21,000	21,000	27,000
Total	$ 51,000	$ 63,000	$ 81,000
Capital			
A	$ 21,000	$ 21,000	$ 27,000
B	21,000	21,000	27,000
C	9,000	21,000	27,000
Total	$ 51,000	$ 63,000	$ 81,000

The partnership holds all of its assets for investment. What is the result to the parties if the partnership distributes Land 1 to A in complete liquidation of his interest in the partnership? Land 2 to C?

4. The balance sheet of equal partnership ABC is as follows:

	Adjusted Basis	Book Value	Fair Market Value
Assets			
Cash	$ 30,000	$ 30,000	$ 30,000
Land 1	12,000	12,000	15,000
Land 2	18,000	18,000	6,000
Land 3	21,000	21,000	27,000
Land 4	30,000	30,000	21,000
Total	$111,000	$111,000	$ 99,000
Capital			
A	$ 37,000	$ 37,000	$ 33,000
B	37,000	37,000	33,000
C	37,000	37,000	33,000
Total	$111,000	$111,000	$ 99,000

The partnership was formed with cash contributions and holds all of its assets for investment. No § 754 election is in effect. In a liquidating distribution, C receives Land 2 and Land 3. What is the result to the parties? What is the result if instead C receives Land 2, Land 4, and $6,000 in cash?

5. The balance sheet of equal partnership ABC is as follows:

	Adjusted Basis	Book Value	Fair Market Value
Assets			
Cash	$ 72,000	$ 72,000	$ 72,000
Business Asset	21,000	21,000	30,000
Self-Created Goodwill	0	0	15,000
Total	$ 93,000	$ 93,000	$117,000
Capital			
A	$ 31,000	$ 31,000	$ 39,000
B	31,000	31,000	39,000
C	31,000	31,000	39,000
Total	$ 93,000	$ 93,000	$117,000

The partnership was formed with cash contributions. C receives $39,000 cash in liquidation of his partnership interest. The partnership has a § 754 election in effect. What is the result to the parties?

6. The balance sheet of equal partnership ABC is as follows:

	Adjusted Basis	Book Value	Fair Market Value
Assets			
Cash	$ 18,000	$ 18,000	$ 18,000
Land 1	19,000	20,000	18,000
Land 2	18,000	22,000	18,000
Total	$ 55,000	$ 60,000	$ 54,000
Capital			
A	$ 20,000	$ 20,000	$ 18,000
B	16,000	20,000	18,000
C	19,000	20,000	18,000
Total	$ 55,000	$ 60,000	$ 54,000

A, B, and C formed the partnership by contributing $20,000 cash, Land 2, and Land 1, respectively. The partnership thereafter invested $2,000 of its cash in improving Land 2, but otherwise has had no activity. The partnership holds all of its assets for investment and has a § 754 election in effect. What are the tax consequences to the partners and the partnership if the partnership makes the following alternative distributions more than seven years after its formation?

a. Partner A receives $18,000 cash in complete liquidation of his partnership interest.

b. Partner B receives Land 1 in complete liquidation of her partnership interest.
c. Partner C receives Land 2 in complete liquidation of his partnership interest.

7. The balance sheet of equal partnership ABC is as follows:

	Adjusted Basis	Book Value	Fair Market Value
Assets			
Land 1	$ 850,000	$ 850,000	$ 80,000
Land 2	400,000	400,000	120,000
Total	$1,250,000	$1,250,000	$ 200,000
Capital			
A	$ 250,000	$ 250,000	$ 40,000
B	250,000	250,000	40,000
C	750,000	750,000	120,000
Total	$1,250,000	$1,250,000	$ 200,000

The partnership was formed with cash contributions and holds all of its assets for investment. C receives Land 2 in liquidation of his partnership interest. A § 754 election is not in effect. What is the result to the parties?

8. Following a 50 percent decline in the value of equal partnership ABC, D purchases C's one-third interest for $10,000. No § 754 election is in effect. Immediately following D's purchase, the balance sheet of the partnership is as follows:

	Adjusted Basis	Book Value	Fair Market Value
Assets			
Land 1	$ 20,000	$ 20,000	$ 10,000
Land 2	20,000	20,000	10,000
Land 3	20,000	20,000	10,000
Total	$ 60,000	$ 60,000	$ 30,000
Capital			
A	$ 20,000	$ 20,000	$ 10,000
B	20,000	20,000	10,000
D	10,000	20,000	10,000
Total	$ 50,000	$ 60,000	$ 30,000

Assume that the values of the partnership's assets remain unchanged following D's purchase. Some years later, without any change in values, the partnership distributes Land 3 to D in complete liquidation of her partnership interest. What are the tax consequences to the partnership and the partners if a § 754 election is made in connection with this distribution?

MATERIALS

H.R. Rep. No. 103-826, Part I
103rd Cong., 2d Sess. 187-89 (1994)

. . .

Partnership Distributions of Marketable Securities

Present Law

Neither a partnership nor its partners generally recognize gain upon a distribution of partnership property to a partner (sec. 731(a)(1) and (b)). A partner is required to recognize gain, however, to the extent that the amount of money distributed exceeds the partner's basis in its partnership interest immediately before the distribution (sec. 731(a)(1)). Thus, in general, if a partnership distributes cash to a partner in an amount that exceeds the adjusted basis of the partner's interest in the partnership, the partner must recognize gain; but if the partnership distributes marketable securities to the partner in lieu of cash, the partner can defer recognizing gain.

A partner's basis in property distributed in a non-liquidating distribution is the lesser of the partnership's adjusted basis in the distributed property or the partner's adjusted basis in partnership interest (reduced by money distributed in the transaction) (sec. 732(a)). A partner's adjusted basis in its partnership interest is reduced by the amount of money and the basis of property distributed to him in a non-liquidating distribution (sec. 733).

In a liquidating distribution, the partner's basis in the distributed property equals the partner's basis in the partnership interest (reduced by money distributed in the transaction) (sec. 732(b)).

A partner that contributes appreciated property to a partnership is required to include pre-contribution gain in income to the extent that the value of other property distributed by the partnership to that partner exceeds its adjusted basis in its partnership interest (sec. 737). This rule applies if the distribution is made within five years [raised to seven by statutory amendment in 1997] after the contribution of the appreciated property.

Reasons for Change

Concern has arisen that taxpayers can exchange interests in appreciated assets for marketable securities while deferring or avoiding tax on the appreciation, by using the present-law rules relating to partnership distributions. The present-law rules permit a partner to exchange, tax-free, his share of appreciated partnership assets for an increased share of the partnership's marketable securities. This transaction is the virtual economic equivalent of a sale of a partner's share of the partnership's assets. If the taxpayer were to exchange an interest in an appreciated asset for cash, he generally would recognize gain on the appreciated asset; yet if the taxpayer receives a partnership distribution of marketable securities, which are nearly as easily valued and as liquid as cash, he can avoid gain recognition.

This distinction in tax treatment between cash and marketable securities elevates form over substance, causes taxpayers to choose the form of transactions for tax reasons rather than economic reasons, and may not promote accurate income measurement. Rather, the present-law rule merely permits taxpayers to defer or avoid tax.

To limit the deferral or avoidance of taxation upon the receipt of marketable securities by a partner with unrealized appreciation in his partnership interest, the bill provides that the receipt of marketable securities in a partnership distribution causes the partner to recognize gain from the disposition of its partnership interest, to the extent that the value of the securities exceeds that partner's adjusted basis in its partnership interest. Thus, gain is recognized in the same manner, as if the partner had received money in lieu of securities.

Exceptions are provided under this rule. It is acknowledged that certain partnerships are formed for the purpose of holding marketable securities for investment or for sale to customers. Thus, an exception is provided in the case of a distribution of marketable securities by an investment partnership to a partner who did not contribute any property to the partnership other than money or securities or other similar property. In addition, it is not intended that a partner be taxed under the provision on the partnership's gain attributable to his share of the partnership's marketable securities distributed to him, because he has not exchanged his share of any other partnership asset for an increased share of the partnership's marketable securities. Thus, an exception (structured as a limitation on gain recognized under the provision) applies, to the extent that the gain that would otherwise be recognized under the provision does not exceed the distributee partner's share of the partnership's built-in gain (if any) with respect to securities of the type distributed to him. Further, the bill provides an exception for a distribution of marketable securities if the distributed security was contributed by the distributee partner (except to the extent that the value of the distributed security arises from marketable securities or money contributed to an entity to which the distributed security relates). Finally, the bill provides regulatory authority to except distributions when the distributed security was not a marketable security when acquired by the partnership.

Because the partnership tax rules provide a great deal of flexibility, and taxpayers can arrange their affairs so as to take advantage of this flexibility, the bill grants to the Treasury Department regulatory authority to prescribe rules that effectively prevent taxpayers from avoiding the intent of this provision (as well as to provide relief from the application of the provision, where appropriate).

CHAPTER 25

Partnership Mergers and Divisions

PROBLEM AREA 25

INTRODUCTION

Most of the federal tax consequences of partnership mergers and divisions lie buried beneath the language of the Internal Revenue Code. The only statutory mention of the topic occurs in § 708(b)(2), which serves only to identify (incompletely) the partnership that is deemed to survive in a merger or division. At first blush, this identification might seem significant only for administrative purposes, such as determining which partnerships must apply for new tax identification numbers after one partnership splits into more than one. A moment's thought suggests further consequences, such as the bunching of income that may attend the termination of any partnership that is not deemed to continue after the transaction and the termination of tax elections previously filed by such partnerships.

The real importance of determining which partnership continues, and which partnership or partnerships terminate, is that this identification is the first step in determining what is deemed to have taken place in the merger or division. As illuminated by expanded Regulations published in 2001, only one (at most) of the constituent partnerships in a merger can survive for tax purposes, and all of the other partnerships are deemed to have transferred their assets and liabilities to that partnership. Although more than one of the partnerships resulting from a division can survive for tax purposes, the 2001 Regulations provide rules for choosing the "divided partnership" from among the survivors, and that partnership is deemed to have transferred portions of its assets and liabilities to the other resulting partnership(s). These transfers are deemed to take place for tax purposes whether or not they actually occur under governing state law. For example, assume that the Redco partnership transfers all of its assets and liabilities to the Blueco partnership in a transaction treated as a merger for tax purposes in which Redco is deemed to survive under § 708(b)(2)(A), because the former partners of Redco own more than 50 percent of the interests in Blueco following the transfer and the former partners of Blueco do not. Despite what actually happened, the tax law will treat the transaction as a transfer by Blueco of all of its assets and liabilities to Redco in return for partnership interests in Redco.

The 2001 Regulations allow taxpayers to depart from this mandatory "assets-over" construction in only one instance. If a terminating partnership in a merger or the continuing partnership in a division actually distributes assets to its partners, who immediately contribute them to the continuing partnership in the merger or to a recipient (non-continuing) partnership in a division, the distribution and contribution will be taxed in accordance with their form as an "assets-up" transaction. As explored in the questions in this Problem Area, this can be useful where the outside basis of the partners exceeds the partnership's basis in its assets or to avoid potential problems under the anti-mixing-bowl (AMB) provisions of §§ 704(c)(1)(B) and 737.

If the parties do not choose to follow the assets-up form (or if they engage in a "formless" transaction under governing state law), the following steps are deemed to take place in a merger of two partnerships:

1. The terminating partnership contributes all of its assets and liabilities to the continuing partnership in exchange for interests in the continuing partnership; and

2. The terminating partnership distributes the interests in the continuing partnership to its partners in liquidation of their interests in the terminating partnership.

The tax consequences of the merger to all parties are determined, generally, by applying the normal partnership tax rules to each of the transaction steps that is deemed to occur. In this respect, the tax law of partnership mergers departs from that applicable to corporate mergers. Subchapter K has no provision akin to § 368 in the corporate realm. It contains neither a definition of the term "merger" nor any provisions establishing special tax treatment for this transaction. This is not an impediment to partnership mergers. Unlike in the corporate context, where the transactions composing a merger would be heavily taxed absent special non-recognition rules, the generally benign rules that apply to partnership contributions and distributions allow the typical partnership merger to proceed as a lightly taxed or entirely non-taxed transaction.

The application of the AMB provisions to partnership mergers is an area of recent and somewhat controversial developments. In a 2004 Revenue Ruling (later withdrawn) and Proposed Regulations issued in 2007, the Service has determined that the deemed contribution in transaction step 1 creates a new layer of § 704(c) gain in the assets contributed by the terminated partnership, which may be subject to tax under the AMB provisions upon a distribution of property by the continuing partnership during the seven years following the merger. No new § 704(c) layer arises in the assets of the continuing partnership, presumably because they are not treated as transferred in the transaction. Importantly, the 2007 Proposed Regulations confirm that the distribution in transaction step 2 does not result in the immediate imposition of any AMB tax liability.

If the parties do not choose to follow the assets-up form, the following steps are deemed to take place in the division of one partnership into two:

1. The divided partnership contributes a portion of its assets and liabilities to the recipient partnership in exchange for interests in the recipient partnership; and

2. The divided partnership distributes the interests in the recipient partnership to its partners. If the division is pro-rata among all of the partners, this distribution will not change their respective interests in the divided partnership. If it is not, the distribution will result in the reduction or liquidation of one or more of the partners' interests in the divided partnership.

As in the case of partnership mergers, the tax consequences of these steps are determined by applying generally applicable partnership tax rules. Unlike in the case of mergers, however, these rules may not be benign. For example, if the division is not pro-rata among all of the partners, § 751(b) is likely to apply. This should not be surprising: a non-pro-rata distribution of property by a partnership holding § 751 assets generally brings § 751(b) into play. Section 751(f) preserves this result if the distributed property is a partnership interest.

In this respect, the tax consequences of a partnership division should be the same as, and certainly no worse than, the tax consequences of a distribution of the property held by the recipient partnership. When it comes to the application of the AMB provisions, however, the results may be far worse. Normally, the reach of the AMB rules extends only to the built-in gain or loss that exists at the time of contribution of property to a partnership – the so-called "original" § 704(c) gain or loss. The AMB rules do not reach gain or loss that arises thereafter, during the period that the partnership owns the property. Said differently, the AMB provisions do not apply to reverse § 704(c) layers. Thus, on a distribution of property by a partnership, the maximum exposure under the AMB provisions is measured by the original § 704(c) gain or loss.

In a division, however, the contribution that is deemed to occur in transaction step 1 may be a contribution for purposes of the AMB provisions. Indeed, following the approach of the Proposed Regulations for mergers, it certainly is such a contribution. As to mergers, these Proposed Regulations state explicitly that the distribution that is deemed to occur in transaction step 2 of the merger is not an occasion for the imposition of tax under the AMB provisions. There are currently no Regulations or other guidance specifically addressing the application of the AMB provisions to partnership divisions. In its commentary on the 2001 Regulations, however, the Service has indicated that it is not inclined to write a similar exception for partnership divisions.

Barring a change of heart on the part of the Service, it appears that the AMB provisions may (and perhaps already do) apply more broadly and aggressively to partnership divisions than to regular partnership property distributions. It may seem odd that merely "packaging" distributed property in a partnership should dramatically change the tax consequences of the transaction. But this observation begs the question of which way this discontinuity should be resolved. If the AMB provisions apply to the entire built-in gain or loss at the time of a partnership division, can their application to ordinary property distributions be far behind?

PROBLEM 25

QUESTIONS

1. Individuals A and B own equal interests in partnership AB, which has a net asset value of $300,000. Individual C owns 90 percent, and individual D the remaining 10 percent, of partnership CD, which has a net asset value of $200,000. Which partnership, if any, is treated as the continuing partnership if AB and CD merge pursuant to the merger provision of governing state partnership law?

2. Partnerships AB and CD are as described in question 1. above. In addition, C owns 90 percent, and individual E the remaining 10 percent, of partnership CE, which has a net asset value of $300,000. Which partnership, if any, is treated as the continuing partnership if all three partnerships merge under governing state law? What if the net asset value of CE is $200,000?

3. Under the facts of question 1. above, describe the transactions that are deemed to take place for federal tax purposes in each of the following alternatives.

a. AB and CD merge pursuant to the merger provision of governing state partnership law.

b. CD distributes all of its assets to its partners in liquidation of their interests and immediately thereafter C and D contribute all of the distributed assets to AB in exchange for AB partnership interests.

c. CD distributes its principal business assets to its partners as a current distribution and immediately thereafter C and D contribute all of the distributed assets to AB in exchange for AB partnership interests. CD alternatively (i) transfers its remaining assets to AB in exchange for AB partnership interests, which it distributes to C and D in liquidation of their CD interests or (ii) retains such assets for investment.

d. AB distributes all of its assets to its partners in liquidation of their interests and immediately thereafter A and B contribute all of the distributed assets to CD in exchange for CD partnership interests.

e. AB distributes all of its assets to its partners in liquidation of their interests. AB's assets are such that they can be owned and operated independently by A and B, who do so for a period of time. Thereafter, A and B contribute all of the distributed assets to CD in exchange for CD partnership interests.

f. AB transfers all of its assets to CD in exchange for CD partnership interests, which AB distributes to its partners in liquidation of their AB partnership interests.

g. C and D contribute all of their CD partnership interests to AB in exchange for AB partnership interests.

4. Oldco, a partnership, owns ten parcels of real estate held for investment, each valued at $10,000. The partners have the following percentage interests:

A	40%	D	20%
B	20%	E	10%
C	10%		

Oldco has no liabilities. In each of the following transaction structures, identify the continuing partnership(s), if any, and describe the transactions that are deemed to take place for federal tax purposes.

a. *"Forward spin-off."* Oldco transfers one parcel to a newly formed LLC, Newco, and immediately makes a pro-rata, current distribution of all of the Newco interests to A, B, C, D, and E.

b. *"Forward split-off."* Oldco titles four parcels in the name of CDE, a partnership in formation. C, D and E relinquish their respective interests in Oldco for interests in CDE.

c. *"Forward split-off"* with a twist.

(i) Same as b. above, except that, as part of the transaction, C, D, and E contribute cash or other property to CDE.

(ii) Oldco transfers two parcels to D in liquidation of D's partnership interest. Immediately thereafter, D forms a new partnership, DF, with unrelated individual F. D contributes the two distributed parcels to DF; F contributes cash.

d. *"Reverse split-off."* Oldco transfers six parcels to a newly formed LLC, Newco AB, and immediately distributes the interests it obtains in exchange for these parcels to A and B in liquidation of their respective interests in Oldco.

e. *"Mixed split-off."* Oldco transfers one parcel to D in redemption of one-half of D's interest, and one parcel to E in liquidation of E's interest. D and E immediately transfer the distributed parcels to new partnership DE. Oldco then titles two additional parcels in the name of CD, a partnership in formation. C and D relinquish their respective interests in Oldco for interests in CD.

f. *"Split up."* Oldco transfers two parcels to a newly formed LLC, Newco BD, and immediately distributes the Newco BD interests it obtains in exchange for these parcels to B and D in redemption of one-half of their respective interests in Oldco. Oldco then transfers three additional parcels to another newly formed LLC, Newco BCD, and immediately distributes the Newco BCD interests it obtains in exchange for these parcels to B, C, and D in liquidation of their respective interests in Oldco.

5. Partnership AB was formed several years ago with cash contributions to hold land for investment. Currently, its balance sheet is as follows.

	Adjusted Basis	Book Value	Fair Market Value
Assets			
Land	$100,000	$100,000	$600,000
Liabilities			
Recourse mortgage	$ 80,000	$ 80,000	$ 80,000
Capital			
A	10,000	10,000	260,000
B	10,000	10,000	260,000
Total			
Liabilities & Capital	$100,000	$100,000	$600,000

Partnership CD was formed three years ago with cash contributions and operates a small manufacturing operation in rented space. Currently, its balance sheet is as follows.

	Adjusted Basis	Book Value	Fair Market Value
Assets			
Cash	$ 20,000	$ 20,000	$ 20,000
Inventory	40,000	40,000	60,000
Equipment (original cost $200,000)			
	$130,000	$130,000	$180,000
Total	$190,000	$190,000	$260,000
Liabilities	$ 0	$ 0	$ 0
Capital			
C	95,000	95,000	130,000
D	95,000	95,000	130,000
Total Liabilities & Capital	$190,000	$190,000	$260,000

Neither partnership has made an election under § 754. The parties wish to expand CD's manufacturing operation into a new plant constructed on AB's now vacant land. To facilitate this business plan, AB and CD merge under the applicable state merger statute. The partners have the following ownership percentages in the ABCD partnership resulting from this merger:

A 33.3%   C 16.7%

B 33.3%   D 16.7%

a. For federal tax purposes, what transactions are deemed to take place as a result of this merger? What are the tax consequences to the parties?

b. How, if at all, does § 751(b) apply to the merger?

c. Are any of the parties to this merger subject to tax currently under the "anti-mixing-bowl" (AMB) provisions of § 704(c)(1)(B) or § 737?

d. Construct a combined balance sheet for the ABCD partnership. What are the continuing implications of the merger under § 704(c)?

e. Will a distribution of the inventory to A in the year following the merger invoke the AMB provisions? Assuming that the value of the inventory remains $60,000, what will be the tax consequences to A, B, C, and D?

f. Will a distribution of $60,000 of land to C and D equally in the year following the merger invoke the AMB provisions? What will be the tax consequences to A, B, C, and D?

g. The parties have chosen to use a "formless" merger under state law to complete this transaction. Would there be any federal tax advantage to adopting explicitly an "assets-up" structure, whereby the assets of one of the merging partnerships are actually distributed to the partners of that partnership, for immediate contribution to the other partnership?

h. Assume that CD has valuable licenses to use intellectual property that it would lose if it is not, for state-law purposes, the surviving partnership in the merger. How should the transaction be structured? What are the federal tax consequences of the restructured merger?

6. Following the merger described in question 5. above, the parties are unable to agree to the details of a business plan for the expanded manufacturing facility. The land continues to appreciate in value and the current balance sheet of the ABCD partnership is now as follows.

	Adjusted Basis	Book Value	Fair Market Value
Assets			
Cash	$ 20,000	$ 20,000	$ 20,000
Inventory	40,000	60,000	60,000
Equipment (original cost $200,000)	130,000	180,000	180,000
Land	100,000	600,000	780,000
Total	$290,000	$860,000	$1,040,000
Liabilities	$ 80,000	$ 80,000	$ 80,000
Capital			
A	10,000	260,000	320,000

	Adjusted Basis	Book Value	Fair Market Value
B	10,000	260,000	320,000
C	95,000	130,000	160,000
D	95,000	130,000	160,000
Total Liabilities & Capital	$290,000	$860,000	$1,040,000

The impasse is unbroken after months of negotiations, and the parties decide to go their separate ways. A and B remain interested in the manufacturing operation and bargain to retain it, while C and D are willing to take a portion of the land in exchange for their entire interests in the ABCD partnership. Accordingly, ABCD subdivides its land and titles unencumbered land worth $320,000 in the name of CD, a partnership in formation. C and D then relinquish their respective interests in ABCD in exchange for interests in CD.

a. For federal tax purposes, is the form of these transactions respected?

b. How, if at all, does § 751(b) apply to the division?

c. Are any of the parties to the division subject to tax currently under the AMB provisions?

d. Construct the balance sheets for the AB and CD partnerships resulting from the division. What are the continuing implications of the division under § 704(c)?

e. The parties have chosen to engage in an "assets over" division. Would there be any federal tax advantage to explicitly adopting an "assets up" structure, whereby the ABCD partnership distributes the land to C and D, for immediate contribution to the CD partnership?

f. Assume that the terms of the land subdivision require ABCD to retain ownership, for state-law purposes, of the land to be owned by C and D, but impose no such restriction on the remainder of the land. How should the transaction be structured? What are the federal tax consequences of the restructured division?

MATERIALS

Notice 2009-70, 2009-2 CB 255
Section 704(c) Layers Relating to Partnership Mergers, Divisions and Tiered Partnerships

. . .

SECTION 1. PURPOSE

The Internal Revenue Service invites public comments on the proper application of the rules relating to the creation and maintenance of multiple layers of forward and reverse section 704(c) gain and loss to partnerships and tiered partnerships, including in the context of partnership mergers and divisions.

SECTION 2. BACKGROUND

As discussed in greater detail below, the IRS and Treasury Department issued Proposed Regulations in 2007 addressing the consequences under sections 704(c)(1)(B) and 737 of certain partnership mergers. The IRS and the Treasury Department received a number of comments in response to these Proposed Regulations expressing concern about the proposed treatment of section 704(c) layers in connection with a partnership merger. In addition, the IRS and the Treasury Department have become aware that practitioners are taking positions based upon different interpretations of the current tiered partnership rules (Treas. Reg. § 1.704-3(a)(9)). A number of practitioners suggest that the tiered partnerships rules may need to be clarified and similar rules be provided with respect to partnership mergers. The IRS and Treasury believe that further study of certain aspects of the application of section 704(c) is necessary before finalizing the Proposed Regulations. . . .

Section 704(c)(1)(A) was enacted as part of the Tax Reform Act of 1984 . . . . Congress determined that "special rules are needed to prevent an artificial shifting of tax consequences between the partners with respect to pre-contribution gain or loss. This is particularly important since the various partners may have different tax positions." . . .

Section 704(c)(1)(B) was enacted as part of the Omnibus Budget Reconciliation Act of 1989 (P.L. 101-239). It was Congress's view that the prior law made it "possible for partners to circumvent the rule requiring pre-contribution gain on contributed property to be allocated to the contributing partner." . . .

While section 704(c)(1)(B) addresses the recognition of gain by the contributing partner if property contributed by the partner is distributed to another partner, section 737 addresses the tax consequences when a partner who contributed built-in gain or loss property receives a distribution of other property. . . .

Sections 737(a) and (b) were enacted as part of the Energy Policy Act of 1992 . . . as a result of Congress's concern that "a partner who contributes appreciated property to a partnership may be able to avoid or defer the recognition of gain with respect to that property through the mechanism of having the partnership distribute other partnership property to him in partial or complete redemption of his interest while the partnership continues to own the contributed property." . . .

On August 22, 2007, the IRS and the Treasury Department published in the Federal Register . . . a notice of proposed rulemaking, consistent with Notice 2005-15 . . . , providing that (1) section 704(c)(1)(B) applies to newly created section 704(c) gain or loss in property contributed by the transferor partnership to the continuing partnership in an assets-over merger, but does not apply to newly created reverse section 704(c) gain or loss resulting from a revaluation of property in the continuing partnership, and (2) for purposes of section 737(b), net precontribution gain includes newly created section 704(c) gain or loss in property contributed by the transferor partnership to the continuing partnership in an assets-over merger, but does not include newly created reverse section 704(c) gain or loss resulting from a revaluation of property in the continuing partnership. . . .

The Proposed Regulations include several examples. Example (3) of the Proposed Regulations (see Treas. Proposed Reg. § 1.704-4(c)(4)(ii)(F), Example (3)) involves a situation where built-in gain property contributed to the transferor partnership has both a revaluation loss in the transferor partnership and additional gain upon merger with the transferee partnership. The example concludes that the section 704(c) layers are collapsed in the merger and that upon contribution to the transferee partnership the property had only built-in gain and no built-in loss. . . .

A number of rules in existing regulations may be relevant to mergers, divisions and tiered partnerships. In particular Treas. Reg. § 1.704-3(a)(7)-(9) may apply.

Treas. Reg. § 1.704-3(a)(7) provides rules when a partner transfers his partnership interest and provides a "step in the shoes" approach. . . .

Treas. Reg. § 1.704-3(a)(8) provides special rules for certain specific situations, including the disposition of section 704(c) property in a nonrecognition transaction. . . .

Guidance on allocations with regard to the contribution of section 704(c) property in a tiered partnership structure is provided in Treas. Reg. § 1.704-3(a)(9) . . . .

SECTION 3. DISCUSSION

While no requests for a hearing were received in response to the Proposed Regulations issued on August 22, 2007, the IRS and the Treasury Department did receive comments relating to the Proposed Regulations and took notice of a number of articles published in response to the Proposed Regulations.

Most of the comments and articles address Example (3) which provides that property either has a built-in gain or built-in loss upon merger, not both, and that original section 704(c) gain is reduced by subsequent revaluation losses. Several comments discussed not only the specifics of Example (3), but also the broader implications of the example. In particular, the commentators questioned whether the example implies that a subsequent revaluation loss would reduce prior section 704(c) gains rather than create a new section 704(c) loss layer where there has been no partnership merger. Another comment suggested that the section 704(c) allocations in the example could be different if, for example, the transferor partnership used the remedial method instead of the traditional method. Other commentators expressed concerns that the application of the Proposed Regulations would result in tax allocations after the merger that are not consistent with the economic arrangement of the partners of the transferor partnership. For example, if layers of reverse section 704(c) built-in gain or built-in loss are collapsed in the merger, then a partner who prior to the merger was allocated a net loss for book purposes with respect to the property would not recognize a corresponding tax loss until liquidation of its interest. They contend that if the transferor partnership had continued in existence instead of liquidating, the section 704(c) layers would have been preserved under the tiered partnership rules of Treas. Reg. § 1.704-3(a)(9). Some practitioners believe the results should be the same in a merger.

The IRS and the Treasury Department have also become aware that there are conflicting views among practitioners about how section 704(c) layers should be maintained with respect to tiered partnerships. One view is that an aggregate approach should apply or be permitted such that a tiered partnership arrangement can be "looked through" and section 704(c) applied as if the partners of the upper-tier partnership directly own a portion of the assets of the lower-tier partnership (the Aggregate Approach). Another view is the entity approach under which the upper-tier partnership is treated as owning an interest in the lower-tier partnership but is not treated as owning any interest in the section 704(c) property of the lower-tier partnership (the Entity Approach). Each approach raises different issues and has unique consequences.

After extensive consideration of the concerns raised, the IRS and the Treasury Department believe that comments would be helpful to the development of guidance concerning section 704(c) layers in tiered partnerships and in mergers and divisions. The IRS and Treasury Department believe that it is appropriate to consider the issues regarding section 704(c) layers in general before finalizing the Proposed Regulations.

SECTION 4. REQUEST FOR COMMENTS

The IRS and Treasury Department are seeking comments relating to section 704(c) layers, as well as other section 704(c) issues, with respect to tiered partnerships, mergers and divisions. The IRS and the Treasury Department plan to address these issues as part of a future guidance project. However, the IRS and Treasury Department are not requesting comments on the principles described in Notice 2005-15, 2005-1 C.B. 527.

The IRS and Treasury Department include examples below of the types of comments requested, but comments are requested on all aspect of these issues, not only those matters listed.

Single Partnership with Layers—No Tiers

1. Should any changes be made to the events in Treas. Reg. § 1.704-1(b)(2)(iv)(f), the occurrence of which allow for a revaluation of assets? Should additional events be added?

2. After revaluing property, when, if at all, is it appropriate for taxpayers to net additional differences between value and basis against existing section 704(c) layers and when is it appropriate to create new section 704(c) layers if the layers offset one another (e.g., loss and gain layers)?

3. If a partnership has multiple section 704(c) layers, how should tax depreciation, depletion, amortization and gain or loss be allocated between the layers? When is it appropriate for partnerships to allocate these items to the latest layers first, to earlier layers first or to allocate these items pro rata to all layers for this purpose? Are other methods appropriate? How are these amounts allocated between layers if there are offsetting layers (e.g., how should depreciation be allocated between layers if a property has both a $100 gain layer and a subsequent $100 loss layer)?

4. What other section 704(c) issues are raised relating to section 704(c) layers, e.g., when partnership property is revalued?

Tiers of Partnerships with Layers

5. Are changes necessary to Treas. Reg. § 1.704-3(a)(7) and (8) to address compliance with section 704(c) and maintenance of section 704(c) layers when

property is either contributed to a partnership or transferred to a partner in a tiered partnership structure?

6. Are there different considerations in making property revaluation decisions in tiered partnership structures than in a single partnership (*e.g.*, should a revaluation of an upper-tier partnership constitute a revaluation event at the lower-tier partnership and should revaluation be dependent upon whether the upper-tier partnership has a significant interest in the lower-tier partnership)? Does the order in which tiered partnerships make property revaluations affect resulting section 704(c) layers and does existing guidance permit taxpayers to make revaluations in the appropriate order as necessary?

7. What issues relating to section 704(c) must taxpayers address in tiered partnership structures? What additional issues should be addressed by the Regulations, including Treas. Reg. § 1.704-3(a)(9)?

8. When should Treas. Reg. § 1.704-3(a)(9) permit taxpayers to use an Aggregate Approach or Entity Approach? What should be the results under these approaches? Should taxpayers be able to use other methods to track section 704(c) layers?

9. Under the Aggregate Approach, how would the section 704(c) layers be maintained by the lower-tier partnership?

10. Is the information necessary to maintain section 704(c) layers under the Aggregate Approach readily available? If the Aggregate Approach is permitted what, if any, additional rules would be necessary so that the partnerships may secure the required information?

11. Under the Entity Approach, if after allocating the upper-tier partnership's distributive share of lower-tier partnership section 704(c) allocations on the sale of an asset at the lower-tier level there are remaining book tax differences in the upper tier partnership, how, if at all, should these differences be resolved at the upper tier level?

Mergers

12. Recognizing that the transferor partnership terminates in a merger, what different issues do mergers raise for the section 704(c) layer rules?

13. Whether the Aggregate or Entity Approach is used in tiered partnerships, how will the approach be affected by a merger of one of the partnerships in a tiered arrangement, including a partnership that directly holds section 704(c) property and a partnership with an indirect interest in the property?

14. Under the Aggregate Approach, how would the transferee partnership maintain the section 704(c) layers of the transferor partnership?

15. Under the Entity Approach, when should the transferee partnership maintain the layers of the transferor partnership, or should each asset have a single section 704(c) layer as a result of the merger?

16. Are there different considerations if the transferor has partnerships as partners or if the transferee partnership is a partner in another partnership?

Divisions

17. What issues regarding section 704(c) layers are raised in a division of a "traditional" single tier partnership and in the division of a partnership that is part of a tiered partnership structure?

18. Assuming a partnership division should not create new section 704(c) property (or section 737 net precontribution gain) when each partner's overall interest in

each partnership property does not change, how should section 704(c) layers be created and maintained when a division is not *pro rata* or other changes in partners or property interests occur at the time of the division?

International Issues

19. What international tax issues are raised on the application of section 704(c) layers to tiered partnerships, mergers and divisions? For example, how should section 704(c) layers be created and maintained in cross-border tiered partnerships and mergers and divisions? Should similar "layers" be created and maintained to track and preserve the character of the gain under international tax provisions, including sections 367, 897, and 1248?

Comments may be submitted on or before February 22, 2010 . . . .